AQA GCSE (9–1) Religious Studies

SPECIFICATION A

Christianity, Hinduism, Sikhism and the Religious, Philosophical and Ethical Themes

Jan Hayes

Every effort has been made to trace all copyright holders, but if any have been inadvertently overlooked, the Publishers will be pleased to make the necessary arrangements at the first opportunity.

Although every effort has been made to ensure that website addresses are correct at time of going to press, Hodder Education cannot be held responsible for the content of any website mentioned in this book. It is sometimes possible to find a relocated web page by typing in the address of the home page for a website in the URL window of your browser.

Hachette UK's policy is to use papers that are natural, renewable and recyclable products and made from wood grown in well-managed forests and other controlled sources. The logging and manufacturing processes are expected to conform to the environmental regulations of the country of origin.

Orders: please contact Bookpoint Ltd, 130 Park Drive, Milton Park, Abingdon, Oxon OX14 4SE. Telephone: +44 (0)1235 827872. Fax: +44 (0)1235 400454. Email education@bookpoint.co.uk Lines are open from 9 a.m. to 5 p.m., Monday to Saturday, with a 24-hour message answering service. You can also order through our website: www.hoddereducation.co.uk

ISBN: 978 1 5104 7997 5
© Jan Hayes 2020

First published in 2020 by

Hodder Education,
An Hachette UK Company
Carmelite House
50 Victoria Embankment
London EC4Y 0DZ

www.hoddereducation.co.uk

Impression number   10 9 8 7 6 5 4 3 2 1

Year   2024 2023 2022 2021 2020

All rights reserved. Apart from any use permitted under UK copyright law, no part of this publication may be reproduced or transmitted in any form or by any means, electronic or mechanical, including photocopying and recording, or held within any information storage and retrieval system, without permission in writing from the publisher or under licence from the Copyright Licensing Agency Limited. Further details of such licences (for reprographic reproduction) may be obtained from the Copyright Licensing Agency Limited, www.cla.co.uk

Cover photo © valeriikalantai - stock.adobe.com
Illustrations by Tony Jones, Oxford Designers & Illustrators
Typeset by Aptara Inc.
Printed in Slovenia

A catalogue record for this title is available from the British Library.

Contents

The study of religions

1 CHRISTIANITY 1

1.1 Beliefs and teachings 4
　Getting prepared 26

1.2 Practices 28
　Getting prepared 53
　Christianity glossary 55

2 HINDUISM 57

2.1 Beliefs and teachings 60
　Getting prepared 79

2.2 Practices 81
　Getting prepared 105
　Hinduism glossary 107

3 SIKHISM 109

3.1 Beliefs and teachings 112
　Getting prepared 136

3.2 Practices 138
　Getting prepared 159
　Sikhism glossary 161

Religious, philosophical and ethical studies

What does the specification say about the themes? 163

4 Theme A: Relationships and families 166
Contrasting beliefs 185
Getting prepared 187
Relationships and families glossary 189

5 Theme B: Religion and life 190
Contrasting beliefs 221
Getting prepared 223
Religion and life glossary 225

6 Theme C: The existence of God and revelation 226
Contrasting beliefs 250
Getting prepared 252
The existence of God and revelation glossary 253

7 Theme D: Religion, peace and conflict 254
Contrasting beliefs 274
Getting prepared 276
Religion, peace and conflict glossary 278

8 Theme E: Religion, crime and punishment 279
Contrasting beliefs 305
Getting prepared 307
Religion, crime and punishment glossary 308

9 Theme F: Religion, human rights and social justice 309
Contrasting beliefs 333
Getting prepared 335
Religion, human rights and social justice glossary 337

Index 338

Acknowledgements 340

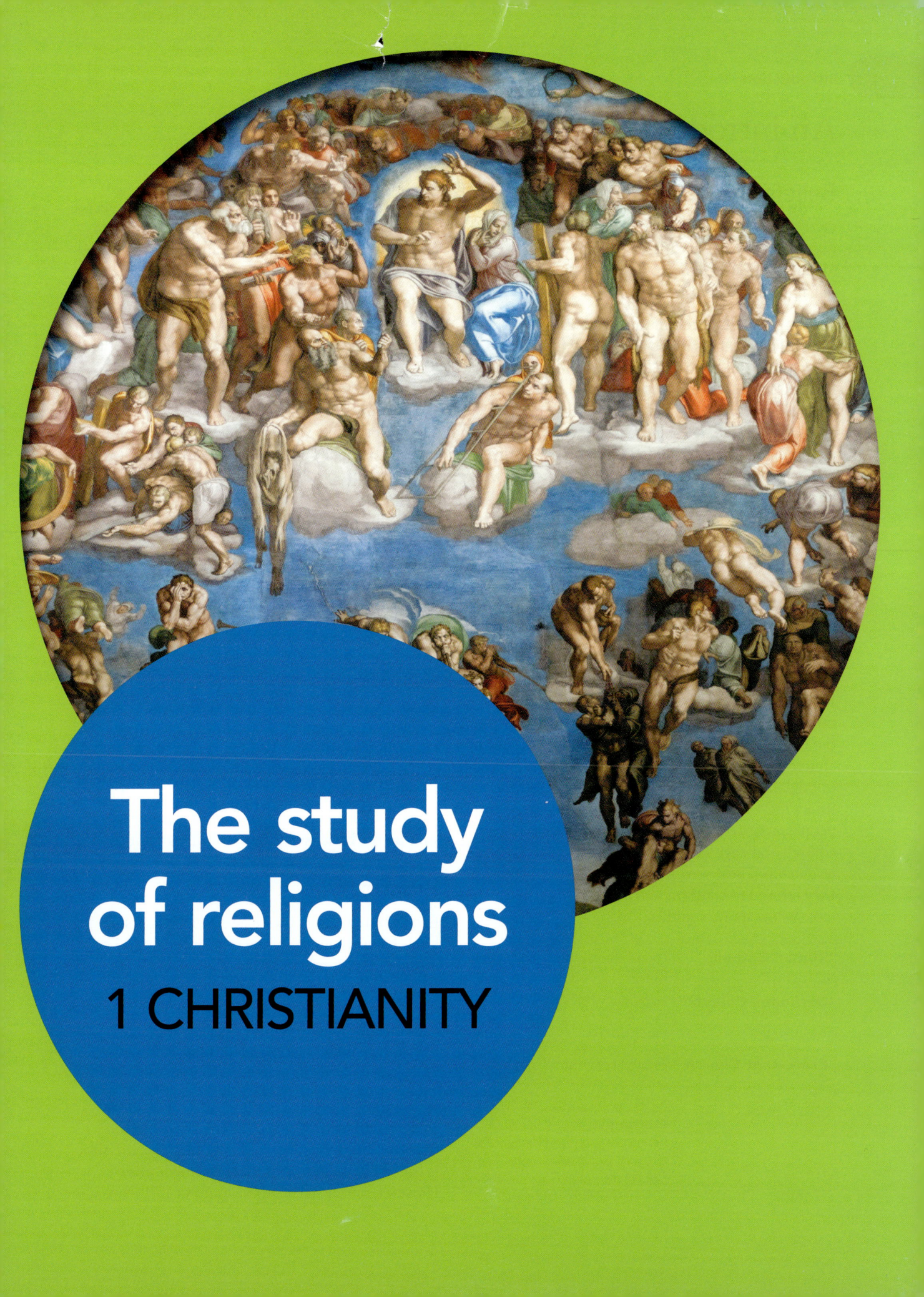

The study of religions

1 CHRISTIANITY

Introduction

An introduction to Christianity

Beliefs and teachings

Over 2000 years of existence, Christianity has seen many changes. Many different groups (**denominations**) belong to it, with different names, but all calling themselves 'Christians'.

The early Christian community established by Jesus soon became known as the Catholic (universal) church; everyone who was a Christian was a Catholic. However, time has seen disagreements about beliefs, leadership, organisation and practices, so new groups have been formed. Each group is known as a denomination. The **Orthodox Church** was the first to break away from the Catholics in 1054CE, which was known as the Great Schism. The main factors causing this were an attempt by Rome to force all Christians to use Latin as their religious language, mistreatment of Orthodox Christians by Western Crusader knights and differences in interpretation of creeds. This created the Eastern Orthodox and the now **Roman Catholic** Church, representing the Church in the East and the West, respectively.

In Europe, until the sixteenth century, people were Roman Catholics. However, a new movement grew up and protested against Rome, becoming known as the **Protestant** movement. European countries set up churches of their own. Hence, in Britain, the Church of England was born, with Henry VIII as its head. As time progressed, many disagreements occurred and people protested against their State form of the Church and began to form new groups with separate leadership. These were known as non-Conformists as they refused to conform to the rules of the State. The table below shows you this:

Roman Catholic	Found worldwide – the largest Christian group
Orthodox Church	Examples of groups – Russian Orthodox, Greek Orthodox, Ethiopian Orthodox
Protestant Church	Example of groups – Church of England
	Non-Conformist – **Methodist**, Baptist, Elim Pentecostal, United Reformed Church, Congregational Church

The **Trinity** is a key belief for all Christians. They believe in one God, who has three persons (aspects): God the Father in heaven, Jesus the Son on Earth (and now with God in heaven) and the Holy Spirit, which is the power of God remaining at work in the world today.

The Bible is the holy book. It is a single collection of 66 books. Now available in most languages of the world, it can be found in old, modern and even children's versions. It is divided into two sections: the Old Testament and New Testament. The Old Testament begins with the book of Genesis and includes 39 books in total. It contains the history of the Jewish people, so we hear about the lives of Adam, Noah, Moses, Abraham, Isaac, Jacob and David, and this history leads up to the life of Jesus (who, remember, was Jewish by birth).

With 27 books in total, the New Testament starts with the four **Gospels** (Matthew, Mark, Luke and John), all relating the life of Jesus. Gospel means good news. Then there are the books and letters that record the spread of early Christianity. The Bible can be interpreted in many different ways.

Many Christian churches have statements of faith (creeds), which were put together by Christian Councils in the early centuries of the Christian Church – for example, the **Nicene Creed** (first written in 325CE, then slightly changed in 381CE) and the **Apostles' Creed** (c. sixth to seventh century CE). They sum up the basic beliefs of the Christian faith.

Practices

Each Church has its own leader, with leadership levels below them to support this individual. The leader of the Roman Catholic Church is the Pope, who is chosen from leaders worldwide and lives in the Vatican City in Rome. The Orthodox Church has the Patriarch, known as the Patriarch of Constantinople. The Church of England has the Queen as its head as a ceremonial leader, but the Archbishop of Canterbury leads in reality.

Church buildings are all different too. From the outside, traditional churches are easily recognisable; it is the more modern ones that you might miss. However, on the inside, these buildings all share some common key features, such as the altar (communion table), the pulpit, the lectern, stained glass windows and, of course, the symbol of the cross. On most occasions, it would be very clear that the building you were inside was a church, but it is not always called a church. You might hear the term cathedral (a church which is often very big and ornate, and is presided over by a bishop) or chapel, or even house churches. Different names, different styles – but all for the purpose of worship of God, and that is the important thing to remember. The church leaders have different names too (for example, priests, vicars, ministers and pastors) but essentially their roles are the same: to look after the people in the community and to lead church services. Most services, though not all, have a combination of hymns, prayers, Bible readings, teachings and sermon, and most churches have some kind of celebration of the meal eaten by Jesus at his Last Supper, which included bread and wine.

The Christian calendar follows the same pattern every year, with events being celebrated at the same time each year. Advent consists of the four Sundays leading up to Christmas (birth of Jesus), Epiphany (when the wise men visited Jesus) is on 6 January, Ash Wednesday (the first day of the 40 days of Lent) remembers the temptations of Jesus, Holy Week (including Good Friday) and Easter remember the death and **resurrection** of Jesus, Pentecost celebrates the gift of the Holy Spirit and the birth of the Church, and Ascension Sunday remembers Jesus being taken up to heaven. There are others, and indeed each Church has variations on how they celebrate each of them.

Sacraments: Some churches, such as the Roman Catholic, Orthodox Churches and some **Anglican** Churches, have seven of these special occasions. They are seen as rites, events of special significance. Many Protestant Churches have two – the **baptism** of a child or adult, and the celebration of the Last Supper – as these are required of Christians in the Gospels. You will learn about these two later.

Key Christian teachings

This is the Apostles' Creed. A creed is a statement that a person believes in. It gives a good outline of everything you need to know for this part of the course.

> I believe in God, the Father almighty,
> creator of heaven and earth.
> I believe in Jesus Christ, His only Son, our Lord,
> who was conceived by the Holy Spirit,
> born of the Virgin Mary,
> suffered under Pontius Pilate,
> was crucified, died, and was buried;
> he descended to the dead.
> On the third day he rose again;
> he ascended into heaven,
> he is seated at the right hand of the Father,
> and he will come to judge the living and the dead.
> I believe in the Holy Spirit,
> the holy catholic Church,
> the communion of saints,
> the forgiveness of sins,
> the resurrection of the body,
> and the life everlasting.
> Amen.

Some things this book refers to, which you might not know:

The Gospels are the first four books of the New Testament – Matthew, Mark, Luke and John. They are called gospel, which means good news, as they tell the story of the life of Jesus.

The **Catechism of the Catholic Church** is a collection of the key teachings which Catholics should believe and follow.

1.1 Beliefs and teachings

The nature of God

Christians believe God has many qualities, many of which we can try to understand in human terms. However, they also believe that, as God is the creator of all, then it is impossible to understand God fully, because as humans we cannot really comprehend the nature of God. You need to specifically know about three qualities, but they are closely linked to many others as well.

God is omnipotent

Omnipotent means 'all-powerful'. God can do anything. Omnipotence is part of being supreme or absolute. It also means God is eternal, because there can be nothing which can overpower or overcome God. Christians believe God's power is used with wisdom, and because God is **omnibenevolent** (all-loving), then this power is used justly and fairly.

'Great is our Lord and mighty in power' *(Psalm 147:5)*

The best example of God's power is the belief that the world was created from nothing, as described in the book of Genesis (see page 10). This also shows us God is **omniscient** (all-knowing), as to be able to create takes intelligence as well as power. The creation was initially perfect, a paradise. Many scholars have said that only God creates; humans reshape or copy what they see around them, taking ideas and using them but never coming up with a totally new thing. In this sense, creation is something entirely divine.

In the Bible, there are many examples of God's power. For example, when releasing the Israelites from their slavery in Egypt, God sent ten plagues upon the Egyptians. In the Gospel stories about Jesus, Jesus claims his power to heal comes from God. They also recount that Jesus himself rose from the dead – the ultimate show of power, proving he was the Son of God.

God is loving

> 'For God so loved the world that He gave his only begotten Son, that whosoever believes in Him shall not perish but shall have eternal life.' *(John 3:16)*

The word used for God is benevolent, or omnibenevolent. It means that God loves everyone regardless of their character or actions. This is an absolute, all-encompassing love which accepts them for good and bad. The Bible says that God's love is limitless – it is constantly there through all time. Humans built a barrier between themselves and God by

Influences

Believing God to be omnipotent, I look at the natural world around me and feel awestruck. A beautiful sunset – God did that; the power of the waves or lightning in a storm – God at work. *If* I believe God can do everything, I pray in the belief that God can help me.

committing sins and not following God's ways. God's supreme act of love was to send Jesus, the Son of God, to die as a sacrifice and **atonement** for those sins. Humans could not break the barrier, only God could – and God's love was the motivation for that sacrifice. It is this love which ensures God is fair in judgement of us – so at Judgement Day, after death (see page 13) when our soul will be judged, God will allow us into heaven as long as we are truly sorry (repentant) for our sins.

Christians believe the love of God is seen all the time in the world. **Miracles** are a way God intervenes to help us. People who do great good, such as Mother Teresa, are said to be reflections of God on Earth, or it is thought that God is working through them. Many Christians talk about feeling comforted by God when they are going through difficult times.

God is just

> 'For I the Lord love justice.' *(Isaiah 61:8)*

This means God is always fair. God sees everyone as having equal worth. God's fairness is absolute, so there can never be any bias held or shown by God. God is omniscient (all-knowing), which makes it possible to be fair in any judgement – after all, God knows everything about everything. God is also transcendent (beyond space and time, seeing all things at once) so cannot be influenced, and can be impartial in any judgements made. This means that God can judge with absolutely no prejudice. Christians believe God hates injustice – so they should always strive to treat others in a just manner.

The most important time when God is just will be at Judgement Day in the afterlife. God will judge between those who have done right and those who have done wrong. God will then deal with each of us based on that judgement.

Since God is all-loving, Christians believe that God's justice is dispensed with mercy. Mercy is when compassion is shown in dealing with someone who has done wrong, so deserves punishment. God understands that humans do wrong, and that circumstances influence us – as long as the person is truly sorry, God will be merciful.

Influences

If I am influenced by my belief that God is love, I want to show that love to others. I try to help when I see help is needed, not for any reward but just to share God's love. I know that God is loving, and whatever I do, I will still be loved, which is a comfort.

Influences

If I believe God is just, I know God will always be just to me. This influences me in the way I deal with other people. I always try to be fair-minded in making decisions, and fair to others – regardless of how they are with me.

The Basics

1. Explain why many Christians say it is very difficult to understand God.
2. What does it mean to say God is omnipotent? Give some examples of this.
3. What does it mean to say God is loving? Give some examples of this.
4. What does it mean to say God is just? Give some examples of this.
5. 'It is impossible to describe the nature of God.' Do you agree with this statement? Explain arguments to agree and arguments to disagree. Then write a justified conclusion showing which of the two sides you think is stronger, and why.

Topic 1.1 Beliefs and teachings

The problem of evil and suffering

Evil and suffering provide the greatest challenge to a person's faith – in the face of terrible evil, how can we believe in God?

The problem

Christians believe God is all-knowing, all-loving and all-powerful. At the same time, they see evil and suffering in the world around them everywhere, as they see people in pain, and they themselves experience it. So how can their idea of God be compatible with their experience of the world? For many centuries, Christian theologians have tried to solve that conundrum – God must be allowing evil and suffering; God could easily have made a world without it, or stop it when it starts. However, this doesn't happen – God lets us experience evil and suffering, but why? No one has managed to come up with an explanation that perfectly resolves the issue – every proposed solution has flaws.

Some suggested solutions to this conundrum

Evil and suffering exist as a punishment for the things we do wrong

Everyone does things they shouldn't, so when we suffer, it is as a consequence of sin. God is punishing us.

Evil and suffering are tests of our faith
In this solution, God allows us to suffer to see if we stay strong in our beliefs. Many people turn more strongly to God at difficult times, finding comfort in their belief or even finding belief.

Evil and suffering exist so that we learn and take responsibility for the world
Christians believe humans were given the duty of stewardship over the creation. This includes helping others. You cannot see something as good unless you can see its opposite – bad – in the world somewhere. There has to be the contrast for either to have meaning. By seeing bad, we can step in and do something to help. Hence, God allows evil and suffering to help us to develop as compassionate beings, which is achieved by taking responsibility.

Evil and suffering exist – just accept that, and that a human will never understand why God allows it
This is the idea that we cannot begin to understand God, so how can we understand the rationale behind what God does or does not allow? People who believe this think you accept the evil and suffering, don't blame God, but look for ways to help others and reduce their suffering.

Is God responsible for it all?
We can split evil into that which comes from the natural world (natural evil), such as disease and natural disasters, and that which comes from humans (moral evil), such as murder and exploitation. All evil causes pain – physical, mental or emotional – which we call suffering. God created the world, so must be responsible for that – though we aren't doing much to look after it! Humans are responsible for moral evil, not God, as God has given humans free will – the ability and licence to make decisions for ourselves, including whether to be selfish and hurtful or kind and caring.

Christians believe we cannot blame God for moral evil. In Genesis 3, the story of the Fall is told – where Adam and Eve disobeyed God and were thrown out of paradise as a punishment. The temptation to disobey and thus do evil was introduced into the creation, and is part of every person – the important thing is to resist it, and living a Christian life helps a person to do that.

> ### Influences
> If a person believes in God, they might decide that any suffering they face is just a test of their faith. This influences them to turn to God in prayer, accepting God's will. Someone else might be influenced by the existence of evil and suffering to do charitable work, trying to help reduce the suffering of others.

The Basics
1. What is the problem of evil and suffering for Christians?
2. Using examples, explain the two types of evil.
3. Explain some of the ways Christians have tried to explain why God allows evil and suffering.
4. 'An all-loving God would not allow evil to exist.' Do you agree with this statement? Explain arguments for and against the statement. Then write a justified conclusion.

Topic 1.1 Beliefs and teachings

The oneness of God and the Trinity

> 'I believe in God, the Father almighty, maker of heaven and earth, and in Jesus Christ his only Son … I believe in the Holy Spirit.' *(Apostles' Creed)*

Christians believe in one supreme God understood through the concept of the Trinity – three persons-in-one. This does not mean that there are three separate gods – the three are one. All three share the same divine nature, and all three are equal. This Trinitarian belief about God makes Christianity quite different from all other religions.

Sounds quite complicated, doesn't it? But that should not be a surprise because how can humans really comprehend God? So the idea of the Trinity symbolises how complex the nature of God really is. It emphasises that God is different from humans, and not fully understandable by us, even if we can make sense of some aspects, like God's omnipotence and benevolence.

> The Trinity has several alternative names. 'Tri' means three, so most names for it include this as part of their wording. Triune God and Tripartite God are two alternative names; it is also called the 'Godhead'.

From this diagram, we can see that the three parts (persons) of the Trinity are the Father, the Son and the Holy Spirit. God is all these, and all three are God. However, each of the three is different from the other two. One way to make sense of this on a simple scale is to think about any student, and the roles they assume in their life. You are sitting in class, learning about the Christian belief of the Trinity. How you present yourself, speak, the skills you use – they are all specifically for the role of student. When you go home, and all schoolwork is done, you probably present yourself differently, speak differently and use different skills – because you are in the role of son/daughter. However, when you go out to spend time with friends, you probably change all those aspects again – the role of friend. There will be more 'persons' to your existence as well. So, in a much more elevated way, God also has different roles, or persons, to make three persons-in-one.

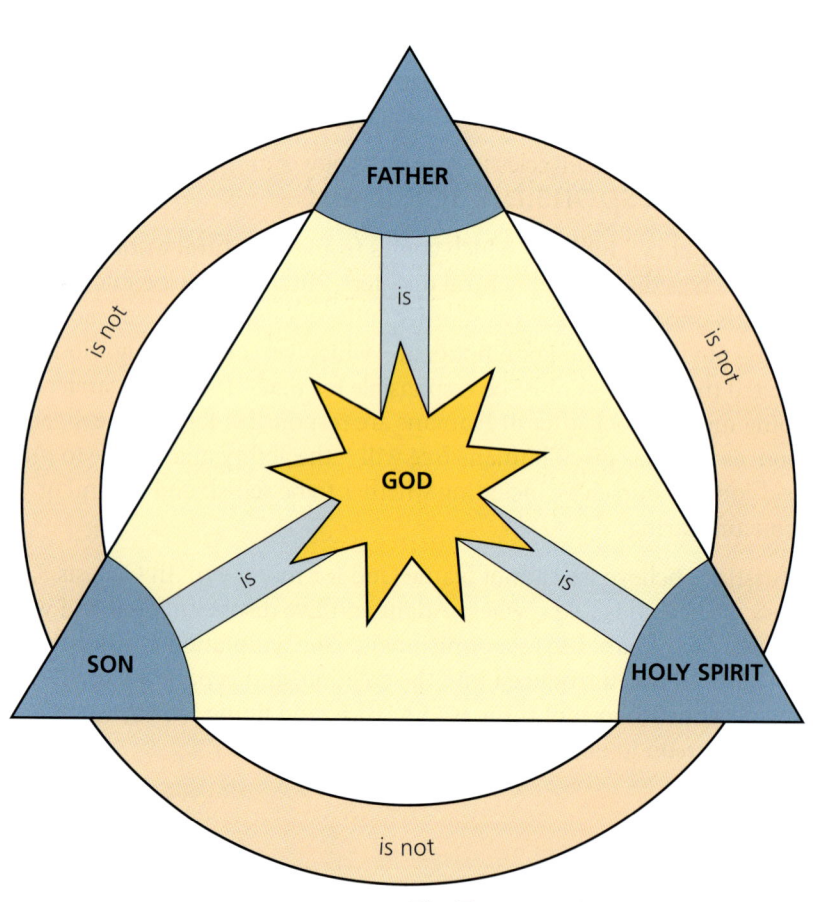

The Trinity can be expressed through this simple diagram

Beliefs about … God the Father

- God the Father is the creator of heaven and Earth, sustainer of the universe. God the Father has no source.
- It is God the Father who blesses Jesus at his baptism, proclaiming him as God's 'beloved Son'.
- It is to God the Father that Jesus prays in the Garden of Gethsemane before his arrest, and to whom he cries out when he is about to die on the cross.
- Jesus taught his disciples the **Lord's Prayer**, which begins 'Our Father …'.
- At his Ascension, Jesus said he was ascending 'to my Father and your Father, to my God and your God' (John 20).

… God the Son

God the Son is Jesus Christ, God made incarnate to live as a human. The Son comes from the Father to bring God's message to Earth so that humans know how to live their lives as God wants them to.

- Jesus performed miracles to reveal the power and glory of God.
- He was born to die as a sacrifice for the sins of humans – his **crucifixion** was an atonement for human sin, which had caused a barrier between us and God, preventing us from getting to heaven.
- Then he rose from the dead, showing his power over death.
- Jesus Christ is the personification of God's love – God's love made flesh.
- The Gospels describe his life. John's Gospel calls Jesus 'logos' or Word, saying the Word was with God at the creation. John (1:2) also says that through Jesus all things were made and without him nothing was made that has been made.

… God the Holy Spirit

God the Holy Spirit is at work in the world all the time. The Spirit comes from Father and Son.

- In Genesis, the creation story tells of how the Spirit of God moved over the void (nothingness) that was before the creation.
- For Christians, they believe that they receive the Holy Spirit at their own baptism, because Jesus told his disciples that they would be baptised with the Holy Spirit.
- Christians believe the Holy Spirit is the source of their strength to keep their faith, to help others, to proclaim their message. They believe God the Holy Spirit is in their hearts, driving them forward and comforting them when in need.
- In John's Gospel, Jesus talks of a Spirit (paraclete) who will replace his presence in the world. It is this which came to the disciples after Jesus' death, giving them the courage to go out into the world and tell everyone about Jesus' message.

Influences

Believing in the Trinity is shown in every Christian's life. They refer to the Trinity in every act of worship; they give and receive blessings in the name of the Trinity. They repeat creeds which describe the Trinity, such as the Apostles' Creed. This belief influences them to live their lives following the message of the Son, Jesus. It influences them to be thankful for God's mercy in sending Jesus, the Son of God. It influences them to think God is always with them as the Spirit, giving a sense of comfort and protection.

The Basics

1. Explain what is meant by the concept of the Trinity.
2. Copy the diagram of the Trinity and make notes about each of the three persons of God around the image.
3. Explain how belief in the Trinity might influence a Christian.
4. 'God the Son is the most important part of the Trinity.' Do you agree with this statement? Explain arguments to agree and to disagree. Give a justified conclusion showing which side you favour and why.

Topic 1.1 Beliefs and teachings

The creation

Christian beliefs about the creation of the world are related in the book of Genesis, chapters 1–3. Christians believe the several stories here describe literally or allegorically how and why God created the world. Genesis 1 describes the making of the world day by day. Genesis 2 focuses on the creation of man and woman, and their place in the creation – that is, that they will be the rulers of it. Genesis 3 describes the Fall – the **original sin** being committed, which results in the fall from **grace** of humans, and their separation from God. God is transcendent, omniscient and omnipotent – to create the world is easily within God's powers.

Genesis 1

Day 1: In the beginning there was nothing but darkness, the Earth was without form and the Spirit of God blew over the restless waters. Then God said, 'Let there be light', and there was light. God said it was good and called the darkness night and the light day.

Day 2: God then separated the firmament from the waters and called the firmament 'Heaven'. The heavens were above the Earth with a space in between.

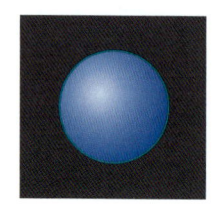

Day 3: God said, 'Let the waters under the heavens be gathered together and let the dry land appear.' God called the dry land earth and the waters seas. God said it was good. God then created vegetation on the land – grass, herbs, and fruits of all kinds from the trees.

Day 4: God said, 'Let there be lights in the firmament to divide the day from the night, the seasons and for the days and years.' God made the moon and the stars for the night and the sun for the day.

Day 5: God created fish for the waters, whales and small fish, and birds to fill the air. God blessed each of them saying, 'Be fruitful and multiply, fill the waters and the skies.'

Day 6: God said, 'Let the Earth be filled with living creatures, creeping things, cattle, beasts of every kind. Let us also make man in our image and give man dominion (power) over the seas, the skies and the earth.' He created male and female alike. God then blessed them and told them to be fruitful and multiply. God had given humans everything and it was all good.

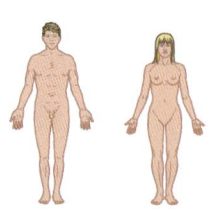

Day 7: God finished the work of creation and rested. God blessed the seventh day and made it holy.

Influences

If I believe that God created the world, I might be awestruck at the power I see around me in the world, and hence the power of God. As the world is God's creation, I will want to show respect to God by looking after it.

Interpreting Genesis

There are a number of ways to interpret Genesis.

Fundamental/literalist approach

Fundamentalist Christians see Genesis as an absolute truth – that is, word-for-word correct. For those holding this interpretation, where there is any dispute with science, it is science that is wrong. They believe in an infallible, omnipotent God, so it is easy to believe that God created the world as per Genesis. When challenged by fossil evidence, for example, these believers would say that God put the fossils in place as a test of our faith. They point to statements in the Bible which say God will give clear information, which needs no interpretation – this is then applied to Genesis, so what it says is what happened. God is not trying to trick anyone.

Genesis as allegory (non-literal)

The majority of Christians from across the different denominations believe that Genesis is allegorical not factual. The intention behind Genesis is to describe the relationship between God and the created world – that the world was created deliberately by a Supreme God, and the world is the place for humans to serve and glorify God their creator. The idea of 'six days' is not meant to be taken as days of our time, rather periods of time, or 'God days' (so geological time descriptions for the phases of creation still fit). This interpretation makes it easier to believe Genesis as well as scientific theories for the origins of the universe.

Genesis as myth

Some people believe that the Genesis creation stories are just ways to express belief in a Supreme God. The stories are inspired by the world we live in and a sense of there being something greater than all of us which was responsible for it all in some way, and that we are special within the world. Really, the stories are giving us messages – the creation was deliberate, we are special, the creation itself is special and we have trusteeship (stewardship) over it.

The role of the Trinity in creation

Belief in the Trinity is reflected in the creation story. On Day 1, we see that God is there, as is the Spirit, which moves over the void. The Gospel of John opens:

> 'In the beginning was the Word, and the Word was with God, and the Word was God. He was with God in the beginning. Through him all things were made; without him nothing was made that has been made. In him was life, and that life was the light of all mankind. The light shines in the darkness, and the darkness has not overcome it.' *(John 1:1–5)*

This is telling us that Jesus is the Word and was there at the beginning of time and crucial to the creation. God is the Trinity, so it makes sense that the Trinity created the world.

The Basics

1. Where do we find the creation stories of Christianity?
2. In your own words, outline the Christian creation story.
3. There are several interpretations of the creation story. Explain each one.
4. Explain the role of the Trinity in the creation.
5. Which interpretation of the creation story do you find most reasonable? Explain why.
6. 'The only important detail in the Genesis creation stories is that God created the world.' Do you agree? Explain arguments for and against this statement. Give a justified conclusion in summary.

Topic 1.1 Beliefs and teachings

Beliefs about the afterlife

According to Christianity, we will each live again after our physical death. Physical death is when the brain dies and organs cease to function; however, Christianity teaches that death is not the end. Rather, it is the point where life on Earth ends, hopefully to be replaced by life with God. This life on Earth is temporary and limited (because of time and space), whereas life with God is eternal, beyond time and space.

In simple terms, Christians believe that, after death, our soul leaves our body. Catholic and Orthodox Christians believe there is then a time of purification, called **purgatory**. Purgatory is for those who have not committed sins which bring eternal damnation (where a person has died without feeling remorse or repentance for their misdeeds in life). Then there is the Judgement Day, when Jesus Christ will judge each person according to their behaviour on Earth. The judgement given results in being placed in heaven for the good/repentant who have been forgiven by God, or hell for the bad/unrepentant. Heaven is eternal bliss with God; hell is eternal damnation. Each of these ideas is expressed in several ways by different Christian groups, so we will look at the key aspects – resurrection, Judgement Day, heaven and hell.

Resurrection

> 'I believe in the resurrection of the body.'
> *(Apostles' Creed)*

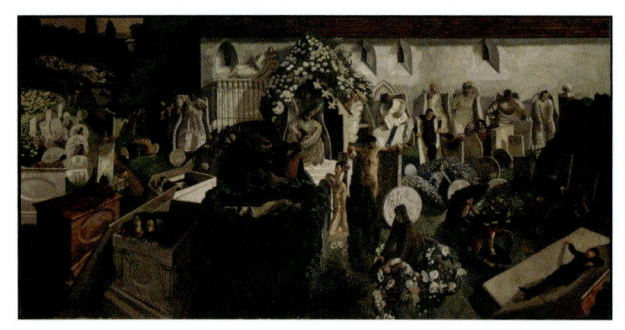

The Resurrection in Cookham Churchyard, by Sir Stanley Spencer

For Christians, the afterlife is about resurrection. The soul is what makes us *us*; it is the special spark which makes each of us unique. Resurrection is the belief that our soul is reborn into some new body. Whether this body is a physical resurrection into a physical body or some other kind is not clear. Traditional ideas speak about the dead coming out of their graves for Judgement Day, which suggests this body gets revived somehow. This has encouraged Christians throughout history to have burials rather than cremations. **St Paul** said:

> 'The body that is sown is perishable, it is raised imperishable. It is sown a natural body, it is raised a spiritual body.'
> *(1 Corinthians 15: 42, 44)*

This is interpreted to mean that we don't climb out of our graves in the same, but rejuvenated, body. Instead, we gain a new, spiritual body, which lives forever, leaving the earthly body to decay on Earth. Throughout a Christian funeral, there are many references to resurrection and an afterlife. This gives those in mourning comfort in the belief that their loved ones are continuing their journey towards God, and that death is not the end.

The hope for resurrection comes from Jesus' resurrection – he had a physical body according to the Gospels. The disciple Thomas was even invited to put his hand inside a wound in Jesus' side which had been inflicted at the crucifixion, so as to have proof Jesus was really back from the dead. That Jesus was physically resurrected encourages the Christian teaching that resurrection for them will also be a physical resurrection.

All through his teaching ministry, Jesus spoke of life after death with God; indeed, several of his Parables are specifically about that, such as the Parable of the Sheep and Goats. This Parable describes Judgement Day, when people are divided up according to the good deeds they did for others during their lifetime. Jesus also said that life after death was 'through him' – you have to believe in Jesus to have life after death.

The Basics

1. Give two understandings of what death is.
2. What is the soul?
3. Briefly describe what Christians believe about life after death.
4. Explain different Christian beliefs about the resurrection.
5. Do you think it is unfair to suggest that only those who believe in Jesus Christ can have eternal life? Explain your answer.

Judgement Day

All Christians believe that there will be a Judgement Day, when Jesus Christ judges the living and the dead to decide if they are worthy of a place in heaven with God. In one of his Parables (stories told to explain a religious idea) – the Parable of the Sheep and Goats (Matthew 25:31–46) – Jesus describes the judgement at the end of time. On Judgement Day, all people are brought together and sorted by Jesus 'as a shepherd separates the sheep from the goats'. Jesus explains that the blessed are going to heaven because they helped him during their lives on Earth:

> 'For I was hungry and you gave me something to eat, I was thirsty and you gave me something to drink, I was a stranger and you invited me in, I needed clothes and you clothed me, I was sick and you looked after me, I was in prison and you came to visit me.' *(Matthew 25:35–36)*

The people say they were not aware they had helped Jesus. Jesus responds that by helping others, they helped him. Those who never helped are condemned to hell:

> 'Truly whatever you did not do for one of them, you did not do for me.' *(Matthew 25:45)*

God is just and merciful, so Christians believe that those who commit sins (i.e. disobey God) can still be admitted to heaven; they just must repent, i.e. be truly sorry. This means that the judgement will take into account what people did to make up for the wrongs they committed.

Many Christians believe in one judgement, done on Judgement Day, which happens at the end of time after the coming of the Kingdom of God on Earth (a time of peace, when all live according to God's ways). However, Roman Catholics believe in two forms of judgement – at death, there is the particular judgement, when souls are judged and sent to purgatory, heaven or hell. Purgatory is for the purification for souls, making them worthy of heaven. Only the truly good or truly wicked will go to heaven or hell at this point, meaning most souls experience purgatory. Praying for the souls of the dead is done in the hope that those prayers will ease the passage through purgatory. The second, final judgement takes place when Christ returns at the end of time. The dead are resurrected, and then judged. All souls are judged according to their belief in Christ, and only those who reject Christ go to everlasting condemnation. Those good souls who did not know of Christ – for example, having lived in a non-Christian country with no information about Jesus – would be saved by the mercy of Christ and the atonement made when he was crucified.

The Basics

1. What is meant by Judgement Day? When does it happen, according to most Christians?
2. What happens on Judgement Day?
3. Outline the Parable of the Sheep and Goats.
4. 'The way to reach heaven is to help others.' Do you agree with this statement? Explain arguments for and against, and then give a justified conclusion showing which side you think is stronger.

Topic 1.1 Beliefs and teachings

| HEAVEN | Goodness / Happiness / Eternal / With God | Punishment / Suffering / Misery / Without God | HELL |

Heaven and hell

Following the judgement, Christians believe our soul will be sent to heaven or hell. Given God is just and merciful, and that most people would be truly repentant in the face of God, then maybe we should expect heaven to hold many more souls than hell.

Heaven is not part of the physical universe: Jesus says, 'My Kingdom is not of this world' (John 18:36). St Paul's letter to the Hebrews tells them that 'heaven is not of this creation'. This makes sense if the resurrection is of a spiritual body, as the universe is a physical universe, not a spiritual one, and science only covers the physical and material world, not any spiritual one.

Heaven is eternal bliss with God, which is interpreted by some to be a timeless existence of goodness and happiness. While most of us imagine heaven as a physical place with abundant food, beautiful gardens and so on, Christians tend to think more of a spiritual existence with God.

Hell is described by some Christians as a place of eternal damnation – a place of suffering and torture. Historically, the Church taught that hell was a place of eternal punishment and suffering, with all souls in torment without end. Many modern Christians do have a problem with that idea, though, because they do not think it is compatible with believing in an all-loving, merciful God. Some of these Christians see hell as temporary – people who have committed truly wicked acts must be punished, as must those who have been generally unkind or bad people. Indeed, Jesus said that every person does wrong at some time – for example, when asking 'those without sin' to cast the first stone at a woman accused of adultery (no one did!). However, some Christians believe that there must be a point for each person at which their punishment is enough for the crimes they committed. God being all-loving and omniscient (all-knowing) would be able to recognise that point and then welcome them into heaven. For some Christians, hell is just nothing – no resurrection, no life with God – it is separation from God forever. They do not believe God would torture even the worst people; rather God would not give them a new life at all.

Influences

Christians believe there is life after death, but that it is decided based on two things – believing in Jesus, and being someone who shows compassion to others. So, Christians follow Jesus' teachings, trying to live their life as he described a good person should. They should also make it their habit to help others however they can. This becomes part of their nature through the transforming influence of the Holy Spirit when welcomed into their life.

The Basics

1. Describe how Judgement Day affects whether a person goes to heaven or hell after death.
2. Explain what is meant by heaven.
3. Explain different Christians' interpretations of hell.
4. Explain, using examples, how belief in the Christian idea of life after death might influence a person in their daily life.
5. 'It is not important for a Christian to believe in life after death.' Do you agree? Explain arguments to agree and disagree. Then write a justified conclusion showing which side you feel is stronger.

The Incarnation and Jesus as the Son of God

A nativity scene showing the Incarnation

Incarnation means 'born in the flesh'. Christians believe Jesus was God, but was born and lived fully as a human. They believe Jesus was actually the Son of God – a part of the Trinity, fully God. John's Gospel begins by saying that Jesus was with God as the Word when God created the world (see page 11):

> 'The Word became flesh and lived amongst us. We have seen His glory, the glory of the one and only [Son], which came from the Father, full of grace and truth.' *(John 1:14)*

So Christians believe Jesus was fully human, but fully divine at the same time. He had to be fully human to be able to live in the world as a man, and to then die. He had to be fully divine to be able to rise from the dead, and mend the relationship between God and humans which had been broken.

Why did the Incarnation have to happen?

Christians believe God had to be born as a human to show God's love. This was done in several ways through Jesus. First of all, Jesus taught people to help them understand how they should live. His message was one of love, summed up in the teaching 'Love your neighbour', which he said was one of the two great commandments, alongside 'Love God'. He also performed miracles to help people but also to show the power of God, as he claimed his power to perform miracles came from God. Finally, he was crucified and died as a sacrifice for humans – an atonement for human sin (see page 23). Christians believe that humans had strayed so far away from how God wanted them to live that they had created a barrier between them and God. This barrier could not be broken by humans, so God sent Jesus, the Son of God, to be sacrificed. Christians believe that the death of Jesus broke down that barrier and made it possible for humans to be reunited with God in heaven after death. Jesus then rose from the dead, showing his divine power, before ascending to heaven, returning to God.

Roman Catholics believe Jesus' sacrifice, which was an atonement, was the key reason for God to come to Earth as the Incarnation. For Protestants, the fact that God walked among humankind as a man, showing love through God's message and miracles, was just as important a reason – and some believe it to be a more important reason.

Christus Victor is the idea that Christ has power over death

> 'For God so loved the world that He gave His only begotten Son, that whosoever believes in Him shall not die but shall have everlasting life.' *(John 3:16)*

Topic 1.1 Beliefs and teachings

Why do Christians believe Jesus to be the Son of God?

The Bible and Christian teachings give Christians many reasons to believe that Jesus was the Son of God. Some examples are:

- Before Jesus was born, his mother, Mary, was visited by the Angel Gabriel. This visit is called the Annunciation, and is celebrated by Roman Catholic and Orthodox Christians. Mary was told that she was 'with child', having been chosen to bear God's Son. Gabriel also visited others and told them of the impending birth of the **Messiah**, the Son of God.
- The birth stories speak of Jesus receiving visitors – wise men and shepherds – who had been led to the birth place by a star and by angels. In fact, if we combine the two versions of the birth, found in Matthew and Luke's Gospels, we see that the whole of creation is represented at the birth – wise men (rich), shepherds (poor), animals (nature) and angels (heavenly hosts). Jesus – as Son of God – completes the set.
- As a boy, Jesus was found at the temple discussing the religious law with the priests. They were astounded at his knowledge and confidence.
- Jesus' power to perform miracles shows he was something special. He healed people (for example, blind Bartimaeus was given sight), raised people from the dead (for example, he raised Lazarus days after he had died) and had control over nature (for example, he calmed a storm on the Sea of Galilee). He claimed this power to have been from God.
- In Mark's Gospel, Jesus is asked if he is the Son of God – he answers, 'I am.' In John's Gospel, he says 'I and the Father are one.' Before his **ascension**, Jesus tells his disciples, 'I came out from the Father and have come into the world, again I go away from the world and go to the Father.' These quotes suggest Jesus claimed to be the Son of God.
- The Apostles' and the Nicene Creeds both sum up Christian belief, and are recited by Catholic, Orthodox and Anglican Christians. They both describe Jesus as the Son of God – it is a central belief for Christians.

Influences

For a Christian, the belief that Jesus was the Son of God gives greater importance to Jesus' teachings. Over the centuries, it has been the main reason for following the teachings – they come from such an important source. *If* I believe Jesus was the Son of God, then I believe what he said to be the truth. Believing Jesus to be the Son of God means I will worship Jesus, as he isn't just a prophet, as religions like Islam believe.

If I believe God was willing to live on Earth as a human, setting aside his divinity, then I feel more grateful for the love he showed through his sacrifice. That gratitude might make me more compassionate to others – I am using Jesus as a role model.

The Basics

1. What does it mean to say Jesus was the Incarnation of God?
2. Explain two teachings about the Incarnation.
3. Why do Christians believe the Incarnation had to happen?
4. Why do Christians believe Jesus was the Son of God?
5. Explain how belief that Jesus was the Son of God might influence Christians today.
6. 'If Jesus was the Son of God, humans can't copy him as a role model.' Do you agree? Explain arguments to agree and disagree, and then write a justified conclusion.

The crucifixion

Jesus' death is central to Christian belief, stated in the Nicene and Apostles' Creeds. He was executed by the Roman method of crucifixion. The story of Jesus' death by crucifixion begins a week earlier than the day Christians call Good Friday. It begins when he enters Jerusalem, with crowds cheering for him, on Palm Sunday, possibly the day that the Jewish religious leaders finally decided they had to get rid of him. Together, the Gospels record some variations in the details of events leading up to the actual crucifixion, which are probably due to the different sources each Gospel writer used.

An artwork showing the crucifixion of Jesus

The events leading up to and including the crucifixion

- The evening before he was crucified, Jesus hosted the 'Last Supper', where he shared bread and wine with his disciples. He said this was his body and blood, and told them to eat it in remembrance of him. This is why Christians share the **Eucharist** (see pages 37–38). He also said Judas would betray him and Peter would deny he knew him.
- Later, while his disciples slept, Jesus prayed in the garden of Gethsemane. He asked God to free him from the suffering he was due to face, but was given no reply, so he accepted God's will as his fate.
- Jesus was arrested after Judas identified him to soldiers, fulfilling Jesus' prediction about betrayal. The disciples began to fight the soldiers to defend Jesus. As a man of peace, and accepting his fate, Jesus stopped them.
- Jesus then underwent a series of trials before the Sanhedrin (religious leaders), Herod and finally Pontius Pilate (the only one with the power to have him executed). Pilate had him whipped, hoping to satisfy the demands of the religious leaders. Seeing no other option, and scared that these men would complain to the Roman Emperor that he was not doing his job, Pilate then washed his hands of Jesus' fate and allowed him to be executed. Soldiers dressed Jesus in a purple robe and placed a crown of thorns on his head – mocking him as a king without power.
- The morning of the crucifixion, Jesus was forced to carry his cross to Golgotha (a hill near Jerusalem, the name of which means 'place of the skull'), where he was to be executed. He was unable to carry his cross all the way, so a man called Simon of Cyrene was forced by the Romans to help him.
- Jesus was crucified between two criminals. One mocked him, the other showed pity for Jesus, who he said was innocent. Jesus said they would be with him in paradise that day.
- Soldiers threw dice for his robe, and made fun of him – telling him to get off the cross if he really was the Son of God.
- On the cross, he asked for something to quench his thirst, and was given sour wine. A spear was stabbed into his side. He asked God, 'Father forgive them, they know not what they do.'
- Jesus cried out, 'Father why have you forsaken me?', and then 'It is finished.' The sky went black, and the curtain in the temple (which hid the holiest part of the temple from non-priests) tore in two to give anyone sight of the interior. One soldier said, 'Surely this man was the Son of God.' Jesus died ('gave up his soul').

Topic 1.1 Beliefs and teachings

Why did Jesus have to die?

We can answer this from several perspectives.

Jewish leaders

At this time, Palestine was controlled by the Romans, who were ruthless in putting down any rebellion. There were many rebellions against Roman rule both before and after Jesus lived. Given the popularity of Jesus, and the fact he drew huge crowds to hear his words, revolutionaries might have been prepared to use Jesus to trigger a rebellion. The Jewish leaders wanted to stop this because it would have brought severe reprisals on all the Jewish people and would have meant them losing their leadership roles in the Jewish community. More importantly, the Romans would have stopped them from carrying out worship as prescribed in the Torah, which was a key duty. In other words, Jesus was a potential threat to them.

More importantly, Jesus had challenged the religious authority of these leaders. He said and did things they felt to be against their religion, even **blasphemy** (insulting God) and at the very least he allowed people to think he was the Messiah (the chosen one sent by God). Blasphemy was punishable by death under Jewish law.

Christians

Christians now believe Jesus had to die because that was why he was alive. Jesus was the Incarnation, the Son of God. Only Jesus' death as a sacrifice was capable of breaking down the barrier that humans had generated between themselves and God. This barrier was forged from sin and selfishness; his death made atonement for that sin and broke the barrier, allowing humans to be reunited with God in heaven (see page 23).

Influences

If I believe Jesus was crucified for my sake, I will be thankful for that sacrifice – it gives me the chance to be reunited with God. I might show my thanks by doing things for others, such as using some of my wealth to sponsor a child in a developing country. I would also worship Jesus as God, and during Lent (the period leading up to Easter) spend time in prayer and reflection about what Jesus did for me. Daily reflection and meditation help to calm a person, as well as giving them a chance to better understand the whole idea of sacrifice.

The Basics

1 Why is the crucifixion an important event for Christians?
2 Outline the events leading up to and including the crucifixion.
3 Explain some reasons why Jesus 'had to die'.
4 'No person can be blamed for the death of Jesus.' Do you agree? Explain arguments to agree and to disagree. Write a justified conclusion, showing which point of view you support and why.

The resurrection

The resurrection is the term given to Jesus rising from the dead. Just as the crucifixion is central to Christian belief, so is the resurrection, also stated in the Creeds. For many Christians, this is the most important point of Jesus' life. It is celebrated on Easter Sunday (see pages 43–44).

All four Gospels record the resurrection, and a series of appearances after it. After Jesus died, his body was taken down from the cross and moved to the tomb of Joseph of Arimathea. Nothing could be done to prepare it for full entombment because it was the Sabbath, so it was wrapped in a shroud and laid in the tomb. The intention was that, when Sabbath was over, female followers would come to tend to the body before the tomb was sealed. So, on the Sunday after Jesus' crucifixion, Mary and others went to do this work, only to find the stone rolled away from the tomb, and the tomb itself empty. In Matthew's version, they are told by angels that Jesus has risen and that they should go and tell the disciples the news. In John's version, Mary sees a man she assumes to be the gardener and asks him where he has hidden the body. He then reveals himself as Jesus.

This altar is dominated by an empty cross – the symbol of Jesus Christ's resurrection

Later, Jesus reveals himself to all the disciples while they are hiding in an 'upper room', afraid of being arrested like Jesus was. Following this, there are several other resurrection appearances, which include Jesus continuing to teach his message and giving them the duty to do that in the world.

The crucial point is that Jesus had risen from the dead – as he said he would. His power over death shows he was the Son of God, and that God's love for Jesus is absolute. Christians believe that Jesus rising from the dead shows that they can have a life after death, in heaven with God – that death is not the end.

Influences

Christians must believe in the resurrection. This helps them believe in life after death, so when someone close to them dies, they know that person will be with God and that they will see them again, which comforts them. It is also the proof that Jesus was the Son of God, so validates all their other Christian beliefs. For Christians, Easter is the most important festival because of this event.

Topic 1.1 Beliefs and teachings

The ascension

Of the Gospels, Luke (24:50–53) and Mark (16:19) mention the ascension, which is when Jesus ascended to heaven to return to God. The Acts of the Apostles also include a longer version of the story (1:1–11). It is also found in the Creeds, so is a core belief for Christians. It is celebrated on Ascension Thursday.

Forty days after his resurrection, Jesus appeared to his disciples for the final time. He led them to the village of Bethany, where he blessed each one. He told them to return to Jerusalem and that they would receive the Holy Spirit (an event which is now celebrated at Pentecost), which would help them to preach his message everywhere. They then watched as he was 'taken up' to heaven, hidden by a cloud. As they continued to gaze towards heaven, two angels interrupted their thoughts, asking why they were looking in that direction – Jesus was gone but would return.

The ascension marks the end of Jesus' earthly ministry. His 'human' life had ended at the crucifixion, but the ascension marked his return to full glory as God. This might have been the first time that the disciples saw him as his true self – indeed, the accounts both suggest the disciples were in awe when they saw this event.

An artwork showing Jesus ascending to heaven

Influences

If I believe in the ascension, my belief that Jesus was the Son of God part of the Trinity is confirmed. This makes what he taught even more important because it is teaching from God, so I follow that teaching. At the ascension, Jesus gave his disciples a task to preach his message – believing this might make me want to do the same, to talk to people about Jesus' message.

The Basics

1 Describe the resurrection events.
2 Explain two reasons why the resurrection is an important event for Christians.
3 Describe the ascension.
4 Explain two reasons why the ascension was an important event for Christians.
5 'The resurrection is the most important event for Christians.' Do you agree? Explain arguments to agree and to disagree, before coming to a justified conclusion as to which point of view is stronger, and why.

Sin

Sin is an act which goes against God's laws. Sins are acts which hurt God and hurt others. The result of sin is that it separates a person from God. Sin was the reason that there was a barrier between humans and God; in other words, a barrier to **salvation** (see pages 24–25). This barrier prevented humans from being allowed into heaven with God. God was incarnated as a human – Jesus – to break the barrier down because humans could not do it for themselves. Jesus' death was the atonement that made up for that sin, making it possible to be reunited with God (see page 23).

> 'For all have sinned and fall short of the glory of God.'
> (Romans 3:23)

Everyone commits sins – big ones, little ones, deliberately or by default. Jesus said there were two great commandments – 'Love God' and 'Love your neighbour' – so anything which goes against either of these can be considered a sin. For example, for many, to deny God's existence is to insult God, so that would be against 'Love God'. Committing murder takes a life, and emotionally hurts many people – it is blatantly not 'Love your neighbour'. Both of these would be sins.

Roman Catholics see there being two kinds of sin – mortal and venial. Mortal sins are deliberate breaches of God's law on serious matters – for example, blasphemy, adultery or murder. They are considered to seriously offend God, throwing the love for us back in God's face, causing separation from God. If a person dies without having truly repented for these sins, they cannot go to heaven. They are called 'mortal' sins because they cause the 'spiritual death' of the soul. Venial sins are wrongs which upset God – for example, gossip or telling small lies (which do not lead to serious consequences). They are thought to weaken the soul – that is, they make it more likely that worse sins will be committed.

All Christians believe the crucial thing is to try not to sin, and to be truly sorry when you do. They believe that you can make up for sin by repenting of the wrongs already done, doing good deeds and by worshipping God. For many Christians, the sacraments of **Confession** and Eucharist are good ways to say sorry to God, and so have a 'clean slate' with God (see pages 34 and 37–38).

Influences

Belief in sin influences Christians in many ways. They will try to know and understand what is and what is not a sin. This helps them avoid committing sin through ignorance. They will accept that humans are frail and are likely to sin, but can reduce how much they sin by being mindful of God. This might make them pray very often. Many young Christians use the phrase 'What would Jesus do?' as a guide in their lives, helping them avoid sin. Many Christians do good deeds to make up for sin – they might act humbly, offer apologies for wrongs, and be proactive in doing good.

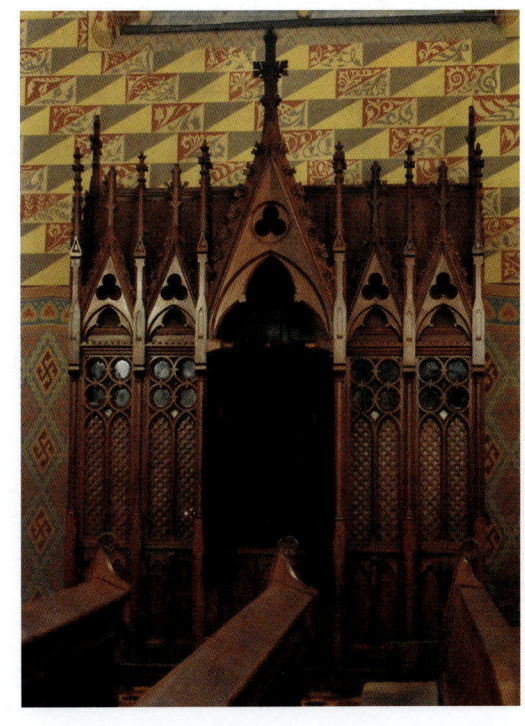

Roman Catholic churches have Confession boxes. These are linked cubicles for the purpose of confessing sins. The priest sits in one side, hidden from all, while the believer enters the other and seeks forgiveness for their sins privately and without the priest knowing their identity. They are there given tasks of penance

Topic 1.1 Beliefs and teachings

Original sin

For Christians, evil came into the world through the Fall, which we can read in Genesis 3. This is the story of Adam and Eve eating from the Tree of Knowledge in the Garden of Eden. God had forbidden them to eat from this tree, but a serpent persuaded Eve that there was no harm in eating its fruit. Eve persuaded Adam to taste the fruit. At this first show of disobedience, the two understood they had done wrong, so when God visited, they hid. God knew what they had done and threw them out of the Garden of Eden, telling them they would now have to fend for themselves. Man would have to work the land to get food; woman would struggle with childbirth; both would grow old and die.

The term 'original sin' was coined by Irenaeus, a Greek theologian of the second century CE. He said that all humans had the capacity to sin, and this 'ability' had itself come from that original sin by Adam and Eve. They realised they could disobey God, and then went ahead and did so – this is the first (so original) sin, which became the mind-set for humans going forward.

The Orthodox Church believes everyone inherits this original sin. Baptism is done to wash a baby clean of it. The Roman Catholic Church believes we inherit the capacity to sin, not Adam and Eve's actual sin – we then give in to temptation to commit sin. The Anglican Church sees sin as totally personal, and nothing to do with Adam and Eve; rather, it is part of the human condition, which can be fought against by living a 'life with Christ'. In complete contrast, **Quakers** focus on the 'inward light' of humans, that there is something of God in everyone. Sin, for them, comes from our abuse of our free will, not an inbuilt capacity to sin.

Adam and Eve in the Garden of Eden choosing to break God's rule that they should never eat of the Tree of Knowledge

The Basics

1. What is sin?
2. Using examples, explain how sin breaks Jesus' two great commandments.
3. Using examples, explain the two forms of sin which Roman Catholics believe in.
4. Explain two reasons why sin is such a big issue for Christians.
5. In your own words, retell the story of the original sin.
6. Explain two contrasting understandings of the impact of original sin.
7. 'It doesn't matter what you do, God will forgive you.' Do you agree? Explain arguments to agree and to disagree, including Christian arguments.

Atonement

You have already read this word a lot in your studies so far. It is really important in Christianity. It is one of the main reasons God was incarnated as Jesus Christ on Earth.

> 'For God so loved the world that He gave His only begotten Son, that whosoever believes in Him should not die but should have everlasting life.' *(John 3:16)*

Christians believe that, when Jesus was crucified and died, his death was an atonement, or making up, for the huge number of sins done by humans, which had separated us from God. If you think of 'atonement' as 'at-one-ment', it helps you to understand the term in its Christian sense – Jesus' sacrifice made humans be 'at one' with God again, so reconciled with God, or back on the right terms.

This image, *Bridge of Life*, shows the idea of atonement through a picture story. The human on the right of the image, kneeling, seeks forgiveness from God for their sin. Through the death of Jesus, symbolised by the cross, a bridge to God is created, and – at their death – the human can walk across because they have said sorry for sin, and Jesus' death has made atonement for them as well. Once on the far side, they are with God in heaven, having a new life, hence bridge to life. The cross is empty, as Jesus is with God in heaven, having conquered death.

The crucifix is a symbol of both sacrifice and atonement. It shows Jesus dead on the cross – his death was the atonement: he was a sacrifice for our sake. For Roman Catholic and Orthodox Christians, it is the most powerful symbol for Christianity, and many carry with them that symbol in the form of jewellery or **rosary** beads.

atonement
/əˈtəʊnm(ə)nt/
noun
1 the action of making amends for a wrong or injury
2 in Christian theology – the **reconciliation** of God and humankind through Jesus Christ

Bridge of Life by the Gospel Graffiti Crew

Roman Catholic rosary beads

The Basics

1 What is meant by atonement?
2 How was Jesus' death an atonement?
3 Explain two ways in which atonement is important to Christians today.
4 'Believing in the atonement, Christians should always make up with those who wrong them.' Do you agree? Explain arguments for and against this statement.

Topic 1.1 Beliefs and teachings

Salvation

Salvation is being saved from the consequences of sin, so that it becomes possible to be reunited with God in heaven after death. So salvation is about getting into heaven. Just because Jesus made atonement for sin by his death, it does not mean there is an automatic pass into heaven – Christians believe a person has to be sorry (repent) for their own sin. Christians believe there are a number of ways to gain salvation.

Salvation through law

> 'Obey what I command you today.' *(Exodus 34:11)*

'Salvation through law' means following God's laws all the time, the idea being that a person gains salvation by always doing what is right by God's laws. The original sin (see page 22) was Adam disobeying God's law (to not eat from the Tree of Knowledge), leaving humans in need of salvation. So it is logical to think that, by keeping God's laws, salvation can be obtained. God's laws are found in the Bible, and in other sources of authority accepted by the Church – for example, for Catholics, it is the words of the Pope. The Bible is the most important source to help humans understand what God wants them to do; in other words, to teach them right from wrong in God's eyes.

Salvation through works (action)

> 'A man may say, you have faith, and I have works; show me your faith without your actions, and I will show you my faith by my actions.' *(James 2:18)*

Jesus emphasised that a person needs to show their beliefs through their actions (works). He said it was not enough to just have beliefs: they have to set an example and be role models, following his own example. This has motivated Christians over the centuries to do good – setting up orphanages, schools and hospices, and doing a lot of social care. You can see it in modern schemes such as **food banks** and **street pastors** (see page 46), as well as in the work of Christian charities (see pages 51–52). By doing good, they might also hope to be rewarded by God with salvation.

Salvation through grace

> 'For by grace you have been saved through faith. This is not your own doing; it is a gift of God, not a result of works, so that no one may boast.' *(Ephesians 2:8–9)*

God's grace is God's unconditional love for each person, given in spite of the fact we might not deserve or have earned it. This is brought by the sacraments, which are considered outward

Andy: I believe in the power of the Holy Spirit. When I go to worship, I feel the Spirit bless me.

Zara: I was baptised as a child, but then went through an adult baptism. I wanted to be born again into a life with God, which was given to me through making that commitment.

Dewi: I do my best to be a good person, following laws – both God's law and man's law – and living a morally right life.

signs of inward grace (see page 34). Orthodox and Catholic Christians keep all of the seven Sacraments. Most Christians observe the two sacraments of baptism and communion, bringing God's grace. Baptism is the beginning of life with God, and communion allows a person to say sorry for wrongs, and get a fresh start. In the case of communion, the person is making a conscious effort to 'be right with' God, and so taking responsibility for their own salvation. Many Christians take communion weekly, constantly renewing their promises to God.

Salvation through the Spirit

> 'He saved us, not because of the righteous things we have done, but because of his mercy. He saved us through the washing of rebirth and renewal by the Holy Spirit.' *(Titus 3:5)*

Before the ascension, Jesus told his disciples he would leave the Holy Spirit as a guide and comforter. Christians believe the Holy Spirit is the presence of God's grace in their hearts, and as a result they will be transformed by the Spirit.

Evangelical Christians believe that wherever Christians come together to worship, the Holy Spirit is with them, as Jesus said that was so. They allow the Spirit to work through them, so worship can be very joyful and expressive, including clapping, laughter, singing, dancing, speaking in tongues, healing, etc.

Helena: *I believe in Jesus, but I also believe that I have to earn salvation. I make every effort to do things for the church and others.*

Teemu: *I believe that only God can give me salvation. My belief in God, and love for God means He will welcome me to His kingdom.*

Paul: *Love God, live a morally upright life by doing good. That will bring me salvation – with God's grace, that is.*

Influences

Christians believe in salvation, and this influences them to be thankful for Jesus' sacrifice, without which they could not have salvation. This leads them to do many things – obey God's laws, show compassion for others through good deeds, keep the sacraments to be blessed by God's grace, and worship.

The Basics

1. What is meant by the term salvation?
2. Explain how each of the following bring salvation according to Christians – law; works; grace; Holy Spirit.
3. Read each of the speech bubbles to identify which kind of salvation is being suggested by each person. Explain each.
4. 'Salvation by grace is the most important way to gain salvation.' Do you agree? Explain your arguments before presenting a different point of view. Then write a justified conclusion to show which argument is stronger, and why.

Getting prepared

The Beliefs section of an exam paper is made up of five questions. Here you can read the wording, some tips for doing well and some examples of each.

1.1 question – Multi-choice: 1 mark

For example:

A Which **one** of the following means sin?

  a Breaking the law

  b Disobeying God

  c Hurting someone

  d Bad behaviour

B Which **one** of the following is not a means of salvation?

  a Works

  b Grace

  c Festivals

  d Law

> **Tip**
>
> Lots of these are definition questions, so make sure you know the meaning of all key words.

1.2 question – 'Give two …': 2 marks

This tests knowledge (not understanding).

For example:

A Give **two** of the parts of the Trinity.

B Give **two** beliefs about atonement in Christianity.

> **Tips**
>
> Keep your answer to a minimum: give only two words, or phrases. Example A could be answered simply by 'God the Father, God the Son', or in a longer version, 'God the father created the universe, God the Son was Jesus who died as a sacrifice for sin.' The shorter version takes less time, but gets the same marks.
>
> The exam paper gives prompts of '**two**' to remind you to give two answers.

1.3 question – Influences: 4 marks

This is testing your understanding of how what a person believes affects what they think/say/do – how it influences them.

For example:

A Explain **two** ways in which belief in God's creation might influence Christians today.

B Explain **two** ways in which belief in heaven and hell might influence Christians today.

> **Tips**
>
> You get a mark for each way, plus an additional mark as you explain each way: 2 + 2.
>
> The question wants you to say, 'If a Christian believes _____, then they will (think/say/do) _____.' Don't make the mistake of explaining the belief itself.
>
> Using examples is a good way to explain in this question because it shows how the influence is acted upon.

1.4 question – Beliefs and teachings: 5 marks

For example:

A Explain **two** Christian teachings about the nature of God.

Refer to sacred writings or another source of Christian belief and teaching in your answer.

B Explain **two** Christian teachings about the resurrection.

Refer to sacred writings or another source of Christian belief and teaching in your answer.

Tips

You get a mark for each teaching, plus an additional mark for each explanation. The final mark is for giving a relevant teaching which you will probably already have done! As this question is about teachings, as long as you give an accurate teaching or its source, the fifth mark should be very easy!

'Teaching' doesn't mean you have to give quotations; you could give beliefs or concepts.

You will need to know the key terms – because that is what you are being asked about; if you haven't learned what the resurrection is, you can't answer Example B here!

1.5 question – Analysis and evaluation: 12 marks, plus 3 marks for the quality of written English (SPaG)

For example:

A 'For Christians, the Trinity is the most important Christian belief.'

Evaluate this statement.

In your answer, you should:
- refer to Christian teaching
- give reasoned arguments to support this statement
- give reasoned arguments to support a different point of view
- reach a justified conclusion.

B 'The crucifixion of Jesus is more important than his resurrection.'

Evaluate this statement.

In your answer, you should:
- refer to Christian teaching
- give reasoned arguments to support this statement
- give reasoned arguments to support a different point of view
- reach a justified conclusion.

Tips

The question wording gives you a great way to check your answer – use the different bullet points to check you have done all the things you need to do.

If the statement says something is 'best', 'most important' or gives any kind of value words, then challenge it by saying, 'It depends what is meant by …'. This is a good technique to make your brain think more widely in answering.

You have to give an agree side and a disagree side in your answer – failure to do so will cost you any mark above Level 2 (6 marks out of 12). Similarly, failure to explain anything you write will also keep you stuck at Level 2 at best.

By giving and explaining all arguments for one side, then doing the same for the other side, you write a clearer answer which is easier to mark.

'Justified conclusion' is a posh way of asking you to say whether the agree or disagree side is stronger, and why you think that. It doesn't mean for you to rewrite arguments you have given already! So one side might have more arguments, might be clearer, might be more compelling/persuasive or might fit with what you already think. These are all useful ways to justify a conclusion. Sometimes, you just can't decide – and it is okay to say that as well.

1.2 Practices

Public worship

'Make a joyful noise unto the Lord … come before His presence with singing … enter into his gates with thanksgiving, and into his courts with praise: be thankful to him, and bless His name.' (Psalm 100)

Public worship is worship done in groups, rather than in ones or twos. It doesn't mean worshipping in a public area. Worship usually, but not always, takes place in a Christian place of worship – church, chapel, cathedral, etc. Acts of worship can take place in public places – when the congregation has come together somewhere bigger than a church – for example, a congregation having a Christmas service in the local shopping centre, or an act of worship held in a park or stadium when the Pope visits a country.

Worship is important because it is praise of God. Christians are showing their devotion to God, and having a chance to hear and better understand God's message. Jesus said that wherever a few gather in his name, then his Spirit is with them – so getting together to worship was part of Christian tradition from the very beginning, as well as bringing the Holy Spirit to the group.

All Christian worship is based around the Bible, as this is considered to be the word of God or inspired by God, containing Jesus' teachings and those of the early Church. The service will usually include:

- Bible readings (often one each from the Old and New Testaments)
- hymns (inspired by or using words from the Bible)
- prayers (including the Lord's Prayer from the Bible)
- a sermon (inspired by a Biblical message or based on a Biblical story).

The different Christian denominations follow different forms of worship. For the course, you need to know about each of the following – liturgical, non-liturgical and informal.

*My name is James. I am an Anglican Christian. In our church, we use **liturgical worship**. This just means we have a set programme to the service, with set wording for much of it, which follows the Book of Common Prayer, which dates back to 1549 (though it has been updated a few times). We each follow what the vicar says as we read the service from this book, and say aloud some statements as guided by it. The Bible readings and prayers are set for each service – so you could go into any Anglican Church and hear the same ones. They follow a themed approach, which follows the 'Church Year'. Of course, the vicar's sermon isn't fixed – they have to stick to the theme, but they will have written their sermon themselves. I like this kind of worship because I feel comforted and confident by the familiar structure of it. It feels very proper as it is quite formal – I am getting it right.*

1 Christianity

*My name is Grace. I attend a Methodist Church, where we use **non-liturgical worship**. That means we don't have a set pattern with set words and readings. For each service, our minister will decide a theme, and then build a service around that theme. Sometimes it is obvious, like at Christmas, but they are always relying on the Spirit to inspire their work. The service has a familiar pattern in terms of hymns, prayers, readings and sermon, so you know what happens next, but not the exact content of it. I like this kind of worship because it is always fresh. Often it gives a perfect, timely response to things that are happening in the world, helping me as a Christian to reflect on them, and on what God might want me to learn or do. I feel that I have been able to give praise to God and take peace from these services, so setting me up for the week.*

*My name is Nat. I attend a Community Church, where worship is guided by the Spirit. There is no fixed pattern, and no fixed words; it is **informal worship**. So the theme of the day (which is really a kind of message to us as Christians) is chosen for each service, and the hymns, prayers, readings and sermon are chosen to fit with that theme. We might sing several hymns together, or have prayers by a few people. Some of the service might be to listen to someone playing music or singing; I have seen screenings of Christian bands from other parts of the world within a service. The point is, we are showing our love and devotion for God, coming together to praise God and be filled with the Spirit – and the Spirit moves us to proclaim our love in different ways. I love the vibrancy of these services, and the emotions they bring out – I always leave feeling refreshed and revitalised.*

The Basics

1 What is worship?
2 Explain the use of the Bible in worship.
3 Explain each of the three types of worship – liturgical, non-liturgical and informal.
4 Explain the benefits of each type of worship.
5 'As long as it is focused on the Bible, it does not matter what kind of worship a Christian does.' Do you agree? Explain arguments to agree and disagree, including different Christian perspectives.

Topic 1.2 Practices

Private worship

Christians believe a person can worship God at any time, anywhere – as God is everywhere and always with them. Private worship is a person's worship which is guided completely by themselves, and not as part of a formal act of worship for a congregation. It is personal – between them and God. It takes as many forms as there are people choosing to do it, because it is personal. Hence, people do this at different times, for different reasons, using different things to support their worship or as a focus for their worship. It is an important kind of worship because it shows the devotion of an individual. Some would say this is harder because people have to make more time for it, and think more about it, as well as actually leading and doing the worship. It shows a person's personal commitment to God, but this commitment is tailored to exactly what they need to say and do. Some would say this is the most honest form of worship because the person has no distractions and cannot just go through the motions of public worship.

Someone praying alone before a crucifix in church

Although I go to church on Sundays, on many days I take time out to read some passages from the Bible. It might be something we heard at church, or something random. I find having a bit of quiet time and just reflecting on the words makes me feel closer to God, calmer and more assured of God's love for me.

I worship God alone most days. I will give time in prayer, telling God my thoughts. If I tell God my cares and worries, I feel they are lightened – God has taken my load from me, or at least is helping me to bear it. I share my joys as well. I must thank God for the good that happens in my life. I feel that when I pray to God, my relationship with God is strengthened; I feel comforted by that.

Praying to God in private is very important to me. I can be completely honest in what I say and how I say it. I can take as much or as little time as I want (in a service, the time is fixed and I sometimes feel it wasn't enough or was too much for what I needed to say). There are no distractions for me – like when Jesus left his disciples in Gethsemane to go and pray alone. This is a powerful time.

I will go to church at some point during most weeks to pray and reflect before one of the statues there. Sometimes it is because I want to ask God for something – I find talking it through with God usually helps me to see a way forward. Being in church, the atmosphere helps my devotions because everything is there for God – you don't need a formal act of worship to get that feeling.

I use the Book of Common Prayer when I do my private devotions to God. I like the language, and I know I am on the right track with it. I read it at my own pace, and think about the words I am reading. I feel that I come closer to God, who speaks to me through these words. John's Gospel says that the time is coming when worshippers will worship in spirit and truth, and that is what I feel I am doing when I worship this way.

I use my rosary beads, and pray. Usually, I pray the Lord's Prayer – after all, Jesus gave this when his disciples asked how they should pray. Just holding the beads helps me focus on the words of the prayer. I also recite prayers such as the Grace and Hail Mary, as well as reciting the rosary. Each of these is helped by using rosary beads to count. I do this at the start of each day – fresh day, fresh start.

I meditate each day in the early morning. I focus on a part of the Creed, or some teaching of Jesus, or just God. I have also used images, such as Jesus on the cross. I hope that, by really focusing, I can gain an insight into the true meaning of the words, as well as coming closer to God.

I take time at the end of each day to just think back on what I have done, and whether my day would have pleased God. I start with a hymn – just quietly sung to myself, then pray and reflect. It feels as if I have closed off the day, and can go to sleep at one with God, ready for the new day.

Aids to worship

Many Christians use things to help them focus during their worship, or to focus on. Just holding the Bible while praying helps some people to feel their prayers are stronger and more heartfelt. There might be a statue in church of Jesus' sacrifice that they look at, or a picture which makes them think of God's creation – each allowing reflection on the religious truths they reveal. The rosary is a string of beads with a crucifix attached – each bead is grasped while (a part of) the prayer is said so that prayers may be counted (see page 23). All aids to worship help create the appropriate atmosphere for worship, helping the worshipper to engage more fully.

The Basics

1. What is private worship? How is this different from public worship?
2. Why do many Christians feel it is important to worship God in private as well as through public worship?
3. Describe some of the ways Christians carry out private worship.
4. Using examples, explain two different reasons why a Christian might use aids to worship.
5. 'Private worship is better than public worship.' Do you agree with that statement? Explain arguments to agree and disagree, with reference to Christianity. Write a justified conclusion to show which point of view you feel is stronger and why.

Topic 1.2 Practices

Prayer

Prayer is communication with God; lifting the heart and mind to God. It is a central part of Christian worship, and something many Christians do at least daily, both formally and in their head. By praying, a person is demonstrating their belief that there is a greater being than themselves – many bow their heads when they pray as a sign of submission.

When a Christian prays, they are trying to strengthen their relationship with God, so that they come closer to God. Perhaps through prayer they can have a revelation of God, or gain better understanding of a quality of God. Many Christians pray as a way of reflecting on their actions and ideas, opening themselves to the guidance of the Holy Spirit in understanding the creation and religious truths. For many, prayer is a source of comfort because they do feel that they have come nearer to God.

Christians believe that prayer can make a person 'right with God'. It is their chance to say sorry – and mean it – for any wrongs they have committed. By saying sorry (repenting), they can receive God's forgiveness. Even the worst of people can get that forgiveness because God is merciful and all-loving (see pages 4–5).

> 'Do not be anxious about anything, but in everything, by prayer and petition, with thanksgiving, present your requests to God. And the peace of God, which transcends all understanding, will guard your hearts and your minds in Christ Jesus.' *(Philippians 4:6–7)*

Within prayer, a Christian does one or more of the following:

- thanks God – for example, for good health
- praises God – for example, for the created world
- confesses sins – for example, saying sorry to God for speaking unkindly about others
- asks God for help for oneself – for example, praying for good exam results
- asks God for help for others – for example, praying for victims of a natural disaster.

Set prayers

Liturgical worship includes set prayers – these are prayers in which the wording is fixed; all a person need do is recite them. These are considered to be perfect without any need to change the wording at all. An example is the Grace, often said before meals; another is the Hail Mary, used by Catholics when praying the rosary. The most famous of all is the Lord's Prayer.

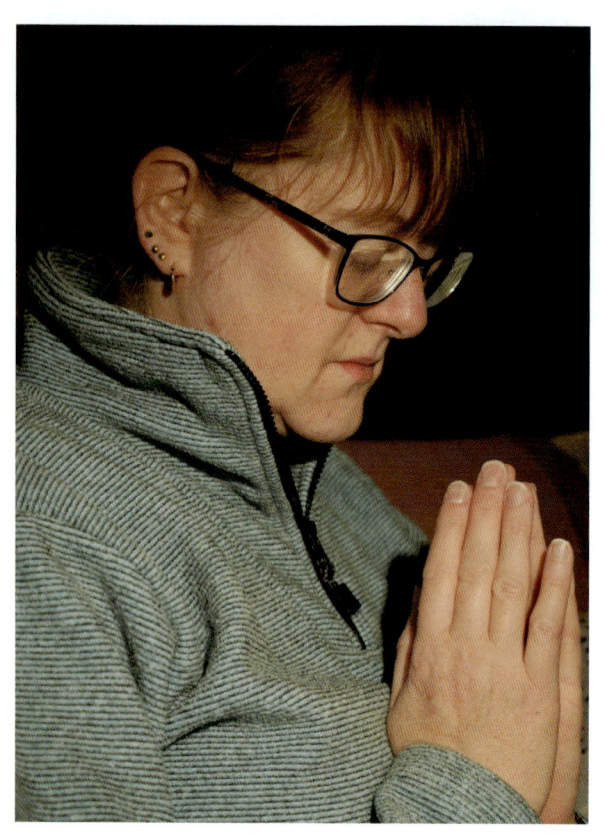

Bowing one's head and holding hands together is a common position for prayer

Informal prayer

As prayer tries to get that personal connection with God, it is often very informal and spontaneous. This is called extemporary prayer – people say what they feel is right and what they feel they need to say in their prayers. This means the prayer is made up completely by the person doing it, and while it might use themes which set prayers use, it is in the person's own words. For example, while some Christians say the Grace before eating, others thank God in their own words. If a person is praying to God for something specific, they will usually use their own words – even if they start or end by using a set prayer. During worship, evangelical Christians invite the Holy Spirit to guide their prayers, as they believe they are led by the Spirit in what they say during prayer.

Jesus and prayer

In Matthew 6:5–8, Jesus tells his followers not to be boastful in their prayer, not to stand so that everyone can see them. Rather, he says, prayer is between God and the individual, and should be private. In Matthew 7:7–11, he encourages his followers to ask God for things – seek and you will receive – which shows God's love. Luke 18:9–14 advises people to be humble before God, so that when God judges, it will be done mercifully. The most famous advice from Jesus about prayer is what we know as the Lord's Prayer.

Jesus' disciples asked him how they should pray. His answer was to give them the Lord's Prayer. It does all five of the things mentioned earlier – praise God, thank God, say sorry, request for self and request for others. It is the single prayer which every Christian in the world, throughout history, both knows and uses. Each phrase within it has a special meaning.

Our Father in heaven,	This prayer is to God the Father (Trinity), the Creator.
Hallowed be your Name.	'Hallowed' means 'praised', so straightaway the person is showing respect to God.
Your Kingdom come.	A plea for the Kingdom of God to come – a time when there is peace everywhere.
Your will be done, on Earth as it is in heaven.	The hope that everyone everywhere will keep God's laws – this will happen when the Kingdom of God comes.
Give us this day our daily bread.	Asking God to make sure they do not go hungry – both physically and spiritually.
And forgive us our trespasses, As we forgive those who trespass against us.	'Trespasses' are sins; here the person is asking for forgiveness for themselves, as well as the determination to forgive others who wrong them.
And lead us not into temptation	Asking for God's protection from being tempted into sin.
But deliver us from evil.	Asking God for protection against the evil of the world.
For yours is the kingdom, the power, and the glory, for ever and ever.	This acknowledges that, as God is so powerful, everything previously requested is possible.
Amen	Hebrew word meaning 'so be it', essentially showing the prayer is ended.

The Basics

1. Why do Christians pray?
2. Explain different ways in which Christians show their respect to a greater power when praying.
3. Explain, using examples, what is meant by set prayer.
4. Explain, using examples, what is meant by informal prayer.
5. Explain what Jesus taught about prayer.
6. Why is the Lord's Prayer considered to be the 'perfect' prayer?
7. 'Informal prayer is the best form of prayer for Christians.' Do you agree? Explain arguments to agree and disagree, before coming to a justified conclusion.

Topic 1.2 Practices

The sacraments

The sacraments are rituals which are 'external signs of inward grace'. When a Christian goes through one of these rituals, they receive the grace of God – a blessing. Different groups of Christians keep up to seven sacraments. Orthodox and Catholics keep all seven, believing all were at least implied in the teaching of Jesus. Most Protestant groups keep two as they say Jesus only instructed these two (baptism and Eucharist) to be kept. Some – Quakers and Salvation Army – keep none, as they say that the stories are just descriptions of what happened to Jesus, not duties for Christians to follow.

Why keep the sacraments?

- They are at least implied in Jesus' teaching, so keeping them is following his lead.
- They are key rituals for Christians, so by keeping them, Christians live a full religious life.
- They mark the key stages of life from birth to death, so Christians have God's blessing throughout their lives.
- Receiving the sacrament is a way to receive the gifts of the Spirit, and so strengthen faith, which is important, especially in difficult times.

What are the seven sacraments?

Baptism	Welcoming a person into the faith by immersing them in water. The water represents a new birth; new life in Jesus.
Confirmation	The person confirms the decision made by their parents at **infant baptism**, and accepts the faith for themselves. The ceremony includes the 'laying on of hands', where the vicar/priest puts their hands on the head of the person and blesses them.
Eucharist	Remembers the Last Supper, where Jesus gave bread and wine to his disciples, saying it was his body and blood. Represents Jesus' sacrifice and atonement for human sin; gives a sense of a fresh start to all who participate.
Reconciliation	Confession of sins, requiring true repentance. Represents forgiveness from God.
Healing	Two forms – a blessing on the sick, or the Last Rites for the dying person. A form of spiritual healing.
Marriage	The joining of a man and a woman in holy matrimony; their relationship is blessed by God and they become 'one flesh', never to part.
Ordination	A person committing their life to the religious path – as a priest, monk or nun. The blessing from God is meant to give the ordained one special gifts which are necessary to their new role.

The Basics

1. What are the sacraments?
2. List each of the sacraments, saying what it is and what it represents.
3. Why do Christians keep the sacraments?
4. 'All Christians should keep the sacraments.' Do you agree? Explain arguments for more than one point of view.

The sacrament of baptism

Baptism welcomes a child or an adult into the Christian faith – a public announcement of commitment. Parents make this decision on behalf of their baby; as an adult, the person makes the decision for themselves. Baptism is done in the name of the Father, Son and Holy Spirit, thus showing belief in the Trinity. It is a rite of dedication, where a promise is being made to bring up the child or live according to Jesus' teachings.

Infant baptism

This is the baptism of a baby at the request of its parents, who vow to bring it up in the faith.

Paschal candle: given to the baby so that it can 'receive God's light'. Jesus said 'I am the way, the truth and the light', so this candle reminds that Jesus' message gives light to see the right way to live.

Water is used in the ritual. It is poured over the head of the baby three times, and the sign of the cross is marked on its forehead. In the Orthodox Church, the baby is fully immersed in the water. The water has been blessed and is used to symbolise the washing clean of sin, as well as a new birth to Christ.

God-parents: in the Catholic, Orthodox and Anglican traditions, they must be practising Christians. If anything were to happen to the parents, the God-parents would be responsible for the religious upbringing of the child.

White garments signify the purity of the baby and are a symbol of being clean of sin.

Chrism oil is used in the Orthodox, Catholic and Anglican traditions. It is smeared onto the forehead of the baby – anointing it with God's blessing.

The ritual is carried out at a font – a stone bowl which holds the blessed water. These are often near the entrance to the church, showing the baby is welcomed at the door and representing the doorway to a new life.

Topic 1.2 Practices

Believers' baptism

This happens in many Protestant traditions and reflects the belief that a person must be old enough to understand their commitment if they are to take it seriously. Some Protestant groups only use **believers' baptism**, for this reason, and because Jesus was an adult when he was baptised. Before going through the ritual, a person will have followed a study course so that they understand the key beliefs and the responsibilities they will take on by making this commitment. Whereas infant baptism is a ceremony which takes place as part of or at the end of a normal Sunday service, believers' baptism is a service in its own right.

Baptistry: Some churches have their own pool for baptism within the church; many prefer to go to flowing water (a river, stream or the sea) to copy Jesus' baptism in the River Jordan.

Full immersion: Jesus was fully immersed in the River Jordan, and so this is copied for adults. It is seen as the proper way; a new birth. The person steps into the water at one end, is fully immersed in the name of the Father, Son and Holy Spirit, and exits at the other side.

White garments: For the actual baptism, many people wear old clothes, and then get changed into new, often white clothes after the actual baptism. These reflect having been washed clean of sin, but also their new life in Christ. Some even take a new name as their baptism name.

The testimony: All adults baptised will give a speech after their baptism to the congregation. They explain their decision – what led them to make it, and how it will change their life. Members of the congregation, by being there, are agreeing to help them in their spiritual journey.

The Basics

1. What is baptism?
2. Explain different reasons why Christians get baptised.
3. Explain the different elements of an infant baptism.
4. Explain the different elements of a believer's baptism.
5. Compare and contrast the two forms of baptism.
6. 'All babies of Christian parents should be baptised.' Do you agree? Explain arguments for and against this statement, including reference to Christian arguments. Write a justified conclusion showing which argument you find to be strongest, and why.

The sacrament of Eucharist

The Eucharist is the ritual which remembers Jesus' Last Supper, which took place on the evening of his arrest, the day before he was crucified. He was in an upper room with his disciples and broke bread for them. He gave pieces of the bread, and some wine, to each disciple, telling them to eat and drink in remembrance of him. He said that the bread represented his body, broken for them; the wine represented his blood, spilled for them. Christians have copied this ritual ever since.

This is probably the sacrament that Christians keep most often, some even taking part in it daily, though for most it is a weekly or monthly event. There are a number of names for this ritual: Catholics call it **Mass**, Orthodox Christians call it the **Divine Liturgy**, Anglicans call it **Holy Communion**, and Nonconformists call it the **Lord's Supper**.

In the Nonconformist churches, any person can participate in this ritual, receiving bread and wine. However, in the Catholic and Anglican traditions, a person must have been confirmed before they are eligible.

> ### The Anglican Holy Communion
> The Anglican service follows the words and instruction of the Book of Common Prayer. It begins with a prayer, then Bible readings. The Nicene Creed will be spoken aloud, followed by prayers and the peace (where everyone wishes each other peace). Then the vicar prepares the bread and wine, praying over it before people step forward to receive it as a sacrament and blessing.

Why is it important?

- Keeping this sacrament follows Jesus' command to 'do this in remembrance of me'.
- It is an act of cleansing, so that a person can again be 'at one' with God because they have recalled Jesus' sacrifice, which they are thankful for, and are sorry for their own wrong-doings.
- It symbolises the new covenant between God and man; the fresh start given by Jesus.
- For many, the consuming of bread and wine is a symbol for feeding the soul, which is what belief in God gives.

The Catholic Mass

The Liturgy of the Eucharist forms the second part of the Mass at every Mass service. These take place every day, so Eucharist can be done daily. Offerings of money are given, which are brought to the altar with water, wine and wafers of unleavened bread (hosts). Unleavened bread is made without yeast, which is what Jesus would have eaten at the Last Supper, as it was the Jewish Passover. The wine is poured into a chalice with some drops of water, representing the union of the divine and human sides of Christ, somehow becoming Christ's actual body and blood (**transubstantiation**). The hosts are lifted to heaven to be blessed, as is the chalice. The priest ceremonially washes his hands. The Sanctus prayer is said, and the sign of peace made. The priest consumes the host and wine himself. He then offers the host to each congregant, who bows and makes the sign of the cross. They then return to their seats to pray and reflect.

The priest preparing the bread and wine for Mass

Topic 1.2 Practices

The Nonconformist Lord's Supper

Often this is a completely separate ceremony, coming after the main Sunday service once a month, when anyone not wishing to participate has left the church. The minister will call congregants to the altar to participate. Once there, the minister reads the text of the Last Supper and prays. Each person is given their own glass of wine or a wine substitute (many do not use wine) and a piece of bread (not a wafer) broken from a single loaf. Often the bread is leavened – made with yeast so that it rose, to symbolise life and the resurrection. Bread and then 'wine' are given to each person to consume, and the minister reminds them that Jesus said 'Do this in remembrance of me.' These represent Jesus; they do not become his body and blood. They recite the Lord's Prayer together, followed by personal reflection.

Pastors preparing the bread and wine for the Lord's Supper

The Orthodox Divine Liturgy

Bread and wine are prepared on the altar, which is hidden from view behind the iconostasis (a wall of images behind which only priests may go). The bread (made with yeast to represent life) is divided into four parts, three of which are blessed by the saying of the Eucharistic prayer. Orthodox Christians believe that Jesus is then present in some way in the bread and wine. After Bible readings, prayers and a sermon, first the Bible and then a chalice containing both the bread and wine are brought out. Everyone is invited to share this, and they receive a spoonful of the mixture. The fourth portion of bread is taken to people who were not able to attend.

A priest gives bread mixed with wine to an Orthodox Christian

The Basics

1. What is the Eucharist?
2. Describe the event from which the Eucharist originates.
3. Why is the Eucharist important to Christians?
4. Describe Eucharist rituals from two different Christian groups. What are their similarities and what are their differences?
5. 'The Eucharist is the most important act of worship for Christians.' Do you agree? Explain arguments for and against that statement. Write a justified conclusion showing which point of view is stronger.

Pilgrimage

Pilgrimage is a special journey to a sacred place. The journey made represents the hardship brought by being devoted to God. For many Christians, pilgrimage allows them to exercise greater effort in that devotion – for example, walking long distances to reach the place of pilgrimage, such as the walk to Canterbury. The time taken for this journey is a chance to reflect on one's life, and so develop spiritually. Some say it is a chance to 'recharge spiritual batteries' as they feel immersed in their religion. Pope Benedict XVI said that going on pilgrimage 'is to step outside ourselves in order to encounter God where he has revealed Himself' – in other words, to try to encounter God.

In Christianity, there is no duty to make a pilgrimage; pilgrimage is done entirely from the free will of each individual. There are many reasons why many Christians do go on pilgrimage: they may want to show their devotion to God, use the pilgrimage as an apology to God, seek something from God or just experience that special place. The actual places have become places of pilgrimage because of a person or event they are associated with. For example, many Christians want to go to Jerusalem and walk the route Jesus took on his way to his execution. They go at Easter, as that is when Jesus was executed.

The Catholic pilgrimage to Lourdes

Lourdes is in France. In 1858, a girl called Bernadette Soubiroux claimed to have had 18 visions from a lady who spoke to her of the **Immaculate Conception**. Bernadette had followed instructions by this lady to clean out a blocked spring and drink the water, which cured her ill health. Her friend also bathed her broken arm in it – which was healed. A priest who questioned Bernadette became convinced she had seen the Virgin Mary because of her account and the specific words used, which he did not believe she had the ability to know or use. Lourdes became a place of pilgrimage, particularly for those looking to be physically healed (seeking a miracle), and over time, more and more have flocked to the site.

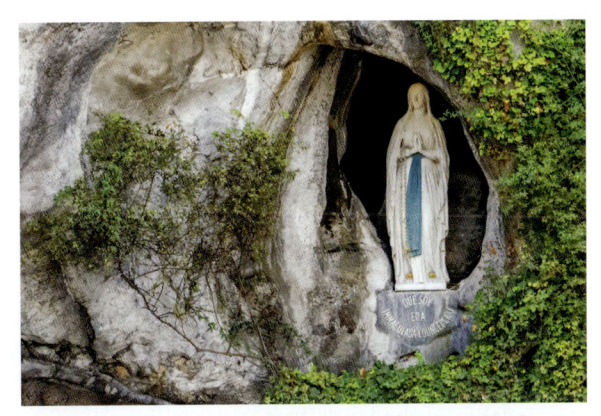

The grotto at Lourdes, a place of pilgrimage for Catholics

The grotto where Bernadette saw the visions has become the focal point for the Mass to be held. A significant number of small shops sell souvenirs of Lourdes, including bottles of the holy water from the spring. A massive edifice has been built to contain the whole area, which includes several churches, administrative areas, accommodation for the sick and baths to allow bathing in the holy water. Every day, the sacrament procession is held, which ends with the sacrament of healing.

While people come to see the place where Bernadette saw the Virgin Mary, for many visitors it is for the chance of a miracle that they make the pilgrimage.

Topic 1.2 Practices

Iona – a different kind of pilgrimage

The island of Iona, a place of pilgrimage for Christians of all denominations

Iona is an island used as a pilgrimage venue by Christians of all denominations. In 563CE, St Columba settled there and set up a monastery, from which monks went out into England to preach Christianity. It became a pilgrimage site in the fifteenth century because of St Columba, but later fell into disrepair. In 1938, the site was rebuilt by men training to be ministers, and a new community began – the Iona **ecumenical** community. Ecumenical means 'worldwide church' – it is for any and all Christians.

Iona now has a global membership, and a way of life committed to peace, justice and fighting for the environment. People visit for short or long periods of time, with each day spent in prayer, Bible reading and stewardship of the land. This is a working pilgrimage, not just a visit or some kind of spiritual tourism. As a pilgrimage site, it is really a place for retreat and refocusing on one's faith, where the pilgrimage is to a principle or concept, rather than because of a specific person/event.

The Basics

1. What is pilgrimage?
2. Explain different reasons why Christians go on pilgrimage.
3. Explain Lourdes as a place of pilgrimage.
4. Explain Iona as a place of pilgrimage.
5. 'Pilgrimage has no value in the modern world.' Do you agree? Explain arguments for and against this statement, before writing a justified conclusion.

Festivals

Christians celebrate a number of festivals to do with the life of Jesus or events from church history. Some Christians celebrate festivals specific to their denomination. For example, only Orthodox Christians celebrate the baptism of Jesus, and Roman Catholicism has many Saints' Days. A festival is a time of remembrance, often joyful, which has a strongly religious element to its activities. For the course, you need to know about two Christian festivals – Christmas and Easter.

The Annunciation – when the Angel Gabriel told Mary she was to have a child, the Son of God

Christmas – celebrating Jesus' birth

Christmas has become the biggest festival in the UK. Schools and offices close for a period of time; it is now normal to spend huge sums of money on gifts for others; TV and media have special programming; everywhere you go, the **secular** images of Christmas are to be seen – Santa, Christmas trees, sleighs and so on. However, Christmas is a Christian festival which celebrates the birth of Jesus on 25 December (or 6 January for Orthodox Christians). The religious side of the festival pre-dates our modern, secular enjoyment of it. The Christmas story is found in the Gospels of Matthew (M) and Luke (L):

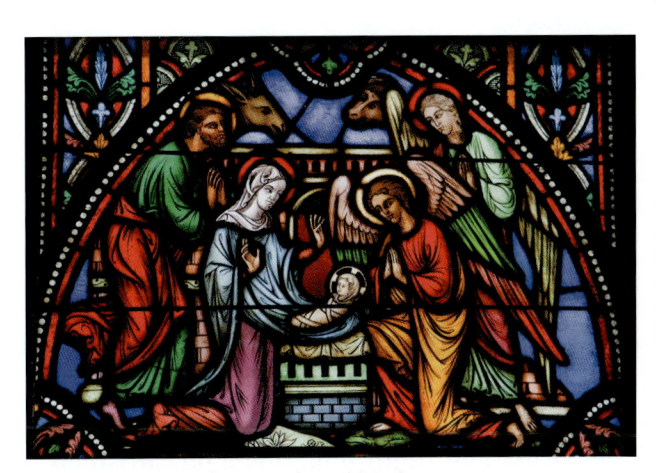

A nativity scene showing Jesus' birth

- The Angel Gabriel visited Mary and told her she had been chosen to have God's child. (L)
- The angel visited Joseph to explain Mary's pregnancy. (M)
- Joseph and Mary went to Bethlehem for the census; there was no room to stay in, so they stayed in a stable. (M, L)
- Jesus was born amidst the animals of the stable. (M, L)
- An angel visited shepherds and told them to visit Jesus – so they did. (L)
- An angel visited wise men from the East, telling them where Jesus was and that they must not return to the court of Herod (who they had visited, expecting the new king to be at his palace). They took gifts of gold, frankincense and myrrh. (M)
- The family fled to Egypt to avoid Herod's command that all baby boys be killed. (M)

Topic 1.2 Practices

The Midnight Mass service at church on Christmas Eve

A Christingle

The celebrations begin at midnight on Christmas Eve with Midnight Mass (or Watchnight service). Then on Christmas Day morning, hymns are sung and sermons given which are focused on the Christmas story and message, Christingles (oranges decorated with cloves, fruit and a candle) are given to the children, and nativity plays may be performed. This is a traditional way to teach children the story of Jesus' birth. The church will have been decorated with religious symbols and is traditionally very full of light. In the Christian Church as a whole, there is a focus on helping the poor. Many Christians will decorate their homes with religious symbolism – for example, a nativity scene – and send religious cards, rather than cards with snowmen, robins, Father Christmas, etc.

There is much symbolism in the religious celebrations.

- Lights/candles represent Jesus coming into the world as the 'light of the world'.
- Jesus born in a stable represented by the nativity scenes shows the humility of Jesus the Son of God born into poverty yet coming through love. This was the Incarnation (see page 15).
- The giving of gifts represents the gift of the Son of God to the world (also shown in the gifts of the shepherds and kings).
- The wise men's gifts were symbolic – gold showed Jesus to be a king (wealth), the frankincense that he had religious importance (it was used to anoint priests) and the myrrh a foretelling of his death (it was used as an embalmer).
- A Christingle represents the world, the four seasons, the fruits of the world as gifts from God and the blood that Jesus would shed to save the world.
- The fact that angels, animals, and rich and poor people were there shows that the whole of God's creation witnessed and celebrated the coming of the Son of God to the world.

Why is Christmas important?

- It remembers Jesus' birth – so the start of the Christian religion.
- It is a time of hope, recalling Jesus coming to the world as a light for God's message.
- It is a time of giving, thinking of others – much charitable work is done by individuals and the Church as a whole. For example, many churches are opened to provide food and shelter for the homeless.
- It is a time to remind non-Christians of Christian beliefs, and to invite them to share in that joy.

The Basics

1. Outline the origins of the Christmas festival.
2. Explain how Christians celebrate Christmas.
3. Explain why Christmas is important to Christians.
4. 'Christmas has lost its religious importance in the modern world.' Do you agree? Explain arguments to agree and disagree, before writing a justified conclusion.

Easter – remembering Jesus' sacrifice

The Christian festival of Easter comes at the end of what is known as Holy Week – the last week of Jesus' earthly life. Holy Week begins with Jesus' triumphant entry into Jerusalem, when crowds hailed him as a king, and the religious leaders finally decided they needed to get rid of him. Christians remember this day as Palm Sunday and will take crosses made from palm leaves home from the service as a reminder both of the way the crowds greeted him and of the fate which was to come for him. On Maundy Thursday, Christians remember the events of the day before Jesus was executed – the Last Supper, his prayers in Gethsemane, his arrest and the trials. A special service in the evening includes the Eucharist because Jesus held his Last Supper on this night. The altar will be cleared of all items, and the church specially 'un-decorated'. It is traditional to cover crosses with shrouds, and flowers are removed or not put on display. This is because the next day is the day Jesus was executed, so it prepares the church for the saddest of days.

Good Friday

Good Friday is a sombre day for Christians, as it recalls the crucifixion of Jesus. Not only was this a terrible experience in which Jesus suffered greatly, but it also reminds Christians that he was forced to suffer because of how humans behave. This gives a sense of sadness and guilt. However, at the same time, there is thankfulness that they will now be able to go to heaven after death. For the story of the original Good Friday (see pages 17–18).

How is Good Friday observed?

Christians might spend part of the day in prayer or reflection. Services are held at the church, particularly the Easter Vigil, which takes place in the late evening in Anglican, Catholic and Orthodox Christianity. The congregation meet at the church but, at many churches, they wait outside, and the church is kept in darkness. The priest/vicar will deliver a service there while members of the congregation hold lit candles (representing Jesus – the light of the world). They then make a procession around the whole church. At midnight, the doors to the church are opened, and the church will be flooded with light, shrouds will have been removed and flowers placed – this all suggests light and life. Altogether, the service has four parts: the Service of Light, followed by the Liturgies of the Word, Initiation and Eucharist. Christians are celebrating Jesus' resurrection from the dead.

Many Protestant groups also have a service on this evening. The actual act of worship is non-liturgical, but is still focused around the sacrifice made by Jesus for everyone.

A Good Friday church service

Topic 1.2 Practices

Easter Sunday

An Easter Sunday church service

This day remembers when Jesus rose from the dead. The women followers had gone to Jesus' tomb to prepare his body, only to find it gone – he was alive. You can read the story of the original Easter Sunday on page 19.

How is Easter Sunday observed?

Christians attend church services, the theme for which is always life and light – this is the day Jesus rose from the dead, the day his true power as Son of God was shown. Christians believe that, as Jesus conquered death and was resurrected, so they can be resurrected after death. This makes Easter Sunday a joyful celebration, when many sermons urge Christians to think about how they can help others, following Jesus' example of being a 'light to the world', and bringing hope and justice to those in need. Nowadays, the media will often screen the sermons given by leading religious figures, such as the Pope, the Orthodox Patriarch and the Archbishop of Canterbury. The Pope will give his sermon across St Peter's Square in Rome, and thousands will attend as a form of pilgrimage.

Many churches give out eggs to the children – either chocolate or hard-boiled, painted eggs. These represent the stone which had been rolled away from Jesus' tomb but, perhaps more importantly, represent life. In the Anglican, Catholic and Orthodox churches, the Eucharist is obligatory for all those who have been confirmed.

Easter is the most important festival for Christians, as the death and resurrection of Jesus are the central teachings of Christianity. All Christians know that Jesus' death was an atonement for the sins of humans, and that by his death, heaven was again opened to all as the barrier of sin between humans and God was removed (see page 23).

The Basics

1. What is Holy Week?
2. Explain the origins of each of these days – Maundy Thursday, Good Friday, Easter Sunday.
3. Explain how Christians observe each of those three days.
4. Explain why Easter is an important festival for Christians.
5. 'Easter is the most important festival for Christians.' Do you agree? Explain arguments in support of this statement and arguments for another point of view. Write a justified conclusion showing which side you think is stronger.

The church in the local community

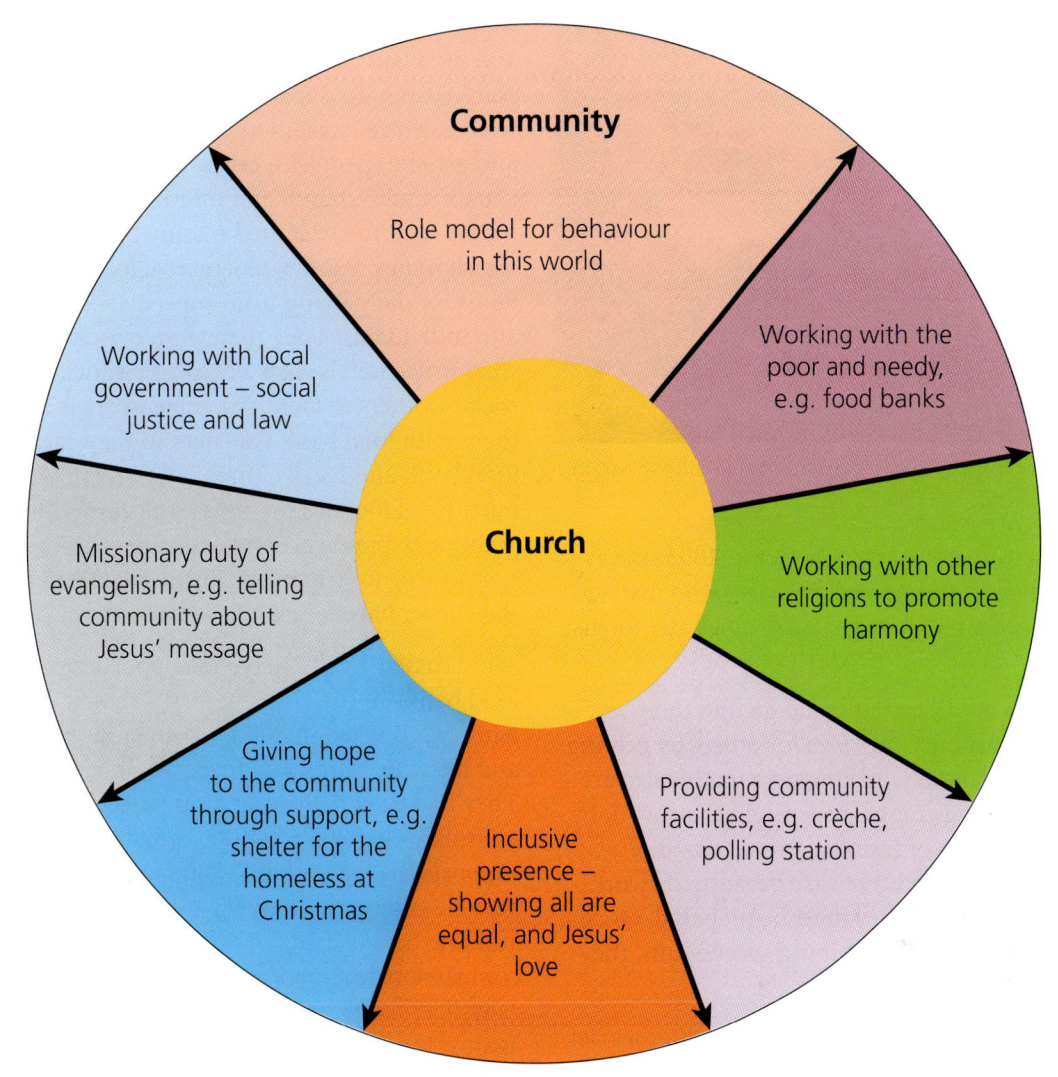

Community / **Church**

- Role model for behaviour in this world
- Working with the poor and needy, e.g. food banks
- Working with other religions to promote harmony
- Providing community facilities, e.g. crèche, polling station
- Inclusive presence – showing all are equal, and Jesus' love
- Giving hope to the community through support, e.g. shelter for the homeless at Christmas
- Missionary duty of evangelism, e.g. telling community about Jesus' message
- Working with local government – social justice and law

Some of the ways the church works within its local community

Each church stands in a secular community, as well as being a community of believers in its own right. Most Christians believe their church should be involved in the life of the whole community. They see their church as a part of that community, not a separate element which happens to be placed there. In his life, Jesus spoke to and helped people anywhere he met them – he did not just confine his words and actions to those who had become his followers. He taught that Christians must help the poor to show God's love, providing for both spiritual and earthly needs. For Christians, just believing in God is not enough; Jesus told them that 'faith without action is pointless', so they have to apply their beliefs and do something good. Similarly, after the creation, Genesis says that God made humans his stewards, giving all humans the role of looking after the world. When we consider that life is sacred for Christians, we can combine those two ideas to show that stewardship must include looking after other people, not just the natural world.

Churches work independently and together to be involved in their local community. They contribute at a pastoral level to support many groups – for example, allowing their church hall to be used as a community centre, a crèche and a meeting place. Many churches are used as polling stations for elections. Churches often host community groups for art, reading, yoga and so on. Joint initiatives might include working with the homeless and linking with people of other religions to aid mutual understanding. Many churches contribute to discussions and decisions in local politics.

45

Topic 1.2 Practices

Street pastors

Street pastors work in the community helping those in need

The street pastors movement began in 2003, and is now governed by the Ascension Trust, who manage 20,000 trained street pastors in 270 cities and towns in the UK.

Street pastors are Christians who go into their community to show God's love for others by helping, listening and generally making sure that people are safe in the evenings/night. They begin their work by completing 12 days of training over a period of months. The training is not easy because the work they do is not easy, so they must be prepared. Once they have completed this training successfully, they are commissioned for the role.

Each evening, a town's street pastors meet for a brief prayer session, asking for God's blessing. They then go out into the community to work with those who are out – mainly people who are clubbing, drinking and socialising. This means they often deal with people who are drunk, have been in fights or have got into trouble.

> 'Therefore, my beloved brothers, be steadfast, immovable, always doing the work of the Lord, knowing that in the Lord your efforts are not in vain.'
> (1 Corinthians 15:58)

Food banks

Many churches have now set up porch box schemes and food banks. Porch box schemes encourage the congregation to donate (mainly) food items, which – from a central collection area – are then parcelled up and given to people in crisis. These schemes are usually multi-church and multi-denominational initiatives and are staffed mainly by volunteers from the churches. Food banks receive food and other items for daily living from supermarkets, companies and individuals. They then work closely with local care professionals such as health visitors, schools and social workers to identify people in crisis and issue them with food bank vouchers so they can go to the food bank and receive three days' worth of nutritional food. Many food banks also offer additional, practical compassionate support and signposting to help people break free from poverty so they never have to use a food bank again.

The Trussell Trust's network supports two-thirds of food banks in the UK. The first Trussell Trust food bank was opened in 2000, when Paddy Henderson and his wife, Carol, saw there was a need in the UK. They had been delivering food parcels to Bulgaria in a similar scheme since 1997. Today the Trussell Trust supports the network of 1,200 food bank centres to provide emergency food and practical, compassionate support, as well as campaigning against the structural issues that lock people into poverty to help create a future without the need for food banks.

The Basics

1. Describe some of the ways the church is involved in its local community.
2. Explain why Christians believe they must help in their local community.
3. Describe the work of food banks.
4. Describe the work of street pastors.
5. 'Churches should just focus on the people who come to worship.' Do you agree? Explain arguments for and against this statement, and then write a justified conclusion.

Mission, evangelism and church growth

> 'Go into all the world, and preach the Gospel to all of creation.' *(Mark 16:15)*

Christianity is a missionary religion. Before he ascended to heaven, Jesus told his disciples to go out to all nations and preach his Gospel. He gave Christians a duty to tell people, and to convert them into believers. This duty still exists.

Mission means 'sending'. It is the idea that Jesus sent his followers out into the world to go everywhere. To go to others – including non-Christians – and tell them about Jesus' message is a duty. This is why some Christians are very open and not at all secretive about their faith and beliefs. Indeed they are proud of them, and want to share that pride with others.

Evangelism is to give the message to others while trying to persuade them it is the true path; in other words, trying to convert non-Christians to be Christians. Throughout the history of Christianity, where a Christian country has explored and taken control over other countries, Christianity has been introduced to those peoples. The empires of Britain, Spain and Portugal all established Christianity as the main religion in every country they conquered; those of Germany, Belgium and Netherlands likewise. In every case, these Europeans believed that they were helping their new subjects to be able to go to heaven. Also, missionaries from many Christian denominations went to live in other countries to convert people – often risking their lives in doing so. These forms of evangelism could be cruel and intolerant of other faith systems, and they were always closely linked to invading forces. This missionary activity helped establish Christianity in some way. Christianity exists in almost every country in the world today. Africa and Asia are the areas where Christianity is currently expanding most. This is due to evangelism within those countries as the religion has developed to become more relevant to the lives of people there. However, there is a lot of missionary work going on in the UK and other countries where Christianity is the principal religion, as Christians try to fight the decline which has taken place over the last 30 years.

Church growth is exactly what it says – increasing the size of the church community. Mission and evangelism contribute to this greatly, as they convert people to Christianity, as well as encouraging lapsed (those who no longer practise) Christians to return to the church community.

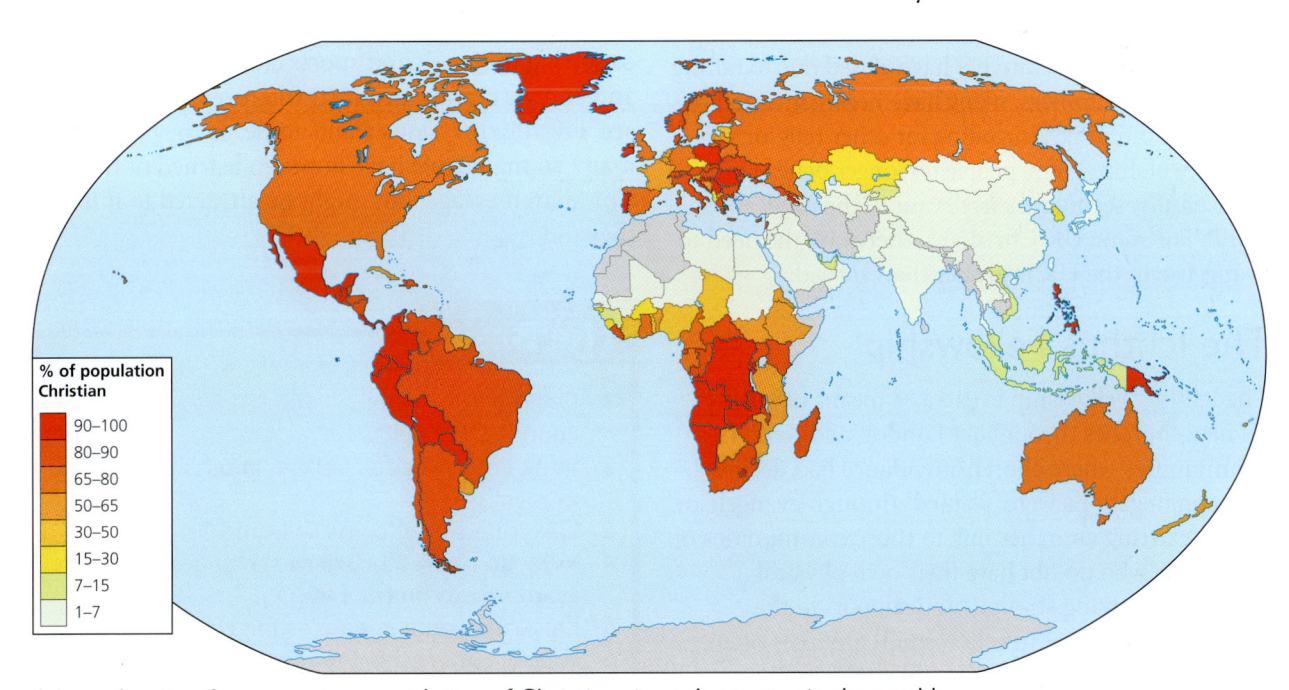

A map showing the percentage population of Christians in each country in the world

Topic 1.2 Practices

*I belong to the **Church Army**. I trained to be a Church Army evangelist. We talk to people about Christ, trying to bring them into Christianity. We do this in the poorest areas, showing God's love for all through our actions. The Holy Spirit helps me to tell them how Jesus has changed my life, how he can change theirs, and it gives me strength to help them in theirs.*

I work for the European Church Mission. I have been living in the UK, but I am Dutch. We have been building church communities here. Our role is to bring Jesus' message in a new way to the congregations, helping renew faith and persuading people of God's love through Jesus' message. Our aim is to see the people of Europe transformed through Jesus Christ.

I am a missionary for Serving in Mission, which is a worldwide missionary organisation. Actually, there are over 4,000 of us in over 70 countries in the world. I have worked in Bolivia and in the Philippines so far, as a teacher of English. My missionary role is to teach Jesus' message, converting others to my faith. It is a dual role – helping the country's development and evangelising.

In the UK, there are now more Christians than ever before in British history, but a lot of this is to do with the UK population being much larger than in the past. As a proportion of the whole population, the percentage of Christians is the smallest ever: just 38 per cent of the population describe themselves as Christians compared to 50 per cent in 2008 and 66 per cent in 1983. Many churches have closed due to falling congregation numbers, many have been converted into other buildings, including for other religions to use for worship. Many people no longer believe in Christianity, seeing it as irrelevant in the modern world. For some UK Christians, therefore, the need to evangelise in the UK is greater than abroad.

The Ichthus Fellowship

The Ichthus Fellowship began as a means of setting up new churches throughout London and Kent. In communities where church attendance had declined, new congregations were 'planted' through evangelism. Today, existing churches link to those communities of Christians who do not have their own physical building, so giving strength and support to the believers. They meet in cells – small groups – often meeting in houses, for prayer and study; in congregations for acts of worship; and in celebrations, where several congregations come together. Their central focus is to worship God.

Fresh Expressions of Church

Fresh Expressions of Church is an initiative aimed at encouraging people to become Christians by going to them in their spaces. For example, going to skate parks to talk about Jesus, holding informal acts of worship, meeting in local cafés for study and prayer or setting up youth and sports clubs, which begin and end with prayer. In fact, wherever young people are, Fresh Expressions wants to be, as they know that many young people have not even learned of the Christian message, but might be attracted to it if they did.

The Basics

1. Define these words – mission; evangelism; church growth.
2. Why do Christians believe in mission and evangelism?
3. Describe some forms of evangelism.
4. Why do many Christians see church growth as important in the UK?
5. Describe some initiatives for church growth.
6. 'Church growth is the most important task for the church today.' Do you agree? Explain reasons to argue for and against this statement.

The worldwide church – working for reconciliation

Reconciliation is the restoring of good relations after a dispute. You have learned that Christians believe that Jesus' death was a sacrifice (see page 5), an atonement for the sins of humans which had created a barrier between them and God and prevented them from going to heaven (see page 23). Jesus' death broke through the barrier, making it possible for humans to be reunited with God in heaven. This was a reconciliation.

Throughout Jesus' life, he encouraged reconciliation by accepting outcasts, such as Zacchaeus the tax collector, and healing those people rejected by the Jewish people, such as the Samaritan woman.

Christians take up this work all around the world, whether locally, nationally or internationally, seeing it as a duty to try to bring peace and harmony to a troubled world.

The ecumenical (worldwide) movement is seen to have begun with a call from Nathan Soderblom (Archbishop of Uppsala, Lutheran Church of Sweden) to all Christians to unite and work for world peace during the First World War. The Church needed to be a source of hope and comfort after Europe had been devastated. After the First World War, it was thought that the Church could bring great positive change to the world, through Christians uniting globally.

World Council of Churches

This organisation brings together churches, denominations and church fellowships in more than 110 countries, uniting over 500 million Christians. From the first Council in 1948, it has tried to show that all Christians are one united faith, sharing the same basic beliefs and so the same duty to show love and compassion for everyone. This has led to an attitude of working together and their efforts to 'heal the world'. As one group, it aims to carry out mission and evangelism, and actively works to heal and reconcile, seeking justice and peace and breaking down barriers between conflicted groups. At the latest (tenth) Council, they agreed to work together to promote justice and peace in the world as an expression of their belief in the Trinity.

The symbol of the World Council of Churches, www.oikoumene.org

The Basics

1. What is meant by 'reconciliation'?
2. How is Jesus a model for Christians in reconciliation?
3. What is the ecumenical movement?
4. Explain the work of the World Council of Churches.
5. 'Reconciliation is an important role for Christians today.' Do you agree? Explain arguments to agree and disagree.

Topic 1.2 Practices

The worldwide church – fighting persecution

Persecution is hostility, ill-treatment or oppression aimed at a person or group for a period of time. It is a form of injustice. Jesus' message was considered blasphemy (insulting God) by the religious leaders of his time because he was reinterpreting the scriptures, and in a way they had not understood, or did not agree with. This led to them persecuting him, his disciples with him and any Christians after his death. The first 300 years of the religion saw Christians persecuted by the authorities, hunted down as an illegal group, and jailed or executed. The early Church knew very well what it was to be persecuted.

Throughout their history, Christians have responded to their persecution with forgiveness and love, rather than vengeance and hate. Jesus' message from the cross was to ask God to forgive his persecutors – and this is the example Christians follow. The Parable of the Sheep and Goats (see page 13) shows that what a person does for others, they also do for Jesus. Given that Christians believe this, they are encouraged by it to try to fight injustice everywhere. Across most religions, there is the belief that hatred is defeated by love, not retaliation – Christianity is no exception. Jesus spoke of two great commandments – to 'love God' and 'love thy neighbour'. Whenever a Christian speaks out against or does anything to fight persecution (which, by definition, is injustice), then they fulfil that second great commandment and follow Jesus' teachings.

Christians in the modern world challenge the persecution of others – Christian or not. Christians in Afghanistan have become a persecuted group, as have those in the Middle East. Christians across the world welcome refugees from these communities and pressure their own governments to hold these countries to account. In Myanmar (Burma), the Rohingya Muslims have been persecuted, leading them to flee to neighbouring countries such as Bangladesh. Christian groups have sent emergency supplies, and volunteers have gone to work in the refugee camps to help these people. Many Christians join campaigns and protests putting pressure on governments to hold other governments to account when there is an injustice perpetrated on a group.

There are many groups whose work is focused on helping persecuted Christians. Here are four to find out about:

1. The **Barnabas Fund,** whose motto is 'hope and aid for the persecuted church', works mainly with Christians in Muslim countries, channelling money to help them develop their communities. www.barnabasfund.org

2. **Open Doors**, set up by Brother Andrew as a Bible-smuggling operation into the old Soviet Union, continues his work through a global underground network. It is estimated that his work has helped persecuted Christians in over 120 countries. www.opendoors.org

3. **Mission without Borders** works in Eastern Europe, supporting the poorest Christians by providing for their spiritual, educational, emotional and physical needs, and those persecuted for their faith. www.mwbi.org

4. **Aid to the Church in Need**, set up by a Pope, supports persecuted Catholics wherever they are. It focuses especially on those who find themselves living in refugee camps, who have left behind everything in fleeing their own homes, by giving pastoral and physical care. www.acnuk.org

Don't overlook that any work for reconciliation is also a way to fight persecution. By reconciling groups and communities, those within the conflict who have the least power become more fairly treated. Many Christians see reconciliation and fighting persecution as two sides of the same struggle for justice in God's world.

The Basics

1. What is persecution?
2. Explain reasons why Christians might try to end persecution.
3. Choose one of the four named groups above and find out more about them. Present your findings as a fact file.
4. 'All Christians should be active in challenging persecution.' Do you agree? Give explained arguments to support your point of view.

Responses to poverty

Poverty is the lack of basic essentials, so that daily life is very difficult. These essentials include adequate food, clean water, good shelter, adequate education, a job and good healthcare. There are many millions of people all around the world who live in absolute poverty (poverty by any measure used), as well as those who live in relative poverty (poverty by the standards of their own country). Their problems may be from disasters, such as an earthquake devastating a country, or from human activity – for example, civil war. This topic forms part of Theme F, so check pages 326–332 to get a broader understanding of the problem.

Jesus' message was of love and compassion for those in need. Many of those he helped were from the fringes of society, often helpless to change their circumstances. Since Jesus is the role model for Christians, his actions must be copied. He also taught 'Love your neighbour', making it clear that anyone in need should be considered that neighbour, whether friend or foe, known or not. The Parable of the Sheep and Goats (Matthew 25:31–46) says we will all be judged at the end of time, based on our attitude to and efforts for our fellow humans. The Parable says that whatever we do for one of them, we do for Jesus. Consequently, Christians believe that they should always help those in need.

In the UK, Christianity recognises its duty to help the poor. Food banks (see page 46) have been set up by, or linked to, many churches; the Porch Box scheme in Bury collects foodstuffs etc. and issues crisis packs to those in emergency need around Greater Manchester; many Christians all over the UK are involved in local government, including decision-making to help the poorest of their communities.

Across the world, poverty is often more obvious in less economically developed countries (LEDCs). This is because the country has little money for development at any time, so when a disaster strikes, they are even less able to find the money needed to sort out the problem. Often their infrastructure (roads, communication links, energy/water supplies, buildings etc.) are less robust than in developing countries, so are easily damaged. Many Christians help fund disaster relief when a country has urgent and immediate need – for example, after an earthquake, and aid programmes where poor infrastructure and facilities prevent people from breaking out of poverty in many countries. Christian denominations have set up a number of charities to help the poor of the UK and abroad.

Sonja: *I tithe, that is, have 10% of my earnings taken straight from source and paid into a series of charities. This includes sponsoring a child in Bangladesh.*

Mia: *I visit churches and schools to speak about the work of a charity. I help people to understand what is done with the money they give.*

Neil: *For several years now, I have kept a link with a couple of refugee camps. My church collects dried food, water, blankets, toiletries and medicines. Then I drive them over to the camp, to give out to people there. We do this twice a year.*

Marcus: *I co-ordinate the fund-raising at the churches in my community who work in partnership. Together we have been able to support a couple of villages in Burkino Faso.*

Topic 1.2 Practices

CAFOD Catholic Agency for Overseas Development www.cafod.org.uk	Set up in 1962, **CAFOD** is the official overseas aid organisation for the Catholic Church of England and Wales. It provides disaster relief as well as development programmes to people in LEDCs. Projects are suggested by the communities, and the work done with them, so as to empower them. Often one project leads to others – for example, a clean water system in a Brazilian favela leading to the building of health centres and a school. CAFOD is also involved in campaigning to try to change laws and to get more government support for communities overseas. It has an education programme to raise awareness of the causes of global injustice and funds for the work of the organisation.
christian aid www.christianaid.org.uk	**Christian Aid** was originally set up by the British and Irish churches to support refugees at the end of the Second World War. For 75 years, Christian Aid has provided disaster relief and long-term development support for poor communities worldwide, while highlighting suffering, tackling injustice and championing people's rights. It works on projects that are requested and run by local communities and partner organisations. It still supports those affected by natural disasters – for example, tsunami victims in Indonesia in 2018. An important part of its work is political campaigning, recognising that governments have great power to change and influence on issues such as climate change. You might recognise their logo from the red envelopes delivered to many households during Christian Aid week every year.
tearfund www.tearfund.org	Set up in 1968, **Tearfund** began as an initiative of the Evangelical Alliance in the UK. As a Christian charity, Tearfund believes that everyone has an amazing God-given potential to create change. Tearfund works with local churches and Christian organisations around the world to unlock this potential, and bring material and spiritual hope. Tearfund also works with supporters and partners to influence powerful decision-makers around the world, and encourages everyone to live in a way that doesn't harm their global neighbours. An example is Tearfund's 2019 'Rubbish Campaign', which called on Coca-Cola, Nestlé, PepsiCo and Unilever to take responsibility for their plastic waste in poorer countries.

The Basics

1. What is poverty?
2. Explain why Christians believe they have a duty to help the poor.
3. Explain different ways that Christians help the poor in the UK and abroad.
4. Research one of the three Christian organisations in the table (see above) to find out more about their work. Present your findings as a fact file.
5. 'Christians in the UK should focus their help for the poor on those in the UK.' Do you agree? Explain arguments to agree and arguments for a different point of view. Write a justified conclusion showing which side you feel is stronger.

Getting prepared

The Practices section of an exam paper is made up of five questions. Here you can read the wording, some tips for doing well and some examples of each.

2.1 question – Multi-choice: 1 mark

For example:

A How many sacraments do Roman Catholics observe?

   a 2   **c** 5

   b 3   **d** 7

B Which **one** of the following is **not** another name for Holy Communion?

   a Mass   **c** Eucharist

   b Christingle   **d** Lord's Supper

> **Tip**
>
> Lots of these are definition questions, so make sure you know the meaning of all key words.

2.2 question – 'Give two …': 2 marks

This tests knowledge (not understanding).

For example:

A Give **two** forms of worship.

B Give **two** reasons why Christians celebrate Easter.

> **Tips**
>
> Keep your answer to a minimum – give only two words or phrases. Example A here could be answered simply by 'liturgical, non-liturgical', or in a longer version, 'One is liturgical worship which follows a book like the Book of Common Prayer; another is non-liturgical, which means every act of worship is decided for the day itself, not read from a book.' The longer the answer, the more time it takes away from your other answers.
>
> The exam paper gives prompts of '**two**' to remind you to give two answers.

2.3 question – Diversity: 4 marks

This is testing your knowledge of the similarities and differences within religion – how different Christians practise their religion differently; or different elements of something.

For example:

A Explain **two** contrasting forms of Christian prayer.

B Explain **two** similar ways in which Christianity plays a role in the local community.

> **Tips**
>
> You get a mark for each way, plus an additional mark as you explain each of those ways: 2 + 2.
>
> 'Contrasting' in the question just means 'different' – you are not being asked to write about opposites.
>
> Using examples is a good way to explain in this question because it shows you know more than just the key words/terms.

Topic 1.2 Practices

2.4 question – Practices related to teachings: 5 marks

This question wants to know how what Christians do links to what they believe, so you have to be able to refer to teachings in your answer if you want to get full marks.

For example:

A Explain **two** religious activities Christians carry out on pilgrimage.

Refer to sacred writings or another source of Christian belief and teaching in your answer.

B Explain **two** ways in which Christians try to help those who are persecuted.

Refer to sacred writings or another source of Christian belief and teaching in your answer.

Tips

You get a mark for each point you make, plus an additional mark for each explanation. The final mark is for giving a relevant teaching. Sometimes it is difficult to directly answer the question with a teaching. In this case, give your example and say <u>why</u> they would do/say that. This usually allows you to give a teaching. As this question is about practices, it is often difficult to think of a teaching which is readily relevant – this makes it necessary to use more words to clearly show how your chosen teaching is relevant (and so get the credit). Referring to a sacred writing is good practice – for example, 'In Genesis, it says …'.

'Teaching' doesn't mean you have to give quotations; you could give beliefs or concepts.

2.5 question – Analysis and evaluation: 12 marks

For example:

A 'To be a Christian, a person has to do more than just worship God.'

Evaluate this statement.

In your answer, you should:

- refer to Christian teaching
- give reasoned arguments to support this statement
- give reasoned arguments to support a different point of view
- reach a justified conclusion.

B 'All Christians should do something to fulfil their duty of mission and evangelism.'

Evaluate this statement.

In your answer, you should:

- refer to Christian teaching
- give reasoned arguments to support this statement
- give reasoned arguments to support a different point of view
- reach a justified conclusion.

Tips

The question wording gives you a great way to check your answer – use the different bullet points to check you have done all the things you need to do.

If the statement says something is 'best', 'most important' or gives any kind of value words, then challenge it by saying, 'It depends what is meant by …'. This is a good technique to make your brain think more widely in answering.

You have to give an agree side and a disagree side in your answer – failure to do so will cost you any mark above Level 2 (6 marks out of 12). Similarly, failure to explain anything you write will also keep you stuck at Level 2 at best.

By giving and explaining all arguments for one side, then doing the same for the other side, you write a clearer answer which is easier to mark.

'Justified conclusion' is a posh way of asking you to say whether the agree or disagree side is stronger, and why you think that. It doesn't mean for you to rewrite arguments you have given already! So one side might have more arguments, might be clearer, might be more compelling/persuasive or might fit with what you already think. These are all useful ways to justify a conclusion. Sometimes, you just can't decide – and it is okay to say that as well.

Christianity glossary

Anglican another term for the Church of England

Apostles' Creed a statement of Christian belief from the early Church

Ascension Jesus being taken up to heaven on the 40th day after Easter

Atonement the action of making amends for wrong doing; the idea of being at one with God

Baptism a ceremony to welcome a person into the Christian religion

Believers' baptism a ceremony to welcome a young person or adult into the Christian religion using full immersion

Blasphemy speaking badly about a religion or insulting God

CAFOD a charity: Catholic Agency for Overseas Development

Catechism of the Catholic Church a summary of Roman Catholic teaching

Christian Aid a charity working in the developing world providing emergency and long-term aid

Church Army an evangelistic organisation founded within the Church of England

Confession a sacrament in which a Catholic or Orthodox Christian admits their sins to a priest in return for forgiveness (absolution)

Confirmation an initiation ceremony carried out by a bishop bestowing the gift of the Holy Spirit

Crucifixion capital punishment used by the Romans which nails a person to a cross to kill them

Denomination the name for the different branches of the Christian Church

Divine Liturgy the Orthodox form of the Eucharist

Ecumenical relating to the worldwide Christian Church

Eucharist the Christian service/ceremony to recall the Last Supper, in which bread and wine are consecrated and consumed

Evangelical Christian Christians who believe they have a duty to preach Christianity in order to convert others to the religion

Evangelism preaching of the faith in order to convert people to that religion

Food banks charity groups collecting donated food to distribute to the poor in Britain

Fundamentalist Christians who take the Bible literally, i.e. word-for-word true

Gospel the names of the books about the life of Jesus in the Bible: Matthew, Mark, Luke and John

Grace unconditional love that God shows to people, even those who do not seem to deserve it

Holy Communion the bread and wine ceremony in the Church of England

Immaculate Conception belief that Mary was a virgin when she became pregnant with Jesus; held by Roman Catholics and Orthodox Christians

Incarnation God in human form, i.e. Jesus

Infant baptism ceremony to welcome a child into the Christian religion

Informal worship worship which has less formal structure, so can be made up of any set of practices in any order

Iona an island in Scotland with a fourth-century monastery used by Christians today as a religious retreat as it is a place of tranquillity and peace

Liturgical worship a church service with a set structure of worship

Lord's Prayer the prayer Jesus taught his disciples to show them how to pray

Lord's Supper non-Conformist form of the Eucharist

Lourdes a town in France where the Virgin Mary appeared; now a place of pilgrimage

Mass the bread and wine ceremony in the Roman Catholic Church

Christianity glossary

Messiah the anointed one who is seen as the saviour by Jewish and Christian people

Methodist a Protestant Christian group founded by John Wesley in the eighteenth century

Miracles events that have no logical or scientific explanation; these are described in the Gospels as performed by Jesus

Mission an organised effort to spread the Christian message

Nicene Creed a statement of belief used in Christian services

Non-liturgical worship informal structure found in some church services

Omnibenevolent all-loving; God loves each person without exception or prejudice

Omnipotent the idea that God is all-powerful

Omniscient the idea that God is all-knowing

Oneness of God the idea that God is 'One'

Ordination the process by which someone becomes a vicar/priest

Original sin the act of disobeying God when Adam and Eve ate the fruit of the forbidden tree

Orthodox Church a branch of the Christian Church with its origins in Greece and Russia

Persecution continual ill-treatment of someone or a group, even to the point of killing them

Pilgrimage a sacred journey to a sacred place

Protestant a branch of the Christian Church that broke away from the Roman Catholic Church

Purgatory in Roman Catholic belief, the place where souls go after death and before the final judgement; a place of purification through suffering for sins

Quakers the Society of Friends, a Christian group

Reconciliation the process of making people in conflict become friends again

Resurrection the physical return of Jesus on the third day after he died

Roman Catholic the largest Christian group, based in Rome with the Pope as its leader

Rosary a set of beads used to count prayers, especially in the Roman Catholic Church

Sacrament the external and visible sign of an inward and spiritual grace

Salvation the saving of the soul from sin

Secular relating to worldly as opposed to religious things

St Paul a man who taught the teachings of Jesus; originally Saul of Tarsus before his conversion

Street pastors a Christian organisation of people working on city streets at night caring for people who need help or are involved in anti-social behaviour

Tearfund a Christian charity working to relieve poverty in developing countries

Transubstantiation the change in the bread and wine to become the actual body and blood of Christ

Trinity the belief in God the Father, God the Son and God the Holy Spirit

The study of religions

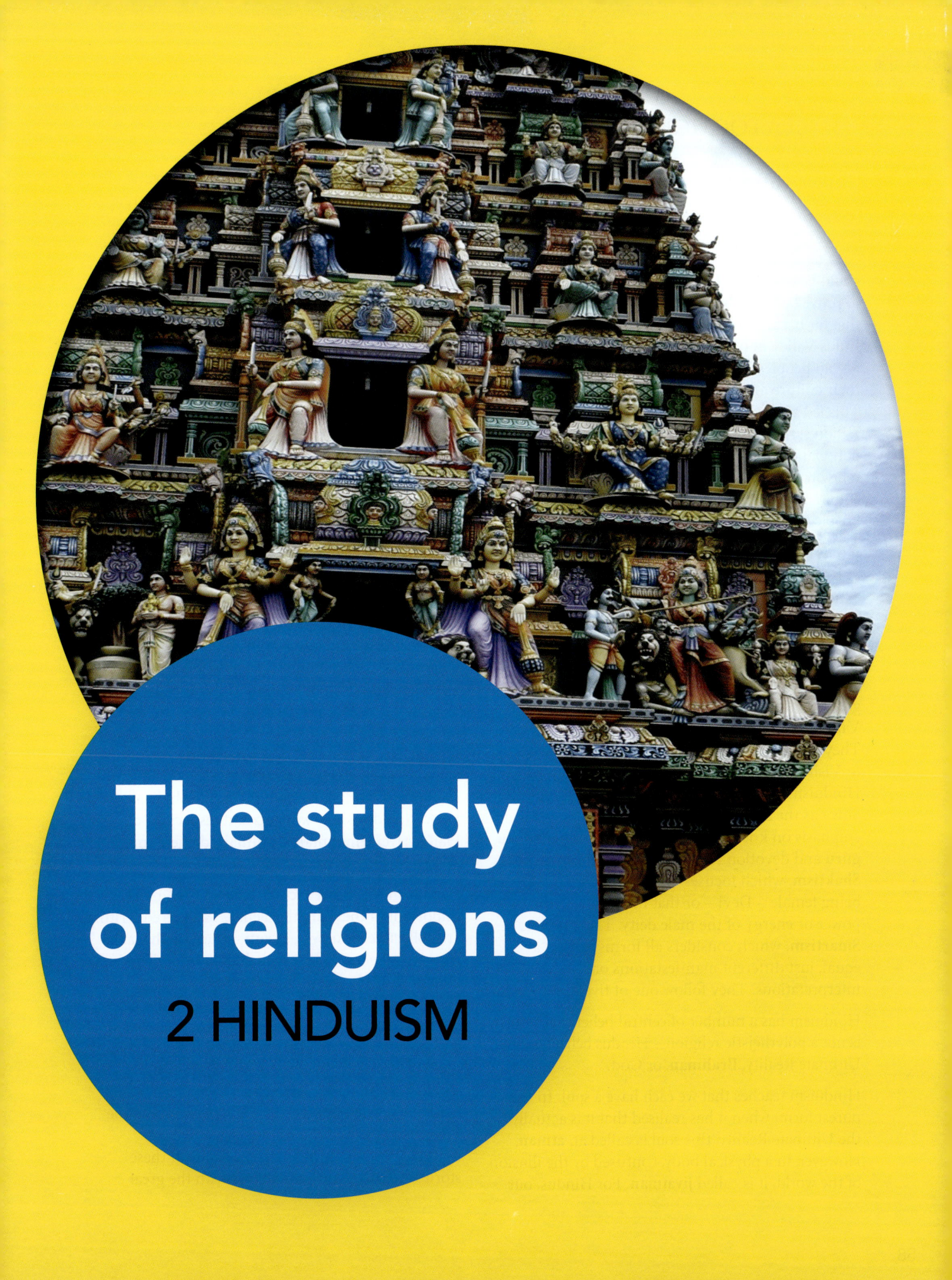

2 HINDUISM

Introduction

An introduction to Hinduism

Beliefs and teachings

Hinduism is the most ancient religion in the world. Scholars have found evidence of the religion dating back to 2500BCE, though some scholars believe it could be as old as 12,000 years, although this is hard to prove because there were no written documents that far back. The religion began in the Saraswati-Indus Valley in Northern India when the Indo-Aryan peoples migrated into this region, mixing their culture and beliefs with those already there. This led to the Vedic period, when the greatest of Hindu scriptures were written. Hinduism is the national religion of India and Nepal, and is the main religion of Bali. However, it is found in most countries around the world now – one in seven people on Earth is a Hindu.

Hinduism has no single founder. Hinduism claims to be a living religion and is founded on the spiritual experiences of many individuals – men and women – over thousands of years. These individuals (sages, rishis, saints and teachers) shaped beliefs over many centuries. From their interpretations of scripture and teaching of those ideas have come the different groups within Hinduism. The four main ones are Vaishnavites, who worship Vishnu as Supreme Lord. They place great emphasis on service and devotion to Vishnu. **Vaishnavism** is the largest group within Hinduism. A second group – **Shaivism** – worships Shiva as the Supreme Lord. Shaivites place great emphasis on knowledge, especially learning from a **guru** and devotion to Shiva. A third group is **Shaktism**, which focuses on the Ultimate Reality as being female – Devi – or that the female is the power or energy of the male deity. The fourth is **Smartism**, which considers all forms of God as equal, just different manifestations or interpretations. They follow one of five main **deities**.

Hinduism has a number of central beliefs. Hinduism is not a polytheistic religion – Hindus believe in one Ultimate Reality, **Brahman**, or God.

Hinduism teaches that we each have a soul. In its purest form, when it has realised that it is actually the Ultimate Reality, this soul is called an **atman**. However, in a physical body, confused by the illusion of the world, it is called **jivatman**. For Hindus, our goal in life is to achieve **moksha**, for our jivatman to recognise its true nature as atman, and to be reunited with Brahman. For some Hindus, our atman is Brahman, which is the only thing that truly exists. However, our atman is so deluded that it does not realise this – that delusion is **maya**. Until our soul (jivatman) realises its true nature, and the true nature of everything, it keeps being born into a life in this world (reincarnation) – this is **samsara**: birth, death and rebirth. When it has the realisation, it achieves moksha – liberation, and becomes reunited with Brahman. Hinduism recognises different pathways (**yoga**) to achieve moksha – **bhakti** (devotion), **karma** (actions), **jnana** (knowledge) and **samadhi** (meditation).

The **Tri-murti** is a Vaishnavite concept of God in the form of three deities – Brahma (creator), Vishnu (sustainer) and Shiva (destroyer). Hindus also believe that there are many lesser deities, such as Saraswati, Lakshmi and Parvati, who are the consorts of the Tri-murti, or their children, such as Ganesha. However, all deities are simply manifestations of the qualities of Brahman, the Ultimate Reality. Vaishnavites also believe that, in times of great need, Vishnu incarnates as an **avatar** (avatara) to save humanity and the **Dharma** (eternal law). Rama and Krishna are two of the most loved avatars. Brahman is within everything, the essence of everything and everyone – human, animal, plant, the physical world. Hence Hindus show worship and respect for all. Plants, rivers, mountains, animals, deities, gurus – all can be focuses of worship.

Hinduism has many sacred writings. The most important of these are the Vedas. The sacred writings are collectively known as **sruti** – that which was heard – collections of revealed knowledge. The Vedas include four hymn sections (Samhitas), ritual handbooks (Brahmanas), and books of religious and spiritual debate (Upanishads). Each of the main groups of Hinduism also follows its own sruti called the Agamas. As well as the sruti, Hinduism has **smriti** – those which were remembered. These include great stories such as the Mahabharata, the Bhagavad Gita and the Ramayana, as well as mythology such as the Puranas. Many of these stories and myths are associated with the great festivals and kept in the memory of all Hindus through their retelling at these events.

Practices

Hindus follow **Sanatana-dharma** – the eternal path. Worship is a duty which should be carried out daily at home or at the temple (**mandir**). Most Hindu families have their own shrine at home to be able to worship each morning. An act of worship includes making offerings to the deity and seeking their blessing. Temples are staffed by priests, often but not necessarily of the Brahmin caste. Priests have been trained to carry out the many ritual acts of worship which are found in Hinduism, as well as being tasked to look after the statues of the deities (**murtis**), which are considered sacred. They also know the scriptures well, and Hindus will seek advice and knowledge from them.

There are many Hindu festivals, though few Hindus celebrate every festival as many are regional or related to a specific deity. However, all Hindus celebrate **Diwali**, an autumn festival which celebrates Rama saving Sita from the demon king Ravanna, who was terrorising humanity, and the couple's return from exile. They also celebrate **Holi**, a spring festival of fun, which recalls the pranks of Krishna, and how Prahlad's devotion to Vishnu saved him from Holika's fire. In the UK, these have become large communal events welcoming people of any religion or none to join in.

Pilgrimage is important in Hinduism as it is an act of complete worship; for many, it is considered a religious duty. Pilgrimage sites usually link to individual deities; however, most Hindus will try to go to **Varanasi** – the longest-inhabited city on earth, home of Shiva and filled with thousands of temples and gurus. Combining both festival and pilgrimage is **Kumbh Mela**, which takes place on a rotation of four sites every third year (hence a 12-year cycle). At Kumbh Mela, two great rivers meet along with a mystical river, and it is believed that entering the river at dawn can bring moksha instantly.

Hinduism is a religion of living as well as of beliefs. There are many personal virtues which Hindus should try to develop within themselves, including cleanliness, self-discipline, honesty, service to others and non-harming (**ahimsa**). By living such a life, moksha can be attained. This has led to many Hindus being vegetarian and trying to bring about social change. These attitudes have led to many projects such as cow protection, social inclusion and women's rights.

2.1 Beliefs and teachings

The Hindu concept of God

Hinduism is *not* a polytheistic religion; that is to say, Hinduism believes there is one Ultimate Reality, Brahman – divine consciousness – *not* many different gods. Brahman is manifested or made known through many forms called deities. This is **Saguna Brahman** – Brahman with forms, also called Ishwara.

Brahman

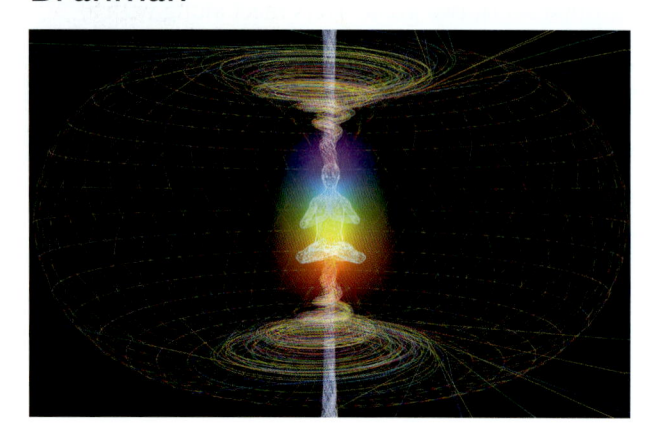

It is impossible to fully or perfectly describe Brahman. However, Hinduism does try to suggest some descriptions of Brahman and the qualities of Brahman – always accepting that these are imperfect descriptions. Only when a person achieves moksha (liberation) is it possible to truly know Brahman.

> 'Brahman is pure consciousness, without parts, without form. In order to help the seeker in his efforts to surrender, symbols and qualities are added to Brahman.'
> *(Upanishads)*.

Given God is so different to humans and is transcendent (beyond the material world, time and space), it makes sense that we could not really imagine or know God. This is **Nirguna Brahman** – Brahman without form. A Hindu's goal in life is to be reunited with Brahman by recognising their own true identity as Brahman. For many Hindus, the way they do this is by building their religious knowledge and trying to understand the concept of Brahman. Brihadaranyaka Upanishad 391 describes individual aspects of Brahman, such as eternal, immanent, transcendent and pure consciousness. Brahman can be understood through these aspects, because we have the words to be able to recognise, simplify and understand these terms. However, it is impossible for a human to understand Brahman fully.

The Three Features of the Divine

The idea of the three features of the divine is an attempt to describe Brahman through three aspects. It is encapsulated by the phrase *sat-cit-ananda*.

- Sat – pure existence: Brahman is everywhere as a non-personal being, part of everything in the universe, eternal. This is God as pure existence. 'Everything is Brahman' (Upanishads). This influences Hindus to show respect and worship to everything – be it the natural world, or any living being.
- Cit – divine consciousness: Brahman is within our hearts, the 'controller within' (antaryami), knowledge. This is consciousness – for example, the realisation of Brahman within.
- Ananda – spiritual supreme contentment: Brahman is beyond everything (transcendent), as the supreme personal and loving God (Bhagavan or Ishwara) who brings spiritual pleasure, or bliss. This encourages Hindus to show great devotion to Brahman – for example, in the form of Vishnu.

2 Hinduism

Different understandings of Brahman as ananda – Supreme Lord

Vaishnavites believe that Vishnu is actually the Supreme Lord, the creator of the universe. They worship him through devotional practices, such as worship. He is seen as pure love. In one creation story, Vishnu lies on a serpent in the great void. From his navel comes a lotus flower, which opens to reveal Brahma. Vishnu commands Brahma to create, so he creates the universe. Later, Shiva destroys it, so that the cycle can begin again.

Shaivites believe that Shiva is the Supreme Lord, pure goodness full of peace and compassion. Study and meditation are important to understand aspects of Shiva and to achieve enlightenment (moksha). It is common for Shaivites to devote their entire lives to this, not getting married or being part of ordinary society, and devoting themselves to a guru in order to learn.

The Tri-murti

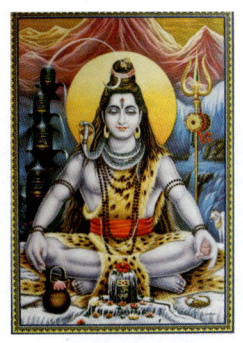

Brahma   Vishnu   Shiva

This is a Vaishnavite concept of Brahman. It sees God as three key forms:

- Brahma – the creator. He is often shown bearded, holding the Vedas and riding a swan. He is the personification of sat (pure existence).
- Vishnu – the sustainer. He is shown having blue skin and wearing yellow clothes. He is the personification of ananda (bliss).
- Shiva – the destroyer. He is seen in the form of Nataraja, Lord of the Dance, dancing in a circle of flames, or as a holy man meditating at Mount Kailash. He is the personification of cit (knowledge; divine consciousness).

Each of the Tri-murti has a consort, or partner (see page 62). Their consort is a deity with powers in their own right, but also represents the feminine energy of the male. Just as the deities have families, so Hindus see it as a duty to have their own family.

Believing in the Tri-murti might lead a Hindu to focus their devotion on one form, so that they worship that form exclusively. All Hindus are influenced to take care of the world in respect for the creative roles of the Tri-murti.

Influences

If I believe that Brahman is everything, then I will see everything around me as being worthy of respect and perhaps worship. Certainly I will be able to worship Brahman anywhere, because Brahman is not confined to any single place.

If I believe that Shiva is Brahman as the Supreme Lord, I will focus my devotion on Shiva. I will attend a Shaivite temple for worship, and I study the scriptures to become closer to a better understanding of Brahman.

The Basics

1. What do Hindus call God?
2. Explain Hindu beliefs about Brahman.
3. Explain the three features of the divine.
4. Explain the idea of the Tri-murti.
5. 'There is no point in trying to understand God.' Explain the arguments a Hindu might give for and against that view.

Topic 2.1 Beliefs and teachings

Male and female deities

The Rig Veda says, 'God is One but wise men call him by many names.' The deities are these names, personifying aspects of Brahman. The Upanishads say a person can believe they have understood Brahman when they understand a deity, but they have not – they should go and study another … and another … Hindus insist that the Ultimate Reality can only be understood through first-hand experience. They cannot be understood by thinking and reasoning, or by the study of scriptures.

Hindus worship the deities, having a particular one to whom they dedicate a shrine at home and devote worship to. Hindu temples are dedicated to one specific deity – usually one of the Tri-murti – but also have shrines of lesser deities. For particular circumstances, they might worship a different deity – for example, making offerings to Parvati in the hope of pregnancy, or to Ganesha when starting a new business. This worship can be more meaningful for them, and be more sincere, as it is for a specific need.

For this course, you need to know about four deities:

Ganesha – the son of Shiva and Parvati, recognised by his elephant head. He is the deity of wisdom and remover of barriers.	Hanuman – the monkey king, known for his strength. He carries a mace to signify that strength. He is a devotee of Rama.
Lakshmi – the consort of Vishnu: the deity of wealth and prosperity, goddess of the hearth and home. Her four arms symbolise the four pathways to moksha (yogas, see pages 94–95).	Saraswati – consort of Brahma: the deity of music, the arts and learning. She is usually seen seated on a lotus (symbolising wisdom) and playing a musical instrument.

Avatars

Hindus believe that Brahman can manifest on earth because Brahman is Saguna Brahman (Brahman with forms) – these incarnations are avatars. 'Avatar' means 'descent'. As an avatar, Brahman is immanent, so can have a direct effect on the world.

Belief in avatars is strongest in Vaishnavism, whose followers believe that Vishnu has incarnated at least nine times, and will do so for a tenth time as Kalki, riding a white horse at the end of the world. The Bhagavad Gita explains avatars by saying that, 'For the protection of the

2 Hinduism

good, and for the destruction of the wicked, for the establishment of Dharma, I am born from age to age.'

There are three levels of incarnation:

- A human who has been given extraordinary powers, such as the Buddha. His role was to protect and explain the Dharma.
- Vishnu personally incarnated but with lesser powers, such as the dwarf Vamana, who defeated the demon king Bali, after he had come to rule the universe.
- A complete incarnation of Vishnu with divine energy, such as Krishna. His role was to restore the Dharma – for example, by guiding Arjuna to know his duty in the Bhagavad Gita.

Rama and Krishna

Rama and Krishna are two of the avatars of Vishnu and probably the most famous and loved.

Rama is the seventh avatar of Vishnu and the hero of the Ramayana. This story tells how a demon king, Ravanna, terrorised the world. Vishnu incarnated as Rama, and his consort Lakshmi incarnated as Sita, Rama's wife. Sita was kidnapped by Ravanna and taken to the island of Lanka where Ravanna had a fortress. Rama, helped by Hanuman and others, searched for her. Eventually a great battle ensued, in which Rama killed Ravanna. Rama and Sita returned home. The festival of Diwali recalls this story (see page 93). Rama represents goodness and strength, the perfect role model for living.

Krishna is the eighth avatar of Vishnu. He is seen in many forms – a baby, a cowherd, playing a flute, a warrior – always with blue skin. He is mentioned in many of the smriti writings, including the Bhagavad Gita, where he is Arjuna's charioteer. This sacred writing tells of their philosophical discussion about the Dharma, and Arjuna's duty to fight in a war, even though it means fighting his own relatives (the story of which is told in the Mahabharata).

Krishna is worshipped as a deity by many Hindus, and there are many temples dedicated to him. ISKCON (International Society for Krishna Consciousness) is a major Vaishnavite sect within Hinduism which has attracted many Western converts.

The seventh avatar of Vishnu, called Rama

The eighth avatar of Vishnu, called Krishna

The Basics

1. Why are deities important in Hinduism?
2. Explain the role of two deities.
3. Explain which deity each of these Hindus might make offerings to
   a a student before exams
   b the owner of a new shop
   c a newly-wed couple.
4. Explain what Hinduism teaches about avatars.
5. Explain how belief in avatars might influence a Hindu.
6. 'It is wrong to say Hinduism believes in many gods.' Explain how a Hindu might respond to that statement.

Topic 2.1 Beliefs and teachings

Beliefs about existence – matter (prakriti) and the three qualities (Tri-guna)

Hindus believe we each have an eternal, inner self – this is called the atman. They believe our atman lives through many lifetimes in this and other worlds – reincarnation. The atman aims to be reunited with Brahman by recognising its true nature as Brahman, the Ultimate Reality, but living in the world makes that very difficult.

Brahman projected itself into two forces – **purusha** and **prakriti**, or male and female energies. From these, everything was created. Prakriti can be simply translated as 'matter', though it is more than that because the word prakriti means something that evolves or reproduces. In other words, prakriti is the primal essence of everything.

Hinduism teaches that Brahman is eternal; also that the soul (jivatman) is born and dies until it recognises its true nature as Brahman. However, humans live in the material universe, which is temporary and ever-changing. Physical existence is part of what prevents the jivatman (soul) from understanding its true nature (as atman), acting as a barrier to attaining moksha (liberation from rebirth) and being reunited with Brahman.

Have you ever felt really lethargic, couldn't be bothered? Or really energised and active so that you couldn't stop? How about contentment – ever felt that? These feelings come from what Hindus call the **Tri-guna**, the three **gunas** or qualities: sattva, rajas and tamas.

> 'The three qualities – sattva, rajas and tamas – are built into human nature. They bind and limit the divinity within the personality.' *(Bhagavad Gita 14:5)*

This quotation describes the Tri-guna – the three elements which make up matter (prakriti). One interpretation says that the three gunas of the Tri-guna define life. So, what are they?

- Sattva is 'goodness', made up of qualities such as awareness, happiness and contentment.
- Rajas is 'activity', made up of qualities such as passion and pain.
- Tamas is 'darkness', made up of qualities such as sorrow, ignorance and obstruction.

Rajas and tamas are opposites, while sattva holds them together. The Bhagavad Gita says that sattva (goodness) is the true nature of the atman, but this is blocked by tamas (darkness); rajas (activity) can increase or remove that blockage. It also says that the gunas act as barriers to knowing the true nature of the atman and everything else, because it is in a person's nature to just focus on how the gunas manifest and to make them unbalanced – for example, wanting more and more luxury, or becoming depressed about a situation. So, we can see the impact of the gunas on any person – a very spiritual person is

Influences

If I believe in the gunas, I will try to be aware of my moods. I want to regulate them, and be in an even temperament. To do this, I might meditate every day – I know that meditation helps a person keep a control of their emotional state.
I will recognise that we must get a balance to the gunas – we cannot get rid of any whilst living as a human. Achieving moksha extinguishes the gunas so I accept but try to manage the effects of the gunas now.

dominated by sattva; someone who finds fault in everything by tamas; a person who is always changing and active by rajas. If you think about it, we can all be very lazy and unmotivated (tamas), but then find a reason to get active and pull ourselves out of that mood (rajas), to finally get a sense of well-being and contentment (sattva). On a small scale, we each go through these phases. That having been said, some people never seem to be motivated, others never seem able to sit still – Hindus would say the gunas are out of balance and are a barrier to their spiritual evolution. However, the path to moksha lies through all the gunas – start by being unaware of the truth (tamas), then start to look and work for it (rajas) and finally achieve it (sattva).

The three gunas can be explained in terms of the Tri-murti. Shiva is rajas – passion; Vishnu is sattva – goodness; Brahma is tamas – ignorance.

Hindus believe that a person's personality and mood are both affected by the Tri-guna. Whichever of the Tri-guna is strongest influences their mood, so if rajas is strongest, they might feel full of energy; if sattva is strongest, they might be very calm. This can explain why we react differently in similar situations on different days, why we have 'good days' and 'bad days'.

SATTVA

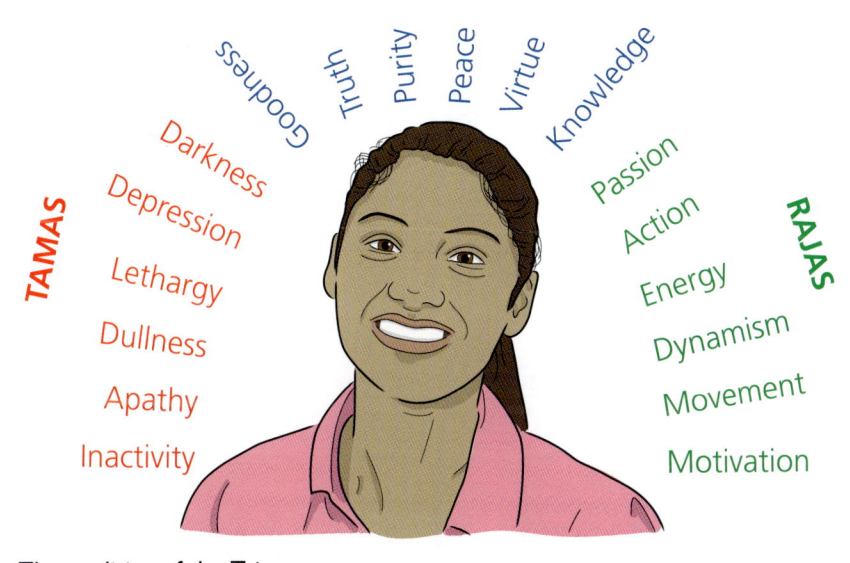

SATTVA: Goodness, Truth, Purity, Peace, Virtue, Knowledge

TAMAS: Darkness, Depression, Lethargy, Dullness, Apathy, Inactivity

RAJAS: Passion, Action, Energy, Dynamism, Movement, Motivation

The qualities of the Tri-guna

The Basics

1. What is prakriti?
2. Say what the Tri-guna are, and use examples to show how they can be seen in humans.
3. Explain Hindu beliefs about the Tri-guna.
4. Explain how belief in the Tri-guna might influence people.
5. 'It is impossible for humans to live a life where the Tri-guna are balanced.' Do you agree? Give reasons for and against your opinion.

Thinking about our world

Don't forget, prakriti is matter; everything in our physical universe is made up of matter. Matter (prakriti) is made up of the Tri-guna. So, everything is affected by the Tri-guna – even our physical world. Those things which are heavy, immovable or unmovable are dominated by tamas: for example, rocks. Those things which are light are dominated by sattva: for example, sunlight and warmth. Those things which are active, such as volcanoes or the sea, are dominated by rajas.

Can you think of any other examples of the influence of the gunas in the world?

Topic 2.1 Beliefs and teachings

Illusion (maya)

'That same self, completely deluded by maya, abides in the body and does everything.' (Upanishads)

The unbalanced Tri-guna create barriers to understanding the true nature of the atman and the universe. Hindus believe that this creates a complex illusion (maya), which humans think of as reality. The Hindu aim of life is to achieve moksha (liberation from rebirth) – the point when the atman sees through the illusion (maya) to understand the true nature of everything, including itself. Hindus believe this illusion makes humans behave in negative ways – being angry, greedy, attached to material pleasures. It also makes people selfish, so that they hurt others deliberately, indirectly or by ignorance.

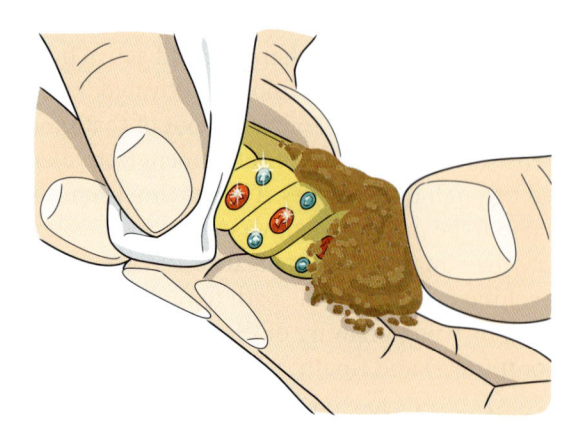

Two analogies can help us understand maya. Firstly, a rishi (an enlightened person who received the Vedas scriptures) called Vashistha described maya as being like dirt. The dirt covers things and hides what they really are. To be able to see what something is really like, you have to clean the dirt away. Hence, the illusion we have created must be wiped away to see the true nature of everything (that everything is Brahman, including the atman).

Secondly, the rope analogy – the Vedas describe the universe as an illusion which appears as a snake. A man, walking in the dark, sees a snake on the path; terrified, he turns and runs. Next morning, nervously, he walks the same path to find that the 'snake' is actually a rope. Fears gone, he carries on his way. Hence, maya (illusion) – like the effect of the darkness – makes us see everything around us as something it is not; we do not see its true nature, so we act differently.

'In a dream state, the atman is completely deluded by maya.' (Upanishads)

The analogies of dirt and of the coiled snake

Influences

Belief in the Tri-guna and in maya might influence a Hindu to meditate each day. Meditation brings about a calmness which can help them to stay in a more even mood throughout the day – helping to balance the excesses of the Tri-guna. It might also make them study the scriptures, such as the Vedas, because these help a person understand the truth and so reduce and remove the barriers of the Tri-guna and maya. The great teacher Shankara said that maya makes a person feel limited and bound, but studying the Vedas lifts that feeling.

The Basics

1. Use examples or analogies to explain maya.
2. Explain Hindu beliefs about maya.
3. How might believing in maya influence a person?
4. 'Maya (illusion) is always bad.' Explain reasons for and against this statement before writing a justified conclusion.

Many worlds

The Vedas says, 'There are innumerable universes besides this one, and although they are unlimitedly large, they move about like atoms in You.' This concept of many universes is called a multiverse.

Hinduism teaches the existence of three worlds (or universes).

- The first is the one we inhabit – the physical universe. Reincarnation happens here.
- The second is an astral or mental plane of existence. Spirits, angels and enlightened souls exist here, who are constantly helping those in the first world. A person can communicate with these beings via worship.
- The third is the spiritual universe in which the greatest fully-enlightened beings exist.

Each atman (eternal soul) originated from Brahman in the spiritual worlds and was then incarnated as part of the process of birth, death and rebirth (samsara) on earth – as jivatman. Reincarnated through many lifetimes, the jivatman evolves to finally realise its true nature (as atman), and is then reunited with Brahman in the spirit world.

Those Hindus devoted to Krishna say that there are three main destinations in the spiritual realm.

- Goloka – the home of Krishna, inhabited by those who are filled with love of Krishna. For these believers, it make sense to be fully devoted to Krishna in this lifetime, so as to be reincarnated to live in blissful contentment in Goloka devoted to Krishna. The Bhagavad Gita says, 'the supreme destination, that place which, having attained it, one never returns – that is my Supreme abode'.
- The Vaikuntha planets ruled by Vishnu, where his devotees can be reborn. These worlds are described as paradises where couples fly around, eternally singing praises to, and of, Vishnu.
- The space in which the spiritual planets float, caused by Krishna's grace. Those souls which have not yet come to love Krishna or Vishnu reside here temporarily between incarnations.

The Basics

1 Explain what is meant by the term *multiverse*.
2 Explain Hindu beliefs about spirit worlds.
3 How might believing in spirit worlds affect a Hindu?
4 'It is better to focus on a good life now than a spirit world later.' Do you agree with that statement? Explain your reasons. What might a Hindu say?

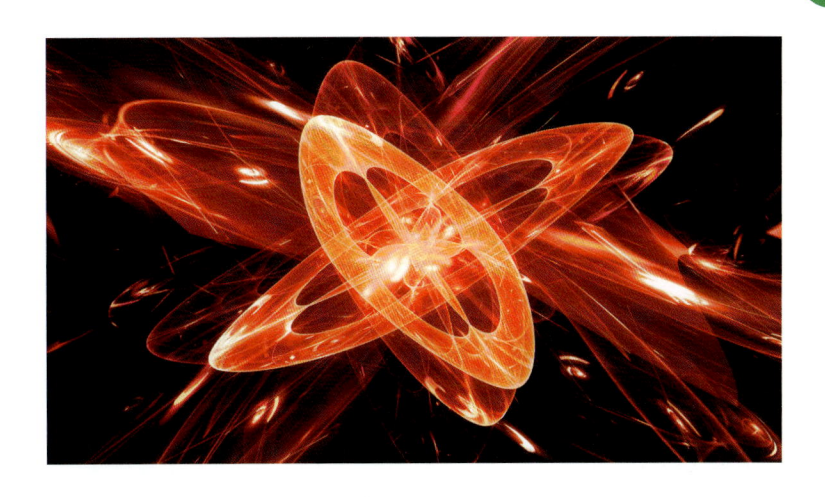

Influences

If a person believes in the three worlds, they should want to become enlightened. Those worlds are much better than our physical world and the suffering it brings. So, they might show more devotion to the path of achieving moksha. For example, this might be done by worshipping a deity such as Vishnu very devotedly; it might be done by studying the scriptures to better understand Brahman. For a Hindu who worships Krishna, they might devote their entire existence to the worship of Krishna in the hope they will be reborn in Goloka, rather than being born again on Earth.

Topic 2.1 Beliefs and teachings

Hindu cosmology

Cosmology is a term referring to ideas of how the universe began. Hinduism has many stories which try to explain this. The earliest stories suggest creation from nothing by Brahman, while later stories attribute creation to one or more of the Tri-murti. Hinduism sees time as cyclical, with no beginning or end. This is similar to the scientific *pulsation hypothesis theory* – the universe is created from nothing, expands and then retracts back to nothing; it then recreates, expands and contracts. It does this forever – like a pulsating mass.

The Rig Veda (sruti scripture) says that at the beginning of time there was a state of nothingness: inertia. There began a vibration and from this all creation sprang.

> 'In the beginning was the non-existent, from which the existent began.' *(Rig Veda 10.129)*

The Rig Veda also tells the Hymn of the Cosmic Man, Purusha, the soul of the universe. The whole universe – everything that has ever been or that is – is part of Purusha, as are the spirit worlds (see page 67). Purusha had a son, who was sacrificed by the gods. He created the birds and animals, and then he himself was divided to form everything else.

In a Vaishnavite story, we find Vishnu sleeping on a coiled snake which floats over the great void (nothingness). He wakens and a lotus flower grows from his navel. The flower opens and there is Brahma. Vishnu commands Brahma to create, and so begins the universe, which lasts for a day of Brahma's life (4.32 billion years). When Vishnu returns to sleep, the universe will end – waiting for the process to begin again.

The Cycle of Four Ages

We now know Hindus believe in something similar to science's pulsation theory – universe, growth, contraction, nothing: repeat for ever. Hinduism teaches that, when the universe exists, we can split the time of its existence (one Brahma day) into four phases or ages (**yugas**). Starting off as perfection, each age gets weaker, but shorter – like when you exercise, starting off doing

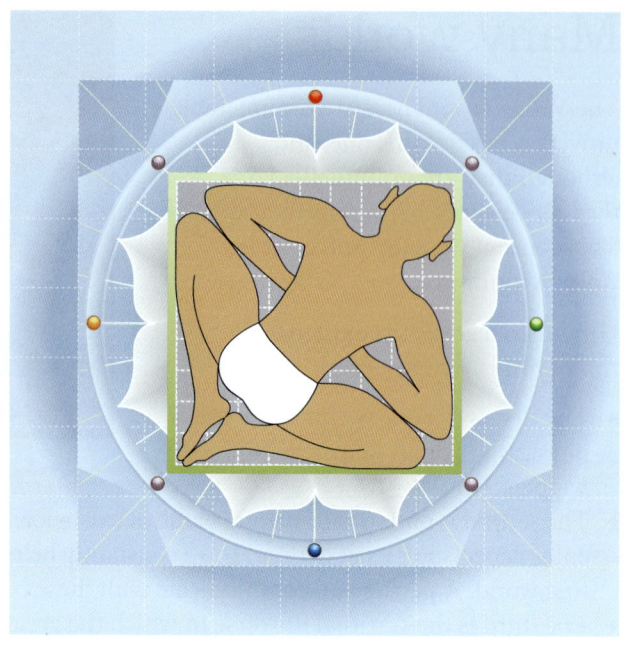

A mandala showing Purusha, the cosmic man

your best, but as you tire mistakes and fatigue take over, until eventually you just need to rest. The four yugas, in the order in which they happen, are:

1 Satya-yuga – lasting 1,728,000 years, this is the golden age. It is an ideal world, where every person is a highly spiritual, pure being; everyone has full concern for everyone else, and all live very long, completely virtuous lives. It is a perfect time.

2 Treta-yuga – lasting 1,296,000 years, this is the silver age. Empires are created, but this also brings war. The world is now 75 per cent virtuous; so 25 per cent is not.

3 Dvapara-yuga – lasting 864,000 years, this is the copper age. Darkness (tamas) affects the world, so there is disease and growing discontentment. Only half the world is virtuous.

4 Kali-yuga – lasting 432,000 years, this is the iron age. This is the most corrupt of ages as there is only virtuousness in a quarter of the world. It is the age of darkness and ignorance, when humans destroy their world around them because they are so selfish, religion is ignored – even ridiculed – and leaders are corrupt. During this age, humans need help from the deities more than ever. We live in this yuga.

Many worlds, many inhabitants

On page 67, you learnt that Hindus believe in a multiverse. One scripture describes 14 worlds – seven higher worlds inhabited by beings who have achieved moksha and are liberated from rebirth; and seven lower worlds which are hells, inhabited by those who need to suffer because of their bad actions. Humans live in the lowest of the higher worlds. The Vedas tells us there are three worlds – the world we inhabit, the physical world; the atmosphere; and the world of the deities (heavens).
In any belief about worlds, the point is always to evolve the atman, so that it moves up to the higher worlds; the difficulty – especially in the Kali-yuga – is avoiding being selfish and bad, which pushes the atman downwards.

Hinduism believes that there are all kinds of beings, from the serpents in the lowest world all the way up to Brahman in the highest. Remember Brahman is all, so the whole idea of worlds is just Brahman. Each kind of being is another evolving soul (atman) – they are just evolved to different degrees. They include the deities, fully enlightened souls, humans, animals, ghosts and hell-beings.

Influences

As Hinduism has many stories of creation, a person might choose to accept scientific theories which are similar in idea, e.g. the pulsation hypothesis theory. Believing in the **Cycle of Four Ages**, they would recognise that this is a time when it is difficult for people to live virtuous lives, but they must try even harder to do so. They might show greater devotion to the deities in the hope of protection from them, and in the hope of rebirth into one of their worlds.

The Basics

1. Explain some Hindu teachings about the origins of the universe.
2. Explain the Cycle of Four Ages.
3. What evidence is there in the world that we now live in Kali-yuga?
4. How might belief in Hindu cosmology influence a Hindu?
5. 'It is impossible to believe both Hindu and scientific theories about the universe.' Do you agree? Explain reasons for and against this view.

Topic 2.1 Beliefs and teachings

Beliefs about the nature of human life – the concept of the atman

> 'He cannot be seen, but he is the seer; He cannot be heard, but he is the Hearer; He cannot be thought, but he is the Thinker; He cannot be known, but he is the Knower. He is the Internal Ruler, your own immortal Atman. Everything else is destroyed except the Atman.' *(Bhagavad Gita)*

Hindus believe that our true self is the atman – we could call it our soul. For Shaivites, this atman works to be reunited with Brahman; for Vaishnavites, it is part of Brahman. The atman is the individual inner self, the essence of every person, pure consciousness, and it cannot die, it is immortal.

Hindus believe that a human is made up of their body, mind, intellect, ego, personality and atman. Of these, only the atman stays the same, because it is eternal, indestructible and absolute – the others are ever-changing. The body grows, ages, dies and returns to dust. The mind is quite self-obsessed and is affected by the corrupt world we live in, building up the ego and leading to negative qualities, including selfishness. Think of how you have changed – even just the change in what you have learnt studying RE from year 7 to GCSE. You have changed immeasurably in every way.

Hinduism teaches that a person might at some point become dissatisfied with life and come to feel there is something more – they have a growing awareness of their atman within. This is the beginning of their spiritual quest. They will then try to seek the truth of things and of themselves. Talking to a teacher or guru would help, as these people have a greater knowledge and understanding and can act as guides.

Influences

Believing in the atman, with its link to Brahman, is really important. Since everyone has an atman, everyone is special, so should be treated well. Similarly, if the whole planet and all beings on it also have some form of atman, then they too are special, and should be treated well. You can see that, from this single belief, a Hindu might see it as their duty to look after the world, to speak out against those who abuse it, to care for animals, be vegetarian, give time for helping others, and so on. There is nothing small about this one belief – it is all-encompassing.

The Basics

1. What is the atman?
2. Explain what Hinduism teaches about the atman.
3. Explain how belief in the atman might influence a Hindu's attitude to themselves; to others; to other beings; to the world.
4. 'Belief in the atman is the most important of all Hindu beliefs.' Do you agree? Give reasons to support your point of view.

Samsara – the process of reincarnation

Hindus believe we have free will. This is what makes us different to all other forms of life. We can choose what we say or do – good or bad. Through those choices, we cause or reduce suffering – our own or that of others.

Reincarnation is the constant cycle of birth, death and rebirth – Hindus call this process samsara. Hindus believe that the atman lives through many lifetimes. Each lifetime is shaped by the actions of previous lifetimes – a belief called karma (see page 72). Hinduism teaches that until the atman realises its true nature as an eternal, sacred being, it will continue to be reborn into physical worlds.

> 'After death, the soul goes to the next world, bearing in mind the subtle impressions of its deeds, and after reaping their harvest returns again to this world of action. Thus, he who has desires continues to be subject to rebirth.' *(Vedas)*

So what is it that continues between lives? Hindus believe that we each have a 'subtle body': this is the combination of our energy and mind surrounding the atman. In between physical lives on Earth, this subtle body could go to a heaven to enjoy the rewards of good deeds done, or could go to a hell to suffer for bad deeds done. Remember Hindus believe in many worlds, which include heaven and hell realms (see pages 67–69). Having used up the harvest of those deeds by spending time in those places, the subtle body is reborn as a physical body. This world is often called the 'world of action', which helps us to see that we control how much good or bad we do, and how much closer to escaping the cycle of samsara we will get. The reason we continue to be reborn is that our ego still exists, so that the atman still sees itself falsely – it is still affected by maya (illusion) and the Tri-guna are unbalanced (see pages 64–66).

The cycle continues until the jivatman achieves moksha (liberation). This is the point at which the atman fully realises its true nature – that it is an eternal, pure consciousness which has no attachment to any emotion or desire. Depending on the form of Hinduism a Hindu follows, they believe the atman then becomes reunited with Brahman (Vaishnavism) or recognises that it is actually Brahman (Shaivism).

The wheel of samsara

> ### The Basics
> 1. Explain what the wheel of samsara is for Hindus.
> 2. Explain how belief in the wheel of samsara might influence a Hindu in their daily lives.
> 3. 'Believing in reincarnation makes a person behave better in this life.' Do you agree? Explain reasons showing you have thought about more than one point of view.

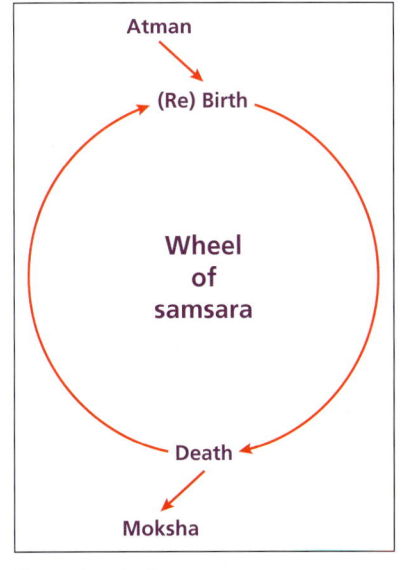

Topic 2.1 Beliefs and teachings

The law of karma

Hindus do not believe there is a God who acts as a judge of us when our earthly lives are over. Instead, they believe in the law of karma, which is part of natural law – that everything has a consequence. Hindus believe that all of our thoughts, words and actions – deliberate or not – have some sort of consequence for us (and others).

Everything we do comes from choices we make, i.e. from our free will – for example, choosing to disobey a parent's instruction to tidy our bedroom, or from habits we have – for example, the habit of leaving homework until the last minute. We can shape both of these to be more positive than negative more of the time – if we want to. We can consciously choose to think before acting and include the good it brings as part of the decision-making; for example, accepting that working at the last minute generally leads to poorer work than work which is planned and not rushed. Plus, one can become the other – so, for example, I do clean my bedroom when I am told to. Later, I anticipate being told and, wanting to forgo the hassle, do it anyway, just before the order comes. Eventually, I don't even think about being told – habit formed.

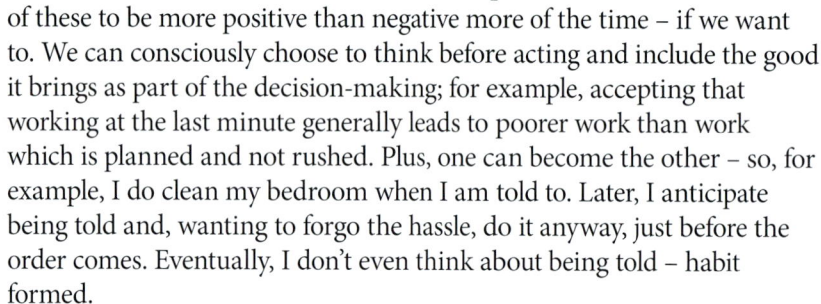

Hinduism splits our actions into papa (negative) and punya (positive). Free will allows either, and we reap the harvest of both in this lifetime, the next or future lifetimes as part of the system of reincarnation (samsara – see page 71).

> 'These actions which cause hurt and suffering to any other living beings are to be considered papa (sin, demerit, unskilful action); and punya (virtue, merit, skilful action) is defined as those actions which bring joy and happiness to others.'
> *(Mahabharata)*

It isn't just about what a person does that affects their karma, though. Of course, what they do catches up with them – what goes around comes around. However, there are natural forces in the world, and other people – they are not just cardboard cut-outs! They live their lives and do things, and these have an impact on us, regardless of the karma we do or don't own. Good things and bad things can just happen!

Generating good karma comes through using free will positively, helping others, not being motivated by what we get out of an action, being devoted to the deities, showing respect to all life, and so on. It is covered by the quotation from the Mahabharata on this page: do that which does not cause suffering to others – but more especially, you could say that do which causes good for others.

The Basics

1. What is the law of karma?
2. Explain what Hinduism teaches about karma.
3. Using examples, explain papa and punya.
4. Explain how belief in free will might influence a Hindu.
5. 'You don't have to be a Hindu to believe in karma.' Explain different points of view toward this statement.

Moksha – liberation from the wheel of samsara

Moksha is liberation from the wheel of samsara. For Hindus, it is the ultimate aim of life – never again to be reborn, and reunion with Brahman. There are four aims – Dharma, **artha**, **kama** and moksha (see pages 76–77). Hindus believe there are four pathways or yogas, to achieve moksha – through action, knowledge, meditation and devotion (see pages 94–97). So, moksha is freedom.

> 'Lead me from the Unreal to the Real.'
> *(Vedas)*

The word 'moksha' comes from two Sanskrit words which together mean destruction of delusions. Hindus believe the world as we see it is not real (maya – see page 66), so to break free of it requires our atman to destroy the illusion and to see things as they really are, realising its true nature as Brahman. So, moksha is self-realisation.

Different Hindus interpret the idea of moksha in different ways. We are going to consider two interpretations using analogies from Hinduism.

A Shaivite analogy might be that moksha is like the drop of water which travels to and merges with the ocean. The huge ocean represents God; the drop is the atman becoming part of God.

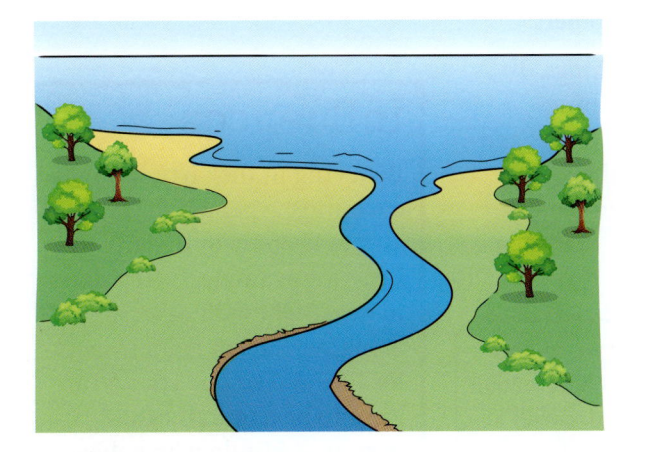

A Vaishnavite analogy might be the green bird in the green tree. While it looks like part of the tree, it is actually separate. So in moksha, the atman is reunited with, but not part of, Brahman.

Some Hindus believe a form of moksha can be achieved while still a human – this is jivanmukti. They describe non-attachment to desire and emotion, living in the world, but not allowing their experiences to lead to any form of wanting or craving. Those who have achieved it are happy alone, live compassionate and virtuous lives without any regard for reward. They are happy to give up everything.

Hinduism also teaches that it is impossible to achieve moksha without having a guru who has themselves realised moksha in their lifetime – a self-realised one. Imagine going somewhere you have never been – you would need guidance to find it. If the route could also be dangerous, that guidance is even more important. A guru is like the guide – they know the path, so can teach you to follow their footsteps. By following them, you reach your goal more quickly and easily, avoiding the barriers and pitfalls which we fall over without clear direction.

The Basics

1. What is moksha?
2. Explain the difference between Shaivite and Vaishnavite ideas of moksha.
3. Explain what jivanmukti is.
4. 'To achieve moksha, a person needs a guru.' How true is that in Hinduism? Explain arguments for and against.

Topic 2.1 Beliefs and teachings

The personal virtues

Virtues are positive, morally good behaviours. For Hindus, the scriptures talk about many virtues which – if practised – bring good karma and help in attaining moksha. You need to know about practising the virtues as a general idea, and about six specific virtues.

Humans have free will, and so can choose to practise the virtues – or ignore them. They can choose to keep the virtues in a selfish way – or use them to help others. This is why free will affects suffering – it reduces it, or creates/increases it. Reading the scriptures gives a Hindu knowledge of the virtues, and helps them to understand the importance of virtues in achieving moksha. By not reading the scriptures, a Hindu remains ignorant of the virtues (what they are, why they are important), and that ignorance leads to suffering – their own or that of others.

The virtues come from recognising that Brahman is in all things. To accept this reality means a person must show respect to all things. Respect includes non-harming, not discriminating, helping others and showing respect for all forms of life, such as by protecting the environment. So by knowledge, a person behaves in a way to reduce suffering for themselves and others – they understand that 'Brahman is all', and want to show respect.

> **Ahimsa** – non-harming. This is non-violence in thought, word and action. Any violence is papa: it will generate negative karma. It leads to suffering, often for the perpetrator as well as the victim. Belief in ahimsa will influence the language we use and the way we behave; more specifically whether we eat meat, how we treat others, our care for the environment. *If you believed this, how might it influence your daily life?*

> **Respect** – since Brahman is in everything, we should show respect for everything. Nothing and no one should need to earn respect. Life is sacred and must be protected. *If you believed this, how might it influence your attitude to people you don't know?*

Influences

Believing in the virtues might encourage a person to try to always keep them in daily life – for example, by trying to be patient with others, being vegetarian from respect for life, and so on. They will want to be a morally good person. A Hindu who believes in the virtue of ahimsa might try hard not only to avoid hurting others, but also to actively seek to help those in need. For example, they might work as a doctor, or might devote time to charity work.

Empathy – this means having a regard for the needs or feelings of others, and how their experiences affect them. It is more than just feeling sorry for them because empathy makes us do something to help. Empathy leads to compassion (loving kindness). *If you believed this, how might it affect your attitude to victims of natural disasters?*

Mind/sense control – this is about showing calmness and patience: for example, not giving in to negative emotions such as greed or anger. These can lead to becoming attached to material things or the outcomes of actions, which push us further from moksha. *If you believed this, how might you behave when in dispute with someone?*

Humility – this is about not being proud or boastful. Hindus believe that everyone is on a spiritual journey; even if not everyone is working at it. We should be humble because we have not completed that journey, and because to be anything else shows a lack of sense control. *If you believed this, how would it affect the way you treat your elders and teachers?*

Love – this is the next step from ahimsa, respect and empathy as those virtues lead a person to want to help others. Showing love by helping others is punya: generating good karma. It also reflects sense control as it is the opposite of greed, anger and selfishness. It reflects humility as we help others without wanting reward or thinking of ourselves as better than them. *If you believed this, how would it change your daily life?*

> 'Do not do to another what you do not like to be done to yourself; that is the gist of the law – all other laws are variable.' *(Mahabharata)*
>
> 'The neighbour is, in Truth, the very self – and what separates you from him is mere illusion.' *(Upanishads)*

How do the virtues reflect these teachings?

For me, humility is the most important. If I do not believe myself to be more important than others, then I will be kinder to all. I will look to work with others, and not against them. I will accept all. From this virtue come many other virtues you see – but it starts with humility.

For me, I try to practice ahimsa in everything I do. Non-violence in my speech, my thoughts and my actions. So I speak and act kindly, I show compassion, I do not eat meat or use anything which causes the life of another being to be taken.

There is no virtue that I think is most important. Self-control is needed because sometimes other people do not make it easy to keep calm. Empathy is needed if I am to really want to help others. Love – where do I start – it is everything, and from it comes everything. The scriptures described the virtues, so they must all be important.

The Basics

1. What is meant by 'virtue'? List some Hindu virtues.
2. Why is it important for Hindus to keep the virtues?
3. The virtues can be said to be interlinked – explain how this is so.
4. How might belief in each of the virtues influence a Hindu?
5. 'Respect is the most important of the Hindu virtues.' Do you agree? Explain arguments for and against that statement.

Topic 2.1 Beliefs and teachings

The four aims of human life (purusharthas)

During a Hindu's life, there are four aims or goals for which they should strive. These are:

1. Dharma (piety and ethical living): making sense of the human condition and resolving it.
2. Artha (wealth): creation of wealth.
3. Kama (pleasure): fulfilling legitimate desires.
4. Moksha (liberation from samsara): reunion with Brahman.

Dharma is the first aim of life. The Dharma is guidance for moral and ethical living. It is formed of three principles for living: being truthful (satya), not harming others (ahimsa) and living simply (bramacharya). Dharma is what makes Hindus fulfil their duties in life – it is the belief that duty is important. A Hindu's duty will vary depending on the stage they are at in their life. *What duties do you have in the different roles in your life – as a student, a son/daughter, a friend? How are those different from the duties of your teachers and parents?*

Artha is wealth. Everyone needs to have money – we cannot function in society without it. We need money to pay for all our needs, whether they are the basic needs such as food and shelter, or 'needs of comfort' such as extra clothes, books, a phone, etc. Money is something humans use as a measure of success. Even a religious person needs money – especially if they have a family to care and provide for. In some stages of life, money is an absolute necessity. Money can also help a person to pursue spiritual goals – for example, paying to go on pilgrimage, paying for offerings, donating to charity, all of which, for a Hindu, generate positive karma. *How, though, might money be a burden?*

Kama is fulfilling legitimate desires, including sensory pleasures, but also craving or desire for other forms of satisfaction – fame, power, knowledge, wealth and so on. Everyone wants to be happy, as they feel that this brings contentment to their lives. Kama is about that pursuit of happiness; kama makes a person try harder, do more, set themselves higher goals and standards. However, it is easy to allow kama to become a distraction – and never become content. Of course, if a person is content, they can focus on the pursuit of moksha. *How might living a simple and ethical life (Dharma) affect this goal for a Hindu?*

> Moksha is liberation from samsara (see page 73). This is the ultimate goal for every Hindu. Any person can work towards achieving moksha in their life; indeed, following the other three aims helps bring moksha closer. However, most people will not be able to achieve moksha in their lifetime. Hinduism is about disciplining oneself to become aware of Brahman in everything, and to be compassionate to oneself and everything because of that. This will lead to both a deeper understanding of God and a greater devotion to God. Those who give up ordinary life to study with a guru, or to focus on religious practice, are making moksha their single aim. *How difficult might it be to focus on achieving moksha for a Hindu?*

Stages of life

Hinduism splits life into four stages, though not everyone follows all the stages. These are called the **ashramas**.

- Firstly, the student stage, when a person is growing up, takes on their religious responsibilities and begins to learn about their religion.
- Second, the householder stage – Hindus are expected to marry and have a family.
- Third, the retirement stage, when a Hindu's responsibilities to their family are reduced because their children have grown up and have families of their own; Hindus might involve themselves more in the life and religious practice of the community as a whole.
- Finally, the renunciate stage, when a person gives up all material possessions and all attachments to focus completely on their spiritual path and achieving moksha.

In modern society, few go beyond the third stage, as our responsibilities seem to last longer, and it is more difficult to renounce everything. However, there is a strong Shaivite tradition of focusing one's entire life and energies on achieving moksha, as well as Vaishnavite traditions of following a guru and a life of devotion (e.g. to Krishna). In each of these stages, the four aims are still present, but a person might focus more on some than others in any stage – for example, a householder needs to earn money (artha) to support his family, whereas a renunciate has clearly given up artha and kama to focus on achieving moksha.

Influences

A Hindu who believes in the purusharthas might see all four as legitimate aims at different times of their life. They always want to fulfill the aim of Dharma as it is a code for living. When married, it is important to earn money (artha) so that the family can be looked after, but also to have a comfortable life (kama). Ultimately by fulfilling these aims a person comes closer to meeting the aim of moksha.

The Basics

1. Explain each of the four aims of life for Hindus.
2. What are the four stages of life (ashramas)? Why don't all Hindus follow all four?
3. Explain how a Hindu might be influenced by belief in the aims at different stages of their life.
4. 'All Hindus should focus on the aim of moksha.' Do you agree? Explain different views on that statement before reaching a justified conclusion.

Topic 2.1 Beliefs and teachings

Sanatana-dharma versus Varnashrama-dharma

Dharma is moral and ethical thinking and living. It is God's divine law which is made up of knowledge and actions – by knowledge, a person chooses positive actions. The duties are like repaying debts – to God (hence to worship God), to religious leaders (who help in the pursuit of moksha), to parents (for life and upbringing) and to the world (as we rely on both society and the environment).

These are two ways to view the Dharma.

Sanatana-dharma

Sanatana-dharma means 'eternal dharma' – it is the name by which many Hindus call their faith (not Hinduism). It means that Hinduism had no beginning, no single founder – it is a combination of eternal truths. These truths make up the Vedas (sruti scriptures – see page 58). Sanatana-dharma covers duties which are absolute and unchanging, and which apply to every person – regardless of their age, stage in life, role or class. The atman of each person owns this duty, which is to perform **sewa** (service) to self, others and God. The personal virtues (see pages 74–75) are all ways that the atman shows its urge to fulfil that duty in relation to others and the world around them – summed up as 'harm never; help always'. Through worship – a daily responsibility for a Hindu – they show sewa to God.

> 'The eternal duty towards all creatures is to not harm in thought, action or word, but to be compassionate and generous toward them.' *(Mahabharata)*

The Basics

1 Explain what Hinduism teaches about Sanatana-dharma.
2 Explain what Hinduism teaches about Varnashrama-dharma.
3 For each form, how might belief in it influence a Hindu?
4 'It is more important to believe in Sanatana-dharma than Varnashrama-dharma.' Explain arguments to agree and disagree with that statement

Varnashrama-dharma

This is a system described in the Vedas but which is now seen as outdated for the modern world by many Hindus, not least because of its link to the Varnas, which no longer define society. We can see it as an equation:

Goals of life:
1 Dharma (ethical living)
2 Artha (wealth)
3 Kama (pleasure)
4 Moksha (liberation)

=

The stages of life (ashramas):
Student
Householder
Retiree
Renunciate

+

Social divisions (Varnas):
Brahmin (priests, teachers, intellectuals)
Kshatriya (police, soldiers, administrators)
Vaishyas (farmers, businessmen, merchants)
Shudras (artisans, workers)

In **Varnashrama-dharma**, each stage (ashrama) and social group (varna) has specific duties, so their Dharma depends on both. In other words, each person's Dharma is different. A student must focus on learning to live ethically; a householder on acquiring wealth to support their family, and enjoying the pleasures of a family; a retiree lets go of artha and kama to turn their minds to the pursuit of moksha; a renunciate is focused on attaining moksha. In this system, it is also believed that brahmins follow all four goals; kshatriyas follow the first three; vaishyas the first two; shudras follow only the goal of wealth to support their families.

Getting prepared

The Beliefs section of an exam paper is made up of five questions. Here you can read the wording, some tips for doing well and some examples of each.

1.1 question – Multi-choice: 1 mark

For example:

A Which of the following is the name for the Ultimate Reality?

   a Brahma   **c** Brahman

   b Saraswati   **d** Ganesha

B How many goals of life are there for Hindus?

   a 2   **c** 4

   b 3   **d** 5

Tip

Lots of these are definition questions – so make sure you know the meanings of all key words.

1.2 question – 'Give two…': 2 marks

This tests knowledge (not understanding).

For example:

A Give **two** of the three features of the divine.

B Name **two** deities in Hinduism.

Tips

Keep your answer to a minimum – give only two words, or phrases. Example A could be answered simply by 'Bhagavan, antaryami', or in a longer version, 'Hindus believe that the divine is in everything which exists; they also believe that the divine is within our hearts.' The second takes longer to write but – and gets just the same mark. It is better to use this time in the longer questions.

The exam paper gives prompts of '1' and '2' to remind you to give two answers.

1.3 question – Influences: 4 marks

This is testing your understanding of how what a person believes affects what they think/say/do – how it influences them.

For example:

A Explain **two** ways in which belief in the atman might influence Hindus today.

B Explain **two** ways in which belief in Sanatana-dharma might influence Hindus today.

Tips

You get a mark for each way, plus an additional mark as you explain each of those ways – 2 + 2.

The question wants you to say, 'If I believe ____, then I will (think/say/do) ____.' Don't make the mistake of explaining the belief itself.

Using examples is a good way to explain in this question because it shows how the influence is acted upon.

Topic 2.1 Beliefs and teachings

1.4 question – Beliefs and teachings: 5 marks

For example:

A Explain **two** Hindu teachings about samsara. Refer to sacred writings or another source of Hindu belief and teaching in your answer.

B Explain **two** Hindu teachings about the four aims of human life. Refer to sacred writings or another source of Hindu belief and teaching in your answer.

Tips

You get a mark for each teaching, plus an additional mark for each explanation. The final mark is for giving a relevant teaching, which you should already have done! As this question is about teachings, the fifth mark should be very easy!

'Teaching' doesn't mean you have to give quotations; you could give beliefs or concepts.

You will need to know the key terms – because that is what you are being asked about; if you haven't learnt what the four aims of human life are, you can't answer Example B!

1.5 question – Analysis and evaluation: 12 marks, plus 3 marks for written English (SPaG)

For example:

A 'Moksha (liberation from rebirth) is the most important teaching in Hinduism.'

Evaluate this statement.

In your answer, you should:

- refer to Hindu teaching
- give reasoned arguments to support this statement
- give reasoned arguments to support a different point of view
- reach a justified conclusion.

B 'Hindus should show devotion to Vishnu because he helps humans when they are in need.'

Evaluate this statement.

In your answer, you should:

- refer to Hindu teaching
- give reasoned arguments to support this statement
- give reasoned arguments to support a different point of view
- reach a justified conclusion.

Tips

The question wording gives you a great way to check your answer – use the different bullet points to check you have done all the things you need to do.

If the statement says something is 'best', 'most important' or gives any kind of value words, then challenge it by saying, 'It depends what is meant by…'. This is a good technique to make your brain think more widely in answering.

You have to give an agree side and a disagree side in your answer – failure to do so will cost you any mark above Level 2 (6 marks out of 12). Similarly, failure to explain anything you write will also keep you stuck at Level 2 at best.

By giving and explaining all arguments for one side, then doing the same for the other side, you write a clearer answer which is easier to mark.

'Justified conclusion' is a posh way of asking you to say whether the agree or disagree side is stronger, and why you think that. It doesn't mean for you to rewrite arguments you gave already! So one side might have more arguments, might be clearer, might be more compelling/persuasive or might fit with what you already think. These are all useful ways to justify a conclusion. Sometimes, you just can't decide – and it is okay to say that as well.

2.2 Practices

Places of worship: the temple (mandir)

Hindus worship at the mandir, or temple. Temples are very sacred spaces, often very ornate, always full of statues (murtis) and other symbols of Hindu belief. Religious rituals happen at the temple, led by priests, who have trained for many years to be able to perform them.

The word 'mandir' means 'dwelling'. It is considered to be the home of a deity on Earth – hence the space being so sacred. Each one has at least one murti which has been designed and made following the strict guidelines in the Shilpa Shastra scriptures. These guidelines begin with the material to be used (wood etc.), then the process of making (which includes many rituals) and finally the actual consecration at the mandir when the deity is supposed to infuse the murti itself. The mandir will be dedicated to that one deity – though will usually have murtis for a number of other deities as well.

The temple space is always surrounded by some barrier, usually a wall, and most temples are very ornately decorated with colourful statues of the Hindu deities. Entry into the temple will be through a high and ornate door or gate, making the point to the worshipper that they need to be respectful. The tower gateway itself may be made up of many statues of many deities – colourful and imposing. At the far end of the temple space, in the most elaborate of the shrines, will be the garbagriha, which is the central dwelling place of the deity to whom the temple is dedicated. It is here that daily acts of worship (**puja**) take place. Most temples follow a similar floor-plan, though each temple is uniquely decorated.

Temples are tended by priests. Years ago, all priests came from the Brahmin caste (see page 78); however, that is not true now. Western converts to Hinduism as well as non-Brahmins have undergone the studies and training to be a temple priest, so many temples have non-Brahmin priests. Priests tend to the main deity, which is treated as if it were a living being – 'waking' it early in the morning, washing and dressing the murti, making offerings to it. Priests carry out rituals during the day – fixed rituals, such as morning worship, as well as individual rituals, such as blessing a new baby. They are also available for advice and guidance to worshippers on religious matters and on how to resolve issues as a Hindu.

A Hindu temple from the outside

Inside a Hindu temple

The central shrine in a Hindu temple

Topic 2.2 Practices

Temples always have several lesser and smaller shrines to other deities than their main one. These are often deities associated with the main deity – for example, a shrine to Hanuman in a temple dedicated to Vishnu or Krishna. They will usually be arranged along the sides of the temple leading from doorway to central shrine. Worship at side shrines is usually personal worship (see page 86).

Around the temple, there are usually many symbols of the religion and worship – for example, sacred plants such as the lotus (representing moksha), offerings of fruit and flowers, key quotations or **mantras** as decoration, stories from the lives of deities and avatars, such as the story of Rama and Sita. Most temples are uniquely and highly decorated both outside and inside.

Priests leading ritual worship in a Hindu temple

The whole of the temple is meant to inspire devotion in the worshipper. It gives symbols and clues about the beliefs and teachings of Hinduism. It gives a worshipper access to the deity because the deity is present within the murti. When Hindus pray or make an offering to the deity, their offering is blessed by the deity – they can have some of that back, for example, as blessed food or flowers.

Why are temples important in Hinduism?

- They are dedicated to, so are the abode (home) of, a deity.
- Worshippers can fulfil their daily duty to worship at a temple.
- Worshippers can access priests for advice and guidance at a temple.
- Temples are focal points which show the devotion of the community to the deities.

Worshipping outdoors

In India, shrines in the outdoors are commonly seen. These are small shrines set up and dedicated to the deities. In many villages without access to a temple, small shrines are set up to allow people to fulfil their duty to worship, and as guardians for the village. These are not usually ornate, sometimes even as simple as a pile of stones or a single tree. Anything can be a focus for worship (see pages 85–86).

The Basics

1. What is the Hindu name for their place of worship? What does that name mean?
2. Explain the different features of a Hindu temple.
3. Explain why Hindu temples are important places.
4. Why are shrines also found outdoors in Hinduism?
5. 'Hindu temples inspire Hindus to worship.' How far can you agree with this statement? Explain your reasoning.

2 Hinduism

Worship in the home

Hinduism is a religion which places great emphasis on the importance of worship at home, perhaps more than any other religion does. Most families have their own shrine. This might be on a shelf in a room they use, or even a room devoted to the purpose of being a shrine room.

Why worship at home is important

- Worship is a daily duty for Hindus, and not everyone can get to the temple everyday.
- Having a home shrine allows a Hindu to worship at the beginning of the day – the most auspicious time.
- By worshipping often, devotion is shown to the deity and this might bring reward, such as helping to achieve moksha.
- Worshipping at home ensures the whole family continue to keep the religion, emphasising its importance for living.

Home shrines come in different forms

B Around the murti may be statues of the same or other deities – for example, deities associated with their chosen focus. These are for personal worship.

A The central or largest part of any shrine is always a statue (or image) of the deity, called a murti. This is the deity to which the household shows their greatest devotion, called a kula-devi, and is the focus of their daily worship (see pages 84–85). Here we see Ganesha.

C There may also be other symbols of Hinduism. For example, the aum symbol. There will be a bell (to awaken the presence of the deity) and incense (representing the sweetness of Hindu Dharma). There will also be offerings – light, incense, flowers, water, food – as these are made at each act of worship.

D An arti lamp with its light is used as part of the act of worship. It is found on a metal tray along with flowers, a small bell, incense burner, and a water pot.

83

Topic 2.2 Practices

Caring for the home shrine

Any shrine is a sacred space. Generally, Hindus do not wear shoes in their house; certainly they will be barefoot in their shrine room, or standing before a small shrine. Any food they eat is offered to the deity so as to be blessed and made pure. If the family has a shrine room, any pets and activities such as smoking or drinking alcohol will not be allowed in there; the intention being to maintain this sacred and pure space. While a daily activity in the temple is the washing and dressing of the deity, in the family shrine this happens just once or twice a week.

'Truly the Self is in the heart.' *(Chandogya Upanishad)*

'This is Prajapati (Lord of all beings), this heart. This is Brahman. This is all.' *(Brihadaranyaka Upanishad)*

'The heart is the abode of all things, and the heart is the support of all things.' *(Brihadaranyaka Upanishad)*

The space of the heart

All worship should be done from the heart; this is what makes it sincere. When Hindus talk about the space of the heart, they don't mean the physical heart which beats in pumping blood around your body. It isn't something which shows up on an x-ray or ultrasound scan. They mean the core of your being, your very essence, knowledge and consciousness. You have learnt that Hindus believe their Self is the atman; they believe that the atman resides in the heart, as does Brahman – which are separate or the same depending on the form of Hinduism (see page 70). The space of the heart is where a person can experience the love of God, and from where they express their love for God; it is where a person develops their love and compassion towards others, and their devotion to God. Of course, worshipping in the space of the heart means a Hindu can worship anywhere – temple, home or outdoors.

The Basics

1. Explain why home shrines are important in Hinduism.
2. Describe a Hindu home shrine.
3. Explain Hindu teachings about the 'space of the heart'.
4. 'Hindus should always worship at a shrine.' Do you agree with this statement? Explain reasons for and against it, and come to a justified conclusion.

Focuses of worship and representations of the divine

Hinduism as a religion allows many paths to achieving moksha, so it makes sense that there can be many 'focuses of worship'. Remembering that 'Brahman is all', it is also easy to see how anything could become a focus of worship for a Hindu. For the course, you have to know about five aspects of this, and why they are important. These are met on the next few pages. Each one links to several of the beliefs you studied in the first section on Hinduism.

One God (personal or non-personal)

In Hinduism, there is one Ultimate Reality, or God. God is at once personal and non-personal, immanent and transcendent (see page 60). For most followers of Western religions (Christianity, Judaism and Islam), or those who have learnt something about those religions, to focus worship on one God makes absolute sense. A Hindu might focus on Vishnu or Shiva as Supreme Lord, making their offerings and devotion to that deity. They might try to understand Brahman better through scripture. We could see this focus as a Hindu going to the absolute source of all their beliefs.

The many deities, gurus and other elders

The deities represent aspects of Brahman (see pages 61–63). Focusing on one specific deity allows a Hindu to be very specific in their worship – for example, a student using Saraswati as a focus for their worship at exam time as Saraswati is the deity of learning.

Gurus are teachers; more than that, they are experts with a higher level of religious understanding than ordinary Hindus. The Sanskrit term 'guru' means 'the one who dispels the darkness and takes toward the light', showing their crucial role in helping a person come closer to achieving moksha. A guru must accept a person as their disciple/student, and that person must then follow their guru's command and teachings absolutely. In this way, the guru becomes the focus of the person's worship or devotion.

Elders may be one's parents or grandparents, or elder members of the community. They are in the third stage of life (see page 78). These people have all lived longer than us, and have more experience of life, as well as a better understanding of living as a Hindu. They deserve our respect, which we show by listening to their advice, treating them well, caring for them and so on. This respect and devotion to elders makes them a focus of worship.

Holy land, hills and rivers

'Ether, air, fire, water, earth, planets, all creatures, directions, trees and plants, rivers and seas, they are all organs of God's body. Remembering this, a devotee respects all species.'
(Bhagavad Gita)

The whole of creation is a manifestation of Brahman – even the physical landscape. Hindu stories link the deities and events to many places; these places became seen as sacred. Shiva's home is considered to be Mount Kailash in the Himalayas; Vrindavan was the home of Krishna as he grew into a man; Kumbh Mela takes place at the convergence of sacred rivers, including the Ganges, which is itself considered a deity. These places are special and to go to them brings blessings, especially when they are difficult to get to. Many Shaivites will go on pilgrimage to Mount Kailash; many Vaishnavites make pilgrimage to Vrindavan; Kumbh Mela hosts the biggest pilgrimage of any religion (see page 100); and it is very common for Hindus to ask for their ashes to be scattered in the River Ganges after being cremated beside it.

Topic 2.2 Practices

Sacred plants and animals

Many plants are considered sacred in Hinduism. They are usually associated with a deity, or have medicinal qualities. The tulsi plant (holy basil) is a very valuable medicine and is closely associated with Vishnu. The peepal tree (sacred fig) is also used for medicine and was the tree beneath which the Buddha meditated until enlightenment – the Buddha is considered an avatar of Vishnu in Vaishnavism (see pages 62–63). Banyan trees are found near many temples, were mentioned in the Bhagavad Gita and give shade to travellers.

Each deity has an associated animal – for example, Ganesha is linked with a mouse. In India, monkeys seem to be attracted to temples, and the cow is a sacred animal, being used in special ceremonies at temples and homes, and always protected from harm (see page 102).

The murti as a material representation of God

Temple statues of deities are specially made and consecrated (see page 81). These statues are called murtis and are believed to hold the essence of the deity within them. They are a physical, material representation of God. Every religious person, when attending their place of worship, focuses on something – for Hindus, it is the murti. The murti represents God, or an aspect of God; the actual statue itself is not the focus of the worship. Many different forms of worship take place at the temple or shrine focused on the murti (see pages 87–90).

The importance of having different focuses of worship

- Hindus believe that Brahman is all and that the atman returns to Brahman upon achieving moksha. So having Brahman as the focus for worship is really getting to the point of everything Hinduism believes.
- People are different and find themselves in different situations at different times. Having many different options as a focus of worship allows everyone to worship sincerely. It also means any person can gain blessings, which brings good karma.
- Any form of worship is a form of bhakti (devotion), which is one of the paths to achieving moksha (see page 96).
- Given Brahman is all – including the created world – respect for all of life and the environment itself are part of being a Hindu. It is not possible to have something as a focus of worship and then treat it badly.

The Basics

1. Hindus believe 'Brahman is all'. How might this affect ideas about what counts as a focus of worship?
2. Explain contrasting focuses of worship for Hindus.
3. Explain the importance of having different focuses of worship for Hindus.
4. 'For Hindus, the only proper focus of worship should be God.' Do you agree? Explain reasons to support more than one point of view, before writing a justified conclusion.

Forms of worship

'People may worship me in any form they wish. The form does not matter to me; only the quality of the love which is expressed in worship.' (Bhagavad Gita)

Worship is any action taken to show recognition of the divine. Worship takes effort and sincerity – a person cannot just do it by accident. For a Hindu, there are many forms of worship – just as with many focuses (see pages 85–86). Being able to worship in many different ways means that any person can find a way they prefer. When a Hindu worships at a shrine, the deity is believed to become present therein.

Why worship is important in Hinduism

By worshipping Vishnu, I show my love and devotion for him. By doing this, I receive love from Vishnu.

The Vedas scriptures tell us we should chant the Gayatri mantra at three different points in the day – before sunrise, before noon and before sunset. So worship is a duty for a Hindu – duties are there to be fulfilled.

Any worship shows we acknowledge Brahman is all; the worship connects us to Brahman, no matter what the focus is.

Worship helps me to understand what my religion teaches me, and helps me to become more pure. This is important for my spiritual journey to moksha.

I find that worship leaves me feeling calmer, so I can manage the rest of the day better.

Worship is part of life for me. Since I was a child, I was taught I should worship and how to do that. A day without worship would be very strange to me; I see worship as a daily priority.

Topic 2.2 Practices

Puja

Puja means adoration or worship – it is showing devotion to the deity through their murti. It is a ritual form of worship, i.e. it follows a specific process. Puja happens several times daily in every Hindu temple. Many Hindu families do puja at their own home shrine in the morning.

Hindus doing puja

What is done	Why it is done
A bell is rung.	To awaken the presence of the deity, and invite the deity to accept the worship.
While chanting mantras, water is offered to wash the murti, then cloth or a sacred thread is put over the murti, or water is sprinkled around the shrine.	To show respect and to honour the deity; to purify the shrine.
A tilak mark is made on the forehead of each worshipper. Offerings are made – flowers, leaves, fruit, water, rice, sweets. Incense is burned.	To show love and respect to the deity, just as any guest to the house would receive food. The tilak represents the worshippers' desire to achieve moksha. Incense represents God as it spreads everywhere. The tilak is placed on the forehead, which is the part of the body that becomes active when a person becomes enlightened.
A lighted lamp (arti) is waved before each worshipper.	To allow them to take a blessing from the deity. Light represents moving from the darkness of ignorance to the light of truth.
Camphor is lit in a small dish.	To represent the burning away of the ego, which must happen so as to achieve moksha.
Blessed food (prasad) is taken back from the shrine by each worshipper.	The final act to end the puja.

Arti ceremony

The arti (or arati) ceremony is a ceremony of light; the main element is a lighted lamp. This ceremony is performed at least twice daily in every temple, five times in big temples. The first ceremony will be before dawn, the last after dusk. Families also carry out arti ceremonies at their home shrine – twice daily.

The priest will hold a tray on which the lit arti lamp has been placed along with (usually) flower petals, water and incense. A conch-shell may be blown to start the ceremony, before a short prayer is said or sung (often to the music of drums, bells and gongs). This prayer thanks the deity, reminding the worshippers that God is everywhere. The lamp is waved before the statue of the deity (murti) in a clockwise manner – following the natural rhythm of the Sun in the northern hemisphere – to infuse it with the deity's blessing. The priest then passes the tray around the worshippers, or moves around them with it. Each one will hold their hands, palms down, briefly over the flame, before then touching their head and eyes – this brings the blessing from the flame to themselves. The ceremony often ends with the conch-shell being again blown.

The Arti lamp

Significance – first and foremost, this is the most commonly held ceremony: every Hindu experiences it daily. Also, this is the ceremony which awakens the presence of the deity – reminding everyone that Brahman is all. As well, the symbolism of light is that light dispels darkness – the teachings help to see the truth; the flame burns away the ego.

Havan

The **havan** is a ritual which purifies a place or venture. The central element is the fire, which represents the fire god Agni, and all the participants will sit around this. The priest or person leading the ceremony must sit facing north. During the ceremony, many prayers are said and mantras chanted. Four bowls are filled with water, which is used to wash hands and to sprinkle around the group. The fire is ceremonially lit, using camphor and ghee. Then different items are offered to the fire (tossed into it), including lotus seeds, fruits, flowers, sandalwood chippings, honey, ghee and herbs. An arti completes the ritual.

The havan (fire) ceremony

Significance – the ceremony is meant to sacrifice the ego for spiritual progress, so each time anything is offered to the fire, the word 'Swaha' is uttered ('I sacrifice my ego'). This ceremony is believed to bring an end to hardships, including financial and health issues. It is also believed to bring success to new beginnings.

Darshan

Darshan means viewing – it refers to a worshipper looking at the statue or image of the deity. The belief is that when the worshipper looks at their focus of worship – a statue, an image, a guru, etc. – they receive a blessing because that focus is looking back at them. Darshan is seeing and being seen. During meditation, a Hindu can visualise a deity, and this is also darshan. A Hindu presents themselves, bows their head and puts hands together or prostrates (lies flat) before the deity, then makes an offering, which might include prayers.

Significance – for all Hindus, it is comforting to believe that as they see, so the deity sees back; it gives a sense of being loved by the deity. Shaivites believe that the darshan given by gurus can help a Hindu to develop spiritually; it will burn away ego, helping them to meditate and to move closer to moksha.

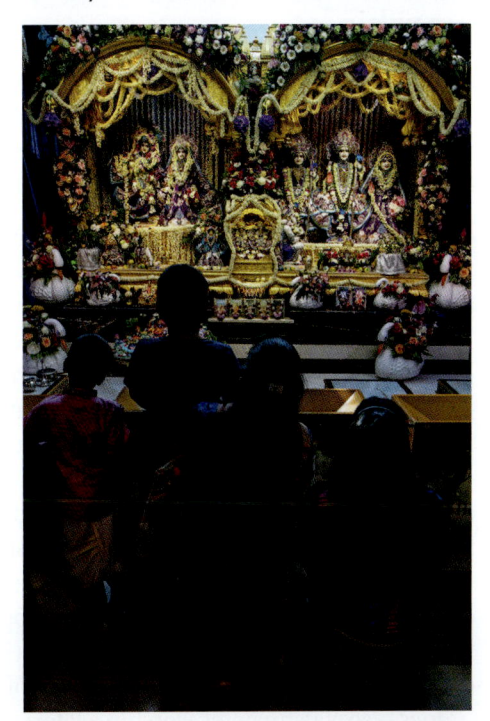

Darshan – seeing and being seen by the deity

Bhajan/kirtan

Bhajan means adoration, while **kirtan** means glorification. This is the singing of hymns and repetition of mantras to music in praise of God. It is done in small groups, or even the whole congregation of worshippers at times.

Significance – singing hymns of praise is a form of devotion and is central to Vaishnavite worship and to bhakti yoga (see page 96).

Singing bhajans in the temple

Topic 2.2 Practices

Japa/mantra

Japa is meditation using mantras – which are short phrases of special importance, such as Om Nama Shivaya (adorations to Lord Shiva). A Hindu might use a set of prayer beads (mala) to make sure they repeat this mantra the right number of times. There are 108 beads in the mala, and these are often made of tulsi wood (Vaishnavite version) or Rudraksha beads (Shaivite version).

Significance – reciting mantras helps a Hindu to focus their mind on the deity, and so express their love for that deity; they can train themselves to have greater self-discipline through this. Meditation is believed to bring insight and help spiritual progress, as well as being an expression of devotion to the deity.

Differences between Shaivite and Vaishnavite worship

Firstly, it is important to say that the basics of each different form of worship are similar for both Shaivites and Vaishnavites; both groups do all the forms. Differences might be in their interpretation of what or why they are doing something – this comes from their beliefs.

- Shaivites see Shiva as the Supreme manifestation, whereas Vaishnavites see that as Vishnu. Each group focuses worship on that deity.
- Shaivism strongly suggests the soul must be awakened by a teacher, a human; whereas Vaishnavism stresses complete surrender to Vishnu (or avatar), i.e. a deity. All Hindu boys have a religious teacher for their student stage of life, but it is more common for Shaivites to have a personal teacher who they follow as adults. Most Vaishnavites follow the teachings of a saint or other great holy man as their teacher.
- Each has specific significant and sacred places, and worshipping at either brings great merit, but each has specific places – for example, Shaivites at Mount Kailash; Vaishnavites at Vrindavan.
- A key practice for Shaivites is siddha yoga (self-discipline); whereas for Vaishnavites it is chanting and hymns (japa/kirtan).
- Shaivism does not teach the existence of avatars, whereas Vaishnavism does – so Vaishnavites worship avatars as deities (for Shaivites, these are just extraordinary humans, not deities).

A Hindu devotee uses beads in performing japa

The Basics

1. Why is worship important for Hindus?
2. Why do different Hindus do different forms of worship?
3. Explain what happens during each of the following forms of worship – puja; arti; havan; darshan; kirtan/bhajan; japa/mantra.
4. For each form of worship, explain why it is significant.
5. Explain how Shaivite and Vaishnavite worship differs.
6. 'Puja is the only form of worship a Hindu need do.' Explain arguments to agree and to disagree with that statement. Explain which you find to be the stronger point of view.

Sacred festivals

Hinduism has many festivals, though not all are celebrated by all Hindus – some are kept by certain groups, some are regional. Hindu festival celebrations in India and in the UK have differences – because India is a Hindu country. India is a Hindu country, so that the Government and all of society are celebrating a festival, for example some festivals are public holidays in India (but not in Britain). Different families celebrate the same festival in different ways because of their family traditions. All this reminds us that Hinduism is an inclusive, pluralistic religion, accepting difference and embracing it.

It is true, though, that festivals share one central theme – that good will triumph over evil, so that the Dharma (this is, the correct moral order) is restored.

There are three groups of festivals – those linked to a deity or guru, celebrations of lunar/solar events and harvest celebrations. This GCSE course focuses on two of the main festivals, celebrated by Hindus everywhere in the world – Holi and Diwali. You need to know why and how they are celebrated.

Common activities in celebrating festivals

Festivals are times for families and communities to come together. In the UK, huge fairs are held in local parks in Hindu communities – everyone is welcome, Hindu or not. The festival days are a time to wear new clothes, give gifts and share special foods and meals. The stories behind the festivals are told, and shown on TV channels. Hindus attend the temple for darshan and puja several times. Giving to charity and charity work is encouraged. Processions of temple deities are held.

My children love Holi. We get up early to go to the mandir; they love to be with their grandparents listening to the bhajans and receiving blessings from the arti ceremony. At home, we will tell them how Lord Vishnu protected Prahlad. They are too young to understand the meanings yet, but in time, they will.

At the mandir, Diwali is a very busy time, with many more worshippers coming in. Service to others is an important thing for Hindus; we show compassion and love by this, and we can come closer to moksha. I help to prepare the items for our Holi procession, which shows non-Hindus the joy our religion brings.

As a priest, I help lead puja at Holi in the mandir. We have many worshippers, and all the set pujas are very busy – everyone wants to share the arti ceremony. People will also take this time to seek advice and guidance.

I welcome all my extended family to eat in my home at Diwali. After the serious joy of the mandir, we eat all kinds of special foods, and join our community in their celebrations. Faith, fun and family – what is better!

The Basics

1. What is a festival? Name two Hindu festivals.
2. Why do Hindus celebrate festivals differently?
3. Describe some of the ways in which Hindus celebrate festivals.
4. 'For Hindus, worship is the most important way to celebrate a festival.' Do you agree? Explain reasons for and against that statement.

Topic 2.2　Practices

Holi

'Holi tells us that your own cleverness will bring you to the flames.' *(Acharya Prashant)*

Holi is a two-day festival held in spring. The first day of the festival is Holika Dahan, remembering the Vaishnavite story of Holika and Prahlad.

Prahlad was the son of a demon king called Hiranyakashipu, who commanded everyone to worship him. However, Prahlad refused as he was devoted to Vishnu as Supreme Lord. In his fury, the king ordered Prahlad be killed. He asked his sister, Holika (who, having been blessed by the deities, was protected from fire), to help to kill Prahlad. She took Prahlad into a flaming pyre. Prahlad chanted the name of Vishnu, who rewarded him for his devotion by transferring Holika's protection to Prahlad. He survived the fire unhurt, but Holika burned to death.

This story shows the power of devotion (bhakti) to Vishnu; also that good conquers evil. Holika is also a metaphor for the negativity we each have within ourselves – Hindu devotion is believed to be the fire which rids us of that negativity.

On the first day of the festival, bonfires are lit with effigies of Holika on them, recalling this story. Hindu communities everywhere enjoy fireworks and bonfires on this night. Grains from the winter harvest are roasted and eaten. Worship at the temple is encouraged.

Throwing coloured powders at Holi

The second day is Rangwali Holi. This is the day of Holi that many non-Hindus often know something about. In the morning, people gather in public places and chase each other around, throwing coloured powders and water at each other. This is why it is also known as a festival of colour. Its origins are in a story about Rama Krishna (one of Vishnu's avatars), whose skin was blue. He loved Radha but felt conscious of the colour difference between them, so Krishna is said to have gently painted her face to make it the same as his. He is also known as a prankster, so the throwing of paint fits his character. This activity reminds us that everyone is the same – all are equal as barriers disappear for the throwing of coloured powders. It is a day of fun, with music, singing and dancing common after the morning's activities. In the UK, there are many Holi parties where you can buy packets of powder to throw at other people.

Diwali

The story of Diwali when Rama defeated the evil demon, Ravanna

Diwali is a five-day autumn or harvest festival. It is also known as the Festival of Lights because it is traditional to put rows of electric lights or small ghee lamps (divas) along paths and around windows and doors.

Diwali recalls the story of the Ramayana (smriti scripture), and this story is retold by families at the temple and on TV every year. Rama, seventh avatar of Vishnu, incarnated with his consort, Sita. Sita was kidnapped by a many-headed demon king, Ravanna, and taken away to the island of Lanka. The monkey king, Hanuman, and others helped Rama search for her, and eventually tracked her down. Ravanna refused to give Sita up, and so a great battle ensued between the forces of Rama and those of Ravanna. Hanuman had to find medicines to heal the many wounded on Rama's side. Eventually, Ravanna was defeated – Rama gave him the chance to surrender, but he refused. Rama killed Ravanna. Reunited, the couple returned home and, as they went, villagers lit the way with small lamps (hence the tradition of lighting lamps now).

The underlying theme of this festival is that good conquers evil. Hindus are reminded that Vishnu comes to restore the Dharma through incarnating as an avatar because Ravanna's rule brought fear to all humans. The lights symbolise the prayer 'Lead me from darkness to light', which is the intention behind being religious. Rama's wife, Sita, is set as the role model for wives – she never gave in to Ravanna, always believing Rama would find her. The whole story is seen as a metaphor for each person: Ravanna being the evil intentions any person can have, and Rama the battle to drive them out and be a good person.

Also celebrated at this time is Lakshmi, goddess of prosperity. A special puja dedicated to Lakshmi is performed at mandirs. Business people will have their account books blessed in the hope of a successful new year of business. It is also common to attend the mandir to make puja, and do the havan ritual of throwing grains into the fire. Away from the mandir, there is music and dancing, and communities celebrate as families and together as communities. In the UK, large festivals are now held in many parks, inviting anyone to join the festivities; for example, Trafalgar Square (London) has been hosting such events since 2001, with 35,000 people attending in October 2019.

The Basics

1. Why do Hindus celebrate festivals?
2. What common activities are undertaken in celebrating a Hindu festival?
3. In your own words, retell some of the stories behind the festivals of Holi and Diwali.
4. Explain why each of these festivals is important in Hinduism.
5. 'Diwali is the most important Hindu festival.' Do you agree? Explain different points of view regarding this statement, showing which you think to be the stronger.

Topic 2.2 Practices

The four paths towards yoga (union with the divine)

The goal in life for Hindus is to achieve moksha, which is realising one's true nature and thus achieving union with the divine. Hinduism is an inclusive religion, and just as there are many focuses of worship and many ways to worship, there are also many paths to achieve moksha. This all reflects that anyone can find the way which suits them. Hinduism's priority is the search for Truth, not to say one way is the only way. Given the belief in reincarnation (see page 71), humans need many lifetimes to even begin to see the truth, let alone understand it. Belief in reincarnation allows a belief that different paths could be followed in different lifetimes.

Karma yoga – the path of action

Service to others in the temple

Service to those in need

> 'Strive constantly to serve the welfare of the world; by devotion to selfless work one attains to the supreme goal in life. Do your work with the welfare of others in mind.'
> *(Bhagavad Gita)*

This yoga is based on following one's duty to give selfless service to others. Karma is the energy generated by our thoughts, words and actions – and can be positive (punya) or negative (papa). It makes sense that by always living a morally good life, showing compassion to others, a person must evolve spiritually, and come nearer to moksha. At first, they might have to continually remind themselves to behave this way, but with that effort it becomes their normal way of life.

> 'Your work is your responsibility, not its result. Never let the fruits of your actions be your motive. Nor give in to inaction.'
> *(Bhagavad Gita)*

Karma yoga is about being selfless – doing things for the sake of doing them and because they are needed, not to gain a personal reward.

I choose karma yoga as my path in life. I trained as a nurse, and have volunteered in several emergency situations. For example, I went to the Congo in Africa to help out when there was an Ebola crisis as they did not have enough medical staff. However, everyday in my work in a UK hospital, I can also do selfless service – it is the attitude with which I do my work.

Through karma yoga, the Hindu comes to understand that their ability to act in this way is actually a gift from the divine, because living and behaving this way makes a person see others as their equals, breaks down barriers and helps them to appreciate that God is all. This is the path every single person can take. In the Bhagavad Gita, Krishna presented this way as a young man's way.

Jnana yoga – the path of knowledge

I chose karma yoga as my path in life. We have many visitors to our temple, so I act as a voluntary guide. At festivals, I help to decorate the temple, and organise the processions. We regularly go into the community to take food to the poorest, and I help with that. I do this simply because it is right to do so.

The path of knowledge

'By realising God, one is released from all fetters.' *(Vedas)*

Some might say that ignorance – or not knowing – is the worst problem in the world; or that a little bit of knowledge is dangerous. Jnana yoga is the path by which a Hindu – recognising they know little – studies sacred texts to learn more about the true nature of all things, of themselves and of Brahman. They achieve moksha through learning and thinking. There are three stages in jnana yoga:

- study of scriptures, which requires a teacher because the scriptures and their message are so complex
- reflecting on what has been read and learned to make proper sense of it
- meditation to fully understand the difference between the material world and reality.

I chose jnana yoga as my path in life. I have studied the scriptures since childhood from my Sacred Thread Ceremony. I have studied under different teachers, learning as much as I could before I needed to find someone more knowledgeable.

I chose jnana yoga after my children had grown up and made their own families. I wished to turn my focus to the scriptures and come nearer to achieving moksha. Sometimes I explain our beliefs to my son or my grand-children. I believe we are all students at some level.

As they are absolutely dedicated to this path, a person choosing it will live a very disciplined life, often following very strict rules and routines. They control their emotions and desires tightly. They meditate daily. They will be careful with their food, ensuring it follows Hindu beliefs about food which helps and heals, rather than that which is not good for a healthy body and mind. Given the scriptures are difficult to follow, anyone who chooses this path would need to be intelligent. In the Bhagavad Gita, Krishna describes it as a mature man's path.

Topic 2.2 Practices

Bhakti yoga – the path of devotion

The path of devotion, shown here by ISKCON members to Lord Krishna

Bhakti comes from a Sanskrit word which means to adore or worship God. This is perhaps the most followed of the yogas. It is sometimes described as 'love for love's sake', or the path of the heart, and is about devoting the whole of oneself and one's life to the Divine. Everything is done out of love for God; being afraid of the consequences of not doing something is not the driving force behind behaviour. Since this is the case, service to others, compassion, love and acceptance of others develops naturally.

Any Hindu can follow bhakti yoga – Vaishnavites show devotion to Vishnu and/or his avatars; Shaivites to Shiva and his family; Shaktis to female deities such as Durga or Kali. Always the end goal is to experience love in its highest form – by reuniting with God, which is a state of bliss.

Those following this path will use chanting, mantras, prayers and kirtan as part of their worship. They will also study scriptures, reflecting on their meaning and how they can live their life by them. Any person, of any age and in any place can follow this path.

I chose bhakti yoga as my path in life. I am part of an ISKCON group and we worship Krishna. We know our love and devotion will be repaid by Krishna.

I chose bhakti yoga as a devotee of Kali. I attend the temple every day, and join acts of worship with others. Singing and praying with others brings a wonderful feeling inside. I feel contented and at ease when I leave the temple.

Astanga yoga – the path of meditation

'For one who does not meditate there is no peace; and for one lacking peace where is the happiness?' (Bhagavad Gita)

Astanga refers to the eight stages which make up raja (king) yoga. It is the path of self-discipline through practice of meditation and yoga exercises. It requires total focus and commitment for a person to be successful. The eight stages lead systematically to moksha – the first two are about self-control of mind and body; then two stages of physical and mental exercises for a healthy mind and body; then three increasingly difficult levels of meditation; and the final stage is complete realisation of the truth and the real self, and thus union with the divine.

This path is not just about meditation, or about exercise – which the word 'yoga' is associated with in the Western world. It includes all other yogas within itself – for example, the first stage encourages moral living, which reflects karma yoga. The second stage includes study of scripture and devotion to God, reflecting jnana and bhakti yoga. However, astanga goes beyond those, expecting them to become habitual ways of life, and builds on them into meditative practices. The meditation leads to moksha, but without the good habits of those early stages, moksha would be impossible to achieve.

I chose astanga yoga as my path in life. I have used all the other paths in my goal to achieve moksha making them part of my daily life. Astanga is really the next step.

I chose astanga yoga when I saw the peace which one of my spiritual teachers had achieved. I also wanted that peace. Astanga is not easy though. I have followed it for many years, and am now working through the meditation stages.

Why are the yogas important?

- Each of the yogas can lead to moksha. Moksha (liberation) is the goal of Hindu belief and practice.
- They allow many different routes to the same goal, so everyone can find a way that suits them. Different people have different opportunities in their life, and different personalities suit different paths.
- They have each been proven to work over time by gurus, saints and others. This gives the evidence that they work, so thousands of Hindus follow the path set by these gurus and saints.
- They develop the follower to be a compassionate member of society. Compassion is a key virtue in Hinduism, and central to Hindu practice. Being compassionate can only be good for society.
- They are recommended by the scriptures, which are the holy books of Hinduism. These scriptures, especially the Veda and Upanisads, are very highly respected because they are seen as the truth from God.

The path of meditation and self-discipline

The Basics

1. What are the four paths to union with the divine?
2. For each path, explain what it is, and how a follower might keep that path.
3. Explain why a person might say that the yogas are similar to each other.
4. Explain how a person's personal circumstances (age, lifestyle, wealth, etc.) might influence their choice of yoga.
5. 'For Hindus, meditation (astanga yoga) is the best path to union with the divine.' Explain different points of view for that statement. Write a conclusion in which you show which point of view is the strongest.

Topic 2.2 Practices

Pilgrimage

> 'A pilgrim must go with total surrender, with a total faith in God, that it is only by God's grace that he can finish the pilgrimage.' *(Ma Yoga Shakti)*

A pilgrimage is a journey to a place of religious importance. Very often the journey to that place is seen as part of the pilgrimage, with the pilgrim preparing themselves to be in the right frame of mind when they are at that place, or undergoing hardships to get there. This is part of the devotion which makes a person go on a pilgrimage. As the Vedas say, 'All his sins disappear; slain by the toil of sacred journey', showing the journey to be as important as the actual place being visited.

Hinduism has many, many places of pilgrimage. They might be linked with the deities: the resting place of a deity, such as Mount Kailash, where Shiva is said to meditate, or the birthplace of an avatar, such as Vrindavan, where Krishna spent his youth. They might be linked to a Hindu saint or guru: for example, Swaminarayan Hindus journey to the temples which their founding guru, Swaminarayan, himself established in Islamabad and other cities. They might be a great temple, such as the new ISKCON temple at Vrindavan. They might be places of deep religious importance, such as the Ganges, a place of pilgrimage especially associated with the act of scattering the ashes of a close relative.

A Hindu can choose to make pilgrimage or not – there is no rule about making a pilgrimage in the religion. However, the making of a pilgrimage brings great merit, and so positive karma. It has become part and parcel of being a Hindu to make a pilgrimage at some time, for some personal reason.

Why is pilgrimage important for Hindus?

- To gain positive karma: with the right frame of mind, every minute spent at a place of pilgrimage (and the time spent journeying to it) could be considered as an act of worship.
- It shows devotion to the deity: Hindus believe the deity gives blessings and love back to the pilgrim for their devotion – for example, by making offerings to Shiva in any of the thousands of temples at Varanasi.
- Many Hindus believe that pilgrimage can help with healing illness, and with removing hardships and barriers in life.
- Many Hindus believe that sins are repaid by making certain pilgrimages – for example, at Kumbh Mela, or by bathing in the Ganges at its source in the Himalayan mountains.
- This physical journey is believed to be a mirror of the spiritual journey – just as the pilgrim goes to this sacred place to connect with the divine, so their spiritual journey takes them to the source of the divine within themselves, their atman.

> *As a Hindu, I do not have to make pilgrimage. However, I have been on several pilgrimages in my life. Why is that? Well, going on pilgrimage allows me to be fully immersed in my faith – something that does not happen anywhere else. The sights and sounds are unique. These places feel spiritually powerful to me. I am at the very place where something or someone truly great was. When I am back home, and think of that pilgrimage, I can again experience the joy and calm I felt. This is a special feeling.*

The Basics

The next two pages may also help you to answer these questions.
1. What is meant by the term 'pilgrimage'?
2. Explain why pilgrimage is important in Hinduism.
3. 'It is not important for every Hindu to make pilgrimages.' Do you agree? Explain your answer, showing you have thought about more than one point of view. Write a justified conclusion to show which view is stronger.

Varanasi

Varanasi is a city in north-west India. In the world, no other city has been continuously inhabited for longer – people have lived there since at least 2000BCE. Millions of pilgrims go to Varanasi every year as it is the holiest site for Hinduism. Legend has it that Shiva established Varanasi as his sacred place after defeating Brahma, and that he used a pillar of light to mark the place. There are hundreds of temples in this city, dedicated to many different deities, but it is considered the city of Shiva. Pilgrims often go to visit many different temples and join acts of worship in a number of them.

The River Ganges, which is believed to be a deity, flows through Varanasi. Hindus believe that if they bathe in its sacred waters, sins can be repaid and positive karma gained. Hence, many pilgrims come to the Ganges to bathe. In the morning and evening, pujas are held at the banks of the Ganges on the ghats (the steps at the side of the river which lead you down to it) to worship Mother Ganga.

There are hundreds of temples in Varanasi, many of which have been rebuilt several times over their long history. The most famous is the Kashi Vishwanath Temple, which is dedicated to Shiva and is one of the 12 holiest Shaivite temples in the world. This temple is always very busy with worshippers – thousands daily. Shaivism teaches that a visit to this temple can help a person achieve moksha. Some Hindus will go to Varanasi just to be able to visit a great many temples and do darshan (see page 89) at each.

Varanasi has many holy men and gurus as well as priests to whom pilgrims come for guidance and advice. A person might go to Varanasi just to spend time with gurus so that they can better understand the teachings of their religion. They might seek the blessings of a holy man on their marriage, or for a business venture and so on – the idea being that blessings given here are stronger.

Hindus believe that when a person dies they have a better chance of a better rebirth, perhaps even of achieving moksha, if their ashes are scattered in the Ganges. It is very common for Hindus to seek to have their funeral cremation done on the ghats beside the Ganges, and so there are many cremations taking place throughout the day in many places on the ghats.

The Basics

1. Why might Hindus go to Varanasi as a pilgrimage?
2. Describe the different activities a Hindu might undertake if they go to Varanasi.
3. 'Only Shaivites need go to Varanasi for pilgrimage.' How far do you agree? Explain reasons for and against that statement before writing a justified conclusion.

Topic 2.2 Practices

Kumbh Mela

Kumbh Mela takes place in each of four sites over a 12-year period so happens every three years. While other mela pilgrimages are first recorded in 644CE, the Kumbh Mela itself is first recorded around the seventeenth century.

A mela is a fair – a gathering of people to buy and sell goods. Kumbh Mela is the great fair, with religion being its central element. It happens at the places where the River Ganges and the River Yamuna meet: Allahabad, Haridwar, Nashik and Ujjain. Once every 12 years, at Haridwar, it is believed that the River Saraswati (a mystical river) also converges with the other two, making this the biggest of the four events. The last time this took place was in 2013, and it was attended by about 100 million people. This is the world's biggest pilgrimage – in fact, it is the largest gathering of people on the planet.

Pilgrims bathing in the water at Kumbh Mela

Origins of the Kumbh Mela

The Puranas scriptures tell of a jar of nectar which could give immortality. In ancient times, demi-gods and demons fought over it, chasing each other to have possession of it, and drops spilled at the four places which now host the Kumbh Mela, making them sacred places. Hindus believe that the waters at these places during Kumbh Mela have mystical powers and are able to heal, to cleanse pilgrims of their sins, and even to allow a person to achieve moksha.

Kumbh Mela is an opportunity to receive teaching from holy men

Kumbh Mela events

Attending the Kumbh Mela are many different groups from within Hinduism. Camps are set up by warrior monks, individual gurus with their followers, and those who normally shun everyday society will arrive; groups from Hindu communities come from their mandirs; ordinary Hindus make the pilgrimage alone or with their families. This is a gathering of every group within Hinduism.

Kumbh Mela is a great market/fair at which many religious items can be bought and sold

Pilgrims have the chance to join in acts of worship – singing bhajans, joining in pujas, darshan, through seeing holy men and holy women. They can buy religious items. They can seek advice and guidance from holy men (sadhus), as so many sadhus attend.

The most important element of the pilgrimage is bathing in the river. On the day of the new moon, the warrior monks walk in procession to the river, and are allowed to be the first in. Being first in at the dawning of the new day is believed to bring moksha. Bathing there on this day is believed to undo lifetimes of negative karmic acts.

The Basics

1. What is Kumbh Mela?
2. Explain why millions of Hindus attend Kumbh Mela?
3. Describe the activities a Hindu might participate in when they go to Kumbh Mela?
4. 'Kumbh Mela is the most important pilgrimage for Hindus.' Do you agree with that statement? Explain reasons to agree and disagree before writing a justified conclusion.

Hindu environmental projects

'The Earth is my mother, I am the Earth's son.' *(Atharva Veda)*

The created world – even though it is maya (illusion) – reflects God and is part of God. Hindus must try to see God in all things, and by doing this, they show greater respect to them. A Hindu looking at the world in this way will try to protect the environment. Mohatma Gandhi summed up the Hindu attitude well when he said that the earth, air, land and sea are not things we inherit from those who have passed, but rather they are on loan from the people of the future. In other words, we have a duty to look after the world for our children, and our children's children.

There is a story in which Krishna defeats a poisonous serpent. This serpent had made its home in a watering pool, making it so toxic that anyone who went near it died. Krishna caught the serpent and sent it to the ocean, then cleaned up the pool so people and animals could use it again. This can be seen as a metaphor for the damage that can be done to our environment, and our need to fix the problems we have caused.

You have already learnt that pilgrimage is important in Hinduism (see pages 98–100). Imagine the damage so many people can do when they make pilgrimages: the infrastructure of the pilgrim area, the demands pilgrims put on its systems and resources, the damage the numbers of people can do just by passing through. Many Hindu places of pilgrimage now work hard to conform to the guidelines and expectations of the Green Pilgrim Network – ensuring sustainable pilgrimage. Places of pilgrimage have set up recycling and other sustainable projects to try to show due respect to the environment while also protecting the right to make pilgrimage.

The Bhumi Project includes Hindus worldwide who work in 'a spirit of co-operation, devotion and service' to take care of the environment through many different projects. For example, there is a Green Temple guide, which helps temples to run sustainably and in environmentally friendly ways.

THE BHUMI PROJECT

> **The Basics**
>
> 1. Why should Hindus have a regard for the environment?
> 2. Explain two ways in which Hindus show their care for the environment.
> 3. 'For a Hindu, looking after the environment is their most important duty.' How far do you agree? Explain your reasons.

Topic 2.2 Practices

'Cow protection'

Most people (even when they know nothing else about Hinduism) know the cow is a sacred animal for Hindus. In India, cows wander freely in the streets; in many Indian states, it is forbidden to hurt or kill a cow; retirement homes for cows exist.

Krishna was a cowherd in his youth

Why is the cow sacred to Hindus?

The cow symbolises all of the natural world – the earth provides for and nourishes us without asking for anything in return, and so does the cow. Hindu scriptures remind us that the cow is a great provider – of milk and all the products coming from milk; of dung, which can be used as fuel for fires and as a fertiliser. The cow is a hard worker, helping plough fields, move goods and so on. It is not necessary to kill a cow to get many good things from it.

A cow decorated for festival celebrations

Cows have religious significance – Krishna, Vishnu's avatar, was a cowherd in his youth. ISKCON, the Krishnan movement, take their duty to look after cows very seriously. At festivals, cows are dressed up with garlands and paints, and paraded. One festival is dedicated to cows – Gopashtama festival. Milk and ghee (a type of butter which comes from milk) are used extensively in Hindu temple rituals.

The cow has a docile nature, making it easy to work with, and also allowing it to symbolise ahimsa (non-violence). It is also strong and works hard for its masters – the qualities of strength and service being key Hindu traits.

How do Hindus show their belief in 'cow protection'?

- Most Hindus do not eat beef (meat from cows), even if some might eat meat from other animals.
- There is an organisation in India which is trying to make the killing of cows illegal across the whole country – Project Mother Cow.
- Retirement homes (goshallas) and fields have been created for cows; there are over 3,000 goshalas in India. In the UK, there is one at Bhaktivedanta Manor (the UK home of the Krishna Consciousness movement, ISKCON).
- At festivals, cows are given special feeds, to show them respect and thanks. They are often dressed elaborately and used as part of the festival processions.

The Basics

1 What is meant by the term 'cow protection'?
2 Explain why Hindus believe the cow should be looked after and protected.
3 Explain some of the ways in which Hindus show their respect for cows.
4 'For Hindus, cow protection is the most important environmental action they can make.' Do you agree? Give reasons to show different views. Write a justified conclusion.

Charities promoting well-being, social inclusion and women's rights

'I am proud to tell you that I belong to a religion in whose sacred language, Sanskrit, the word *exclusion* is untranslatable.' *(Swami Vivekananda)*

'One person is not another person. What is he then? He is unique.' *(Swami Prajnapad)*

'Brahman is all.' *(Vedas)*

Hinduism teaches that everyone is equal, even if different. Each person is on the same journey to achieve moksha – just at different points on the journey. Atman and Brahman are intended to be reunited eventually – which is true for every sentient being. Also Hinduism teaches that the world around us is imbued with Brahman's essence, so is worthy of respect. This is because the only reality is Brahman (see page 60). As a country develops and becomes richer, it is better able to see the problems within its society, and to try to fix them. Hinduism encourages this attitude of making things better for more people because of the beliefs about the atman and Brahman. Additionally, helping others – especially without desire for reward – brings positive karma and helps a person in their own rebirths.

Sewa Day (sewaday.org)

This UK-based organisation encourages everyone to do something for someone else – an act of kindness without thought or expectation of reward. Annually there is a Sewa Day, when many groups get together to complete bigger projects. Most of the projects help the most vulnerable in society – the homeless, those in hospitals and hospices, those in disadvantaged areas. Sewa is central to Hindu living, but it reflects Hindu beliefs that every life is special and sacred, because Brahman is all. Sewa Day promotes well-being, by making its volunteers think of others, not themselves, and so aid the well-being of those others.

Working for social inclusion – Sulabh International

Set up by Dr Bindashwer Pathak, this organisation combines technology with social idealism. In India, even though the caste system (Varnas) is illegal, there are still traces of it. One of the organisation's projects works with those 'Untouchables' whose job it is to clear toilets without running water ('scavengers') – a dirty and unhygienic job, which also reinforced their very low status in society. Resolving this needed several levels – toilet technology which cut out the 'scavenger' role; rehabilitation of the users and the 'scavengers'; training for the ex-'scavengers' and support to get other jobs; education of their children so they did not feel born to be 'scavengers'. The final phase is a social one – social adoption – as scavenger families are publicly adopted by families of higher social standing, and spend time together. This final phase helps remove the barriers and builds greater tolerance – it is done out of compassion and has no financial cost.

Dr Pathak's organisation does much more than this – see www.sulabhinternational.org

Women's rights

In the time of the Vedas, women were given equal rights with men (the first image of God was as a female). The prophets were both men and women, but during the Middle Ages women were given the role of housekeeping and men became the rulers of the household.

> 'Her father protects (her) in childhood,
> her husband protects (her) in youth,
> and her sons protect (her) in old age; a
> woman is never fit for independence.'
> *(Manusmriti)*

This quotation from Hindu scriptures suggests that women are dependent upon men, never independent from them, encouraging a culture whereby women are educated to a lesser level and have fewer rights than men.

The Vedas scriptures suggest that a woman's primary duty is in having children and looking after the home. This means that men work to earn the money – and this gives men more power, reducing women's rights. However, for a nation to be successful on the world stage, it needs to empower women, ensuring they can contribute to the country's development. So, as society changes, some Hindu women's lives – especially in cities and in Western communities – improve, though many in villages continue to face great difficulties.

Hinduism is a living religion and continues to evolve with time. Modern Hindu women are now given full freedom to be active members of society in India and elsewhere. Unfortunately, in the villages, women are still mistreated and underprivileged but the changing economic landscape of India is slowly bringing about change everywhere.

Some of the many women's groups in India include:

- Commit2Change – seeks to provide education for orphaned girls, because the best way to get girls out of the poverty cycle is to educate them. Being educated brings more and better job opportunities; having a (better) job helps improve a person's life.
- Sayfty – rape is a huge issue in India; Indian laws do not protect women well enough against rape, so Sayfty educates women in keeping themselves safe and in self-defence techniques.
- WASH United – there are massive taboos around menstruation (periods), and a big issue with availability of sanitary products to manage periods (period poverty). WASH United educates girls so they understand that menstruation is not a disease, and provides sanitary products for them.
- Sarvajal sets up 'water ATMs' in rural areas where water is scarce. (In Sanskrit 'Sarvajal' means 'water for all'.) Women are the ones who collect water in Indian traditional society, so Sarvajal means women can get clean water from nearer their homes at affordable costs. They can protect their families' health, and gain time back as they no longer have to make the longer journeys for water. This means that some are able to work in small co-operatives to earn money for their families.
- Women on Wings – creates jobs for women in rural India, so that they can support their families and communities. This helps girls and women escape the cycle of poverty: poverty encourages child marriage, forced prostitution, and girls and women being sold as a slaves.

The work of all these charities might seem strange to people living in the UK, but they are all essential in India. They are each changing women's lives, their opportunities and their futures on a daily basis. Indeed, thinking about the UK more carefully, the work of some of these charities is also relevant here – rape, period poverty, sexual exploitation are all things we read about in the news.

The Basics

1. Explain why Hindus should not show discrimination against others.
2. Describe how different Hindu charities are helping the vulnerable in society.
3. Explain how different charities are helping to support women's rights.
4. 'The best way to solve inequality is to show compassion.' How far do you agree? Explain reasons for different points of view. Write a justified conclusion.

Getting prepared

The Practices section of an exam paper is made up of five questions. Here you can read the wording, some tips for doing well and some examples of each.

2.1 question – Multi-choice: 1 mark

For example:

A Which **one** of the following is not a form of Hindu worship?

   a puja   c moksha
   b darshan   d havan

B Which **one** of the following is the Hindu festival of lights?

   a murti   c Diwali
   b Holi   d Kumbh Mela

Tip

Lots of these are definition questions – so make sure you know the meanings of all key words.

2.2 question – 'Give two…': 2 marks

This tests knowledge (not understanding).

For example:

A Give **two** focuses of worship for Hindus.

B Give **two** places of pilgrimage for Hindus.

Tips

Keep your answer to a minimum – give only two words, or phrases. Example A could be answered simply by 'sacred plant, murti', or in a longer version, 'One focus of worship is sacred plants such as the tulsi or holy basil, which has medicinal properties. Another is a murti or statue of the deity which has been dedicated so that it has the essence of the deity within it.' The longer the answer, the more time it takes from your other answers.

The exam paper gives prompts of '1' and '2' to remind you to give two answers.

2.3 question – Diversity: 4 marks

This is testing your knowledge of the similarities and differences within religion – how different Hindus practise their religion differently; or different elements of something.

For example:

A Explain **two** contrasting paths to union with the divine (yogas).

B Explain **two** similar ways in which Hindus worship the divine.

Tips

You get a mark for each way, plus an additional mark as you explain each of those ways – 2 + 2.

'Contrasting' in the question just means 'different' – you are not being asked to write about opposites.

Using examples is a good way to explain in this question because it shows you know more than just the key words/terms.

Topic 2.2 Practices

2.4 question – Practices related to teachings: 5 marks

This question wants to know how what Hindus do links to what they believe, so you have to be able to refer to teachings in your answer if you want to get full marks.

For example:

A Explain **two** contrasting ways in which Hindus celebrate Diwali. Refer to sacred writings or another source of Hindu beliefs and teachings in your answer.

B Explain **two** contrasting ways in which pilgrimage is important for Hindus. Refer to sacred writings or another source of Hindu beliefs and teachings in your answer.

Tips

You get a mark for each point you make, plus an additional mark for each explanation. The final mark is for giving a relevant teaching. As this question is about practices, it is often difficult to think of a teaching which is readily relevant – at times you might have to give a lot of explanation to clearly show how your chosen teaching is relevant.

'Teaching' doesn't mean you have to give quotations; you could give beliefs or concepts.

2.5 question – Analysis and evaluation: 12 marks

For example:

A 'The only place a Hindu needs for worship is the space of the heart.'

Evaluate this statement.

In your answer, you should:
- refer to Hindu teaching
- give reasoned arguments to support this statement
- give reasoned arguments to support a different point of view
- reach a justified conclusion.

B 'It is more important for a Hindu to meditate than to do good actions.'

Evaluate this statement.

In your answer, you should:
- refer to Hindu teaching
- give reasoned arguments to support this statement
- give reasoned arguments to support a different point of view
- reach a justified conclusion.

Tips

The question wording gives you a great way to check your answer – use the different bullet points to check you have done all the things you need to do.

If the statement says something is 'best', 'most important' or gives any kind of value words, then challenge it by saying, 'It depends what is meant by…'. This is a good technique to make your brain think more widely in answering.

You have to give an agree side and a disagree side in your answer – failure to do so will cost you any mark above Level 2 (6 marks out of 12). Similarly, failure to explain anything you write will also keep you stuck at Level 2 at best.

By giving and explaining all arguments for one side, then doing the same for the other side, you write a clearer answer which is easier to mark.

'Justified conclusion' is a posh way of asking you to say whether the agree or disagree side is stronger, and why you think that. It doesn't mean for you to rewrite arguments you gave already! So one side might have more arguments, might be clearer, might be more compelling/persuasive or might fit with what you already think. These are all useful ways to justify a conclusion. Sometimes, you just can't decide – and it is okay to say that as well.

Hinduism glossary

ahimsa non-violence in thought, word and action; a personal virtue in Hinduism

artha wealth; one of the four human goals in life

arti an act of worship in which light is offered to the deities

ashramas four age-based life stages described in Hindu scriptures

astanga one of the yogas or paths to union with the divine; meditation

atman the true Self; immortal and divine part of each person

avatar an incarnation of a deity, such as Rama and Sita as incarnations of Vishnu

bhakti one of the yogas or paths to union with the divine; devotion

bhajan form of worship; singing hymns

Brahman the Ultimate Reality, God

Cycle of Four Ages (yugas) belief that time is cyclical through Four Ages; each Age is shorter and more corrupt than the last, before the cycle restarts

darshan a form of worship which involves seeing (and being seen by) a deity or holy person

deities personifications of the qualities of God; aspects of the divine

Dharma duty; morality; religion

Diwali a Hindu festival held in autumn; festival of lights

gunas (which make up the Tri-guna) the three qualities which everything in the universe has

guru teacher

havan a form of worship utilising fire; the fire ceremony

Holi a Hindu festival held in Spring

japa a form of worship involving the recitation of a sacred word or phrase

jivatman the Self in the physical body; a person's 'soul'

jnana one of the yogas or pathways to union with the divine; knowledge/study

kama (pleasure) one of the four goals of human life

karma the law of action

kirtan a form of worship; singing hymns of praise

Kumbh Mela gathering of Hindus which takes place every three years in a 12-year cycle of four venues

mandir a Hindu temple; Hindu place of worship

mantra a short statement/phrase with spiritual importance when repeated

maya illusion; the true nature of the universe

moksha liberation from the cycle of samsara (rebirth); loss of ego entirely

murti physical representation of the divine; statue or image of a deity

Nirguna Brahman God without form; impersonal form of the divine

prakriti matter; the physical element of all things

puja act of worship

Purusha Vaishnavite concept; cosmic man who was sacrificed by the gods in order to create the universe

samadhi meditation

samsara the wheel or life; birth, death and rebirth

Saguna Brahman God with form; personal God which can be described or an image made

Sanatana-dharma eternal law; belief that Hindu teachings are for all people at all times

sewa selfless service to others; social service, help of the needy

Shaivism major Sect of Hindus who follow Shiva as the Supreme Lord

Shaktism a group within Hinduism which shows devotion to the female power of the deities

Hinduism glossary

Smartism a group within Hinduism which considers all forms of God as equal

smriti Hindu scriptures which were passed down by word of mouth, including stories of the deities

sruti Hindu scriptures which were revealed to sages and gurus

Tri-guna the three qualities which govern all things (tamas, rajas and sattva)

Tri-murti Vaishnavite understanding of God as three – Brahma (creator), Vishnu (sustainer) and Shiva (destroyer)

Vaishnavism biggest Sect within Hinduism who follow Vishnu as Supreme Lord

Varanasi city of Shiva; most important city for the Hindu faith, on the banks of the River Ganges

Varnashrama-dharma Hindu law which is based on the four Varnas and four ashramas

yoga a pathway to union with the divine

The study of religions

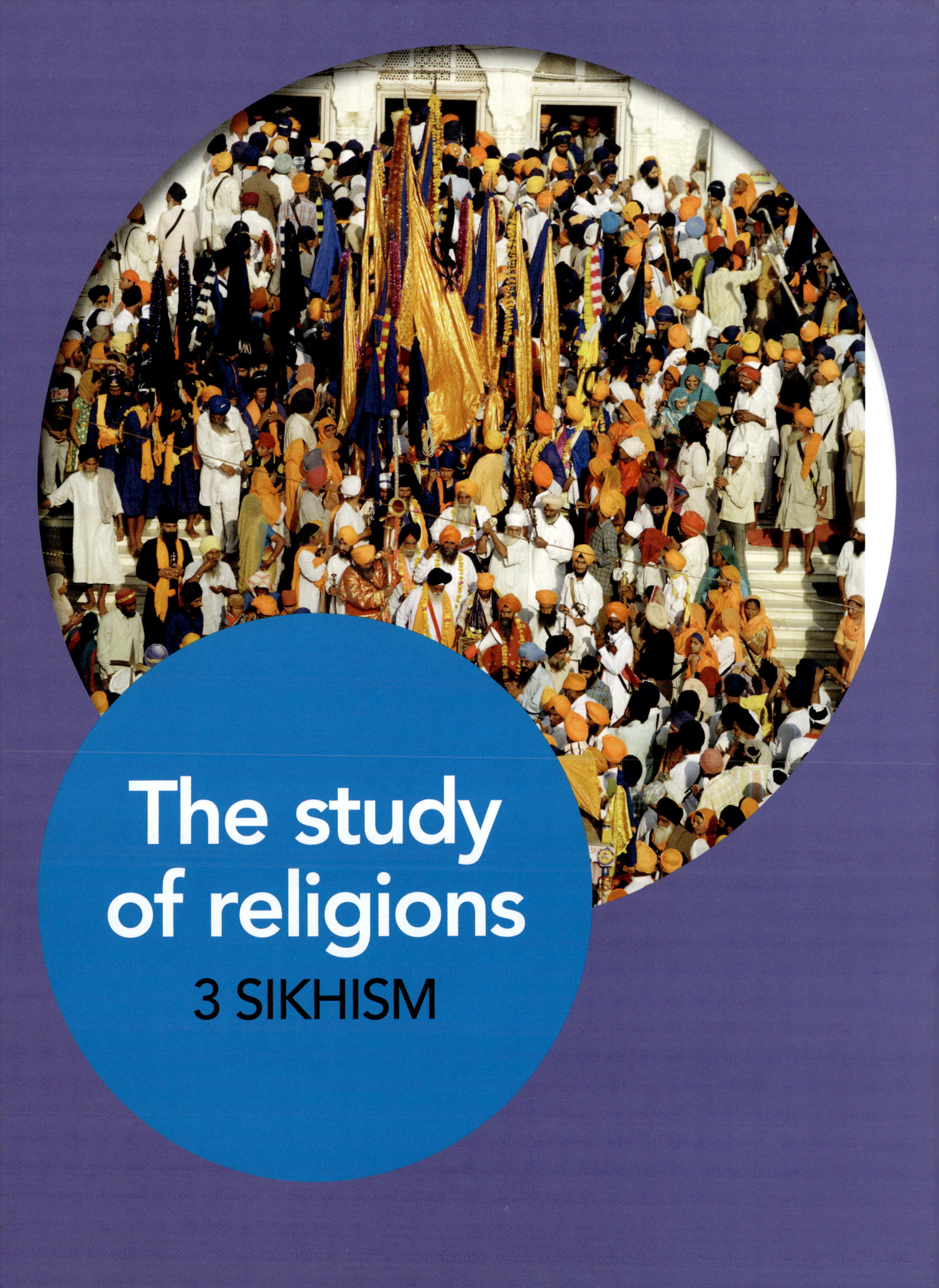

3 SIKHISM

Introduction

An introduction to Sikhism

Beliefs and teachings

Sikhism is the youngest of the major world faiths. It was founded in India by Guru Nanak, who was born a Hindu in 1469. He showed signs of rejecting his Hindu upbringing quite early when he refused the Sacred Thread ceremony (an initiation ceremony), though his teachers were astounded by his ability to recall and discuss the scriptures. He learned to read, write and speak several languages. He had a religious experience, claiming to have met God, and later travelled extensively across Asia learning about other religions and talking with their followers. He settled back in Kartarpur, in north India, where he set up the first Sikh community – and so the religion began.

Sikhs believe that God created everything and is manifested in everything. Their holy book, the **Guru Granth Sahib (GGS)**, begins with the **Mool Mantra**, written by Guru Nanak. It describes God. Copies of the Mool Mantra are found in every Sikh temple and home, this being a statement of belief. The Guru Granth Sahib was compiled by Guru Gobind Singh, and is made up of poems and hymns by a number of the Ten Gurus, as well as by some Hindu and Muslim mystics. It is considered as the word of God, never to be changed, and the layout of every copy as well as its wording is the same wherever in the world it is used or read.

The Sikh community was led initially by the Ten Gurus, starting with Guru Nanak and ending with Guru Gobind Singh. All are considered humans with special qualities, evolved through all of the stages of **mukti**, and so able to explain about God and how Sikhs should live their lives. A central teaching by all was that every person is equal, and Sikh practices are designed to reflect that. The final Guru, Guru Gobind Singh, set up the **Khalsa**, which was a new form of Sikh devotion to God. Following specific rules for living, wearing the **Five Ks** and acting as role models for others, these are the **amritdhari** Sikhs who have completed the **Amrit Sanskar** ceremony to make that step.

For Sikhs, the goal of human life is to be reunited with God. This is called mukti – liberation from the bondage of the **Five Vices** of ego. Sikhs believe in rebirth – that we are each born into many lifetimes. During each lifetime, we do good and bad, and this generates **karma**. That karma shapes the next lifetime. To achieve mukti, a Sikh must be **gurmukh** (God-centred), and not **manmukh** (self-centred). The whole religion is based around living in a way that is focused on God. Sikhs believe in five stages of mukti, and also that there are clear barriers to mukti, which are negative character traits (Five Vices).

Practices

Sikhs worship in a **gurdwara**, which is home to a copy of the Guru Granth Sahib. The gurdwara is recognisable by its saffron flagpole and flag, which are displayed outside. Worship takes place every day and Sikhs may attend whenever they wish. The main day of worship in the UK is Sunday. Worship is focused on the Guru Granth Sahib, which is treated as if it were a living Guru. An act of worship begins early in the morning, and continues throughout the day; Sikhs attend as and when they wish, and stay as long as they wish. Some gurdwaras hold this formal worship every day, others just on Sundays. Acts of worship involve the reading of the Guru Granth Sahib by a **granthi**, music played by **ragis** to join people with the word through singing hymns, the sharing of **karah parshad** (holy food) with everyone and eating at the **langar**. The langar is the communal kitchen set up by Guru Nanak and made a duty by Guru Ram Das (the fourth Guru). The gurdwara is looked after by a committee and/or the **Sangat**, which is the religious community and its leadership. Many of these people are sewadars – volunteers who give their time and efforts as a form of sewa (selfless service to others – which is a duty for Sikhs). Members of the Sangat are meant to support each other, especially in building faith.

Sikhs should live good lives. There are many virtues they should cultivate within themselves in the goal to achieve mukti because for Sikhs the whole point of human life is to truly know God, achieving bliss. **Nam Japna** is meditating on the name of God; Sikhs should try to keep God in mind at all times. **Kirat Karni** is living an honest lifestyle, i.e. having a job which helps not hurts others or the world, and living in a morally good way. **Vand Chakna** is about service to others – through charitable giving (most Sikhs give 10 per cent of their income to the gurdwara) and **sewa** (selfless service to others).

For Sikhs, there is no duty to complete pilgrimage; however, many Sikhs do go to the Golden Temple at Amritsar, especially for festivals such as **Vaisakhi**. The Golden Temple is linked with many key figures and events of Sikhism, making it a special place for all, and the centre of the Sikh religion.

Sikhs celebrate many festivals and **gurpurbs**. Two are key – **Divali** (festival of lights) and Vaisakhi (when Guru Gobind Singh created the Khalsa). In the UK now, it has become common for Sikhs to share these festivals with the wider community, setting up park events with music, fairs and food. Worship is always the beginning for these festivals, though. The births and deaths of the Gurus provide dates for gurpurbs, which are festivals connected with the Gurus. An Akhand Path is the reading from start to end of the Guru Granth Sahib continuously. Taking about 48 hours, these precede the celebration of every festival and gurpurb, and are also held for special family occasions.

3.1 Beliefs and teachings

The nature of God in Sikhism

ੴ
ਸਤਿਨਾਮੁ ਕਰਤਾ ਪੁਰਖੁ
ਨਿਰਭਉ ਨਿਰਵੈਰ
ਅਕਾਲ ਮੂਰਤਿ ਅਜੂਨੀ ਸੈਭੰ
ਗੁਰ ਪ੍ਰਸਾਦਿ
॥ ਜਪੁ ॥
ਆਦਿ ਸਚੁ ਜੁਗਾਦਿ ਸਚੁ॥
ਹੈ ਭੀ ਸਚੁ
ਨਾਨਕ ਹੋਸੀ ਭੀ ਸਚੁ॥੧॥

There is One God
Truth is His name, He is the Creator
He is without fear, He is without hate
He is timeiess and without form
He is beyond birth and death
The enlightened One
He can be realised by the Guru's Grace
Meditate on the Name
He was true when ages commenced
He is true now
He will always be true

This is a photo of part of the universe. It is the Helix nebula, also called the 'Eye of God'. Nebulas are giant clouds of dust and gas far away in space

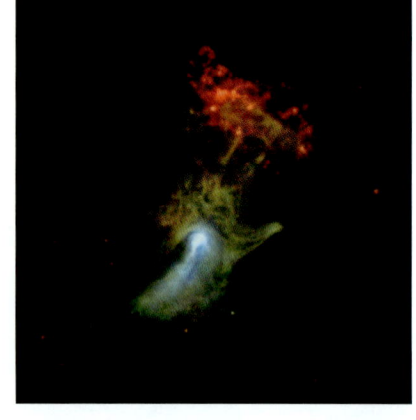

This is a photograph of another part of the universe. It is called the Hand of God nebula

If you were to go to a gurdwara, you would see the Mool Mantra, which is prominently displayed; if you went into a Sikh home, you would see the Mool Mantra. It is the first part of the first shabad (hymn or chapter) of the Sikh holy book – the Guru Granth Sahib. The first line – Ik Onkar – is used as a symbol for the religion, and displayed in art, decoration and worn as jewellery. It was written by the founder of Sikhism, Guru Nanak, and taught by him as a way to begin to understand God. It is a description of God, and as such can tell us everything about the nature of God for Sikhs. Of course, the rest of the Guru Granth Sahib tells us more about God, but really it is expanding and explaining the Mool Mantra. The Mool Mantra is the Sikh declaration of faith.

Why is the Mool Mantra important to Sikhs?

- The Mool Mantra is the foundation of Sikh belief, and from it everything else flows.
- By believing the Mool Mantra, a person is a Sikh – all their practices come as a result of believing it.
- It gives Sikhs an understanding of God at a basic level.
- It reminds Sikhs that, even though they can find words to describe God, God is still beyond a human being's full understanding, and hence should be worshipped.
- Following the lead of Guru Nanak, every Sikh will recite the Mool Mantra daily at least once.

What does the Mool Mantra say about God?

Phrase	Meaning
There is One God	There is only one God, so God is supreme and absolute (unchanging). God has no partners, nor is split into different forms. Since God is supreme, God is omnipotent (all-powerful), omniscient (all-knowing) and benevolent (all-loving). There can be nothing greater than God, which means humans cannot really understand God. Guru Nanak said, 'The Lord is contained high up in the sky and down below in the nether regions too. How can I tell of the Lord?' The number 'One' is used to emphasise that every form of spirituality (or religion) is focusing on the same One being.
Truth is His name	God is the one pure reality or Truth. Everything we see or experience is affected by our ego, which has been corrupted by the Vices (greed, anger, pride, lust and materialism). These are part of human nature. Only God is uncorrupted, so only God is Truth.
He is the Creator	Sikhs believe God created everything in the universe. As God is One, God did this from His own power and had no help.
He is without fear	God is omnipotent (all-powerful) and fears nothing/no one because God is beyond all such negative traits.
He is without hate	God is all-loving; no matter what someone does, God still loves them because God will not hold a grudge, discriminate or show bias. This also means that God will be merciful to all, and operate fairly and with justice.
He is timeless and without form	God is eternal, without beginning or end – existed always (past, present and future). Time has no effect on God, as God is beyond time and beyond space (transcendent). This means God sees all things happening everywhere and at all times. Without form means that God is neither male nor female. It is traditional to refer to God as 'He' in English so Sikhs follow this, but that does not mean they consider God to be male ('He' is just a convention). God is not in one place but is like a force or energy that is everywhere. 'Without form' reminds us that every image we have of God is putting a limit on Infinity, so while it may be useful in some ways, we always have to push beyond it to know God, as no description is really accurate.
He is beyond birth and death	Again, God is transcendent. The things which affect us, to cause us to be born and to die, do not apply to God. This means God is unlike humans.
The enlightened One	God sees the true nature of all things. God is omniscient (all-knowing). God lives in a state of constant bliss – the clarity of enlightenment (which is the aim for humans).
He can be realised by the Guru's Grace	God reveals Himself to humans, and so allows them some understanding of God. Humans only know of God, or experience God, because and when God wants them to. Humans are reliant on the grace (blessing) of God for their knowledge and experience. The fact that humans can get a glimpse of God, and that God bestows his grace on humans, means that God is immanent – involved in the world.
Meditate on the Name	This is a reference to Nam Japna – the Sikh duty to stay aware of God at all times. By meditating on God's name, a Sikh shows devotion and comes closer to mukti (liberation), which is the goal in life.
He was true when ages commenced, He is true now, He will always be true	Again stating that God is eternal, beyond time and space and so beyond birth and death. God always was, is and will be. Since everything else is changing and impermanent, and humans are subject to the Vices, this is again saying that God is Truth – the one reality.

Topic 3.1 Beliefs and teachings

Guru Nanak and the Mool Mantra

Guru Nanak travelled extensively across Asia on four huge teaching journeys. He met people of other religions, particularly Hindu, Muslim and Buddhist, but it is likely that he met Christian and Jewish peoples as well because both religions existed in some of the places we know he travelled to or through. As a young student, his teachers said how intelligent and insightful he was, that he understood very complex religious ideas easily, and could challenge explanations they gave. On his teaching journeys, he would have been able to talk about the beliefs of other religions with their followers, helping him to see clearly what he himself believed.

Guru Nanak also experienced God and the grace of God; he was lost for three days and when found (in a state of bliss) he said he had been with God. Hence, Guru Nanak was able to use all this to phrase the Mool Mantra and give a clear description of God. So, the Mool Mantra gives the Sikh interpretation of what God is like, but – as Guru Nanak himself said – it can never be completely right as humans simply do not have the ability to really comprehend God.

Influences

If a person believes the Mool Mantra, they will devote themselves to gaining knowledge of God. They would realise that God is the Supreme Being, and so want to worship him. They would recognise that God is responsible for everything that exists, and is both powerful and loving. This might influence them to look after the world around them, and to show love and compassion to others.

For many Sikhs, believing the Mool Mantra creates a sense of awe and wonderment within them – this whole world, the universe and everything come from God, so reflect God. When they look at the things around them, which are interconnected and interdependent, they might see such beauty and design that they feel gratitude to God.

If a Sikh believes God is without hatred, then they must try to reflect that in their own treatment of others. They could make sure they avoid being unkind and discriminatory towards others; for example, not be prejudiced. They could go further and get a job which tries to bring justice to people who have been unfairly treated – for example, working in the police force, being a doctor, teaching others, and so on.

The Basics

1. What is the Mool Mantra? Who wrote it?
2. Where would you expect to see the Mool Mantra?
3. Explain what the Mool Mantra teaches about God.
4. Explain what these words mean when describing God:
   a. One
   b. Transcendent
   c. Immanent
   d. Eternal.
5. Explain how believing the Mool Mantra might influence a Sikh today. Consider the Mool Mantra as a whole, and then consider individual parts of the Mool Mantra in writing your answer.
6. 'The only thing a Sikh needs to understand God is the Mool Mantra.' Do you agree? Explain reasons to show different points of view. Write a justified conclusion, showing which point of view you find to be stronger.

God the Creator

'There was darkness for countless years. Neither earth nor sky; there was only His will. Neither day nor night, sun nor moon. God was in deep meditation. There was nothing except God.' *(Adi Granth 1035)*

'The Lord and Master supports the weave of the fabric of the universe … The entire creation came from Him … All the creation is His body … Through and through He is blended with His creation.' *(Guru Granth Sahib [GGS] 294)*

The Mool Mantra (see pages 112–114) is the opening part of the first shabad (chapter or hymn) of the Guru Granth Sahib (the holy book of Sikhism). It is a description of God written by Guru Nanak.

Sikhism does not have a creation story in the way that Christianity does (the Genesis creation story – the seven days of creation by God from nothing). Guru Nanak taught that the universe is a mystery which humans cannot comprehend. The Mool Mantra begins by saying that there is one God, who is the creator. Guru Nanak taught that we can know that God created everything, and that God is part of everything – beyond that, we struggle to know much!

Guru Nanak taught that, before the universe existed, only God existed. The Mool Mantra teaches that God is timeless, and that God always was, is and will be. God was without any physical form, and without any partner. God was meditating. This means God is separate from the universe, transcendent.

The Guru Granth Sahib says that the universe exists because God wanted it to exist. It was the will of God (hukam) which formed the universe. The universe is not just real, it is 'beauteous' says the Guru Granth Sahib. When God willed the universe to exist, he put his essence into everything – simply, God is part of everything; the universe is a physical manifestation of God himself. So God is both part of and separate to the universe – as humans we cannot understand this, only believe it. The relation between God and the universe is similar to that between our minds and our bodies. We are just made up of chemicals, yet we cannot help but have a sense of mind, of being. In the same way, God is the Mind or Being of the Universe.

Influences

Believing that God is timeless and absolute, a Sikh can think about the universe and accept God made it. They do not need to be worried that we cannot explain how God made it – after all, any scientific description is just a theory, open to change and alteration, even open to being scrapped as wrong. They can appreciate the beauty and feel a sense of wonder when they see images of the universe, such as the Helix nebula and Hand of God nebula (see page 112).

If God created the universe then it follows that he will care for it and look after it, so believing God is the creator gives a sense of security. A Sikh's focus should be on living a gurmukh (God-centred) life in order to play their part in this creation.

The Basics

1. What does it mean to say God is timeless?
2. Look back at the Mool Mantra (pages 112–114). What does the Mool Mantra say about God in relation to the universe?
3. Explain Sikh beliefs about the origins of the universe.

Topic 3.1 Beliefs and teachings

The implications of believing God created the universe

I believe God created the universe by His will. The universe only exists because of God's will. So I am dependent on God's will. I know God is without hate, and so God is merciful, but I must be grateful because I exist by the will of God. I show my gratitude by worshipping God at the gurdwara.

*I believe God is manifested in the whole of creation. I am constantly amazed by nature – its beauty and design – and am reminded that God did all this, and God **is** all this. I try to look after the world around me to show my deep respect for God. I have a job as a conservation worker helping to restore natural habitats, and I feel like this is a good way to show my respect.*

I love looking at pictures of the universe. This makes me think of God, because God created the universe and is part of it. However, it is so vast, I can't make real sense of it. I mean, we have pictures of planets that would take millions of years to even reach they are so far away. That reminds me of God – so vast that I can't make sense of Him. I am in awe.

The universe is God. Anything I do is a symbol of my love for God. I know God loves me because I just have to look at the magnificent world He created for us. I try to show my love by treating the world with respect – all the usual stuff, recycling and so on. I am a vegetarian out of respect for life, and love for God.

The Basics

1. Explain how belief in God as creator might influence a Sikh.
2. Explain how belief in God manifested in the universe might influence a Sikh.
3. 'Looking after the world should be a religious duty for Sikhs.' How far do you agree with that statement? Explain your reasons.

The nature of human life

Sikhism teaches that it is impossible for humans to properly understand why God created humans. Humans can only know the aim of life. Sikhism teaches that a person can never become God, nor merge with God. God and humans are different.

Humans are made in the image of God, infused with God's divine spark or essence – which we can call the soul. We are the highest point of the creation – 'O Man, you are supreme in God's creation' (GGS). Humans are the only part of creation that can achieve salvation (being set free of negative karma from actions and their consequences).

From that belief, it is easy to realise that the aim of human life is to evolve spiritually through truthful, moral and disciplined living so as to become in tune with God. Hence a person becomes a sort of super human, in touch and in tune with God, knowing God's will and carrying it out, showing compassion in their dealings with all others. This person is also not affected by the Five Vices (see page 123) and does not show any haumai (self-centredness, pride or ego – see page 124). This is mukti (liberation) (see page 121).

It is difficult for a human to achieve the aim of life. When born into this world, we are all subject to haumai. This creates a barrier between a person and God. Also, the world encourages the Five Vices – greed, anger, pride, lust and materialism. If you think of how society encourages people to behave and live, you can see it is easy to become more selfish and more tied down by the Vices. However, Sikhs believe that by living a morally good way, and remaining mindful of God at all times, we can overcome these barriers. The Guru Granth Sahib says: 'Haumai is a great malady. The remedy is to attune oneself with God.' Whether being a good person makes someone think more of God or vice versa, these are the two crucial elements of Sikh living. The Guru Granth Sahib also says that having 'obtained the privilege of human birth, now is your only opportunity to meet God'. The goal of Sikhism is to take advantage of that opportunity.

Influences

Sikhs believe that the goal of human life is to be liberated. This can only happen if a person lives a life devoted to God (gurmukh). This belief leads Sikhs to study the teachings of the Gurus and the Guru Granth Sahib – to better understand God. It leads them to live in a way which is truthful, humble and compassionate – recognising the equality and special status of every person. This might affect the job they do, the way they interact with others, in fact, every aspect of their day-to-day living.

The Basics

1. Explain the aim of human life for Sikhs.
2. Explain what Sikhism teaches about humans as a part of creation.
3. Explain how the Five Vices act as barriers to achieving the goal of human life (mukti).
4. 'Haumai (self-centredness) is the worst quality of a person.' How far do you agree with this statement? Explain arguments showing you have thought about more than one point of view.

Topic 3.1 Beliefs and teachings

Sikh virtues

Virtues are qualities of a person which are considered to be morally good. They are valuable because they are based on principles, and shape a person's behaviour positively. Sikh teachings describe many virtues, so a Sikh should try to develop them in themselves, making them their habitual way of thinking and acting. By doing this, a person is more likely to achieve mukti (see page 121), as they act as defence against haumai (ego, the barrier to mukti) (see page 124). For a Sikh, it is not enough to just show devotion to God; they also have to live a virtuous life. The virtues are very inter-connected, and so a person would be developing them together, not one at a time.

> 'As many are the vices, so many are the chains round one's neck. One removes vice with virtue, for virtue is our only friend.' *(GGS)*
>
> 'Devotion without virtues is impossible.' *(GGS)*
>
> 'Practise truth, contentment and kindness; this is the most excellent way of life.' *(GGS)*
>
> 'In the society of the holy, one becomes holy, and one runs after virtues, forsaking his sins.' *(GGS)*

Wisdom

Wisdom is knowledge gained through study and life experiences, and then reflected upon deeply. It takes into account situations and helps a person to make fair judgements. Wise people remain open-minded, recognising that they don't necessarily know best in every situation. Hence wisdom links closely to humility.

Truthful living

This is about being honest to and with oneself and with others. It is about realising that how we live reveals what we really worship, what the goals and values of our life actually are. Additionally, it is about not being deceitful – that is, doing what you say you will do, saying what you really think and not lying, and not making promises you have no intention of keeping. It also means behaving in a fair way towards all others and not being biased when dealing with others. A natural outcome of this way of living is justice.

Justice

This can mean social justice – the sense of bringing about equality for everyone, which is a central principle of Sikhism (see pages 126–132). Justice is about ensuring the rights of others, and not exploiting others. This leads to fighting for justice through different means, such as the creation of laws. Any person can behave in a just way – that is part of truthful living – and if all of a community or society behave in that way, everything is better for all.

Temperance

This is about not doing anything in excess. Temperance is often associated with alcohol or drug-taking, and is really about self-control. A person who does not practise temperance hurts themselves and others because intemperance leads to selfishness. Temperance links to contentment because it naturally means a person is satisfied with 'enough', not wanting more and more (of anything).

Self-control

Self-control is important in keeping to the path of truthful living. The Five Vices (see page 123) are all about losing self-control – someone says something unkind, and a person's first reaction might be to respond in kind, or to try to hurt them. This is a loss of self-control; it is always better to consider the situation and react calmly.

Patience

Daily life brings many irritations for every person. We might want something to happen more quickly; we might find someone getting in the way of something; time goes slowly … Sikhs acknowledge that impatience can be easy in daily life, as well as in religious life. So it is good to learn patience. Patience also brings courage because sometimes impatience can boil over into anger or aggression, and these are vices to be avoided by Sikhs.

Courage

In Sikhism, this is the moral courage to stick to the path of Sikhism – regardless of what happens. A good example of this is the Gurus who were martyred for their beliefs: Guru Arjan and Guru Tegh Bahadur. Sikhs anywhere in the world can be subject to discrimination and must show courage. It is also about the courage to be truthful – sometimes lies are easier. It is also about the courage to fight for justice and in self-defence, through peaceful means and as warriors. Sikhs wear a small dagger or a sword as part of the Five Ks, demonstrating their willingness to fight.

Humility

To be humble is to avoid behaving in a proud and boastful way; a humble person does not seek glory or fame for anything they do. Sikhs should recognise they are nothing in comparison to God, that no one is better than another, and that they have much to do to achieve mukti. All these things should make a person face the truth that they have no right to be boastful – humility is an outcome of being honest with oneself. This connects with forgiveness as we need to look past the errors that we, and others, will inevitably make.

Contentment

To have contentment is to be satisfied with what one has and with one's lot in life. That does not mean to settle for little or nothing, nor to make no effort in life; it is more about remaining calm: accepting events and their results with a sense of calm. It is about realising that the Universe does not owe us anything, so everything is a gift that we should make best use of. From this point of view, a person can be happier and can act with greater self-control, being less ego-centred.

Influences

I want to achieve mukti and be with God. As a Sikh, I believe that the world offers too many temptations away from mukti and God. However, my faith gives me the goal of mukti, and by keeping the virtues I can be shielded from the temptations – the Vices. So I try to be mindful of God, and be mindful of the virtues. This helps me to avoid the traps of the Vices and ego.

Tasks

Which virtue(s) do each of the following situations make it difficult to keep? Why?
1. Jay saw someone getting treated unfairly by a senior member of the office staff, and the victim was clearly upset by it.
2. Enzo got into trouble at school, and knew his mum would be disappointed with him when she found out.
3. When Aneela got to the shop tills, the check-out assistants were chatting too much with customers, and someone pushed in.
4. Tom is allowed to play on his computer games for only one hour each night after the family meal.

The Basics

1. What do we mean by virtues? What are the Sikh virtues?
2. Explain why the virtues are important for Sikhs.
3. Explain how daily life makes it difficult to keep the virtues.
4. Explain how belief in the virtues might influence a Sikh in their daily life.
5. 'The Sikh virtues are summed up by "just being a good person".' Do you agree? Explain more than one point of view to that statement.

Topic 3.1 Beliefs and teachings

Karma and rebirth

Sikhs believe each person has a soul, which is a divine spark from God. This soul is the part of a person which strives to reunite with God. However, the world is corrupt, and the soul – when born into a physical body – becomes tainted by that corruption, so that it is not aware of its true identity.

> 'We do not become saints or sinners by merely saying that we are; it is the actions that are recorded. According to the seed we sow, is the fruit we reap By God's grace, O Nanak; Man must either be saved or transmigrate.' *(Guru Nanak)*

Karma

Karma is action. In Sikhism, this is the belief that good acts generate positive karma, and bad acts (sins) generate negative karma. The effects of karma differ. We might do something in this lifetime which hurts others, and then get hurt ourselves ('what goes around comes around'), or we might do something in this lifetime which only has an effect in the next. If you imagine a shadow or mark on the soul created by karma, that shadow or mark is still there when the soul is next reborn. Sikhism is very clear that the entire burden of karma can be removed in a single lifetime – the Gurus taught that it need not take many lifetimes to 'wipe the slate clean'. How is this so? Guru Nanak said this is possible by being truly sorry for sins committed, by living a moral, truthful life, and by showing absolute devotion to God. Hence, the Sikh way of life is designed to do all these things.

Rebirth

The Sikh goal in life is to achieve mukti, to be reunited with God. It is only by God's grace that a person can do this. The Guru Granth Sahib teaches transmigration of the soul, or rebirth – that each soul will live through many lifetimes, beginning with the simplest of sentient beings – 'For several births you were a worm, for several births an insect, for several births a bird or an animal.' Finally, it tells us that the soul is born as a human: 'After ages you have the glory of being a human.' Humans differ from all else in creation, according to Sikhism, because of several key qualities:

- the ability to reason – thinking and decision-making
- the ability to understand right and wrong
- the ability to know God
- the capacity to achieve mukti.

It is up to humans to use these qualities to live in the right way, to gain God's grace and so to achieve mukti – the ending of rebirths.

Influences

If I believe that in my life I generate karma which shapes my rebirth, I will want to make a better rebirth more likely. As a Sikh, I am devoted to God and follow the teachings of the Gurus. This includes worship and selfless service to others (sewa). By focusing on God, I am more aware of my actions and how they please God or not. I can be more careful to live by the virtues. I am trying to be good, and avoiding being bad – to get the right kind of karmic consequences.

The Basics

1. Explain the Sikh terms karma and rebirth.
2. Explain how belief in karma might influence a Sikh in their daily life.
3. 'Belief in karma is the most important Sikh belief.' How far do you agree? Explain reasons showing more than one point of view.

Mukti – liberation from rebirth

Mukti is the aim or purpose of life in Sikhism. It is an end to the cycle of rebirth in which a soul transmigrates into one lifetime after another. Sikhs believe that only the grace of God can make this happen; that grace is gained when a Sikh lives a truthful life, dedicated to helping others achieve mukti, and devoted to God. This is what Sikhs mean when they say a person is gurmukh (God-centred) and a 'servant of God'.

Mukti can be achieved as a human. The Gurus were gurmukh; they had achieved mukti while alive.

Another interpretation of mukti is that it is salvation, or deliverance from the prison or barrier of ego that shuts out the Grace and Presence of God. As the person is so God-focused, and does everything for God and for the sake of others, God grants them salvation from being reborn again. In many ways, this means a person should not be focused on achieving mukti – rather they should focus on showing devotion to God, and serving God (and others). Mukti becomes a by-product of that, rather than the aim. The Guru Granth Sahib says, 'I crave not for a kingdom, nor even for mukti; What I long for is the lotus feet (of the Lord)'.

Why do Sikhs want mukti?

- They are taught this is the goal of human life.
- Achieving mukti is to be reunited with God and have everlasting bliss.
- Achieving mukti is to be the perfect servant of God.
- Mukti is absolute contentment and bliss – free of all suffering and worries.

Mukti as positive and negative

In a negative sense, mukti is 'getting rid of' certain characteristics, such as suffering, ignorance, rebirth, passion, desire, materialism and other negative characteristics.

In a positive sense, mukti is the full understanding of oneself; the realisation of the true nature of the self as the divine spark. This brings everlasting peace, bliss and contentment.

You can think of it as a tug-of war – the world and your ego against the desire for mukti. You could also think of this in terms of 'push and pull' – Sikhism teaches that by being more focused on oneself and the world, we are pulled away from mukti; by focusing on God and service to others, we push ourselves closer to mukti.

> ### The Basics
> 1. Explain Sikh beliefs about mukti.
> 2. Explain why mukti is an important belief in Sikhism.
> 3. Explain how mukti has positive and negative aspects.
> 4. 'A Sikh should concentrate on devotion and service, not mukti.' Do you agree? Explain reasons for and against that statement; then write a justified conclusion.

The tug-of-war for mukti

Topic 3.1 Beliefs and teachings

The five stages of liberation (the Five Khands)

Guru Nanak said that there are five stages of liberation; the idea being that a person goes through a spiritual journey during which specific levels are reached. He described them in the Japji Sahib, which is a poem and prayer that Sikhs recite every morning, and which describes God. The five stages are shown in the following table.

The five stages of liberation (the **Five Khands**)

Stage	Description	Impact of believing in this (influence)
First stage: **Dharam Khand** The realm of duty 'The Earth exists for dharma to be practised.' (Guru Nanak)	This is the stage in which a person realises there is a God, and that they must act properly towards God's creation. They have a sense of duty (**dharma**), which can also be called piety because they act in this way out of respect for God. By practising virtue, the mind becomes calmer so a person can make better decisions. This is a virtuous circle.	• Behaving in a compassionate way to others, e.g. working as a nurse. • Showing respect for all of God's creation, e.g. being vegetarian. • Showing thankfulness to God, e.g. by worshipping God.
Second stage: **Gian Khand** The realm of knowledge 'Boundless, limitless, infinite.' (Guru Nanak)	In this stage, a person becomes aware of the vastness of the universe and the insignificance of themselves – they are over-awed by a new realisation of God's creation, of the diversity, beauty and scope of it. They are 'mind-blown' by it. In the calm mind, they can hear the voice of the Guru (their intuition/common sense) more and more clearly, from where they find gems of wisdom. This is an experience of God, rather than just knowledge about religion.	• Humility because of how small we are in comparison to God's creation. • Appreciation for what we have, and what the world provides for us. • A desire to know more, e.g. by studying scripture.
Third stage: **Karam Khand** The realm of spiritual effort	Having new insight from the second stage, now the person works harder to get rid of the last traits of their ego, which is holding them back. It is as if their new knowledge pushes them to new heights, fulfilling their duties even more scrupulously. Once at this stage, a person will go on to achieve mukti – this can be thought of as the tipping point of their spiritual journey.	• Devoting more time to fulfilling duties, e.g. spending more time in prayer and worship with the Sangat (see page 135). • Removing the last traces of being materialistic, e.g. by increasing what they give in charity because others have greater need. • Recognising they need to support others, e.g. by sharing spiritual knowledge.
Fourth stage: **Saram Khand** The realm of grace	This is the stage in which a person has full realisation of God all the time. It is a form of bliss granted by God – that is, it comes from God's grace. The person is re-made by God as they were intended to be.	• Believing that nothing can affect them in any meaningful way, e.g. death is not feared as it has no power over them. • Their attitude to everything carries a sense of great calm and peace, e.g. being unruffled by difficult situations.

122

| Fifth stage: **Sach Khand** The realm of truth | The final stage is to be with God in eternal bliss. In the second stage, a person became aware of the vastness and mind-blowing nature of God's creation; in the fifth stage, they see it in reality. It is as if they see all from the divine perspective. They are no longer cut off from God but connected and aligned. This stage cannot be described, just known and understood when it is achieved. | • Believing this stage is possible makes a person keep going on the first and second stages.
• Believing this stage is possible might make a person want to tell others and help others also achieve mukti. |

The barriers to mukti

Rebirth into the material world makes the soul subject to ego and brings many barriers to mukti.

- One of these is maya, or illusion – this is seeing things as we want to see them, rather than as they really are. Maya makes us misinterpret what we see or experience because of our ego and worldly experiences.
- Another of these is haumai, or self-centredness – this is always thinking of oneself and one's needs first; selfishness. It is also the belief that 'I' only need rely on 'me' – that God is unnecessary.

Five other barriers are also known as the Five Vices or Five Thieves. Guru Nanak called them diseases or maladies – things which afflict the human body and soul. They can link to each other, one causing another or making another worse. All of them deflect a person from focusing on God and achieving mukti, as they are a kind of selfishness in themselves. The Five Vices are:

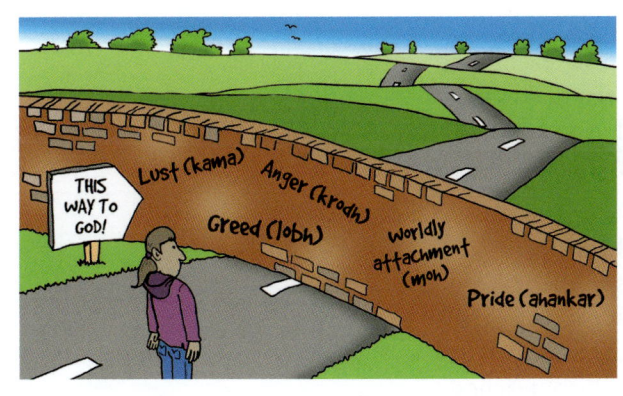

The Five Vices

Each of the Vices begins with a positive emotion which then gets out of control. For example, love is a good thing, but if it becomes lust, it begins to hurt others; it is normal to get irritated in life, but when that turns to anger, it can become violent. In each case, the emotion has been turned into a negative and selfish power.

Influences

Believing in the barriers to mukti makes a person work harder at living a good life. For example, it might mean a person avoids having too much wealth by making sure they share a good proportion with those in need through charities. Seeing lust as a Vice could encourage a person to have sex only within marriage and to avoid situations where temptation might be faced. Believing that all the Vices come from selfishness might make a person involve themselves more in selfless acts, such as helping in the gurdwara.

The Basics

1. Explain the Five Khands.
2. Explain how belief in each of the Khands might influence a Sikh.
3. Explain why there are barriers to mukti and what they are.
4. 'It is too difficult in today's world for a Sikh to achieve mukti.' How far do you agree? Explain arguments for and against that statement, showing you have considered more than one point of view. Give a justified conclusion.

Topic 3.1 Beliefs and teachings

Manmukh – haumai – gurmukh

Manmukh means 'keeping one's face to the mind'. It is being self-centred, a slave to what the mind tells us we want (desires); it is a natural outcome of being born into the world. Sikhism teaches that the distractions of the world encourage a person to become materialistic and selfish, which means they focus less on God.

Think about social media, for example: it encourages us to want more of everything, encouraging greed and attachment/materialism (both Vices). Role models in our society can also be poor examples, flaunting their money and success, encouraging us to copy their words and actions. News in the media can mislead, making us feel anger or hatred towards others because we have bought into a stereotype (an illusion). Society holds money and beauty up as gods – and we chase both for ourselves, rather than trying to make things more equal for more people. Traditional values such as sexual modesty, marriage and family are not seen as important. All of this encourages us to become more self-centred, more focused on materialism and pleasure. This is the world we live in.

> 'The self-willed manmukh separates themselves from God.' (GGS)

The outcome of being manmukh is to be separated from God. Sikhism sees this as a deliberate process, as humans have the capacity to choose.

Haumai is ego, and is another condition of living in the world. It is normal to think of oneself first, and easy to fall into the illusion that 'I am the centre of everything.' If you think of yourself, who are you? What are all the elements which define who you are? Gender, name, family, likes, opinions and so on. While some of these things are seen as fixed (though none of the fixed ones were chosen by you), many are fluid and changeable. If you took away your likes, opinions, your name, family and so on, would you still be you? Most people would say 'yes', because those things are labels, not the real you. So, Sikhism teaches the real you is your self/soul, which is the divine spark. The ego makes you think that all those other things are you – creating an illusion and turning you away from God. The Third Guru, Guru Amar Das called haumai 'the filth which clings to man'.

Sikhism teaches that haumai (ego) is a disease, which is always there affecting us. To get rid of haumai cures the disease. Sikhism teaches that God has created all souls to evolve through many lifetimes (see page 120), and having haumai is part of that evolution; the next stage is to turn to God, thus leaving behind haumai. By turning to God, Sikhism teaches that a person has recognised this 'ego disease', and wants to cure it. Their awareness of the problem and determination to solve it make a cure possible.

> 'Haumai and the remembrance of God are opposites of each other.' (GGS)

Gurmukh means to 'keep facing to Guru' – the opposite of manmukh, and the process to or result of getting rid of haumai. The Sikh way of life

Tasks

Consider these situations. For each decide if it is manmukh, haumai or gurmukh. Then explain why.
1. John committed adultery breaking up his marriage.
2. Sarah worked hard to understand the scriptures, studying daily.
3. Although a good footballer, Iker liked the crowd shouting his name best of all.
4. Steve stole money from his company to fund an extravagant lifestyle.
5. Enoki puts her spare energy into voluntary work.
6. Tom helps others but only after making sure he will himself get something out of it.

is designed to help a person be gurmukh – meditating on the name of God, truthful living and service to others ensure a person 'keeps their face to the Guru' and turns their back on haumai. The ideal human is fully gurmukh, reaching the higher of the Five Khands (see pages 122–123). Becoming this ideal human, this super-human, is the path to achieving the purpose of human life (see page 121).

> 'The gurmukhs … eradicate selfishness and conceit from within … sing the glorious praises of the Lord … Through selfless service happiness is obtained.' *(GGS)*

The analogy of the lotus flower helps explain manmukh and gurmukh. The roots of the lotus flower grow in the mud at the bottom of a pond; from that mud, it draws nutrients which help it to grow and produce beautiful flowers. However, the manmukh are like the roots – focused only on the mud, which is the world we live in. At the other end of the plant is a beautiful flower – nourished by the nutrients from the mud. However, it faces the Sun – this is the gurmukh, always focused on God. Of course, humans live in the world, so have to be part of society, work, survive and so on, but Sikhism teaches that they must keep their face to God.

Influences

A person who believes that people have haumai, and this is a barrier to mukti, will want to reduce the effect of it. Of course, they can see that haumai is part of being human, however, they can also see that Sikhism aims to manage haumai and reduce its control on a person. So they are influenced to live a morally good life, and to show devotion to God. A person who believes in manmukh also believes in gurmukh – they are two sides of the same coin. They will want to live in a gurmukh way as much as possible, so will try to live by the virtues. They might recognise that the way they live is more manmukh than gurmukh, and want to change that. To change they might become a Khalsa Sikh, making new vows and immersing themselves more in their religious practices.

The Basics

1 For each of these terms – manmukh, haumai, gurmukh:
   a explain Sikh teachings
   b explain how belief in each might influence a Sikh in their daily life.
2 'It is not easy to be gurmukh in the modern world.' How far do you agree with that statement? Explain arguments for and against, showing you have considered more than one point of view. Write a justified conclusion to show which point of view you feel is stronger.

Topic 3.1 Beliefs and teachings

The oneness of humanity and equality of all

'The whole of humanity should be viewed as one.' *(Guru Gobind Singh)*

The oneness of humanity

The oneness of humanity is the idea that God created everything and everyone. There is *one* God, and similarly there is *one* humanity. Humans are the high point of creation; the only part of creation which is capable of reuniting with God, of receiving salvation from rebirth (see page 117). Sikhism teaches that oneness means everyone is equal and is capable of receiving God's grace and salvation – whatever their gender, age, wealth, status, job, or any other way society classifies people. This is because of ego – these classifications are all just 'labels', and once all the 'labels' are stripped away, only the soul remains. The soul is the divine spark, God's pure creation, which God brings to life with His presence – and every soul is therefore of equal value to God.

> **Influences**
>
> *If* I believe in the oneness of humanity, I will not consider myself as better than others. I will show compassion for those who are suffering, and try to help them, as I feel I have that responsibility.

'We are all made from one clay.' *(Guru Arjan)*

The Guru Granth Sahib is the holy book of Sikhism. Compiled by Guru Gobind Singh, it contains poems and hymns (shabads) written by many of the Gurus, as well as some from Hindu and Muslim sources. Its central themes are describing God, the equality of all and the path to mukti.

'Women and men, all by God are created. All this is God's play. Says Nanak, all thy creation is good, Holy.' *(GGS)*

'Come, my dear sisters and spiritual companions; hug me close in your embrace. Let's join together, and tell stories of our All-powerful Husband Lord.' *(GGS)*

Equality of all

The Guru Granth Sahib constantly repeats the teaching of equality. Given Sikhism believes in the oneness of humanity, it must also believe in the equality of all, and must strive to make that a reality in the world today. In the times of the Gurus, the wider society did not practise equality – especially in the case of gender (women had far fewer rights than men) and caste (an idea of fixed social classes which affected all aspects of a person's life). The Gurus taught that actions are at least as important as beliefs, so religious practice was shaped to be barrier-less. These practices continue today.

> **Influences**
>
> *If* I believe everyone is equal, then I will show respect to everyone. It will not matter what their age, religion, race or gender. What matters is the way I treat them, and that must be as I would want them to treat me.

The Basics

1. What do Sikhs mean when they talk about the oneness of humanity?
2. Explain how believing in the oneness of humanity might influence a Sikh in their daily life.
3. 'There is nothing more important than believing in the equality of all.' Do you agree? Give reasons and show you have explored more than one point of view, including a Sikh view.

Expressions of equality – Guru Nanak

Guru Nanak founded Sikhism and was the first of the Ten Gurus. He formalised the beliefs of Sikhism. He set the tone for the religion in terms of equality, and there are many examples from his life that show how he rejected inequality.

Rejecting inequality through wealth

Guru Nanak trained as a government accountant but turned his back on what would have been a comfortable life with good money. Instead, he devoted himself to God.

On one of his journeys, Guru Nanak met a very rich man, called Duni Chand, who put up flags each time he had accumulated more wealth. He pestered Guru Nanak for a task and eventually Guru Nanak gave him a needle, which he asked him to look after until they met in the afterlife. The man was delighted and very proud – until his wife pointed out his stupidity. How could he take anything to the afterlife? He realised the truth: wealth can only be of use in this world, so should be used wisely. He gave his wealth away and became a true follower of Guru Nanak. Guru Nanak did not reject this man; instead, he helped him see how his wealth could be a good thing – and the man's actions helped to reduce inequality.

Rejecting inequality through religion

Guru Nanak used to bathe in the river every day. On one occasion, he simply disappeared. His friends and family spent three days searching everywhere for him. On the third day, they saw him bathing in the river in the same place from which he had disappeared. When he exited the river, he was in a state of bliss, unable to speak with them. Eventually he spoke, his first words being, 'There is no Hindu, there is no Muslim. Everyone is the same.' He then recited the Mool Mantra (see page 112) and the Japji Sahib (now a key prayer of Sikhism). During the rest of his life, Guru Nanak never rejected people for their religion, and spoke with people of many religions to understand their faith. His closest friend from a young age and throughout his life, who travelled with him on his teaching journeys, was a Muslim called Mardana.

Topic 3.1 Beliefs and teachings

Rejecting inequality through gender

> 'It is from woman that we are conceived and born. Woman is our lifelong friend who keeps the race going. Why should we despise the one who gives birth to great men?' *(Adi Granth)*

This quote by Guru Nanak makes it clear that men and women should be considered equal, and so treated as equals.

In the early Sikh community which Guru Nanak set up at Kartarpur, women had equality. Women could listen to the Guru's teachings, join the worship and eat at the langar – they were not excluded from anything. At the same time, their rights were protected – sati (where a widow throws herself onto her husband's funeral pyre so she will die) was banned. Guru Nanak spoke out against the poor conditions women were subject to in the wider society, ensuring life at Kartarpur did not allow those to continue.

Women have equal rights to men in leading worship in Sikhism

Rejecting inequality through caste

Guru Nanak set up the langar, which is a communal meal taken at the gurdwara. He realised people were coming from far and wide to listen to him speak about God and truthful living, so he felt it was right to feed them before they began their journeys home. However, he made rules for the langar: the food was to be that which any could eat, hence vegetarian; there would be no seated areas or segregations – everyone would sit on the floor and everyone would eat together, regardless of what caste they were.

At the time, society was split into castes – grouping people according to their family and fixing their opportunities and jobs. As part of this, beliefs about pure and impure food, and about people from some castes being unclean, meant that the castes avoided mixing – and certainly would not have eaten food together. Guru Nanak created a system which completely ignored all that and enforced equality.

Influences

Knowing Guru Nanak rejected inequality, a Sikh should try to do the same in their daily life. They should not show prejudice and should not discriminate against others. For example, they would not act or speak in a racist or sexist way, and would try to be accepting and inclusive of everyone. To go further, they could seek a role or job in which they fight to bring greater equality to society – for example, working in social care, contributing to charities for the poor, doing volunteer work in disaster-hit zones in the world.

The Basics

1. Explain how Guru Nanak rejected inequality due to wealth, gender, religion and caste.
2. Explain how a Sikh might be influenced by learning of how Guru Nanak rejected inequality.
3. 'Equality was Guru Nanak's greatest teaching.' Do you agree? Give reasons and explain your answer, showing you have thought about more than one point of view. You should consider Guru Nanak's teachings about God (see pages 112–114) as an alternative point of view.

Expressions of equality – Guru Gobind Singh

Guru Gobind Singh was the last of the Ten Gurus. He wrote part of the scriptures of Sikhism. He established the Khalsa (see page 147), which was the new level of Sikh commitment. There are many examples from his life which demonstrate belief in equality.

> 'Just as millions of sparks are created from the fire, although they are different entities, they merge in the same fire ... having been created from the same Lord, they merge in the same Lord.' *(Guru Gobind Singh)*

When Guru Gobind Singh was saying this, he meant that God created each person, and their aim in life is to be returned to God. Whilst our lives may all be different, our origins and end goals are exactly the same. Hence we are equal, the same.

Rejecting inequality through wealth

Guru Gobind Singh set up and developed the city of Anandpur. Within the city, all systems and processes worked on the principle of equality. Anandpur became very prosperous, making others see the value of this principle. Poverty in the city was almost unheard of – Guru Gobind Singh's way to reject wealth inequality was to try to eradicate the gap between rich and poor.

He included people of all levels of wealth in his initial five members of the Khalsa (the **Panj Pyare**, or Five Beloved Ones), showing that wealth is not a barrier to commitment to God.

In the society of the time, a person's wealth and status was often revealed by their name. Guru Gobind Singh made the taking of the name 'Singh' (males) or 'Kaur' (females) a condition of becoming a Khalsa Sikh – he himself was originally called Guru Gobind Rai, but changed his name (see pages 147 and 158). This meant people would be unable to judge a person's status by their name and so could not discriminate against them for having the 'wrong' status of name.

Topic 3.1 Beliefs and teachings

Rejecting inequality through religion

> 'Someone is Hindu, someone is Muslim, then someone is Shi'a and someone a Sunni; Recognise the whole human race as one.' *(Guru Gobind Singh)*

Guru Gobind Singh rejected religious divisions. He said that God created all people, and the same divine spark was within all. He saw different religions as different routes to the same God, saying, 'He (God) is in the temple as in the mosque, in the Hindu worship as in the Muslim prayer.' He stressed that the important thing was purity of thought, word and action, not blind faith or keeping rituals which a person neither understood nor believed in.

One of Guru Gobind Singh's closest friends, Budhu Shah, was a Muslim holy man.

Rejecting inequality through gender

Guru Gobind Singh stressed the complete equality of women with men. He allowed women into the Khalsa – they could complete the ceremony of commitment, wear the same clothes and follow the same rules as the men. He gave command of the Khalsa to his own wife, Mata Sundri, who led the Khalsa for many years after his death.

He also allowed women to train as soldiers and fight in battles, calling them great warriors. He called them 'sahibzadey' – sons – for their ferociousness in battle, allowing them to be in battalions and to command battalions. He barred his own soldiers from taking women as slaves/wives if they were captured in battle, something that was normal practice at the time.

The name 'Kaur' gave women their own identity – no longer were they just the wife of someone, taking their name and belonging to them. That name actually comes from kanwar, which means 'Crown Prince' – this went against the normal idea of a princess as a passive woman to be used in brokering alliances but without any power herself.

Rejecting inequality through caste

Guru Gobind Singh set up the Khalsa at Vaisakhi in 1699 (see page 147). At that time, five men offered their heads to him for their religion, becoming the first Khalsa Sikhs. They came from different castes (socio-economic groups) within society – demonstrating the acceptance of all by Guru Gobind Singh, and the equality of all. Significantly, it clearly showed everyone that all that mattered was a person's devotion to God, nothing else. The importance of the Khalsa in Sikhism is shown in that it still exists, and for many Sikhs is the obvious step in their commitment to God. Finally, the festival of Vaisakhi (which is focused on this event) is the most important Sikh festival.

Influences

If a person follows the example and teachings of Guru Gobind Singh, they might have friends of different religions. They might welcome those friends into the gurdwara, for the langar, for example. Believing that Guru Gobind Singh created the Khalsa to bring greater equality, as well as to strengthen a person's devotion to God, they would want to become a Khalsa Sikh.

The Basics

1. Explain how Guru Gobind Singh rejected inequality due to wealth, gender, religion and caste.
2. In what ways might a Sikh be influenced today by the ways that Guru Gobind Singh rejected inequality?
3. 'The most important way that Guru Gobind Singh challenged inequality was with the names Kaur and Singh.' Do you agree? Give reasons and explain your answer, showing you have thought about more than one point of view.

Expressions of equality – the Guru Granth Sahib

The Guru Granth Sahib, holy book of Sikhism

Sikhism has one key holy book – the Guru Granth Sahib – which was compiled by Guru Gobind Singh. It is made up of the poems and hymns of many of the Gurus, with a few poems by Muslim and Hindu mystics, as well as some who claimed to belong to no particular religion. Guru Gobind Singh ordered that this book was never to be changed, as it was the final Guru. It is the holy book used in gurdwaras everywhere in the world – each one set out in exactly the same way, and written in the original Gurmukhi script.

The central themes of the Guru Granth Sahib are:
- describing the nature of God
- the equality of all of humanity because of God's divine spark in all
- how to achieve mukti.

If you look back to the previous pages (127–130), you can spot a number of teachings from the Guru Granth Sahib (GGS) which help you to build a picture of the theme of equality.

The Guru Granth Sahib begins with the Mool Mantra, which states that God has no hatred. This means God does not discriminate – and so neither should Sikhs. In its 1,430 pages, the GGS constantly speaks directly and indirectly about equality.

> 'Recognise the Lord's Light within all, and do not consider social class or status; there are no classes or castes in the world hereafter.' *(GGS)*

> 'The gurmukh looks upon all beings alike, like the wind, which blows equally upon the king and the poor beggar.' *(GGS)*

> 'All beings and creatures are His; He belongs to all.' *(GGS)*

Influences

Since Sikhs believe the Guru Granth Sahib is the word of God, a Sikh should read it to learn God's will. Sikhs should try to understand its words and then apply them in their daily life – for example, by not judging others, by teaching their children to accept those different from themselves and by working to bring greater equality to society. Certainly, they should treat others with respect, regardless of their gender, race or religion – for example, it is common for Sikh communities to welcome non-Sikhs into their gurdwaras, to help them understand the Sikh faith a little and to provide food for them.

The Basics

1. Using quotes, explain what the Guru Granth Sahib (GGS) teaches about equality.
2. 'The words of the Guru Granth Sahib are more important than the actions of the Gurus in fighting inequality.' Do you agree? Explain your arguments, showing you have thought about more than one point of view, before writing a justified conclusion.

Topic 3.1 Beliefs and teachings

Expressions of equality – in Sikhism today

Sikhism stresses the need for equality in all aspects of society, starting with a person's choices and personal behaviour, through to equality shown in the Sikh community, in the wider society and country as a whole, and internationally.

Sikhs sharing food at the langar, or communal kitchen, after worship

Sikh worship (see page 140) demonstrates belief in equality. Anyone may be the granthi (reader of the holy book), so long as they are respected in the community and can read it without faults. The worshippers all sit on the floor before the holy book – no special seats or places are created. After worship, all will eat in the langar – side by side, no barriers.

Sikhs work in many different jobs which include working for justice and equality in society. There are Sikh MPs in the UK Parliament; many more are councillors in local government. Working in social care, education, health and policing, many Sikhs are able to support the vulnerable and to promote equality. Sikh charities such as Khalsa Aid work in disaster-hit and poverty-stricken areas, most of which are not Sikh areas, showing compassion to others and ignoring religious barriers.

Tan Singh Dhesi is Member of Parliament for Slough

The Basics

1. Explain how Sikh teachings of equality have influenced Sikhs in their daily lives.
2. 'Equality is a matter of fairness, not of religion.' Do you agree with this? Explain arguments to show you have considered different points of view, including a Sikh view. Write a justified conclusion.

I am amritdhari – I have taken the Khalsa vows and am committed to achieving mukti through my devotion to God and service to others. Guru Gobind Singh gave Sikhs the Khalsa, and with it a visible reminder of our equality as women with men. I am a surgeon in a big hospital – Sikhism stresses that every person has the right to education and should use the gifts God has given them to help others.

As a Christian, I was invited to a gurdwara in our city, as part of a group from our church. The Sikhs we met were very welcoming and wanted us to understand their religion a bit better. They weren't trying to convert us – just to bridge the gap between our communities. After we had been taken round the gurdwara with everything explained and been given a really interesting talk about Sikh beliefs and practices, we were welcomed into the langar to eat.

Sewa (selfless service to others)

Sewa is a Sikh duty which was set up by Guru Nanak, an essential part of being a Sikh. Sewa is helping others, however that can be done, without thought of or desire for any kind of reward. The point is to serve others with a pure mind – just for the sake of being of service. By doing this, we remove haumai (ego).

We Sikhs believe in the equality of all because everyone is created by God and has the divine spark. We strive to develop the Sikh virtues of humility, compassion, truthful living, and so on. Sewa takes these beliefs and virtues and puts them into practice in everyday life as actions in the service of God and for the service of others.

The word sewa has two implications – service and worship. It is service because it is about helping others, but it is worship because 'God pervades all' (GGS). So to help others is also to help God. Every single Sikh can do sewa – there are no limits.

You see, sewa is the other half of my faith to Simran (meditating on God's name and worshipping God). They are like the two wings of a bird – without one of them, the bird cannot fly. Just so, I need to do both to consider myself a Sikh, and through doing both I will achieve mukti.

'You shall find happiness doing sewa.' (GGS)

'One who performs selfless service, without thought of reward, shall attain his Lord and Master.' (GGS)

'The hands of the gurmukh are blessed, for they toil in the service of God and the sangat ... Ego and pride have been lost through serving others.' (GGS)

All of the Gurus spoke about sewa, making it central to Sikh practices. The Guru Granth Sahib has many teachings about sewa and its importance. All Sikhs learn about the ways to perform sewa at home, in the gurdwara and in their local community. The **Rahit Maryada** (Sikh Code of Conduct) says:

> 'Gurdwaras are laboratories for teaching the practice of sewa ... the real field is the world abroad, sewa recognises no barriers of religion, caste or race. It must be offered to all.'

This reminds Sikhs that sewa is not just something they should do in the gurdwara or even in the Sikh community; rather, the real test is doing sewa for those who are not Sikhs because that means ignoring or breaking down the barriers of society itself.

Topic 3.1 Beliefs and teachings

Three forms of sewa

Tan Body/ physical	This covers any physical efforts to help others. For example, helping out in the langar at the gurdwara – serving food to others. In the community, helping an elderly person to do their shopping. In the wider world, going to a disaster-hit area to give out food and water.
Dhan Money/ material wealth	This is the use of money/material wealth to help others. For example, **daswandh** (tithing) is done by most Sikhs, as instructed by Guru Amar Das, which is gifting 10 per cent of their earnings to the gurdwara. In the community, it might be paying for food for the homeless. In the wider world, it might be giving to environmental charities.
Man Mental	This is the use of mind and intellect to help others. It starts with being sincere when helping. For example, a Sikh might help others to better understand the teachings of the Gurus. In the community, a Sikh might be a lawyer, using their intellect to help bring justice. In the wider world, they might become an MP, serving their community but also contributing to law-making.

Khalsa Aid – sewa in worldwide action

Khalsa Aid is a Sikh organisation, set up in 1999, based in Slough in the UK. It was set up to provide aid to those in the greatest need, whoever they are and wherever they are in the world. All the money Khalsa Aid needs to operate comes from donations, and many of those who go to the countries in difficulty are volunteers, even paying their own travel expenses to get to the affected area.

In 2018, for example, a tsunami hit Indonesia. Volunteers were organised to help in providing food, water and medical aid for the victims. A langar was set up to feed some of those affected, and shelters were distributed for those who had lost their homes. In the Democratic Republic of Congo (DRC), where more than a million people fled fighting as refugees, Khalsa Aid distributed food to four refugee camps, set up schools and paid for a water pump to be installed and maintained for the refugees. Khalsa Aid was also one of the first organisations to help the survivors of the Grenfell Tower disaster in London.

Tasks

Explain the form of sewa each of the following represents.
1 Sanjeet helps in the langar when his parents are responsible for it.
2 Mo goes into schools to teach young people about Sikhism.
3 Emma helps at a soup kitchen for the homeless.
4 Carol donates 5% of her earnings to a charity run by the gurdwara.
5 Tara works for an environmental organisation.
6 Charu trained as a lawyer and works in Legal Aid.

The Basics

1 What is meant by sewa? Using examples, explain the three types of sewa.
2 Explain how believing in sewa influences a Sikh's daily life.
3 Explain, using Sikh teachings, why it is important for Sikhs to do sewa.
4 'Sewa (selfless service to others) is more important than worship in Sikhism.' Do you agree? Explain your arguments, showing you have thought about more than one point of view.

The Sangat (holy congregation of Sikhs)

Guru Nanak used the term Sangat to describe the brotherhood of Sikhs. The 'Sat Sangat' (true or holy congregation) was a space for Sikhs to pray together, carry out religious ceremonies and share religious discussion and instruction. In other words, the role of the Sangat was to protect, support and develop the faith of the Sikhs.

> 'The Sat Sangat is the school of the soul, where the Glorious Virtues of the Lord are studied.' *(GGS)*

The development of religious belief through worship is the primary function of the Sangat:

> 'How does one recognise Sat Sangat? Sat Sangat is where the Lord's name is recited' *(GGS)*

The Guru Granth Sahib says that a person can be known by the company they keep – that is, they are shaped by that company and become like them. Using the example of a person becoming a thief by association with thieves, it encourages a Sikh to stay with the Sangat, in order to become more gurmukh. Being in the company of others who believe the same makes it easier to practise their religion, and to learn more about it – there are no distractions, and no barriers:

> 'In the Sat Sangat, fear and doubt depart.' *(GGS)*

The Sangat take the lead in festivals and gurpurbs (see pages 145–150), which often involve large community events and processions. These need to be arranged, as does worship and the langar, for everyone involved. Seeing oneself as part of the Sangat leads a person to be more involved in its work.

Sikhism is as much about sewa as worship. The Sangat motivates Sikhs to do good deeds – the Sikh Code of Conduct describes the gurdwara as being the laboratory for sewa, meaning the Sangat, rather than the physical building. The Sangat encourages its members to help in the gurdwara – for example, leading services, making food and serving it in the langar, teaching other Sikhs; to help locally in grassroots community work and politics, including helping people with problems they face in their lives; and more widely – for example, by supporting disaster relief campaigns. The principle of equality is ingrained in the Sangat, and hence pushes its members to live ethically and bring greater equality to the world.

Influences

Believing in the importance of the Sat Sangat, those Sikhs who wish to focus more on their spiritual goals might decide to be an active member of it. They could take part in all religious activities. For example, festivals such as Vaisakhi include processions through the community which take organisation and management. They could join in the organisation of worship, for example teaching younger Sikhs, or supporting other Sikhs in their religious studies. They might join the Khalsa. Being part of the Sat Sangat brings a person closer to the practice of their religion and their religious community.

The Basics

1. What is 'Sat Sangat'?
2. Why is the Sangat important?
3. Explain Sikh teachings about the Sangat.
4. 'The most important role of the Sangat is to lead the Sikh community.' Do you agree? Give reasons and explain your answer, showing you have thought about more than one point of view.

Getting prepared

The Beliefs section of an exam paper is made up of five questions. Here you can read the wording, some tips for doing well and some examples of each.

1.1 question – Multi-choice: 1 mark

For example:

A Which of the following is the name of the Sikh holy book?

- a Guru Gobind Singh
- b Guru Granth Sahib
- c Mool Mantra
- d Sangat

B How many stages of liberation do Sikhs believe in?

- a 2
- b 3
- c 4
- d 5

> **Tip**
>
> Lots of these are definition questions – so make sure you know the meanings of all key words.

1.2 question – 'Give two…': 2 marks

This tests knowledge (not understanding).

For example:

A Name **two** qualities of God for Sikhs.

B Give **two** of the barriers to mukti.

> **Tips**
>
> Keep your answer to a minimum – give only two words, or phrases. Example A could be answered simply by 'creator, all-loving', or in a longer version, 'Sikhs believe God is the creator of the world, of all life, of humans – of everything. Sikhs also believe that God loves every person and every being in His creation without prejudice.' The second answer takes longer – which is time you can better use elsewhere on the exam.
>
> The exam paper gives prompts of '1' and '2' to remind you to give two answers.

1.3 question – Influences: 4 marks

This is testing your understanding of how what a person believes affects what they think/say/do – how it influences them.

For example:

A Explain **two** ways in which belief in the Sikh virtue of truthful living might influence Sikhs today.

B Explain **two** ways in which belief in sewa might influence Sikhs today.

> **Tips**
>
> You get a mark for each way, plus an additional mark as you explain each of those ways – 2 + 2.
>
> The question wants you to say, 'If I believe____, then I will (think/say/do)____.' Don't make the mistake of explaining the belief itself.
>
> Using examples is a good way to explain in this question because it shows how the influence is acted upon.

1.4 question – Beliefs and teachings: 5 marks

For example:

A Explain **two** Sikh teachings about karma. Refer to sacred writings or another source of Sikh belief and teaching in your answer.

B Explain **two** Sikh teachings about the importance of being gurmukh. Refer to sacred writings or another source of Sikh belief and teaching in your answer.

Tips

You get a mark for each teaching, plus an additional mark for each explanation. The final mark is for giving a relevant teaching. As this question is about teachings, the fifth mark should be very easy!

'Teaching' doesn't mean you have to give quotations; you could give beliefs or concepts.

You will need to know the key terms – because that is what you are being asked about; if you haven't learnt what gurmukh is, you can't answer Example B!

1.5 question – Analysis and evaluation: 12 marks plus 3 marks for written English (SPaG)

For example:

A 'For a Sikh, being haumai (self-centred) is the biggest barrier to mukti.'

Evaluate this statement.

In your answer, you should:
- refer to Sikh teaching
- give reasoned arguments to support this statement
- give reasoned arguments to support a different point of view
- reach a justified conclusion.

B 'Equality is the most important belief for Sikhs.'

Evaluate this statement.

In your answer, you should:
- refer to Sikh teaching
- give reasoned arguments to support this statement
- give reasoned arguments to support a different point of view
- reach a justified conclusion.

Tips

The question wording gives you a great way to check your answer – use the different bullet points to check you have done all the things you need to do.

If the statement says something is 'best', 'most important' or gives any kind of value words, then challenge it by saying, 'It depends what is meant by…'. This is a good technique to make your brain think more widely in answering.

You have to give an agree side and a disagree side in your answer – failure to do so will cost you any mark above Level 2 (6 marks out of 12). Similarly, failure to explain anything you write will also keep you stuck at Level 2 at best.

By giving and explaining all arguments for one side, then doing the same for the other side, you write a clearer answer which is easier to mark.

'Justified conclusion' is a posh way of asking you to say whether the agree or disagree side is stronger, and why you think that. It doesn't mean for you to rewrite arguments you gave already! So one side might have more arguments, might be clearer, might be more compelling/persuasive or might fit with what you already think. These are all useful ways to justify a conclusion. Sometimes, you just can't decide – and it is okay to say that as well.

3.2 Practices

The gurdwara – its role in the Sikh community

Sikhs worship at a gurdwara. 'Gurdwara' means 'door to the Guru', which is to say that there is a copy of the Guru Granth Sahib inside, so a person accesses the holy book through the gurdwara. Originally, in the time of the Ten Gurus, the word 'dharamsala' was used, meaning 'place of faith'. It was where Sikhs came together to worship. Guru Arjan Dev was the first to use the term 'gurdwara'.

A gurdwara can be recognised by its saffron-coloured flagpole and flag. The flag shows the Sikh symbol – the Khanda. It must have a prayer hall and a langar (community kitchen).

The role of the gurdwara

- To be a place of public worship – hymns are sung (kirtan shabad), and the Guru Granth Sahib is read aloud and explained. It is here the Sangat come together (see page 135).
- To be a place of spiritual/moral support – Sikhs see others keeping the Sikh Code of Conduct (Rahit Maryada) and feel strengthened; the atmosphere is perfect for meditating on the name of God (Nam Japna – see page 141).
- To be a place of sewa – the langar provides food for anyone who comes into the gurdwara, regardless of religion (see page 144); gurdwaras are run mainly by volunteers (sewadars).
- To be a place of learning – most gurdwaras have libraries, allowing Sikhs to learn more about Sikhism; Khalsa Sikhs might teach or guide others; classes in Sikh martial arts, history and others take place at the gurdwara.
- To be a place for the community – community life is an important aspect of Sikhism, and Sikh communities run by the principles of the religion (justice, equality, co-operation, etc.). The gurdwara provides a space for weddings and other ceremonies. On festival days, the gurdwara will be decorated, processions begin here and fireworks are set off from here.

A Sikh gurdwara

Worship in the gurdwara

The Basics

1. What does 'gurdwara' mean?
2. Name three features a gurdwara must have?
3. Explain the different roles of the gurdwara.
4. 'The most important role of the gurdwara in the UK is as a place of worship.' How far do you agree with that statement? Explain arguments showing you have considered more than one point of view.

The religious features of the gurdwara

The gurdwara, or Sikh place of worship, must have a hall for worship and a langar, and is signposted by an orange flagpole and flag adorned with the Khanda. The flag is the Nishan Sahib. The Khanda is the symbol of Sikhism, representing God's power, and indicating the presence of the Guru Granth Sahib in the building.

The Khanda – symbol of Sikhism

Stepping inside a gurdwara, every person is expected to remove their shoes and cover their head before entering the prayer hall (diwan hall). This is to show respect to the spiritual guidance received in the diwan hall.

The diwan hall has no seating – Sikhs sit on the carpeted floor for acts of worship. An aisle splits the room into two halves, traditionally with men sitting on one side and women on the other. At the front will be the **palki**, a raised platform, usually cushioned and decorated with cloths, on which the Guru Granth Sahib is laid each day to be read from. Many older gurdwaras, such as the Golden Temple in Amritsar, have the Guru Granth Sahib in the middle, where the Guru would have been teaching. In these places, women and men sit together. Over the palki is the **takht**, a canopy which is usually highly decorated. Decoration may be seen on the walls – often the Mool Mantra (see pages 112–114) and pictures of Gurus. Anyone going into the diwan hall is reminded of the spiritual nature of this place.

The diwan hall, or hall for worship

The Guru Granth Sahib is laid on the palki and shaded by the takht. From here a person called a granthi will read from it to the congregation

Topic 3.2 Practices

The most important feature in the gurdwara is the palki and takht – the space for the Guru Granth Sahib when not resting. It is always placed at the front and centrally – allowing everyone a good view when the Guru Granth Sahib is read. The Guru Granth Sahib is processed from its resting room (the Sach Khand) each morning to be laid on the palki. When a Sikh enters the room, they go to the palki and prostrate before the Guru Granth Sahib, then leave an offering (food, flowers, money) to show respect and gratitude to the Guru. Everyone will have to physically look up to the Guru Granth Sahib as they worship because it has been raised. This shows respect to the holy book and its words. Over the palki is the takht. Holding a canopy over any person is a mark of status and respect in Indian culture; just so, there is a permanent one over the Guru Granth Sahib in the gurdwara. Together, the palki and takht suggest the power and magnificence of God and God's word. Throughout any service, or when individuals attend the gurdwara, the palki and takht are in their focus as glorifications of the Guru Granth Sahib. At the end of the day, the Guru Granth Sahib is returned to the Sach Khand.

For Sikhs, prayer can be private (on their own) or congregational (with others). It is a duty to worship every day, but there is no rule as to how or where. Most gurdwaras are open every day, some 24/7 – worshippers come when it suits them, some attend every day. The whole of Sunday is given to services at the gurdwara, with people attending when they want and for as long as they want. These services focus entirely on the Guru Granth Sahib and include:

- kirtan shabad (singing of hymns, mainly from the Guru Granth Sahib), led by musicians (ragis) while the worshippers join in or just listen
- a granthi (reader), who reads the Guru Granth Sahib aloud, so that people can hear the word of God and guidance given by the Gurus
- Nam Simran – meditation on the name of God
- sermons about the teachings of the Gurus, and their meaning and application in daily life.

The final service ends with prayers, including a universal blessing, asking for the well-being of the whole of humanity. Karah parshad (sacred pudding) is shared amongst all.

The langar, which is the communal kitchen, is an integral part of Sikh practice (see page 128). The funding, making and serving of food at the langar is sewa (see page 144); eating is a show of equality, as people sit together without any hierarchy. When a worshipper feels they have spent enough time in the service, they go to the langar, which will be open throughout the time that services are taking place.

Reading the Guru Granth Sahib during worship

Rajis leading kirtan shabad

A Sikh prostrates before he takes his place for worship

Private devotion in the gurdwara using a gutka (prayer book)

> ### The Basics
>
> 1. Describe a gurdwara – how you might recognise one, and its key features.
> 2. Explain why the palki and takht are important.
> 3. 'The palki and takht are just decoration in the gurdwara.' How far do you agree? Explain arguments showing you have thought about more than one point of view.

Nam Japna

Sikhs can be split into those who have become Khalsa Sikhs (amritdhari) and non-Khalsa Sikhs (**sahajdhari**). Guru Gobind Singh set up the Khalsa in 1699 (see page 147), at which time a new level of commitment was established for Sikhs. Those who took the vows for this became amritdhari. The amritdhari have more duties as Sikhs than the sahajdhari, and these are detailed in the Rahit Maryada, which is the Sikh Code of Conduct.

> 'Haumai is a great malady. The remedy is to attune oneself with God.' (GGS)

The way to 'attune oneself with God' is by focusing on God, keeping God in mind at all times. Nam Japna is repeating the name of God. It can be done out loud, in a formal setting, or in the mind. This allows a Sikh to keep God in mind and attune themselves with God.

Nam Japna is a duty for all Khalsa (amritdhari) Sikhs, though many non-Khalsa (sahajdhari) Sikhs also do this. It is more than just repeating God's name; it is also:

- getting up before dawn to bathe and then meditate on God's name before the sun rises
- praying at least three times a day, during which specific prayers are to be recited – this is called nitnem ('daily routine'); a Sikh may add other Sikh prayers to these or their own words
- reading a portion of the Guru Granth Sahib
- attending worship at the gurdwara, if possible, where they would be in the company of other Sikhs – the Sangat:

> 'Join the Sat Sangat and meditate on the name of God.' (GGS)

Each activity makes them focus on God. This includes seeing the world and others as creations of God. By always having God in mind, a person is more likely to live by the Sikh virtues, living a morally good life.

Home versus gurdwara

A Sikh doesn't spend their entire life either at home or at the gurdwara, so to constantly think of God, a Sikh must do Nam Japna anywhere/everywhere. The gurdwara is the obvious place to do Nam Japna as it is the home of the Sat Sangat, and there will be others with greater knowledge – though a family might pray together as well. Some is done at home – bathing and meditating before dawn being obvious examples. For many Sikhs, being at the gurdwara makes Nam Japna more special, but it is not practical to do everything there.

Sikh man praying

I prefer to pray at home. I pray at the very start and at the end of each day. Being at home ensures I do not miss these prayers. I also feel it is from me to God – no distractions.

I prefer to pray at the gurdwara. There I am surrounded by the spiritual atmosphere of the diwan hall. I pray alone but others are there doing the same. This gives strength to my connection with God.

I pray at home – it is most convenient for the earliest prayers, so my day is beginning with prayer. However I also pray at the gurdwara, the home of the Guru Granth Sahib, the living Guru.

The Basics

1. Explain what is meant by Nam Japna.
2. Explain the importance of Nam Japna for Sikhs.
3. 'It is impossible to fulfil the duty of Nam Japna by only attending the gurdwara.' Do you agree? Explain arguments which show you have considered different points of view, before writing a justified conclusion.

Topic 3.2 Practices

The role of prayer in the home

'O servant Nanak, some are united with the Guru; to some, the Lord grants peace, while others – deceitful cheats – suffer in isolation. Those who have the treasure of the Lord's Name deep within their hearts – the Lord resolves their affairs.' (GGS 305:4)

Considering Nam Japna as a duty, it is easy to see that most Sikhs will pray at home. The teaching from the Guru Granth Sahib reminds Sikhs that, by keeping God in mind, they benefit – they get a sense of peace, avoid suffering and are helped in their lives by God. It is one of the three elements which make up being a Sikh (see page 156).

Sikh woman showing devotion to God at home

Whether at home or at the gurdwara, Sikhs will use set prayers, used by Sikhs since the days of the Gurus and across the world. These prayers give a sense of tradition, equality and belonging, as well as being a spiritual practice. When praying, a Sikh is trying to connect with God, so the more they pray, the stronger the sense of connection, and the more gurmukh they are. To help them pray, they might use a set of prayer beads, called a mala. This allows them to count the different prayers, or repetitions, they do. Since reading scripture is a form of prayer, a Sikh might take time to read their gutka, which is a book containing excerpts from the Guru Granth Sahib.

Nitnem

Nitnem is the 'daily routine' of prayer. There are five parts read in the course of the day. The first three parts, which may be done together in the morning, take 40–60 minutes and include:

- the Japji Sahib – this is found at the beginning of the Guru Granth Sahib and was written by Guru Nanak; it includes the Mool Mantra
- the Jaap Sahib – this was written by Guru Gobind Singh; it glorifies God
- another hymn by Guru Gobind Singh, the name of which translates as 'With your grace'.

At dusk, the fourth part of nitnem is said. This takes 15–25 minutes. Known as the Rehras Sahib, this is a collection of hymns by the Gurus.

Before bedtime, the final part is said. This takes 5–10 minutes and is the Kirtan, or Song of Praise. It is another collection of hymns by the Gurus.

Sikh prayer is not done in a minute or two. Time must be given to it, which means it demands greater devotion.

The Basics

1. Why might a Sikh choose to pray at home?
2. Explain 'nitnem' in Sikh daily life.
3. 'Prayer at home is a vital part of Sikh life.' How far do you agree? Explain arguments which show more than one point of view. Write a justified conclusion showing which point of view you find stronger.

The role and importance of the Akhand Path

An **Akhand Path** is the name given to the continuous reading of the whole of the Guru Granth Sahib. It takes around 48 hours to do this, and there can be no break at any part of the reading. It must end in the early morning, to allow a formal act of worship to take place. Usually taking place at the gurdwara, some Akhand Paths do happen at a Sikh home. Those requesting the Path will pay for all its costs, which includes a langar for the whole reading time, open to all.

The first complete reading of the Guru Granth Sahib was done for Guru Gobind Singh, after he had decided the contents and order of this holy book. He stood and listened to it read in its current order, eating meals and bathing while listening. He declared it the living Guru, which would replace the human Gurus. This was the first Akhand Path.

In 1742, a female Sikh warrior, Bibi Sundari, lay dying of her wounds and asked for the Guru Granth Sahib to be read. It was done in 48 hours, before she spoke the Khalsa vow and died. Henceforth, it became a tradition to read it in 48 hours.

Why hold an Akhand Path?

The Guru Granth Sahib is the focus of an Akhand Path

An Akhand Path always gives a sense of connection with God, demonstrates thanks to God, shows unity with other Sikhs and gives respect to the holy book and the religion. Some gurdwaras hold an Akhand Path every week; the sound of the words is believed to create a power (naad), which resonates with the souls of all of humanity. Thus it is sewa to all others, and helps the listener to build their relationship with God. It has become traditional to hold Akhand Paths at major life and community events, such as:

- happy occasions, e.g. marriage, the birth of a child, university graduation
- sad occasions, e.g. to mark someone's death
- religious occasions, e.g. to begin festivals such as Vaisakhi, or gurpurbs such as the birthday of Guru Nanak (see pages 145–150)
- historic occasions, e.g. remembering a key date in Sikh history.

The Basics

1. What is an Akhand Path? What happens?
2. Explain the importance of the Akhand Path in Sikhism.
3. Explain Sikh teachings about the Akhand Path.
4. 'An Akhand Path is the best way to show devotion to God.' How far do you agree with that statement? Explain arguments showing more than one point of view.

'Continuously sing the Glorious Praises of the Lord, day and night; singing the Lord's Praises, I cannot find the limits.' *(GGS)*

Topic 3.2 Practices

The langar as an expression of sewa

The langar is the meal shared by all worshippers. Each gurdwara must have a communal kitchen for this function (see page 140).

When Sikhism began, people from different castes or classes would not eat together as this was considered to lead to ritual pollution. Ritual pollution – for example, from women who were menstruating – was considered a block to God, one cause of which was men and women eating together. By starting the langar tradition, Guru Nanak was rejecting the idea of ritual pollution, and encouraging equality, as the langar is shared by everyone, all at the same time and all sitting together.

Guru Amar Das was the third of the Ten Gurus. He did much for equality, including women's equality, which he promoted by appointing women as leaders in a large number of his missionary centres. Guru Amar Das emphasised the importance of equality and community by saying, 'First eat together, then worship together.' He made eating together a compulsory part of worship, so it became a way to break down social barriers. Since one could not worship without having eaten at the langar, it forced people to get to know their fellow worshippers, which is key to seeing others as equals. He refused to meet visitors unless they had shared food in the langar.

> 'That is the discipline of the langar – that even a king and a beggar can sit together, serve and eat the same food, in the same way.' *(Harbhajan Singh Khalsa)*

The langar only serves vegetarian food (no meat, fish or eggs), so any person can eat there, emphasising that all are welcome. While UK gurdwaras might serve their local community and then only on Sundays (Sikh holy day), the bigger gurdwaras in India often serve many more every day. At Amritsar, an average of 100,000 meals a day are served – to anyone who comes.

The three forms of sewa at the langar

The langar is seen as a central tool of sewa. Dhan sewa (financial) is needed to pay for the ingredients. Tan sewa (physical) is clearly done by anyone preparing or cooking the food, serving it or cleaning up afterwards. Man sewa (mental) is done by every person who devotes their work to God, doing it because it should be done, not out of wanting some reward. Everyone can do one or more of those things; they could contribute money towards the cost, or give up their time and energy for free and selflessly. The Rahit Maryada says that the gurdwara is the 'laboratory of sewa', i.e. the place where Sikhs begin to explore how they can complete sewa – the langar is a perfect example of that.

A langar in a UK gurdwara

The Basics

1. Explain the purpose of the langar in Sikhism.
2. Explain Sikh teachings about the langar.
3. Explain how the langar is an expression of sewa.
4. 'The langar is the most important part of Sikh worship.' How far do you agree? Explain arguments supporting different points of view.

Sikh festivals

Significance of Sikh festivals

Festivals are celebrations of important religious events. Sikhs also celebrate gurpurbs, which are celebrations of an anniversary related to the life of a Guru (birth or death). For Sikhs in the UK, these are important times to come together as a religious community, worshipping and celebrating in strength. They are also times when their religion can be shared with the wider, non-Sikh community: for example, Trafalgar Square hosts Vaisakhi each year, with 50,000 people attending in 2019, while the Birmingham Vaisakhi processions attracted over 100,000. These celebrations allow non-Sikhs some understanding of the religion, which is helpful to community relations in Britain.

Guru Amar Das (the third of the Ten Gurus) gave the order that Sikhs should celebrate three festivals by coming together as a community. These were Divali, Vaisakhi and Hola Mohalla. Hola Mohalla is celebrated through competitions in many areas, including the Sikh martial art of gatka.

Divali

The Sikh festival of Divali takes place at the same time as the Hindu festival of Diwali. It is an autumn festival, and as such also a 'festival of lights'. For many Sikhs, it is also known as Bandi Chhorh Divas, which means 'freedom day' or 'prisoner release day'.

Origins of Divali

Guru Hargobind led the Princes from the prison as they all held onto his cloak

The actual cloak which saved the princes, which can be seen in the Sikh history museum at Amritsar

In 1619, the sixth Guru, Guru Hargobind, had been imprisoned by the Mughal Emperor Jahangir. They had become friends after Guru Hargobind saved his life. Jahangir held many men as political prisoners in terrible conditions in a fort, and illness spread amongst them. Political prisoners are those people held in confinement because of their political beliefs, not because they have committed a crime. Jahangir was persuaded to ask Guru Hargobind to go there and pray continuously, so they would get well. Out of friendship for Jahangir and compassion for the prisoners, Guru Hargobind did as he was asked. At the same time – working with the Governor of the fort – he got the conditions for prisoners improved. Eventually, the prisoners got well again, and Jahangir agreed he could leave the fort-prison. Guru Hargobind refused to leave unless 52 princes were also released. Having first refused this request, Jahangir later agreed, but ordered that only those who could hold onto Guru Hargobind were to be allowed to leave. Guru Hargobind had a special cloak made, which had 52 'tails' – one for each prince. With each prince holding a 'tail', every one of them walked out with Guru Hargobind. Hence the festival name of Bandi Chhor Divas, which means 'prisoner release day'.

Guru Hargobind's release was a few days before the Hindu festival of Diwali, but he arrived back to Amritsar on the day of that festival, so the people lit Amritsar up with lamps and candles. Hence it was celebrated on the day of Diwali, and as a festival of light, copied today by huge firework displays at Amritsar.

Topic 3.2 Practices

How Divali is celebrated

Modern celebrations of Divali linked to the duty of worship include the following:

- An Akhand Path is completed leading up to the day of the festival.
- Worship at the gurdwara begins very early in the morning and continues until mid-afternoon.
- Speeches and sermons are given which focus on justice and freedom, and retell the story of Guru Hargobind and the 52 princes.
- Offerings are made to the Guru Granth Sahib, such as money, rice/food, flowers and sweets.
- The flagpole of the gurdwara may be cleaned, with a new flag being flown.

Activities linked to the duty of sewa include the following:

- Charitable giving is encouraged.
- People give their time for free, e.g. doctors at Amritsar (where a huge fair is held for this festival), distributions of food to the homeless.
- Many Sikhs are politically active on this day, using it to highlight cases of injustice in the world.

Family and community celebrations:

- Homes are lit with diya lamps, recalling Guru Hargobind's return.
- Families celebrate with fireworks at home and many gurdwaras organise displays.
- Gifts are given and new clothes worn.
- Families come together to share meals.
- Processions are made from the gurdwara through local communities, culminating in festivals in parks and other community spaces, to which anyone is welcome.

> *Divali is my favourite festival because I remember my grandfather telling stories of Guru Hargobind's bravery and compassion. The way he told it made you feel like you were there.*

> *Divali is my favourite festival because I am involved in all the festive activities – religious and communal. As one of the Sangat, I help with the Akhand Path, the morning's worship, and the procession. It feels good to be so fully involved.*

> *I went to Amritsar last year for Divali, and attended the great fair. It was so good to be there surrounded by Sikhs, at the home of Sikhism. I will never forget it.*

Celebrations in the UK and abroad

Of course, the core of the Divali celebration – why it happens, the religious practices carried out for the festival and the sense of family and community – is the same for Sikhs everywhere. However, there are some differences as Sikhs outside the Punjab live in non-Sikh cultures.

Sikhs in the UK may live in Sikh communities, and so their gurdwara becomes the focal point of celebrations. Sikhs in the Punjab region of India are in a much bigger group and are closer to Amritsar. A three-day fair takes place at Amritsar, so many Indian Sikhs make the journey to attend one or more days at Amritsar. There they will bathe in the pool around the Golden Temple, walk around the Golden Temple pathways and join in the services in the massive diwan halls at Amritsar, where continuous singing of kirtans takes place. Amritsar itself is lit up by many thousands of lights, and a huge firework display takes place.

Sikhs in the UK might need to get time off work to celebrate Divali, whereas Divali is a bank holiday in India.

In the UK, some of the practices of Christmas have been adopted for Divali, such as sending Divali cards. This is much more common amongst British Sikhs than in India.

The Basics

1. Why do Sikhs celebrate festivals?
2. Explain the origins of Divali.
3. Describe the different ways that Sikhs celebrate Divali.
4. 'It is more important for Sikhs in the UK to celebrate festivals than for those in India.' Explain arguments to agree and disagree with this statement.

Vaisakhi

Vaisakhi (also known as Baisakhi) is the biggest of all Sikh festivals and takes place in April each year. Its focus is the founding of the Khalsa by Guru Gobind Singh (called Guru Gobind Rai prior to this event). The focus of celebrations is the Khalsa, and Sikh duties.

Origins of Vaisakhi

Guru Gobind Rai led the Sikhs at a time when they were being treated badly by Hindu and Muslim rulers. He often spoke about Sikhs being prepared to fight for justice and against persecution and harassment. In 1699, at the Vaisakhi festival (a spring festival celebrated by both Hindus and Sikhs), he spoke to crowds of Sikhs about faith, courage and bravery. He asked if any of them would be prepared to die for what they believed in. Eventually, one person came forward, was taken into a tent, and the crowd heard the sound of a beheading. Guru Gobind Rai asked the same question four more times. Each time a person stepped forward and each time the crowd believed them to be stepping forward to their death. At the end, Guru Gobind Rai brought all five people out from the tent, still alive, dressed in saffron (yellow-orange) robes, with turbans and swords. He praised their faith and courage, saying they represented a new kind of Sikh – the Panj Pyare (Five Beloved Ones). They had shown their commitment to the principles Guru Gobind Rai lived by, not just blind faith: for example, by fighting unfairness wherever they saw it.

The Panj Pyare were five men from different groups within society, showing that everyone was welcome and equal. They would dress and act differently to show their new status – this meant they wore the Five Ks and followed a set of rules called the Rahit Maryada, or Code of Conduct. There were taboos they had to avoid, called the Kurahits. These five and others who joined them became known as the Khalsa. They also took on a new name – Singh for men, Kaur for women – to show their equality (see page 158). Guru Gobind Rai and his wife also joined them and he became known as Guru Gobind Singh. Since the Khalsa is able to make rules, it has the status of a Guru – all members of the Khalsa have to follow these rules.

The origins of Vaisakhi

Vaisakhi celebrations in Trafalgar Square

Topic 3.2 Practices

How Vaisakhi is celebrated

As with other festivals, an Akhand Path will be done in the lead-up to the day of Vaisakhi. The actual day begins with a service, starting very early in the gurdwara. It is the most popular day for people to join the Khalsa and the opportunity to receive **amrit** will be provided. The Guru Granth Sahib is brought out to be ritually washed, before being read. Five Khalsa Sikhs representing the Panj Pyare will read five verses of the Guru Granth Sahib (a daily duty, but here done for the festival). Amrit (sugar and water stirred with a kirpan sword and blessed) is distributed for everyone to take a sip, but the Khalsa Sikhs take five sips and restate their Khalsa vows. At noon, karah parshad (sacred pudding) is distributed to all, showing equality. At the end of the service, everyone attends the langar.

There may be a procession associated with Vaisakhi. This is led by the Panj Pyare, who may be on horseback. The whole community joins the procession, which is a joyful celebration of their religion. There may be dancing (bhangra and gidda styles), drummers and bands, as well as the singing of religious songs. As Sikhs are warriors who have taken a vow to fight against injustice, mock duels take place, including the use of swords. There will also be speeches about Vaisakhi – its origins, the Khalsa vows and how to be a devoted Sikh. There is a big emphasis on doing charitable work, or giving to charity, which comes from the teachings about fighting injustice, and respect for all life as God's creation.

It is also traditional to wear new clothes on this day and to give gifts and sweet boxes to relatives and friends.

Many Sikhs go to Amritsar to celebrate Vaisakhi at the centre of their religion. They can do voluntary work in the langar, listen to the Akhand Path at the Golden Temple, join the processions there and enjoy a massive firework display, which happens annually. At Amritsar, any Sikh is surrounded by those of their own faith, so they can enjoy an intense atmosphere of spirituality and celebration.

Celebrations in the UK

In the UK, Vaisakhi has been opened to the wider community of non-Sikhs. In major Sikh centres such as Birmingham and Coventry, there are processions and fairs in large parks – for example, at Handsworth Park in Birmingham, there are funfairs, food tents, arts and crafts, music tents and exhibitions.

Sikhs dressed as the Panj Pyare for the Vaisakhi procession

Vaisakhi is my favourite festival because it represents the greatest commitment to God. Sikhs join the Khalsa at this time, or retake their vows – as if this is the first day of your life.

For me, Vaisakhi is the most important festival. It celebrates the Khalsa and their bravery throughout history. They are warriors who still stand up for justice and for the religion.

I love Vaisakhi because all of my extended family meet up to exchange news and gifts. Then all the community comes together like an even bigger family. To me that sense of belonging is very important.

The Basics

1. For Vaisakhi, explain the following:
   a. the origins of the festival
   b. how the festival is celebrated, including in Sikh communities in the UK.
2. Explain why Sikhs might want to go to Amritsar to celebrate Vaisakhi.
3. 'Vaisakhi is the most important Sikh festival.' Do you agree? Explain arguments to show different points of view on that statement. Write a justified conclusion to show which point of view you find most persuasive.

Gurpurbs

> 'Now being full of loving devotion they celebrate the gurpurbs, and their acts of remembrance of God, charity and holy ablutions inspires others.' (Bhai Gurdas 1:7)

Gurpurbs are celebrations of events in the lives of the Gurus: 'gurpurb' actually means 'celebration of the Guru'. This includes births, deaths and martyrdoms. In India, there are also gurpurbs in the hometowns or places associated with marriage and other events in the lives of specific Gurus. The Guru Granth Sahib encourages gurpurbs by saying, 'Only worthy descendants remember the deeds of the elders' (GGS). Gurpurbs honour those they remember, emphasising the importance of their contribution to the Sikh religion.

In the UK, gurpurbs are one-day celebrations, often focused on the religious messages of the event and/or Guru. They usually take place on the Sunday nearest to the actual date; whereas in India, they are three-day festivals, and a holiday is usually given by the state government so the actual day can be celebrated by all.

The main gurpurbs are:

- Guru Nanak's birthday (November). Guru Nanak was the founder of Sikhism, whose poems and hymns shaped the faith and are found in the Guru Granth Sahib.
- Guru Arjan's birthday (May). Guru Arjan was the fifth Guru. He laid the foundation stones of the Golden Temple, and decided it would have four doors (one on each side) to show that everyone was welcome (see page 152). He set up the practice of daswandh (tithing) (see page 134). He compiled the Adi Granth, which collated hymns of the Gurus before him.
- Guru Gobind Singh's birthday (January). Guru Gobind Singh was the final of the Ten Gurus. He set up the Khalsa (see page 147), reinforcing Sikh teachings of equality in a very practical way. He was responsible for the compilation of the Guru Granth Sahib, and for it being seen as the 'living Guru', replacing humans as a teacher and guide for Sikhs.
- the martyrdom of Guru Arjan (June). Guru Arjan is seen as having created the tradition of selfless sacrifice through being killed for his religion (martyrdom). He was ordered to convert to Islam by the Emperor Jahangir. Having refused, he was tortured in a bid to break his will and his faith. However, he never renounced his beliefs, and died as a result of the torture.
- the martyrdom of Guru Tegh Bahadur (November). Guru Tegh Bahadur was the ninth Guru. He spoke out against the forced conversions of Hindus and non-Muslims to Islam. When three prominent Hindus sought his help against this, he told them to tell the Emperor they would convert when Guru Tegh Bahadur did. He was arrested along with some of his followers. They were tortured and killed in front of him to get him to convert to Islam. He refused and was publicly beheaded – for defending the rights of anyone to have their own beliefs.

Celebrating Guru Nanak's birthday (jayanti)

For me, Guru Nanak's birthday is the most important. He began my religion, so even though I celebrate others, this is the first.

For me, I like Guru Arjan's birthday best. I was in Amritsar – which he had built – for the gurpurb. Made a big impression, lots of good memories.

For me, it is Guru Tegh Bahadur's martyrdom. Standing up against injustice, and fighting for the right to choose your religion – such important principles in the world still.

Topic 3.2 Practices

Guru Arjan

Guru Tegh Bahadur

Guru Gobind Singh

Guru Nanak's birthday

Celebrating Guru Nanak's birthday

Guru Nanak's birthday is perhaps the most important gurpurb as he founded Sikhism. While there is no set way to celebrate, there will be certain activities involved. An Akhand Path will lead up to the day of the gurpurb. An act of worship begins when the Akhand Path ends (early morning), lasting until
mid-afternoon. Stories from the life of Guru Nanak are told, perhaps to emphasise a particular message for that time – for example, stories of his youth if the congregation is young, or of his devotion to encourage the congregation in theirs. Hymns in praise of Guru Nanak will be sung. A langar will, of course, complete the day. Some gurdwaras also do the evening prayers (see page 142), followed by kirtan until about 1.20 a.m. (the time Guru Nanak is said to have been born). Many gurdwaras hold a procession on the day before the gurpurb, akin to those held at Vaisakhi.

The Basics

1. What is a gurpurb?
2. Explain why Sikhs hold gurpurbs.
3. Describe the gurpurb celebrations for Guru Nanak's birthday.
4. 'Guru Nanak's birthday is the only gurpurb Sikhs need to celebrate.' Do you agree? Explain arguments showing different points of view.

Visiting sacred places

For Sikhs, there is no such duty as pilgrimage, even though many Sikhs do choose to make special journeys. Guru Nanak said that physical pilgrimage is unnecessary – 'God's name is the real place of pilgrimage', so focusing on God (Nam Japna, see page 141) is the only necessary form. This is because Nam Japna requires a spiritual journey within oneself, and this is more difficult and more rewarding than travelling anywhere. It is more difficult because it requires self-discipline, in that a person lives through the Sikh virtues. It is more rewarding because it leads to the five stages of mukti (see pages 121–123). Similarly, the Guru Granth Sahib states that, 'There is no sacred shrine equal to the Guru', suggesting that a Sikh should focus their energy on the words of the Guru Granth Sahib.

Guru Gobind Singh advised Sikhs that the only reason to go on pilgrimage is to visit gurdwaras. He did not tell Sikhs to visit historical places, or places linked to the lives of the Gurus. Many of these do now have important gurdwaras close by, and so have become places for Sikhs to visit, especially Amritsar (see page 152). The Guru Granth Sahib recognises that people will make pilgrimage – Sikhism is an Indian religion, and Hinduism gives great importance to pilgrimage, so it is natural that many early Sikhs might be influenced by this. However, the Guru Granth Sahib makes the point that anyone who goes on pilgrimage without being humble, and without focusing on God, will not gain good karma for their actions – 'their actions are useless'.

Having said that, Sikhs do make journeys to sacred places, especially in the Punjab region of India and Pakistan, to the towns and cities which are linked to the Gurus. There are many reasons:

- to visit places of historical importance to Sikhs, e.g. Nankana Sahib in Pakistan, where Guru Nanak was born, with its gurdwara (for the 550th anniversary of the Guru's birth, Nankana Sahib has been awarded a university by the Pakistan government)
- to learn more about the history of their religion, e.g. by visiting the Sikh museum at Amritsar
- to take part in worship at sacred gurdwaras, such as visiting the gurdwara at Anandpur Sahib where Guru Gobind Singh set up the Khalsa
- to do sewa, e.g. by working in the langar at Amritsar
- to join the festival celebrations, e.g. the carnival-like atmosphere of Vaisakhi at Amritsar.

Bathing at Amritsar

Going into the Golden Temple for worship

Firework celebrations for Vaisakhi at Amritsar

The Basics

1. Explain different Sikh teachings about pilgrimage.
2. Explain why Sikhs might make journeys to sacred places.
3. 'Pilgrimage has no value in Sikhism.' Evaluate that statement, showing you have thought about more than one point of view. Write a justified conclusion.

Topic 3.2 Practices

Amritsar – Harimandir Sahib (the Golden Temple)

Amritsar is the largest and most important city in Punjab state. For Sikhs, it is the centre of Khalistan, which is their hoped-for independent Sikh state, and the centre of Sikh spirituality.

The Golden Temple is covered in sheets of gold – hence its name. It has doors on all four sides – to welcome everyone/anyone (equality). A person must step down to the floor of the Golden Temple, and the Guru Granth Sahib is on a raised palki, ensuring each person must look up to it (showing respect).

The whole Golden Temple complex is built on land given to Guru Ram Das by the Emperor Akbar. He created a small pool. Later, Guru Arjan built the Harimandir Sahib (Golden Temple) in its centre, with a single walkway to reach it. All the other buildings came later.

There is a continuous reading of the Guru Granth Sahib daily at the Golden Temple. The holy book is kept in the Akal Takht – a gurdwara which stands facing the Golden Temple – from where it is processed each morning and returned each night.

Activities at Amritsar include: bathing in the pool (for exercise and contemplation); meditating in the Golden Temple or facing it (Nam Japna); visiting the many shrines and memorials which are part of the complex (paying respect); joining in worship in diwan halls (duty); sharing or working in the langar (equality and sewa); visiting the museum and speaking with other Sikhs (learning about the religion).

Amritsar is at its busiest for Sikh festivals, hosting three-day fairs (melas), being decorated with thousands of lights, holding huge firework displays. Many Sikhs want to experience Vaisakhi there in the home of Sikhism.

Tourism is huge at Amritsar – it is not only Sikhs who go there. However, every person is welcomed, allowed to move freely, and is fed at the langar. This is a sacred place for Sikhs, but they share it with anyone, emphasising the message of equality and the acceptance of all. An average of 100,000 visitors per day go, all of whom are provided for at the langar.

Amritsar has seen the martyrdom of many Sikhs who tried to defend their sacred place. For example, massacres in 1919 and 1984 are well-documented. It represents the Sikh belief in and fight for justice.

The Basics

1. What is the Harimandir Sahib?
2. Explain why many Sikhs want to go to Amritsar.
3. Describe different activities Sikhs carry out at Amritsar.
4. 'All Sikhs should visit the Golden Temple at Amritsar.' How far do you agree with that statement? Explain arguments and use teachings to show more than one point of view, before coming to a justified conclusion.

Sikh birth and naming ceremonies

These ceremonies are both done as soon as possible after a baby has been born. The birth ceremony will be done at the hospital or home, while the naming ceremony is done at the gurdwara.

Both ceremonies are important because the parents are making the statement that their child is to be brought up a Sikh and are showing their thanks to God for the gift of the child. As the Guru Granth Sahib says, 'The True Lord has sent this gift.' They are involving God and their religion from the very start of their child's life – which itself reflects the faith and devotion of the parents to God and the Sikh way.

The Sikh birth ceremony (Janam sanskar)

This ceremony is arranged as soon as possible after the baby has been born, so that it does not die without having been brought into the Sikh way of life.

Amrit is prepared in an iron bowl by stirring sugar crystals into water with a kirpan (sword) while reciting prayers. In this process, the water is blessed and infused with the power of God's words.

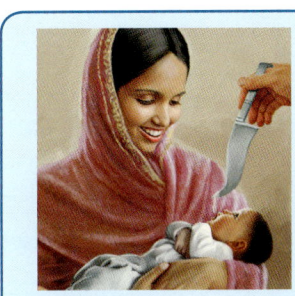

Five drops of the amrit are dropped into the baby's mouth from the end of the kirpan. The amrit is sweet, representing the hope that the child will be sweet-natured. The first thing the child has tasted is holy.

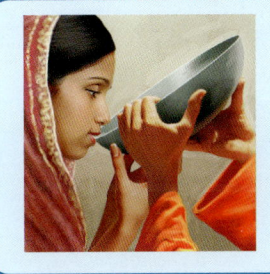

The mother drinks the remaining amrit. She is reaffirming her commitment to Sikhism, but is also taking the blessings of God.

The father whispers the Mool Mantra and the Gurmantar ('Waheguru') into the baby's ears. These are the most important prayers and are the first things the baby hears. This emphasises the importance of the beliefs of Sikhism.

The Basics

1. What is the name of the Sikh birth ceremony?
2. Describe the birth ceremony for Sikhs.
3. Explain the significance of each part of the birth ceremony.
4. 'The birth ceremony is the most important aspect of becoming a Sikh.' Do you agree? Explain your arguments, showing you have thought about more than one point of view.

Topic 3.2 Practices

The Sikh naming ceremony (Naam Karan)

This ceremony is described in the Rahit Maryada (Sikh Code of Conduct), so will follow the same process in each gurdwara. It takes place as soon as mother and baby are fit to attend. The whole community are then involved in the naming of the baby, which is a way for them to acceot their share of responsibility for its upbringing.

Taking the baby to the gurdwara to be named

The process	Its meaning and significance
Everyone attends the gurdwara – parents, family and Sangat.	This shows that everyone welcomes this new child to the community and is happy for the birth. This recognises the belief that God has given the gift of a child: 'The True Lord has sent this gift.'
Parents prostrate before the Guru Granth Sahib and make offerings such as money (dhan sewa), karah parshad and a romalla (cloth to adorn the Guru Granth Sahib).	This shows their thanks to all – money is for the gurdwara, karah parshad for the congregation, romalla for the Guru Granth Sahib. Many families also provide the langar.
Prayers are offered on behalf of the child, and for the child.	All who attend should pray; it is a duty – the child is too young, so this is done for the child. Prayers for the child are to ask for a long and happy life, and that the child will be gurmukh.
Holy water is sprinkled onto the eyes of the child.	This shows the hope that the child will see the truth, and know God.
The granthi opens the Guru Granth Sahib at a random page. They read the first word from the page, and its first letter will be the first letter of the child's name. The parents announce their choice of name, which is cheered by the congregation.	This shows the belief that God guides the decision on a child's name. The cheering of the congregation shows their acceptance and praise for God's guidance.
The child also gains the name 'Singh' for a boy or 'Kaur' for a girl.	Most Sikh names are gender-neutral (used for both male and female), so the name Singh or Kaur helps to identify the gender of the child through their name. It also shows equality (see page 158).
Prayers are read, including the Ardas and Anand Sahib.	This is part of the duty to worship in the gurdwara and allowing the child to hear these prayers in Sangat for the first time.
Karah parshad is issued to all, and the langar welcomes all.	Both are part of normal gurdwara practice, but by being paid for by the parents they also show thanks to the community, and equality of all.

Taking my new baby to the gurdwara allowed everyone in the Sangat to see her, and to welcome her into Sikhism. I know they are her family and will help me to look after her. This makes it more important than the birth ceremony.

Whilst the naming ceremony is important – through the hukam we receive a name for him, and everyone welcomes him. For me, the birth ceremony is more important. It is a more intimate ceremony, and it makes him a Sikh from birth.

The Basics

1. What is the Sikh name for the naming ceremony?
2. Describe what happens in the naming ceremony.
3. Explain why different aspects of the ceremony are important.
4. 'It is through the naming ceremony that parents show their thanks to God for their child.' Evaluate that statement.

Amrit Sanskar – the Sikh initiation ceremony

Guru Gobind Singh and the Panj Pyare, who formed the first Khalsa

Look back to page 147, which describes the origins of the Sikh Vaisakhi festival. The Sikh initiation ceremony dates back to the same event. Guru Gobind Singh spoke to crowds of Sikhs on that day in 1699, and talked about commitment to Sikhism and devotion to God. He asked which people were willing to die for their beliefs. One-by-one, five men stepped forward. They each entered a tent – Guru Gobind Singh allowed the crowd to think they had been killed. Finally, all five exited the tent with Guru Gobind Singh, dressed alike in new uniforms. He introduced them as the Panj Pyare (Five Beloved Ones), who were to represent a new level of commitment for Sikhs.

The Amrit Sanskar initiation ceremony is seen as a pathway to a purer, more spiritual life, as the promises made in the ceremony reflect a deeper commitment to the religion. From that point on, those who have undertaken the Amrit Sanskar ceremony are Khalsa Sikhs, and they follow a disciplinary code in living lives dedicated to achieving mukti.

The ceremony

Sikhs being initiated into the Khalsa

The ceremony takes place in the gurdwara, but – other than the initiates (those who will go through the ceremony) – the ceremony is only open to members of the Khalsa, so is often done in a room other than the main prayer hall. Everyone who attends wears the Five Ks, and five specially chosen Khalsa Sikhs will be dressed in saffron robes, in the style instructed by Guru Gobind Singh. They represent the Panj Pyare.

- There are readings from the Guru Granth Sahib.
- One of the Panj Pyare reads out the duties of Khalsa Sikhs – the initiates must agree to follow them.
- Prayers are said, including the Ardas prayer.
- The initiates kneel with their right knee to show they are willing to fight for the religion. This is the chivalrous 'heroic pose', also adopted by people when knighted by Her Majesty, the Queen, and people proposing marriage.
- The five banis (daily prayers) are recited (see page 142), during which amrit is prepared. Amrit is water to which sugar crystals have been added; this mixture is then stirred with a kirpan (sword). The amrit is made in an iron bowl, representing strength. Hymns are chanted by those present, showing their devotion.
- Each initiate drinks five handfuls of amrit. They will also have five handfuls sprinkled on their hair, eyes and hands. This is a form of blessing.
- More prayers are recited by all.
- Each person shares karah parshad (sacred pudding), which is blessed food or ambrosia. This shows equality.

Topic 3.2 Practices

Extra commitments

Becoming a Khalsa Sikh involves taking on extra commitments to those that all religious Sikhs follow.

1. Take the name Kaur (princess) if female or Singh (lionheart) if male. Many also take the name Khalsa, as it is common for Sikhs to have the names Kaur and Singh from birth.

2. Accept the Guru Granth Sahib as a teacher and guide, studying it daily.

3. All Khalsa Sikhs will wear the Five Ks. Many Khalsa Sikhs wear a loose-fitting shirt and trousers with wide belt for ceremonies and processions, as instructed by Guru Gobind Singh.

4. Live by the three principles of Nam Japna (meditating on the name of God, getting up before dawn to bathe then pray, reciting the five daily prayers – see page 142), Kirat Karni (living a truthful and honest lifestyle, which aims to be more gurmukh) and Vand Chakna (sharing with others, including daswandh, which is giving 10 per cent of income to the gurdwara).

5. Vow to not break the Code of Conduct, which is found in the Rahit Maryada. Prohibited activities are called the Kurahits – these are: not to cut hair, not to eat meat killed in a sacrificial manner, not to drink alcohol/take intoxicants and not to have sex before or outside marriage.

6. Carry out all forms of sewa, including by being an active member of the Sangat, being available to help others in the community and especially to help in religious ceremonies and celebrations.

> 'Waheguru ji ka Khalsa – The Khalsa belongs to God.'

This is a Sikh greeting. It says a lot more than the words show. It is a belief which encourages the vows of the Amrit Sanskar to be spoken and thereafter kept. It shows that the Khalsa is a status which God has created, and so which is sacred. By referring to God, it reminds the speaker and listener that they are representing God as they live their life, so must always do the right thing.

About the Five Ks

Kesh is uncut hair, which is covered by a turban. It shows respect for God.

Kara is a steel bangle. Steel represents strength; the circle of the bangle represents God – without beginning or end.

Kangha is a comb, which represents cleanliness.

Kirpan is a sword, to show a Sikh will fight for justice. As the legal length is restricted to a few inches, it typically looks more like a dagger. A proper-sized kirpan is often worn by Sikh grooms at their wedding, and by Khalsa Sikhs at festival celebrations.

Kaccha are loose-fitting shorts, representing modesty and the willingness to fight in battle.

Amritdhari and sahajdhari Sikhs

Those Sikhs who have undergone the Amrit Sanskar and become members of the Khalsa are also known as amritdhari, which means 'having taken nectar' (see page 155). They have decided to take on the extra commitments through a formal ceremony, and in the eyes of the Khalsa are full members of the Sangat. This is a public commitment, to which they can be held – it is not just between them and God. If they break their vows, they have to face the members of the Khalsa. There they will have to explain their actions, and make apologies to the Khalsa, who will then decide whether there should be a punishment, such as extra sewa. They would then have to go through an Amrit Sanskar to be readmitted to the Khalsa.

British law protects a Sikh's right to wear their turban in their job. Khalsa Sikhs must wear turbans

Not every Sikh decides to take the Amrit Sanskar, often because they are not ready to make the commitment at that point in their life. For example, a convert to Sikhism would need time to study the religion and learn to practise it before they could make what is a life-changing commitment. There is no requirement to become amritdhari, which means no Sikh has to do that – it will be their decision, accepted by the community, whatever it is. Those who have not gone through the Amrit Sanskar are called sahajdhari, meaning 'slow adopter'. These Sikhs have chosen to follow the religion, believe in the Ten Gurus and the Guru Granth Sahib, join in worship and live by the three principles. They might cut their hair and are not bound by the Khalsa vows, so would not face a punishment for breaking any of them. There is an expectation that eventually sahajdhari Sikhs will take the Amrit Sanskar – it is just a matter of when the time is right for them.

I was brought up a Sikh, and became more deeply interested in my faith as I got older. I came to the point where I wanted to show fuller devotion to God, and live by the Sikh Code. So I studied and readied myself to be fit to be amritdhari. Having gone through the Amrit Sanskar, I now keep the 5Ks, and do much more to live as a Sikh, as well as to help others do that.

I was not brought up a Sikh, but later learned about Sikhism. What I learned made sense to me. Now I study the scriptures, and Sikh practices with help from my gurdwara and the Sangat. I think that eventually I will seek to be amritdhari, but I am not ready for that yet. I need to learn more, live longer as a Sikh and then I will be worthy of that commitment. I am sahajdhari.

The Basics

1. Explain the origins of the Khalsa.
2. Describe an Amrit Sanskar ceremony.
3. Explain why it is true that amritdhari Sikhs should be role models for their community.
4. Using an example, explain why a Sikh might choose to remain sahajdhari.
5. 'Every Sikh should join the Khalsa.' Do you agree? Explain arguments showing different points of view, before reaching a justified conclusion.

Topic 3.2 Practices

Kaur and Singh

You have seen that Kaur and Singh are names given to a child at a birth ceremony (see page 153), and that these names are taken at the Amrit Sanskar (see page 155). When Guru Gobind Singh set up the Khalsa, he gave these names to the Panj Pyare and others who also joined the Khalsa. He himself took on the name (his actual name before the Khalsa was Guru Gobind Rai), as did his wife, Mata Jito (becoming Mata Sahib Kaur).

Singh means 'lionheart', coming from the word simha. All males were to take this name, which showed their warrior nature, as Sikhism – by necessity and for healthy living – was a warrior religion. The warrior aspect is especially shown through the Sikh nihangs (or Akalis), the Sikh armed warrior order which was started by Guru Hargobind (the 6th Guru). In Sikh history, they have fought many battles and are considered ferocious warriors.

Kaur literally means 'prince', as it is believed to come from the word 'kanwar'. Women – for the first time – had their own identity, rather than being known by the name of their father/husband.

Why are the new names important?

- Names often link to class, and this was especially true in India where the caste system was very strong in Guru Gobind Singh's time. Guru Gobind was making real what Guru Nanak had said: 'Caste is preposterous … Only the One (God) gives support to all.' The caste system split the whole of society into four groups, plus a group not in the system but below it. Originally, it was just a classification of jobs within society, but over history that became very rigid. People were unable to change from the caste into which they had been born. They were denied opportunities because of their caste, for example, not being allowed into all temples, and being barred from specific jobs. Especially those in lower castes faced prejudice and discrimination because of their caste status. There was a belief in ritual pollution, which meant that castes would not mix, eat together, socialise and so on. If they did, then lengthy rituals to reverse that impurity were needed (according to Hindu religious law), which people did not want to go through. This further reinforced the barriers in society. Sikhism wiped all this away, and the names were part of how that was done.
- For females, Kaur gives them an identity of their own – separate from and independent to their father or husband. In the society of the time, women had no rights, were 'owned' by their father and then their husband, were expected to keep the house and have children, were left uneducated and were even expected to throw themselves onto their husband's funeral pyre (sati). Sikhism rejected all this; 'Kaur' signified that difference for Sikhs.
- Taking a new name after an initiation is like a new start in life – hence the name shows the new start and new commitment.

> **The Basics**
>
> 1. What do the names Singh and Kaur mean?
> 2. When would a Sikh obtain either of these names, and what is the importance of them each time?
> 3. Explain why these names are important.
> 4. 'Having the name "Kaur" or "Singh" shows the most commitment to Sikhism.' Do you agree? Explain arguments to show different points of view. Write a justified conclusion.

Getting prepared

The Practices section of an exam paper is made up of five questions. Here you can read the wording which is used, some tips for doing well and some examples of each.

2.1 question – Multi-choice: 1 mark

For example:

A Which **one** of the following is the Sikh term for meditating on the name of God?

- **a** Vand Chakna
- **b** Mool Mantra
- **c** Nam Japna
- **d** Amrit Sanskar

B Which **one** of the following is **not** a Sikh festival?

- **a** Gurpurb
- **b** Vaisakhi
- **c** Divali
- **d** Amritsar

Tip
Lots of these are definition questions – so make sure you know the meanings of all key words.

2.2 question – 'Give two…': 2 marks

This tests knowledge (not understanding).

For example:

A Give **two** features of the gurdwara.

B Give **two** Sikh festivals.

Tips
Keep your answer to a minimum – give only two words, or phrases. Example A could be answered simply by 'palki and takht', or in a longer version, 'The first feature is the takht, which is at the front and everyone faces, which is the canopy over the place where the Guru Granth Sahib is laid for an act of worship. The second feature is the palki, which is under the takht, which is the actual "throne" that the Guru Granth Sahib is laid on to be read in an act of worship.' The longer the answer, the more time it takes from your other answers.

The exam paper gives prompts of '1' and '2' to remind you to give two answers.

2.3 question – Diversity: 4 marks

This is testing your knowledge of the similarities and differences within religion – how different Sikhs practise their religion differently; or different elements of something.

For example:

A Explain **two** contrasting roles of the Sangat.

B Explain **two** similar ways in which Sikhs express their love for the divine.

Tips
You get a mark for each way, plus an additional mark as you explain each of those ways – 2 + 2.

'Contrasting' in the question just means 'different' – you are not being asked to write about opposites.

Using examples is a good way to explain in this question because it shows you know more than just the key words/terms.

Topic 3.2 Practices

2.4 question – Practices related to teachings: 5 marks

This question wants to know how what Sikhs do links to what they believe, so you have to be able to refer to teachings in your answer if you want to get full marks.

For example:

A Explain **two** contrasting ways in which Sikhs worship God. Refer to sacred writings or another source of Sikh beliefs and teachings in your answer.

B Explain **two** contrasting ways in which a Sikh might fulfil the duty of sewa. Refer to sacred writings or another source of Sikh beliefs and teachings in your answer.

Tips

You get a mark for each point you make, plus an additional mark for each explanation. The final mark is for giving a relevant teaching. As this question is about practices, it is often difficult to think of a teaching which is readily relevant – at times you might have to give a lot of explanation to clearly show how your chosen teaching is relevant.

'Teaching' doesn't mean you have to give quotations; you could give beliefs or concepts.

2.5 question – Analysis and evaluation: 12 marks

For example:

A 'Every Sikh should make a pilgrimage to Amritsar once in their lifetime.'

Evaluate this statement.

In your answer, you should:
- refer to Sikh teaching
- give reasoned arguments to support this statement
- give reasoned arguments to support a different point of view
- reach a justified conclusion.

B 'Sikh festivals are more about fun than religion.'

Evaluate this statement.

In your answer, you should:
- refer to Sikh teaching
- give reasoned arguments to support this statement
- give reasoned arguments to support a different point of view
- reach a justified conclusion.

Tips

The question wording gives you a great way to check your answer – use the different bullet points to check you have done all the things you need to do.

If the statement says something is 'best', 'most important' or gives any kind of value words, then challenge it by saying, 'It depends what is meant by…'. This is a good technique to make your brain think more widely in answering.

You have to give an agree side and a disagree side in your answer – failure to do so will cost you any mark above Level 2 (6 marks out of 12). Similarly, failure to explain anything you write will also keep you stuck at Level 2 at best.

By giving and explaining all arguments for one side, then doing the same for the other side, you write a clearer answer which is easier to mark.

'Justified conclusion' is a posh way of asking you to say whether the agree or disagree side is stronger, and why you think that. It doesn't mean for you to rewrite arguments you gave already! So one side might have more arguments, might be clearer, might be more compelling/persuasive or might fit with what you already think. These are all useful ways to justify a conclusion. Sometimes, you just can't decide – and it is okay to say that as well.

Sikhism glossary

Akhand Path the non-stop reading of the Guru Granth Sahib in its entirety

amritdhari those Sikhs who have gone through the Amrit Sanskar (amrit ceremony) and taken vows as Sikhs

amrit nectar; water and sugar stirred with a kirpan

Amrit Sanskar ceremony of initiation into the Sikh faith, during which a Sikh makes vows and becomes amritdhari

daswandh a tithe; the giving of 10 per cent of earnings to the gurdwara

dhan one of three forms of sewa; financial

Dharam Khand first of Five Khands (levels of liberation); realm of righteous action

dharma duty; religious code of behaviour

Divali Sikh festival; recalls event when Guru Hargobind was released from prison, securing the release of 52 princes at the same time

Five Ks five items worn by Sikhs as symbols of their faith

Five Khands five levels of liberation

Five Vices five negative character traits which act as barriers to achieving mukti

Gian Khand second of Five Khands (levels of liberation); realm of knowledge

granthi person who reads the Guru Granth Sahib during worship

gurdwara Sikh place of worship

gurmukh God-centred; living devoted to God

gurpurbs celebrations of events in the lives of the Gurus

Guru Granth Sahib (GGS) the holy book of Sikhism

haumai pride/ego

karah parshad sacred pudding; given to worshippers at the gurdwara

Karam Khand fourth of Five Khands (levels of liberation); realm of grace

karma the law of action

Khalsa Sikhs who have taken vows of initiation

Kirat Karni one of the three pillars of Sikh life; honest living

langar communal kitchen

man one of three forms of sewa; mental/attitude

manmukh self/man-centred; selfishness

Mool Mantra hymn describing God; written by Guru Nanak

mukti liberation from rebirth; complete loss of ego/pride

Nam Japna meditating on the name of God

palki canopy which is over the throne on which the Guru Granth Sahib is placed in the gurdwara

Panj Pyare Five Beloved Ones; the five selected by Guru Gobind Singh to begin a new level of devotion

ragis musicians who play in gurdwara services to help worshippers understand the Guru Granth Sahib

Rahit Maryada the Sikh Code of Conduct

Sach Khand fifth of Five Khands (levels of liberation); realm of truth

sahajdhari Sikhs who have not undergone the Amrit Sanskar ceremony

Sangat religious community of Sikhs

Saram Khand third of Five Khands (levels of liberation); realm of spiritual endeavour

sewa selfless service to others

takht the throne on which the Guru Granth Sahib is rested for services in the gurdwara

tan a form of sewa; physical

Vaisakhi Sikh festival to commemorate the founding of the Khalsa

Vand Chakna sharing with others; one of the pillars of Sikh life

Religious, philosophical and ethical studies

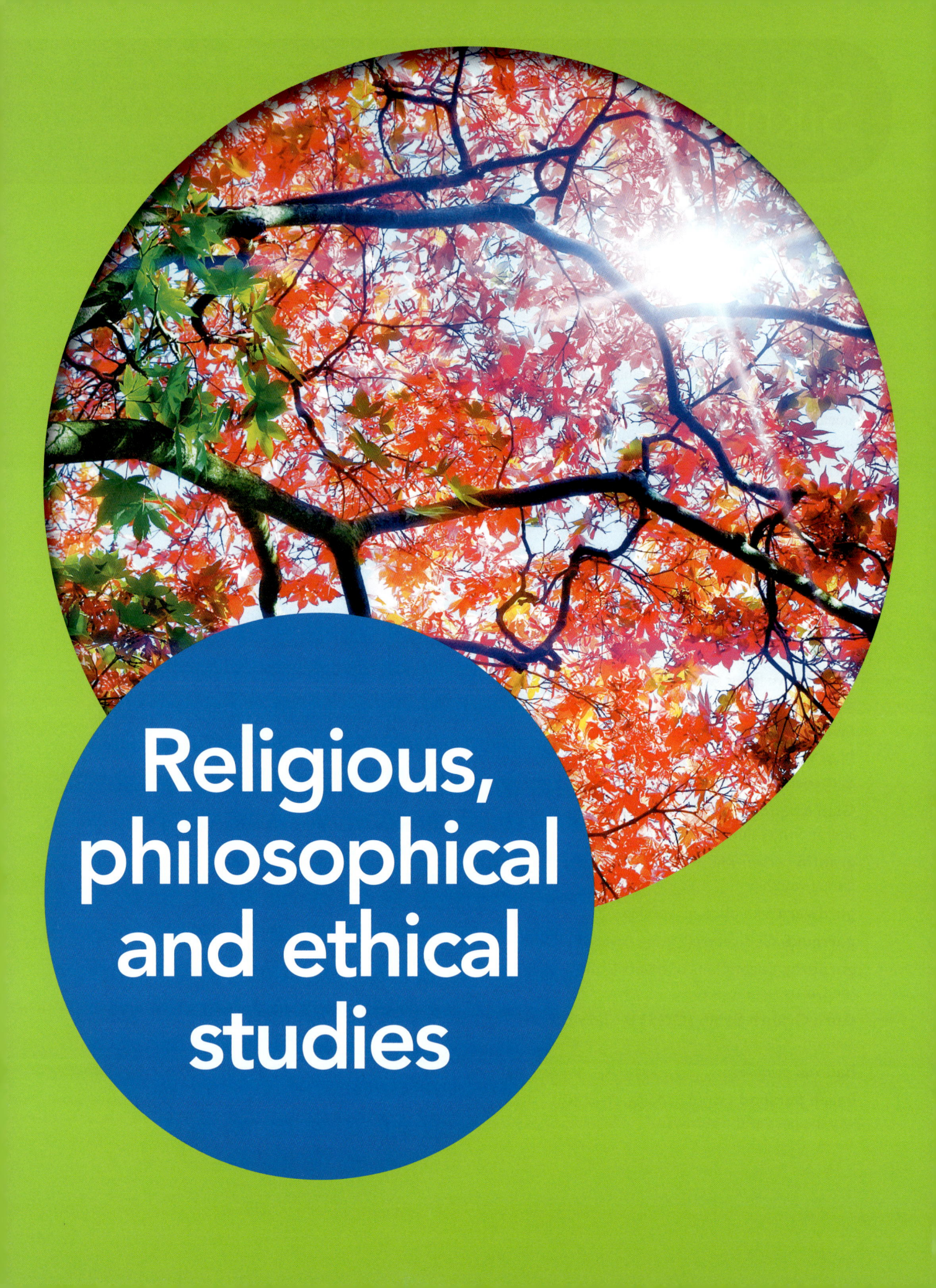

What does the specification say about the themes?

Notes to teachers and students

In all the Themes A–F, you have to study the topics from two different religious perspectives or traditions. These can be consistently the same two throughout all the themes or they can be different religions/traditions for different topics, therefore referring to as many as you want. However, one of the areas of exam question focus will be 'contrasting views' and in these questions you must study two religious traditions. The way to spot this question is that it mentions 'contemporary Britain' in the question, and 'main religious tradition of Great Britain' in the question rider. One of these must be the main religious tradition in Britain (Christianity). This means you **must** give a Christian perspective (generally or a specific denomination) as one of the two religious traditions you refer to in your 'contrasting question' answers. The other might be a different religion or a different Christian tradition.

In each theme three topics are specifically listed in the specification as requiring you to know contrasting beliefs. This means that only these topics can be asked about in the exam through this specific form of question. The table at the foot of the page lists them for you and each of the contrasting areas are addressed in this book at the end of each theme.

In answering these contrasting areas questions for each of the four themes you have studied, you **must** present Christianity as one perspective. It is the main religious tradition of Great Britain.

> **How this question is worded**
> The wording for the question about contrasting views is always written in these two parts:
> - 'Explain two contrasting beliefs in contemporary Britain about …'
> - In your answer you should refer to the main religious tradition of Great Britain and one or more other religious tradition.

> Marks will be awarded as shown in AQA's mark scheme. See the AQA website for details.

What are the 'traditions'?
- They might be religions in their own right – Christianity, Buddhism, Hinduism, Islam, Judaism and Sikhism.
- They might be denominations of Christianity – Roman Catholics, Orthodox, Protestant, such as Anglican (Church of England) or Methodist, or non-Conformist, such as Quakers or Salvation Army.

> **Note**: If one of the chosen themes is Theme C, reference has to be made to Christianity (or a tradition within it) and non-religious beliefs such as atheism or humanism.

Theme A	Theme B	Theme C	Theme D	Theme E	Theme F
Contraception	Abortion	Visions	Violence	Corporal punishment	Status of women in religion
Sex before marriage	Euthanasia	Miracles	Weapons of mass destruction	Death penalty	The use of wealth
Homosexual relationships	Animal experimentation	Nature as general revelation	Pacifism	Forgiveness	Freedom of religious expression

What does the specification say about the themes?

The religious bit …

Religion and religious people have opinions on all issues, just as you do. As this is an RS course, you are going to see the attitudes of the six major religions to the issues studied. Make sure you understand what those attitudes are and what they are based on; in other words, the beliefs and teachings of the religions. In this book, you will be given a small number of beliefs and teachings for each religion on each theme. Quite often, you can use these teachings in a few different themes. If a teaching will apply to more than one theme then you should use it.

Below are some general teachings which you can apply to all the different themes. This cuts down the overall number of teachings you have to learn and ensures that those that you do use, you understand well. However, it is best to use beliefs and teachings which are specific to the themes, as well as the general ones. Do not forget to learn some of those when you meet them later. Copy them into the front of your notebook or file. Then use them as the basis for your work. When you study a theme, refer back to these to help you work out what the attitude of a believer will be to that theme.

☸ Buddhism

1. Rebirth and kamma – our words, thoughts and deeds create energies which shape our future rebirths. We need to make sure these are positive.
2. The Five Precepts (guidelines for living). These are: not harming others (ahimsa); using language kindly; not taking what is not freely given; not clouding our minds; no sexual misconduct.
3. Compassion (loving kindness).
4. The Noble Eightfold Path – the Buddha's system of self-discipline which gives an ethical basis to our actions – for example, Right Speech (using language kindly); Right Action (acting to help, not hurt, others).

ॐ Hinduism

Hindu holy books list many virtues. These include:
1. Ahimsa (non-violence).
2. Self-discipline.
3. Tolerance.
4. Service to others.
5. Compassion.
6. Providing shelter/support to others.
7. Respect for all life.
8. Wisdom.
9. Honesty with others and oneself.
10. Cleanliness.

✝ Christianity

1. Jesus' two key teachings: Love God; Love your neighbour.
2. Equality of all, because in Genesis we are told that God made each of us.
3. Justice (fairness) since everyone is equal, everyone deserves fairness.
4. Forgiveness and love are ideas taught by Jesus and shown in his actions.
5. Belief that God created the world, so it is special as is all life in it. Hence stewardship is an important duty.

☪ Islam

1. The ummah – brotherhood of all Muslims. This means that all Muslims are equal, and deserve equal respect and treatment.
2. That everyone has to follow duties set by Allah (God) – for example, the Five Pillars or Ten Obligations.
3. Shari'ah Law, which is Muslim law stemming from the Qur'an and Hadith and is applied to modern life by Islamic scholars.
4. The afterlife – that Allah has created a paradise which people are rewarded with after death if they have been morally good. Allah has also created a hell, where sinners will be punished.

Religious, philosophical and ethical studies

☪ Judaism

The Ten Commandments which are found in the Torah:
1. Love only God.
2. Make no idols of God.
3. Do not take God's name in vain.
4. Keep the Sabbath holy.
5. Respect your parents.
6. Do not kill.
7. Do not steal.
8. Do not commit adultery.
9. Do not tell lies.
10. Do not be jealous of what others have.

In addition, Jews keep 613 mitzvot, or laws which are all found in the Torah (the holiest of Jewish scriptures, considered the word of God). The mitzvot cover all aspects of life and worship.

☬ Sikhism

1. Sikhism teaches that the divine spark is within all forms of life, so all life is sacred and should be protected.
2. God created everything, so all should be looked after.
3. The absolute equality of all – regardless of class, gender, religion – was taught by all the Gurus.
4. The Khalsa vows – meditation and service to God; not to use intoxicants; not to eat meat which hasn't been ritually slaughtered; to fight for justice.
5. Sewa (selfless service to others) is a religious duty for Sikhs.
6. Sikh ethical virtues – sharing with others, including tithing (daswandh); dutifulness; prudence; justice; tolerance; temperance; chastity; patience; contentment; detachment and humility.

Tasks

Here are some ways that you can help yourself to learn and remember these teachings:
- Check with your teacher which religious traditions you are studying.
- Create a cue card for your religious traditions with the teachings written on them from the boxes above.
- Learn one a day so that you are familiar with each of them, as you will need them in all types of questions.
- Have them with you in lessons to refer to.
- Carry them in your school bag or in your school planner, so you can access them easily.
- Your teacher might give you specific teachings as you study each theme which you can add to the cards.
- The greater diversity of teachings you can refer to, the better your answers will be.
- If you learn them over the duration of the course it will make your final revision much easier as you lead up to your exams.

4 Theme A: Relationships and families

Key elements of this theme

This theme is about personal and sexual relationships, including **heterosexual** and **homosexual** relationships. It goes on to explore how people show their **commitment** through marriage and other forms of **cohabitation** and what the **family** in the twenty-first century looks like. Sometimes relationships end, so the theme also explores **divorce** as well as **remarriage**. Finally, it considers **gender equality**, particularly in the context of roles in the home, but also in society.

Let's talk sex!

Why do people have sex? Love, lust, fun, money, to make life. Can you think of any more reasons? Is it always all right to have sex? When do you think sex is not all right? Under what circumstances?

> Think about the different types of relationships described on the next page. Which ones seem acceptable to you, and which ones do not? Explain why in each case.

It is true to say that society changes all the time in the UK. Fifty years ago, it was illegal to be gay and there was widespread persecution of homosexuals; today it is much more accepted and most young people do not see an issue (whether they themselves are gay or not). Fifty years ago, almost everyone got married and divorce was rare; now fewer than half of us marry and half of those who do get divorced. As society changes, our attitudes to sex may change, although religions tend to keep a more consistent attitude over time, because it is based on beliefs and teachings. For this course, you need to be aware of both secular (what society says/does) and religious attitudes.

> ### Key concepts for this theme
>
> These are the key ideas which come up throughout this theme. You should try to learn them so you can keep referring to them.
>
> **Commitment** – this is an agreement with someone; a promise or pledge. In the case of relationships, it is usually based on being faithful and supportive.
>
> **Responsibility** – with any commitment comes responsibilities. These are the things we have to do as part of the agreement we have made. For example, in marriage it might be that earning money to support the family is a responsibility.
>
> **Contract** – these are binding agreements. Marriage vows and a marriage certificate are evidence of the contract made when two people marry.
>
> **Chastity** – this is the idea of being sexually pure. In a relationship, it would be about being faithful to your partner. Outside a relationship, **chastity** would be about not behaving sexually. Most religious groups believe that sex is only appropriate within marriage, so to be chaste is important.

Religious, philosophical and ethical studies

Sexuality

Age of consent

Age of consent is when you are old enough by law to choose to have sex. It is 16 for anyone. Of course, you could have sex before then – but you aren't considered mature enough to be responsible enough and it is against the law.

Celibacy

I am celibate. I have no sexual partner. I have made a decision to wait until I marry to have sex. If I never marry, then I'll not have sex.

Adultery

Even though we are married, I had an affair. It lasted a few months. It has taken a long time to begin to make up for it. The marriage really took a battering, and is still fragile but we are working at it.

Heterosexuality

We met at school and just fell for each other. Broke up a few times and then drifted apart. But we got back together at a school reunion four years ago and knew we needed to make it work this time. Our relationship is really strong.

Sex before marriage

We all had sexual relationships before being married to anyone. Different circumstances and reasons – part of a relationship, lust – you know, one-night stands – and fun, in a relationship which led to marriage. Everyone else was doing it.

Homosexuality

We met at university and have been together ever since. We are getting married this year. This is a strong, loving, sexual relationship and it works for us.

Tasks

Evaluative questions make up half the total marks. Work out as many reasons to agree and to disagree with each of these statements as you can.
- 'There should not be an age of consent for sex.'
- 'Only married couples should have sex.'
- Take each of your reasons and explain them.

167

4 Theme A: Relationships and families

Contraception and family planning

If you have to learn about sexual relationships and having children you should really know something about **contraception**.

Read the statements and decide why these people use contraception.

I'm not ready to be a dad, but I do have sex. — **Ben**

Sarah — *I'm HIV+ and I don't want to pass that on to my partner. We still enjoy sex.*

We have all the children we want to have, so need to use contraception. — **Effie**

Shane — *Well, I like the feel and the fun of using contraceptives when I am having sex. It's all part of the enjoyment for me.*

The main reason is **family planning**, that is, controlling the size of a family. Ben is preventing his family from beginning, while Effie ensures it gets no bigger. They are planning their families.

Tasks

You are the doctor. Recommend a form of contraception for each of the following:
- Samir – has a family, but knows he could not care adequately for any more children. It is against his religion to have permanent methods of contraception, because that would be changing what God has made.
- Jessica – is married and wants no more children, who she sees as a gift from God. However, her religion does not agree with any artificial methods and she believes permanent methods are against God's wishes.
- Xavier – needs to protect his partner from an STI he carries. He needs to make sure there is no exchange of body fluids during sex.
- Helena – asked for a foolproof (100% safe) form of contraception.

What kinds of contraception are there?

There are many kinds available and they work in different ways. That is why some people use one kind, but not another. Religious people especially will accept the use of some kinds, but not others.

Artificial methods are contraceptive devices which are made and then used, like a condom.

Natural methods are contraceptive practices or behaviours aimed at limiting the chance of pregnancy, such as the rhythm method, which allows a couple to have sex only at the woman's least fertile part of the monthly cycle.

Permanent methods are operations to prevent the production of either egg or sperm permanently. These are the only ones which are guaranteed to prevent pregnancy.

> Try to work out which kind is being described in each of the following statements.

1. The withdrawal method (where a man withdraws from inside the woman before he ejaculates) is a commonly used, but very unsafe attempt to avoid pregnancy.

2. Barrier contraceptives make a barrier between the egg and sperm. If they do not meet, there is no pregnancy. Condoms and caps are two examples.

3. A man can have an operation, as can a woman, called sterilisation. This stops either eggs or sperm being released, so pregnancy cannot happen.

4. A woman's level of fertility varies during her monthly cycle. By working out these cycles of fertility and infertility, a couple can try to avoid pregnancy.

5. Using a coil (IUD) makes the woman menstruate, even if there is a fertilised egg in her womb. So the egg is lost with the blood.

6. Taking the Pill affects a woman's hormones. She should not produce any eggs, so will not get pregnant.

Religious attitudes to sexual matters

☸ Buddhism

- Buddhism, in all its forms, has a very strong **celibate** tradition, with many monasteries and convents. The energy which might have been put into sexual activity is channelled into spiritual activity to try to reach Enlightenment. Having said that, there are many lay Buddhists, who live as families. Sex is seen as natural, but most rewarding as part of a loving, caring relationship, so chastity is encouraged. Using contraception to limit their family size, so practising family planning, can be seen as a skilful act. If a family cannot cope with or does not want a child, then family planning can prevent the suffering a new child might bring.
- For Buddhists monks, sexuality has to be put aside. It is about desire and craving, which the Four Noble Truths explain we must stop if we want to achieve Enlightenment.
- Buddhism encourages people to follow the Precepts, including the Precept to avoid sexual immorality, including **adultery**. Breaking that Precept generates bad karma, and will lead to suffering. Kamma is what determines the quality of the next life.
- Buddhists do not condemn **sex before marriage** or homosexuality, as long as it is part of a loving, caring relationship. Where sex is just based on lust, like one-night stands, then this is craving, which causes bad kamma.

✝ Christianity

Most Christians believe that only married couples should have sex, and only with each other. Chastity is a virtue. Attitudes to the use of contraception vary. There is a celibate tradition within Christianity (monastic life, and the priesthood) which is found mainly in the Catholic tradition.

'Every sexual act must be within the framework of marriage.' The Catholic Church teaches that only married couples should have sex, and the most important reason for sex is to have children. There should be a chance of pregnancy within every act of sex. Protestantism, however, sees sex as an expression of love, with no need for it to lead to pregnancy. Any sex other than between husband and wife is wrong. Sex before marriage is called fornication, and is a sin. The same goes for masturbation, because it cannot lead to pregnancy. Using contraception is against Catholic teaching, because it cancels out the chance of pregnancy, though in Western countries this teaching is often ignored. Most Catholics follow natural methods of contraception.

For some Christians, homosexual sex is thought to be unnatural, and again cannot lead to pregnancy, so it is also a sin and wrong. In places, the Bible also says it is wrong for a man to sleep with another man, which has also been used to show homosexuality to be wrong.

Some other Christians accept sex before marriage in a relationship which is leading to marriage, seeing it as an expression of love. They also stress the need for responsible parenthood; only having as many children as you can properly look after. So the use of contraception is encouraged. Many Christians disagree with sterilisation because that is damaging what God has created (unless for medical reasons).

The Bible says 'Do not commit adultery'; Jesus says that even to look at someone lustfully is wrong, so affairs are also wrong and a sin. Having an affair means you break all the promises you made before God when marrying. Christians do not agree with adultery.

Tasks

Read about religious attitudes to sexual matters for the one/two religions you are studying in this theme.

Remember that contraceptions fall into the following groups:
- those which are artificial
- those which are permanent
- those which are natural

Explain which forms of contraception would be suitable, and why.

4 Theme A: Relationships and families

ॐ Hinduism

For a Hindu man, life is split into four Ashramas or stages. Sexual relationships can only happen in the second stage, which is that of the married householder (grihastha). For the other three stages, the man should remain celibate. This means that women also have sexual relationships only within marriage. Sex before marriage and homosexuality are both against the religion. Sex is seen as a gift from the Ultimate Reality (God), and must be treated with care and respect. It is for enjoyment and to have children.

Chastity is important in Hinduism and all are expected to be virgins before marriage, with their only sexual partner being the person to whom they are married. Two important Hindu virtues are self-discipline and respect, and adultery goes against both of these. Since adultery causes others to suffer, it brings bad karma to the adulterer, and negatively affects their rebirth.

Hindus do not object to using contraception; rather, they encourage it. Family planning is stressed, though Hindus need to have a son to carry out certain religious rituals and this often leads to less use of contraception. During the year, though, there are many days when couples should avoid sex – for example, festivals, full/new moon, holy days. There are up to 208 holy days in total, and this obviously will act as a form of birth control.

☾ Islam

Islam does not agree with choosing never to marry or with monastic lifestyles. It is a religious duty to marry and have children. Every person should be a virgin before marriage, and observe chastity before and during marriage. Celibacy as a life choice is wrong.

If only those who are married have sex, then it is thought that society is protected, because all the issues linked to sex outside marriage are gone. The message is very clear in Islam; only married couples may have sex, and then only with each other. Prophet Muhammad spoke of sex as being special within marriage. He said it was a source of pleasure and provided the blessing of children from God, if the couple so wished. This means that Muslims can and should use contraception. Muhammad also said that couples should only have as many children as they could properly look after – responsible parenthood.

The Qur'an sets out specific punishments for those who have sex before marriage, or who commit adultery, or have homosexual relationships. It calls these people fornicators, and punishment is severe (flogging if single, execution if married). This is still part of Shari'ah Law, and a punishment used in some Muslim countries. In several places, the Qur'an specifically mentions adultery, always saying it is wrong: 'Do not commit adultery. It is shameful and an evil way to act' *(Surah 17:32)*.

Tasks

Look at these couples:

- None of these couples are married. John and Sara only met last week, whereas all the others have been together for months or years. Explain what the attitude of each of your two religions would be to each couple having a sexual relationship.
- What if John and Sara got married? What would be the attitude of each religion about them having sex? What advice might be given by each religion about contraception?

Religious, philosophical and ethical studies

Judaism

The family is very important in Judaism. Anything which goes against this ideal is wrong. Marriage is highly recommended, whereas a life of celibacy is not. The Torah states that woman was made from man to be his companion. This is interpreted to mean marriage.

A sex drive is healthy and sex within marriage is for pleasure and having children. The first command God gave was to 'be fruitful and multiply', which is understood to mean that couples should have at least one boy and one girl. Different branches of Judaism have different attitudes to contraception. Orthodox Jews will accept it for medical/health reasons. They often use the Pill because it does not interfere in the actual act of sex, and does not directly cause the 'wasting of seed' (forbidden in the Torah). Reform Jews accept contraception also for social/economic reasons, so use more forms. For all Jewish people, sex is forbidden at certain times within the menstrual cycle. This acts as a form of birth control.

The Torah lists punishments for sex before marriage, adultery and homosexuality, which are all considered to be wrong. Jewish people are expected to be virgins before marriage and observe chastity all their life. Committing adultery breaks one of the Ten Commandments.

Jewish Law calls homosexuality an abomination. Orthodox Jews still believe this, though they state that homosexuals should not be persecuted. Many Reform and Liberal Jews accept homosexuality if in a loving relationship.

Sikhism

Sexuality is seen as a gift from God, because all beings have sexual urges. However, Sikhs warn against being controlled by your sex drive and believe it should be controlled by marriage. So sex before marriage is wrong, and Sikhs try to protect even against the temptation of it – for example, discouraging dating before marriage. In the Adi Granth, Sikhs are warned to 'avoid that which … produces evil thoughts in the mind.' Married life is seen as the norm and celibacy as a life choice is not encouraged. Chastity, though, is a virtue and highly valued before and within marriage as a form of self-control. Although most Sikhs see homosexuality as wrong (a form of haumai, or selfishness), some accept it as part of what God has created in a person.

In the wedding ceremony, Sikhs make promises, including to be faithful. Those promises are made in front of God. The Rahit Maryada forbids adultery, saying 'the touch of another man's wife is like a poisonous snake', and adultery is one of the Four Abstinences of Sikhism.

When it comes to deciding on which contraception to use, Sikhs can choose for themselves. They are encouraged to follow responsible parenthood (only having as many children as you can properly look after). Sikhs would not use permanent forms of contraception though, except for medical reasons, since these change the body God has given you.

The Basics

Copy and complete this table for each of the two religions you are studying.
You will need to complete the whole row of information for each topic before moving onto the next. You do not know how much writing you will do, so this way keeps it neat and easy to read later when you are revising.

Topic	Agree/disagree	Reasons why
a. Celibacy		
b. Chastity		
c. Sex before marriage		
d. Contraception		
e. Adultery		
f. Homosexuality		

4 Theme A: Relationships and families

Marriage and the family

Marriage is the joining of two people as a legal couple. When done religiously, it is done before God for God's blessing on the **covenant**.

Why do people marry?

You can answer this from your point of view and from what you have learned. People marry for many reasons. Work them out with a partner.

love   **money**   **family expectations**

religious duty   **to legitimise a relationship**

to legitimise a child   **for sex**   **for companionship**

It is likely that a couple who marry do so for many reasons, and their upbringing and culture have a big influence on those.

Who to marry?

Most people would say you marry who you want to. *Is it always that simple though?* Sometimes marrying who you want to has a cost; especially if your family do not approve of the person you want to marry. *Why might that make things difficult?*

Religious people are taught to honour their family and to honour their religion. You might then expect a religious person to marry someone who their family approve of, and someone who shares their religion.

So, should you get parents' approval of your choice, or should it be your acceptance of their choice? The latter is what we call an **arranged marriage**, and means that the parents have found a prospective spouse for their son or daughter. The two meet, while chaperoned, and then decide to go ahead or not with the marriage. Divorce is actually still less common in this kind of marriage than in Western 'love' marriages. Most religious people in the West, especially outside the Hindu, Muslim and Sikh faiths, would feel that getting their parents' approval of their own choice was the better way.

Why the same religion? For Muslims, Sikhs and Jewish people it is traditional to marry someone of the same religion, and it would not be viewed as the best choice by the community if that did not happen. But perhaps the major reason is that if you married someone of a different faith, there would be many clashes, for example in beliefs and attitudes. Which religious building would host the wedding? Which **vows** would be taken? When the time came to have children, which religion would they follow? In any religion, you believe yours is the 'right' way; so why would you marry someone who is following the 'wrong' one?

Tasks

Read these statements. Do you agree or disagree with each? Explain why.

1. The most important reason to marry is to have children.

2. A person should only marry someone their parents agree to.

3. People should always marry someone of the same religion as theirs.

4. There is no point getting married in our modern society.

5. The marriage vows should never be broken.

6. The only good reason to marry is for love.

Roles in marriage

The marriage vows can help us understand the different roles within a marriage. We have all seen or heard people on TV taking their vows; every soap has at least one big wedding a year! So, think of those vows, and you will uncover the roles in a marriage.

> Can you think of the marriage vows or promises? If you cannot, think of how you would expect your spouse to behave when married. It is likely that you will come up with the same set of ideas.

In marriage, a couple promise to each other, either through vows/promises or through a contract, to be good to each other, to be faithful, to love and cherish each other, and to support each other through good and bad, until the marriage is ended by death. If you were setting up an agreement with someone about how you would live the rest of your life together as a couple, you would probably come up with the same or a similar set of values.

Additionally, roles might include who keeps house (cooking, cleaning, etc.), who leads the upbringing of children, or their discipline, who earns money for the family. Traditionally, the man went out to work and the woman stayed at home looking after the home and family. In our society, it is becoming more common for all these tasks to be shared by the man and the woman and even for them to be reversed from what is seen as traditional.

Religions can be very diverse – there are not any hard rules about the roles that husband and wife must take. It is the case, though, that many religious couples follow quite traditional roles – the woman being home-keeper, for example.

The Basics

1. Give some reasons why people get married.
2. Explain what is meant by 'arranged marriage'.
3. Explain why many religious people believe a person should only marry someone of the same religion.
4. Explain beliefs about roles in marriage.
5. 'Extended families are the most effective form of family unit.' Do you agree? Explain arguments for and against this statement.

The nature of families

Nuclear family – this is basically a mum and a dad, plus the child(ren). It is considered a normal family unit in the Western world.	**Extended family** – this is the nuclear family plus other relatives, usually grandparents, living with the family, but can also include cousins, uncles and aunts and so on.
Single-parent family – this is a family of either a mum or a dad, plus child(ren). It is becoming more common to see this kind of family in the UK.	**Polygamy** – this is illegal in the UK. It is where a man has several wives, often having children with each. It is allowable under specific circumstances in the Islamic faith.

4 Theme A: Relationships and families

Marriage ceremonies

☸ Buddhism

Buddhist wedding

Buddhism does not have a set ceremony for marriage, so the ceremonies are completely non-religious.

In some Buddhist countries a couple will visit a monk to have their fortunes read and a lucky date is decided from that reading for their wedding.

Buddhists will follow the local customs of their country for marriage, which may include registering their marriage officially.

Later, the couple might visit the monastery or temple to invite a monk to bless their marriage. He does this by reciting verses from Buddhist scriptures. He also gives them advice about being a married Buddhist.

The couple might then invite the monk to a feast, as a sign of their thanks for his blessing.

✝ Christianity

Christian wedding

Marriage is a sacrament in some Christian traditions; it brings a blessing from God. In the Roman Catholic ceremony marriage takes place as part of the Mass.

The couple will come to church to be united in marriage by the priest. He greets them before the whole congregation.

The priest then reads a homily (a moralising lecture) about marriage and what Christian marriage is.

He asks three set questions to the bride and groom to make sure they understand the responsibilities of marriage.

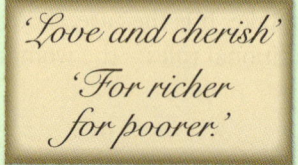

'Love and cherish'
'For richer for poorer.'

The couple make their vows to each other.

The priest declares they have agreed to marry before God and accepts their decision. It is at this point he says: 'What God has joined together, let no man put asunder.'

The rings are blessed and exchanged.

The priest blesses the marriage.

The couple sign the marriage register. This is the civil part of the ceremony.

Religious, philosophical and ethical studies

ॐ Hinduism

Hindu wedding

Find out all about Hindu marriage from **www.vivaaha.org**.

The main ceremony is the last of a series of ceremonies making up marriage, and is the biggest of them.

The groom, his family and friends arrive for the wedding to be received by the bride's family.

Under a specially built canopy, the priest begins the ceremony with a blessing on the couple. The bride and groom give each other garlands.

The father pours out sacred water to show he gives away his daughter, while the priest recites hymns from the Vedas. The groom also accepts his duties and responsibilities as a husband.

The bride and groom face each other. The end of her scarf is tied to his shirt to symbolise their eternal union. They exchange rings.

Holding hands, the couple throw samagree (a mix of sandalwood, herbs, sugar, rice and ghee) into the sacred fire to ask for the deities' blessing on their marriage.

The bride and groom walk four times round the fire, reciting hymns and prayers.

At the end of each circuit of the fire, they both step onto a stone to pray that their marriage will be strong like the stone.

They then take seven steps together round the fire, and with each one exchange a wedding vow.

The ceremony ends with a prayer that the marriage cannot be broken.

☪ Islam

Muslim wedding

Traditionally, Muslim weddings last up to five days, because of the many cultural traditions depending upon which Muslim country or area is involved. We will concentrate on the actual wedding ceremony itself.

The ceremony, which would take place on day four of a five-day celebration, is called nikkah. It is always a simple ceremony and is performed by an imam. Most nikkah are performed at the home of the bride or groom, and not the mosque.

The groom has to declare a mahr (a dowry), showing his respect for the bride. It can include anything she has asked for (for example, money, clothes, even a house). The groom can pay this over time, and is not allowed to take it away; it is hers.

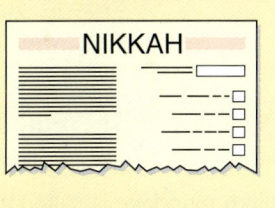

An imam usually leads the ceremony, but it could be any respected male. The bride does not have to be there; she will have given her consent beforehand.

Some couples take vows. They will have signed marriage contracts beforehand about what they expect from the marriage and what the rights of their partner will be.

The imam announces their intention to marry and asks if anyone has any objections. He also recites some verses from the Qur'an, and the Nikkah Khutba, which is about the purpose of marriage.

The consent of the bride is asked for three times by the imam. After it is given, the marriage is complete.

4 Theme A: Relationships and families

Judaism

Jewish wedding

Jewish weddings begin with the signing of the ketubah (marriage contract) in front of four witnesses. It details the legal terms of the marriage.

The bridegroom places a veil over the bride's face, to show he will protect and look after his wife.

They go to the huppah (wedding canopy), where the bride walks around the groom up to seven times.

They drink a glass of wine; the first of seven to represent the seven days of creation, and the start of the building of a marriage.

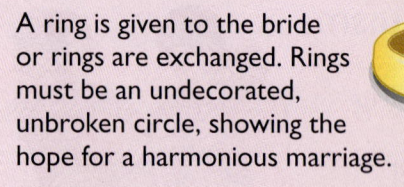

A ring is given to the bride or rings are exchanged. Rings must be an undecorated, unbroken circle, showing the hope for a harmonious marriage.

The rabbi makes a speech about the responsibilities of marriage, and about the couple. Prayers will be said. The cantor will sing.

Finally, the groom crushes a glass under his foot to remember the destruction of the temple, but also to hope that bad luck will not come to the marriage. With this act, the marriage is complete.

Sikhism

Sikh wedding

Visit www.sikhs.org/wedding for more details and pictures about Sikh weddings.

Sikh marriage is called anand karaj. Only Sikhs can have this ceremony. Anyone who is a full Khalsa Sikh can lead the ceremony.

The groom listens to kirtan in the gurdwara as he waits for his bride to arrive. When she arrives she sits on his left in front of the Guru Granth Sahib.

The Ardas prayer will be said to begin the ceremony. This prayer begins and ends all ceremonies.

The end of the scarf is placed in the hands of the bride, while four lavan (verses of a hymn written by the fourth Guru, Guru Ram Das) from the Guru Granth Sahib are read.

When the second lavan is reached, the couple stand, and, groom first, walk slowly around the Guru Granth Sahib. They do this for each lavan.

The Ragis read out the Anand Sahib, and a randomly chosen hymn from the Guru Granth Sahib is read out.

The ceremony ends with the Ardas prayer, and the distribution of karah parshad (blessed food) to all.

Task

Find more detail for all this section. You could check out BBC Bitesize GCSE section, which has specific information on each religion. Try also to find pictures of aspects of the wedding ceremonies to help your recall.

Cohabitation and same-sex marriage

Not everyone marries, but they still have a relationship with someone. So how does that work?

Cohabitation is living together as if married. The only difference is the couple have no marriage licence and legally they do not have the same rights as a married couple (for example, to each other's pension). Not everyone feels the need to go through the marriage ceremony.

Civil marriage registration is about being married, but not through a religious ceremony. It is done at a registry office, and may include promises, but it is not religious. Since March 2014, same-sex couples have been able to marry, meaning they have exactly the same rights as any other married couple.

Civil partnership is the legal registration of a couple (as of 2019). This means that in law they are treated as if married and they have many of the legal protections which a married couple are entitled to.

Attitudes to marriage and cohabitation

Dave: Me and my partner have lived together for 14 years. We have two kids. Marriage is just a piece of paper, and we do not need that.

Jay: We married but we are not religious, so we went to the register office. It was a nice, quiet do – just right for our relationship. It gives us both protection if the relationship fails, but it also gives us benefits while in the relationship – like taxes.

Lucy: We went through a civil partnership last year. As a gay couple, we were never going to be given the same rights as everyone else without this process. For example, now I am legally her next of kin. I couldn't even have visited her in hospital without her family's consent before the civil partnership.

Steve: My partner and I celebrated our gay marriage this year. We have been together 25 years and can finally, publicly, show how we feel about each other.

Musa: I think if a couple love each other then marriage is the key. It is the only appropriate setting for sexual relationships and having children.

Heather: I live with my partner, and we might get married in the future. Right now, we are learning to live together, rather than getting married and then finding out we aren't compatible in that way.

The Basics

1. What is the term for each relationship described below?
   a. Sally and Jane, who legally registered as a same-sex couple.
   b. David and Emily, who have lived together for four years.
   c. Callum and Aneela, who had a register office ceremony.
2. Use information from pages 169–171 for the religion you have studied. What might their attitude be to each of the three relationships in Question 1? Explain your answer.
3. Explain why some people choose not to get married in a religious building when they are in a relationship.
4. How do alternatives to religious marriage differ from religious marriages?
5. 'In the modern world, there is no need for marriage.' What is your opinion on this statement? Include religious arguments in your answer.

Parenting – the purpose of families

You have learned that part of the reason for marriage and the roles within marriage is about children. Think about these questions. *Why do people have children? Are there any specifically religious reasons for having children?*

Reasons why a couple might have children

Shows commitment – shows love – by accident – fulfilment of relationship – duty – family tradition. You probably have more reasons than those, but they are the most common.

What is the purpose of a family?

When two people marry or agree to set up home together, they make a commitment to each other. Very often that includes **procreation** (to have children) and this is just as true for same-sex couples as it is for heterosexual couples. When a relationship includes children, it acquires new purposes and responsibilities. They have a duty now to the children to work harder at issues in their relationship so that the children have stability. In other words, making sure there is a consistency of behaviour and life so the children know what they are coming home to every day, which is a safe and happy environment. Of course, the children have to be protected and cared for. They have to be given every chance to develop as confident and healthy young people, and kept safe from dangers. Part of caring for children includes making sure they have a good education, because that is part of protecting their futures. A good education is the best guarantee that they will be able to have successful, comfortable lives when they are adults. Children have a duty to obey their parents, which is part of showing respect for them. Many religions have teachings about this, such as the Christian and Jewish teaching of 'Honour your father and mother'. All religions emphasise this need for respect in return for their parents' love and commitment to them.

Educating children in a faith

Religious parents are like any other parent in wanting their children to have the best possible start in life. They want their children to be happy and ready to do well in their lives. They also want their children to follow their own faith, so they teach them its beliefs and how to practise it – for example, how to behave by following its rules and how to worship. Many even put their child through some initiation ceremony for the faith – for example, Christians having their children baptised as infants.

For people who are not religious, this might seem unfair and that the parents 'force' the religion on the child. However, religious parents believe their faith is right, and that it is the key to happiness if not in this life, then definitely in the next. They believe that a good afterlife is dependent on love for God and living a morally good life now. They want what is best for their child, and they believe their religion is it. For them, passing on a faith is an act of great love.

Many same-sex couples are also religious believers. If they have children (whether from previous relationships, through treatments such as IVF or by adoption), they will also want the best for their children, including that religious faith.

The Basics

1 Why do many people who marry choose to have children?
2 What are the purposes of families?
3 Explain the roles within marriage, including parenting.
4 'When a couple have children, those children should become their first priority.' Explain reasons to agree and disagree with this statement.

Divorce

Many marriages fail and are legally dissolved. This is what is meant by the term divorce. In the UK, more than one in three first marriages ends in divorce.

Why do marriages fail?

Any difficulties in a marriage can put strain on it – for example, money, arguments, different attitudes or beliefs, affairs, illness, job issues, abuse. When those difficulties become too great for one or both to cope with, they might turn to divorce as a solution.

Should it be easy to get a divorce?

Many religious people might think divorce is always wrong. Many of them do see a need for divorce, but feel that it should not be an easy option, which might encourage people to not even try at their marriage. In 1969, the Church of England was key in getting the divorce laws relaxed. The situation at the time meant people were living in loveless marriages, or separating and being unable to move on. Jesus taught compassion, forgiveness and second chances – allowing divorce is compatible with that. Religions argue that people made a very serious commitment, so should work hard at their marriage, and work even harder when it is in difficulty. Divorce should only be the last option.

Support for marriages in difficulty

Since divorce is not a welcome option, religions try to support couples in these times. Obviously, families will support them – for example, look after the children, listen and help them problem-solve, and so on. Religious people will also do those things, but they might also encourage them through their religion, such as through prayer, reading their holy books, and so on.

UK society also provides marriage counselling services, which allow couples to try to talk through problems or to come to amicable agreements ahead of divorce. This is important because many people feel anger and many negative emotions when their relationship ends, which they need help to get through. Look at www.relate.org.uk, which is a charity which focuses on relationships (of all kinds).

Religious attitudes to divorce

Buddhism

Any vows made are serious and should not be broken easily. Marriage is seen as a thing which keeps society stable, and divorce is discouraged. It is not against Buddhist teachings though.

Buddhism teaches:
- Keep the Five Precepts.
- Be compassionate.
- Thoughts, deeds and actions should always be positive, because they have a kammic value which shapes this and our next lifetime(s).

Divorce has to be seen as the right option. If two people are causing themselves and others great suffering by staying together, this breaks Precepts, creates bad karma and goes against Buddhist principles of compassion and ahimsa.

Christianity

For Roman Catholics, divorce is always wrong. Marriage is a sacrament, which cannot be broken. Promises are made to God and each other to stay together 'until death do us part', and these promises are binding. It is possible to have an **annulment**, which is where the marriage is set aside, as if it never was real.

For most other Christians, divorce is discouraged, but accepted as a last resort. It is sometimes the lesser of two evils, and also a necessary evil so divorcees should not be made villains.

Christianity teaches:
- God hates divorce. (Old Testament)
- 'Whoever divorces … then marries another; it is as if he committed adultery.' (Jesus)
- 'We should forgive those who wrong us, and show love to all.' (Jesus)

Hinduism

Hindu law traditionally does not allow divorce to the Brahmin caste, but it is available to all others. It does happen throughout Hindu society, though is frowned upon.

Hinduism teaches:
- 'I promise never to abandon her, whatever happens.' (Wedding vow)
- Marriage is one of the spiritual stages in life.
- Divorce is granted for specific reasons. (Hindu Marriage Act (1955) and Manusmriti scriptures)

The Manusmriti scriptures said that a man could replace any wife who was quarrelsome or difficult; the law allows for divorce in the case of cruelty, non-production of children and other reasons. Though traditionally disliked, the Hindu religion continues to evolve, so that divorce is now acceptable. However, it is not common, it carries great stigma and it is especially difficult for women who have been divorced. Couples tend to stay together because of these pressures.

Judaism

Marriage is a sacred commitment and union. Although divorce is allowed, it is as a last resort.

Judaism teaches:
- God hates divorce. (Nevi'im)
- 'When a man puts aside the wife of his youth, even the very altar weeps.' (Talmud)
- 'A court can grant a woman divorce, if she can show that she can no longer live with him.' (Maimonides)

Technically, it is easy to get a divorce in Judaism. However, it is not desirable, and every effort will be made to help the marriage stay together. A period of time has to pass which allows attempts at reconciliation. Then the husband will serve the bill of divorce (get); because he put forward the original contract with its promises, it is he who cancels it. The get is written in black ink, with no mistakes and on parchment – it is an official document, and is served before the Bet Din (Jewish Court of Law). Then the marriage is ended.

Islam

Divorce is available to both men and women. However, it is seen as the absolute last resort. Islam teaches:
- 'Marry and do not divorce; the throne of Allah shakes due to divorce.' (Hadith)
- 'If you fear a breach between a man and his wife, appoint two arbiters.' (Qur'an)

A Muslim couple and their families are expected to work hard to fix any problems in a marriage to avoid divorce. There has to be mediation between them, and they have to give time for reflection and to solve problems. If divorce is still the solution, then the man states 'I divorce you' three times before witnesses. He must then wait three months – to be sure his wife is not pregnant, and perhaps to resolve the problems. After that, he must pay the second part of the dowry to show the marriage is ended.

Sikhism

Divorce is not the Sikh way, but is accepted by the faith.

Sikhism teaches:
- Marriage is a sacrament.
- Marriage is the union of two souls and a lifelong commitment.
- 'If the husband and wife dispute, their concern for their children should reunite them.' (Adi Granth)

If a marriage is in difficulty both families will try to help solve the problems – after all, given that many Sikh marriages are arranged, its collapse reflects badly on the families as well as the couple. Divorce used to carry a stigma but this is changing, however, it is still avoided if possible. It is a matter for a person's individual conscience.

The Basics

1. What is meant by divorce?
2. Explain the attitude of religious believers to problems in marriage and divorce.

Religious, philosophical and ethical studies

Remarriage

This can be a person marrying a different partner after a divorce from someone else; this is their second (or more) marriage. It is also sometimes the case that people who divorced later remarry each other. Some people talk about marriage after the death of a partner as being remarriage, others call this a second marriage.

Most people who get divorced think they can have other, positive relationships, and often find themselves wanting to marry again to show their commitment to a new partner. Marriage is the ultimate commitment and the failure of one marriage does not mean that every relationship will fail. It is to be expected that people will look for and try to find happiness again.

> *I have to have sons to carry on my faith and so I will remarry. My first marriage was not blessed with children, and that led to our divorce.*
> **Bilal**

> *Love and marriage go together. I think if the love is strong enough, then a marriage will survive. But just because one marriage ends, doesn't mean never again.*
> **Jesse**

What do you think about remarriage? Do you agree with any of these statements?

Religious attitudes to remarriage

For most religious believers, getting married again after the death of a first partner is not an issue. Of course, they believe the person deserves to be happy and this will help them to be happy. Some cultures disagree with a woman remarrying after her husband has died; they believe she is eternally married to that one man.

If it is marriage after divorce, whether a religion agrees or not depends very much on their attitude to divorce. For those religions which disagree with divorce, of course, remarriage would be wrong. As far as they are concerned, the original marriage still exists. Roman Catholic teaching says that divorce is not recognised by God, so remarriage is not allowed. Other religious believers might allow remarriage, but not allow a religious ceremony. Many Anglican vicars will not perform a marriage ceremony for divorced persons. They recognise that people might have found new happiness, and do believe that marriage forms the basis of a strong, good society. However, they also see the original ceremony as having a sanctity and vows made before God cannot just be laid aside to remake with someone else.

In the Roman Catholic tradition, it is possible to get an annulment of the marriage. This means that the marriage was never proper; this is usually because it was not consummated (no sexual relationship), or because one or both did not properly understand the responsibilities of marriage (for example, when a Catholic marries a non-Catholic and the religion becomes an issue between them). Technically, any marriage after an annulment is not remarriage (there was no first marriage).

> *Sounds silly really, but my wife and I divorced. Then years later we met again and it was love. I think we were too young the first time, but now we are remarrying and it will last this time.*
> **Karl**

> *I have been married four times. Each marriage broke up for different reasons. I am due to marry again in two months.*
> **Nia**

> *After my husband died, I never thought I would find another love. I am so lucky to have met Ben and I think we can be happily married.*
> **Denny**

The Basics

1 What is meant by remarriage?
2 Use information from pages 179–180 for the religion(s) you have studied to explain what their attitude to divorce and remarriage might be.
3 'There is nothing wrong with divorce for religious believers.' Do you agree? Give reasons to agree and disagree, including religious arguments.

Gender equality – gender prejudice

This is prejudice against someone because of their gender. Reread page 173 about the roles in marriage to remind yourself about religious attitudes to roles within marriage.

> Can you work out any reasons why some people might consider the roles in some marriages to be unequal?

Why are some people prejudiced?

Prejudice is the pre-judgement of others based on a characteristic they have, rather than what they are really like. People are often prejudiced because of the way they were brought up; they were taught this kind of attitude and behaviour. There is often an element of tradition. In some societies, women don't hold positions of power and so they are seen as less important. Attitudes are changing but in some cultures that change is very slow. It may also be because of an experience they have had, so their attitude to women was shaped by the women/men they met, or the situations they were in which made them think women/men should be treated in a certain way.

What is the effect of gender prejudice against women?

It can lead to different treatment (discrimination), so that women are given fewer opportunities – for example, by not getting the same chances or promotions at work. It may be that the culture within which they live sets stricter rules for women than for men – for example, where women are not allowed to leave the house, or can only leave when chaperoned, or where girls are not allowed education beyond a certain age; they seem not to have the same rights as men. It may be that women are not allowed to contribute to decision-making or leadership roles, so a female perspective is never considered. Prejudice within power structures can mean that when women are treated negatively, there is no consequence for the perpetrator, and this further encourages that negative behaviour. If you read the newspapers, or watch TV shows, you get the impression that women are the usual victims of violent crime. The year 2014 saw a string of stories about the gang-rape of women in India with little justice served, which has become such an issue it has led to campaigns and actions by women's groups. When no punishments are given to men who commit these crimes, the message seems to be that violence against women is not so bad, which encourages more of it. **Gender discrimination** spans from unkind comments to murder; it definitely has an impact.

Ultimately **gender prejudice** (when experienced through discrimination) makes women feel powerless, which affects their confidence and self-esteem. However, in society, it keeps women less powerful, and makes society work for men rather than for the balance of society. It is true that in the UK, laws exist to prevent gender discrimination, and that employment law is being changed to equalise pay and conditions, so things are getting better for women.

65% OF SECONDARY HEADS ARE MALE

Businesses still mostly run by men

Women outnumber men going to university in the UK

Fewer than 35% of UK MPs are female

Only 30% of girls are educated beyond the age of 12 in the world today

> What impression do you get from these headlines?

The Basics

1. What is meant by gender prejudice?
2. Why are some people gender prejudiced?
3. How does gender prejudice affect women?
4. Look back at page 173 to read about roles within marriage. Do you think these encourage gender prejudice? Explain your answer.
5. 'Gender prejudice cannot be ended.' How far do you agree with this statement? Give reasons to support and argue against it, and include religious arguments in your answer.

Religious teachings about gender equality

☸ Buddhism

- 'If a man denies the possibility of Enlightenment of women, then his own Enlightenment is impossible.' (Lotus Sutra)
- There is no legal basis in Vinaya (monastic) law to deny a woman the right to full ordination.
- The practice of Buddhism is the same for men and women, showing no inequality of demands on either.

✝ Christianity

- Some of the earliest converts and leaders of churches were women – for example, Priscilla at Ephesus.
- 'There is neither Jew nor Gentile, neither slave nor free, nor is there male and female, for you are all one in Christ Jesus.' (Galatians 3:28)
- 'So God created mankind in His own image, in the image of God He created them; male and female He created them.' (Genesis 1:27)

ॐ Hinduism

- 'Good treatment of women is seen as a blessing.' (Laws of Manu)
- 'Where women are honoured, there the gods are pleased.' (Manusmriti)
- There are no differences between men and women on a spiritual level, differences only exist at a physical level because of past lives. (Sruti)

☪ Islam

- Men and women have the same spiritual nature, according to the Qur'an.
- Prophet Muhammad said, 'I command you to be kind to women.'
- 'I shall not lose sight of the labour of any of you who labours in My way, be it man or woman; each of you is equal to the other.' (Qur'an 3:195)

✡ Judaism

- In Progressive Judaism, women can be rabbis, the religious leader at the synagogue and for the community.
- The equality of men and women begins at the highest possible level, as God has no gender. Both men and women were created in God's image. (Genesis)
- Men and women were created equally; their methods of connecting to God through the mitzvot are different but of equal value.

☬ Sikhism

- Men and women may take the role of granthi in the gurdwara, leading the religious services.
- 'Man is born from a woman … woman is born from woman; without woman, there would be no one at all.' (Guru Granth Sahib)
- 'Waheguru (God) is neither male nor female.' (Guru Granth Sahib)

Task

Using the teachings of the religion(s) you have studied above, and from pages 319–321 (about prejudice generally), explain what might be their attitude to gender equality.

4 Theme A: Relationships and families

Attitudes to the role of men and women

Traditionally men have held positions of authority in most religions. They usually are the decision-makers, the leaders in the home, community and religion, and generally have more power. This is true in society generally. Look at the headlines on page 182 and think what they mean in terms of men. Men often have greater responsibilities because of their leading role.

Within religion there is a debate about the role of women. They are treated differently to men and there is often the accusation that women are being discriminated against despite the fact that all religions condemn any kind of discrimination. Here are some examples:

- In Christianity, women cannot be priests in the Roman Catholic Church and the first female bishops in the Anglican Church were only appointed in 2015.
- In Islam, all religious leaders are men and women do not pray at the front of the mosque. Most Muslims believe women cannot be imams.
- In Orthodox Judaism, many women sit separately to men, often upstairs, and do not take part in synagogue services.
- With the exception of ISKCON (the Hare Krishna movement) in Hinduism, all priests are male.
- In Theravada Buddhism, women will pray that their rebirth will be as a man.
- In Sikhism, while either gender may read the Guru Granth Sahib at services, it is unusual to see women fulfilling this role.

If women are denied access to certain roles then this could be said to be discriminatory. However, religion would just say that roles are different but equal. If women are happy with their roles and what they are permitted to do and not to do, then to them discrimination is not an issue. The issue arises when women want to do something as part of their religion but are not allowed because rules or traditions say they cannot.

As time moves on, there are changes being made to traditions but women have to fight hard for those changes. They would argue that if we are all creations of God, then if, for example, a woman wants to devote herself to the service of God and serve the community of believers, would God not want her to, simply because she is a woman? Perhaps a woman could deal with community issues and help people in a different way to a man? Compassion and understanding are key qualities and many women have these.

It all depends on how you view this issue. It is not the same as other forms of prejudice where people inflict hurt and pain on others. However, if you desperately want to do something or be part of something, being denied that because of being female is hurtful.

The Basics

1. Explain religious teaching about gender prejudice. Look at the teachings about prejudice on pages 319–323 to be able to comment on how these might affect attitudes to gender prejudice.
2. Give some examples of sexist behaviour.
3. Should women be allowed to be leaders in religion? Explain two reasons to agree and two to disagree.

Contrasting beliefs

Contraception

✝ Roman Catholic

The Roman Catholic Church's teaching on contraception is that **all sexual acts must be open to procreation – this is natural law**. Anything done to prevent natural law is wrong. In Humanae Vitae, the Pope declared that 'any act which deliberately prevents procreation is an intrinsic evil'. Use of artificial contraception is a deliberate act, and that is a sin. So Catholics should not use contraception.

✝ Anglican

The Church of England does not regard contraception as a sin or against God's teaching. The Lambeth Conference in 1968 stated that **sexual love is good in itself** and that there can be **good reasons for limiting or delaying parenthood**.

✡ Judaism

In Judaism, Orthodoxy accepts the use of contraception for **medical/health reasons**. The 'wasting of seed' is forbidden in the Torah, so the Pill is an acceptable form to use.

☪ Islam

Islamic teaching from Muhammad is that Muslims should practise **responsible parenthood**. They should only have the children they can care properly for.

Question

Explain two contrasting beliefs in contemporary British society about contraception.

In your answer you should refer to the main religious tradition of Great Britain and one or more other religious traditions.

(4 marks)

Sex before marriage

✝ Christianity

Christian teaching generally is that sex should only be experienced within marriage, so sex before marriage is wrong. Sex is a gift from God, for the **purpose of procreation**, but also as a sign of a couple's loving bond. However, this is a **gift to a married couple**. Sex before marriage is seen by many Christians as **fornication**, which is a sin. St Paul said: 'Now to the unmarried and the widows I say: It is good for them to stay unmarried, as I am. But if they cannot control themselves, they should marry, for it is better to marry than to burn with passion.' (I Corinthians 7:9)

☸ Buddhism

Buddhism does not have marriage as a rite of passage – marriages are culturally based events. So sex before marriage – as long as it is within the context of a **loving relationship** – is acceptable.

Theme A: Relationships and families

✝ Anglican

The General Synod of the Church of England recognises the variety of family forms today. It stresses that while marriage is the ideal context, sexual relationships must be **within permanent, loving relationships** (which allows sex before marriage).

✝ Quakers

The Quaker Society sees marriage as the ideal context, but accepts changing society norms. It accepts that a couple can be **faithful to each other in a loving, non-exploitative relationship outside marriage**.

Question

Explain two contrasting beliefs in contemporary British society about sex before marriage.

In your answer you should refer to the main religious tradition of Great Britain and one or more other religious traditions. *(4 marks)*

Homosexual relationships

✝ Quakers

Quakers in the UK fully accept homosexuals into their community and do not condemn those who have homosexual relationships. 'Quakers were one of the first churches to talk openly about sexuality. We feel that the quality and depth of feeling between two people is the most important part of a loving relationship, not their gender or sexual orientation.' The true consideration should be whether there is **genuine (selfless) love** between the couple. They point out that Genesis says that **all people are created in the image of God** – which must include homosexuals.

☪ Islam

Islam sees homosexuality as a **crime against Allah**. Under Shari'ah Law, it is punishable by execution. Prophet Muhammad said 'If you find anyone doing as Lot's people did, kill the one who does it, and the one to whom it is done.'

☸ Buddhism

Buddhism does not condemn homosexual relationships where they are long-term and committed. However, short relationships **based on lust are seen as 'craving' – one of the Three Poisons**. This is unskilful living.

✝ Roman Catholic

The Roman Catholic Church does not accept homosexual relationships. Church teaching classes homosexuality as an 'objective disorder' (only leaning towards sin) and **homosexual relationships as a 'moral disorder'** (committing a sin).

Question

Explain two contrasting beliefs in contemporary British society about homosexual relationships.

In your answer you should refer to the main religious tradition of Great Britain and one or more other religious traditions. *(4 marks)*

Getting prepared

The importance of key words

The key technical words of a theme are the start point of your journey to getting to grips with the content. You need to look at them on three levels. If you do not know the key words, you cannot answer any questions which might include them.

Know definitions for each word

The first question on each theme will require you to answer a simple 1 mark question, and this might be a definition question. You would be given four choices of what a word might mean to pick the right one from.

Here are some examples:

1 Which **one** of the following means a sexual relationship between a man and a woman?

   A homosexual   **B** heterosexual   **C** metrosexual   **D** transsexual

2 Which **one** of the following is meant by the term divorce?

   A separation   **B** ending a relationship   **C** living together   **D** legal ending of a marriage

In larger tariff questions, you need to explain yourself, so need to have fuller definitions of the words.

Have a go at these – they are not a type of question you'll find on your exam paper, but they will help you to practise explaining definitions!

1 Can you explain what is meant by marriage vows?

2 Can you explain what religious believers mean when they say that marriage is a contract?

3 Can you explain what is meant by the term commitment?

Learn the words so you can answer the questions. The key words for each theme are found in a glossary at the end of the theme. For this theme, it is page 189. Why not make your own glossary book, and include **any** word you meet which is new or important? You could do this for any of your subjects as the need to know key words is true for all of them.

The next level

Those words will form the basis of questions worth more than 1–2 marks.
If you do not know the word then you cannot answer the higher value questions.
So, the message remains – **learn the words**.

You could be asked for the religious attitude to, or view on, something. Here are some examples:

1 Explain **two** contrasting religious beliefs about couples living together (cohabitation). In your answer you should refer to one or more other religious traditions. (4 marks)

2 Explain **two** contrasting beliefs in contemporary British society about contraception. In your answer you should refer to the main religious tradition of Great Britain and one or more other religious traditions. (4 marks)

3 Explain **two** contrasting religious beliefs about remarriage. In your answer you should refer to one or more other religious traditions. (4 marks)

A little tougher is to be asked how religious beliefs relate to an aspect of the topic. So for these questions, you need to know the key word to be able to give an answer. Some examples might be:

1 Explain **two** religious beliefs about gender equality. Refer to sacred writings or another source of religious belief and teaching in your answer. (5 marks)

2 Explain **two** religious beliefs about the role of parents in a religious relationship. Refer to sacred writings or another source of religious belief and teaching in your answer. (5 marks)

3 Explain **two** religious beliefs about adultery. Refer to sacred writings or another source of religious belief and teaching in your answer. (5 marks)

And another level …

Half of your marks are for questions which require analysis and evaluation. They are recognisable by a statement, followed by the instruction to argue about it (worth 12 marks). If there is a key word/phrase in the statement which you have to analyse/evaluate, and you do not know it, then you might have trouble answering, again, proving you need to **learn the words**.

1 'Religious believers should never be sexist.'
2 'Ceremonies for remarriage should not be allowed in places of worship.'
3 'Marriage ceremonies are out of date nowadays.'

So, overall, hopefully you see the need to learn the words – start learning.

Relationships and families glossary

Adultery having an affair, a sexual relationship with someone you are not married to

Age of consent the age at which a person is considered old enough to be able to decide to have sex, according to the law

Annulment the cancellation of a marriage

Arranged marriage a marriage of two people which has been arranged and agreed by their parents

Celibacy not having sexual relations; to be celibate

Chastity keeping oneself sexually pure – for example, waiting until marriage before having sex

Civil marriage non-religious marriage ceremony

Civil partnership the legal union of two people; when first passed into law, it covered only same-sex couples, but as of 2019 now covers both opposite-sex and same-sex couples

Cohabitation living together as a couple

Commitment the act of making a promise or pledge

Contraception precautions taken to prevent pregnancy, and to protect against sexually transmitted infections

Contract a binding agreement between two sides

Covenant an agreement based on promises between two sides; often linked to religion, so includes an agreement before and with God

Divorce legal dissolution (ending) of a marriage

Extended family this is the nuclear family plus other relatives, usually grandparents, living with the family, but can also include cousins, uncles and aunts

Family parents and their children as a group

Family planning the planning of when to have a family using birth control/contraceptives

Gender discrimination acting on prejudices against someone because of their gender

Gender equality the idea that men and women are of equal worth

Gender prejudice the idea that men and women are not equal

Heterosexual someone physically attracted to the opposite sex

Homosexual someone physically attracted to the same sex

Nuclear family this is basically a mum and a dad, plus the child(ren)

Polygamy the practice of a man having more than one wife at the same time

Procreation the biological process of a couple producing children

Remarriage marriage a second time after divorce (not usually to the person originally divorced from)

Responsibility a duty; something we have to do, like looking after a younger brother or sister

Sex before marriage sexual relations prior to being married

Single-parent family a family with either a mum or a dad, plus child(ren)

Vows promises made in a wedding ceremony

5 Theme B: Religion and life

Key elements of this theme

In this theme, you will be thinking about **science** and religion; how they compare and how they clash, especially on ideas about the origins of the universe and life. This leads logically to the other parts of the theme as, secondly, you think about the value of the world, including environmental issues and **animal rights**. Then finally, you consider the value of human life, including the issues of **euthanasia** and **abortion**. The key concepts for this theme are split across each part.

Scientific truth *versus* religious truth

Scientific truth

Scientific truth comes from making a **hypothesis**, then testing it to see if it is true. Seeing something happen again and again is important; this is called repeated observation. Think about how you do experiments in science. You write what you are trying to do and what you think will happen. Then you do a lot of testing to check. So your tests confirm or disprove your idea.

Science includes things like $E = mc^2$, or that the Earth is in orbit around the Sun, or that the Northern Lights are a reflection of space dust hitting the atmosphere. In other words, scientific truth is describing our world and how it works.

Science answers the what and how questions; function and process.

Scientific truth is always open to being developed and added to, as we find out more information, or find out new circumstances. It can be challenged and tested by other theories, so is not absolute. It is always conditional, that is, true when based on the conditions in which the testing/observation took place.

Religious truth

Religious truth comes from religions and holy books. We read it, or we get taught it, or some people think they were told by God. Many religions, or versions of a religion, are based on a person's experience of God.

Religion tries to explain things like why we are here, who God is, how we should behave, and what will happen after we die. In other words, it gives us answers to ultimate questions; the questions no one else has an answer for, and which are really important to humans.

Religion answers the why questions; being about purpose and meaning.

Religion, and holy books, can be open to interpretation, but their words do not change. The truth of religion is considered to be absolute, that is, unchanging and relevant for all times.

The Basics

1. What is meant by scientific truth? How is it found?
2. What is meant by religious truth? How is it found?
3. What similarities are there between scientific and religious truth?
4. What differences are there between scientific and religious truth?
5. Which kind of truth is more important? Explain why.
6. 'Religion is about ideas not truths.' Explain reasons to agree and disagree with this statement.

Religious, philosophical and ethical studies

The origins of the universe and life

How the universe began is one of the areas in which it seems that science and religion disagree. You need to know what each side says, and also whether they can agree or not; are they compatible or conflicting kinds of truth?

The Big Bang theory

The **Big Bang theory** is a description of how scientists believe the universe began. Scientists say the universe began about 13.8 billion years ago. There was nothing. Then there was a huge explosion. The explosion made a cloud of dust and gas. It took a long time for the universe to form into what we know of it today; the Sun, stars, planets, and the universe itself. The earliest signs of life appeared millions of years ago, before the land and sea settled. The Earth was very hot, and covered in a primordial soup (a mix of liquids, chemicals, minerals, proteins and amino acids). These fused to give the first life forms, which were simple single-cellular beings. From these, all other life developed, including humans.

> What is the evidence behind this scientific theory? What makes people believe it as a truth?

An explosion causes everything to be flung outwards. Scientists know that the universe is still expanding and that the movement can all be tracked back to a single point. This supports the idea of an explosion; it is as if the explosion is still being felt.

Another bit of evidence is what we call background microwave radiation. Explosions cause radiation and this can still be detected in space.

This was not the first theory of how the universe came to be. As scientists find new evidence, they reshape their ideas. In the case of the Big Bang, it replaced the Steady State Theory as the accepted view of the origins of the universe. There might be another theory waiting in the wings for that extra bit of persuasive evidence – like the Pulsation Hypothesis Theory. That is one of the 'problems' of scientific theory and truth – it is open to change, development and revision. We could say that science is an evolving, changing description of the world and its workings. It is the truth for the time we are in with the knowledge we have.

The Basics

Use this page and page 194 to answer these questions.
1. Outline the scientific theory of the origins of the universe.
2. Outline the Genesis creation story.
3. 'Scientific theories about the origins of the universe are more important than religious stories.' How far do you agree? Explain arguments for and against that statement.

Task

Find out more about the Big Bang theory: who thought of it, what all the evidence was, and whether it is still considered the best explanation of how the universe began.

5 Theme B: Religion and life

Charles Darwin and evolution

Charles Darwin was a natural scientist. He wrote a book called *On the Origin of Species*, published in 1859. This was the culmination of years of research, including travels on the scientific exploration ship, HMS *Beagle*. In this book, Darwin suggested that the world is a place of change, and that the huge variety of creatures and species is the result of thousands of years of change and adaptation (**evolution**). He said that there is a struggle for survival between species because of competing demands and limits of resources like food, space, etc. Where species failed to adapt, they became extinct, so that only the fittest (best-suited) could survive. He called this **natural selection**. Darwin also realised that different places caused different varieties of the same creature to develop, because the places made different demands on the creatures. For example, finches (a kind of bird) have different-shaped beaks depending on whether they live in an area where berries are abundant, or in an area where shellfish are the main food. The great variety of species we see in the world is a result of millions of years of evolution.

We can use an analogy to make the concept easier to grasp.

Look around you at the world and everything in it. *Do things change? Do people change? Is there anything that does not change?*

When you started secondary school, it was a big change from life at primary school. If you have moved from one school to another, that is a big change too. *How did you cope with the difference? Do different people cope in different ways?*

If you went to live in a very cold country, things would be very different for you. You would have to make changes to your life. *What would happen if you did not?*

These are the main elements of evolutionary theory. When we look at the world around us, we can see many, many different varieties of animals, birds, fish and insects.

I see no good reason why the views given in this volume should shock the religious feelings of anyone. (Charles Darwin, On the Origin of Species)

Among the scenes which are deeply impressed upon my mind, none exceed in sublimity the primeval (tropical) forests ... temples filled with the varied products of the God of Nature. No one can stand in these solitudes unmoved, and not feel that there is more in man than the mere breath of his body. (Charles Darwin, 1879)

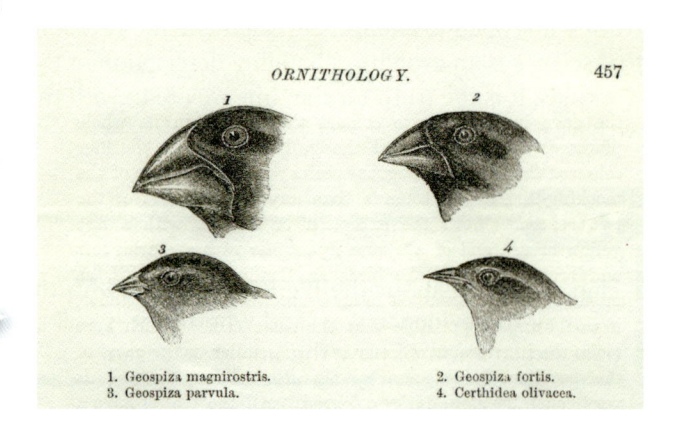

ORNITHOLOGY. 457

1. Geospiza magnirostris.
2. Geospiza fortis.
3. Geospiza parvula.
4. Certhidea olivacea.

Religious, philosophical and ethical studies

If we look at the **environment** in which these species live, we can see there are great differences. For example, some places are much hotter than others.

We can also see that the creatures in an area are suited to that particular environment. For example, a polar bear has special fur, which makes it possible for it to live in cold temperatures.

Environments are always changing – for example, volcanoes may erupt covering the surrounding area with ash, altering the shape of the landscape. Many scientists believe that the world has always been changing. Creatures have had to get used to the change and adapt to it, or they have died. Where a whole species could not adapt, it has become extinct. Where a species did adapt, its biology has changed so that the species survived.

This theory suggests that nothing was designed to look like it does today, or to work in the way it does today. Things have changed so that species could survive, which means it is wrong to believe some power designed things as they are, or to believe the world has always been the same. Many religious people believe that God created the world, so they are at odds with accepted scientific theory.

No God?

You would think that this theory completely discarded God. No longer could people claim the world was the same perfect **creation** of God. The idea of the seven-day creation was also challenged, as evolution suggested that the world developed over many millions of years. So was it time to forget about God? Was science finally getting rid of God?

Darwin still claimed God was involved in all this. In the final chapter of *On the Origin of Species*, he asks where all the intelligence within nature and the complexity and interdependence came from. He finds it difficult to believe that without some sort of guidance, there is not just total chaos. He puts it down to God. God created the original lifeforms with the ability to adapt and change. It is not design down to the fine detail, it is design via intelligence and adaptability.

Now, God is even greater than was first thought; God's creations adapt and change. Many Christians find this something they can agree with – after all, it just adds to the wonder and **awe** felt towards God.

The Basics

1 Who was Charles Darwin? Why is he important?
2 Explain Darwin's theory of evolution.
3 Many people claim Darwin has explained God away, so God is not needed. Why do they say that?
4 Many Christians find it possible to continue to believe in God and accept evolution. How do they do that?
5 Look at the three quotes on pages 192 and 193. What do you think they are trying to say?

[The existence of science is] not a mere happy accident, but it is a sign that the mind of the Creator lies behind the wonderful order that scientists are privileged to explore. (John Polkinghorne, physicist and theologian)

5 Theme B: Religion and life

The Genesis creation story

A creation story is a story telling us how God created the world and universe.

The Christian creation story is written in the Bible. The first book of the Bible is called Genesis, which means beginning, and it begins with God's creation of the world. This version is known as the Genesis creation story, or the Christian creation story, or the seven days of creation story. It is also believed by Jewish and Muslim people. You may have already learned a little about it.

In Genesis, it says that at the beginning there was nothing. God decided to create the world. On each day of this creation, God made a new thing.

On the first day, God created light. God separated light from dark, so that there was day and night.

On the second day, God created the heavens.

On the third day, God collected the water together to give land and sea. God also made plants of every kind grow on the land.

On the fourth day, God created the sun, moon and stars, so that there were lights for the day and the night, and to mark the seasons.

On the fifth day, God created the fish and birds.

On the sixth day, God created animals, and then humans – in God's image.

Finally, on the seventh day, God rested. Each day, God had looked back at the creation and said that it was *good*. God had created a good world.

That creation story is understood in different ways. However it is interpreted or understood, it is what we call a religious truth. Religious truth does not change, it is a truth for all time. Religious people believe this is so because it is a truth which came from God. God is eternal, and without fault, so it must be true.

For some, the creation story as told in Genesis is literally (word for word) true. They believe in an all-powerful, all-loving, all-knowing God – so it is easy to believe that God really could do this in the way described. This is a fundamentalist view of the Bible, and hence of creation.

The order of the creation makes sense: the planet, then vegetation, then fish and birds, then animals, finally man. Genesis perhaps seems a little quick in comparison to what science says, but it was a story first told thousands of years ago. It is told in the only way it could be told, using the language and knowledge of the time, so many believe that the order of the story is correct but the timing is out.

There are some key messages in the story. It is telling us that humans have a purpose; they were deliberately made by the Creator. This was a designed and considered creation – not just an accidental, chaotic happening.

Religious, philosophical and ethical studies

Science ... or religion ... or both?

Can you believe both science and religion on the matter of the origins of life? Read each of these people's understanding of Genesis. Which of them could believe in both Genesis and the Big Bang?

Josh believes the Bible is the Word of God. Everything written in it is absolutely true. God told people exactly what to write. This includes Genesis. So Josh believes that every word of Genesis is true. He believes that the Genesis story is exactly how the world began. It is word for word true. The world was created in seven days by God.

Josh says God can do anything and God is really clever. This means God could create the world. He says we will never understand how, because we are humans not gods, so we should just believe it.

Ronnie believes the Bible is true, but not word for word. He believes God told people things, but they made some mistakes and misunderstood some of what they heard when they wrote them down. So the story in Genesis is right, but not exactly. For example, the story you have read uses the word 'days', but the original language uses a word which means 'periods of time'. Maybe the story was really saying that over a long time, God made the world change and develop. Ronnie believes that. Ronnie believes Genesis is more or less what happened.

Brett believes the Bible is people's ideas about things that happened. He thinks people thought about events and believed that God had been involved. This means that someone was saying how they believed the world began because of God. This means Genesis is not word for word true. Brett still believes God created the world. Scientists did not exist when the story was first told. People had to tell the story in the way that made sense. Genesis makes sense, and it matches the way that scientists say the universe was formed and life developed.

Whether someone could believe both depends on how strictly they follow their religious story. The Big Bang theory and the religious creation story obviously say different things, so a literal understanding of Genesis would make believing both a problem. However, the less literally we take Genesis, the easier it is to see it as a non-scientific way of understanding the world around us. If we think of Genesis as having a message for us, then it is not even answering the same question as science. Science is telling us how, while religion is telling us why.

It is the same with science though; the more completely you believe that theory, the less room there is to believe anything else.

And anyway, who did make the Big Bang go bang?!

The Basics

1 Explain the different interpretations of Genesis.
2 'It is impossible to believe both science and religion when it comes to the origins of the universe.' Explain arguments for and against this statement.

5   Theme B: Religion and life

Comparing these truths

Which is more important, science or religion? If you look at the number of faith schools compared to the number of science schools, you might think religion was more important. If you compare how much time science takes up on your timetable with how much RS does, you might get a different answer. How many science programmes are on TV, compared to religious programmes? What about in the news? Is there more science or more religion? Does either dominate news as a whole or does it all depend on what is happening in the world at the time?

Science, as you have learned, is about hypotheses and testing. It describes observed regularities in the world around us; it helps us make sense of how the world works. Religion is about giving a sense of purpose and meaning to our lives; it can act as a control on behaviour, because of its rules and the promise of an **afterlife**; it gives people a sense of well-being and comfort. *Are those things the same?*

Science and religion are different kinds of truth, telling us different things. So maybe they do not even contradict each other. Many people dismiss religion because it tells us things without scientific proof. However, science works on theories, like the Big Bang – there is evidence for the theory, but not absolute proof. Is there a difference?

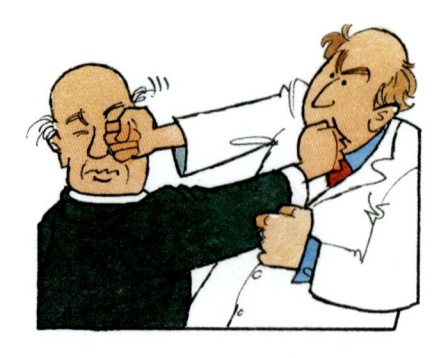

> With a partner, try to work out why society seems to favour science over religion.
>
> You might say because science has proved lots of religious ideas wrong. Or because we live in a modern world. Or because religion is not relevant today. Or that science has greater logic – so is more attractive.

Why does religion still prove strong in the world?

You might have said because it answers questions nothing else can. Or it makes us feel special. Or it is a tradition. Or simply that it is right.

In our society, science holds a high place. It is very important to society's development and improvement right now, and it seems to have overtaken religion for many people. Science does challenge religious beliefs, and this course wants you to explore two of the biggest challenges science has made.

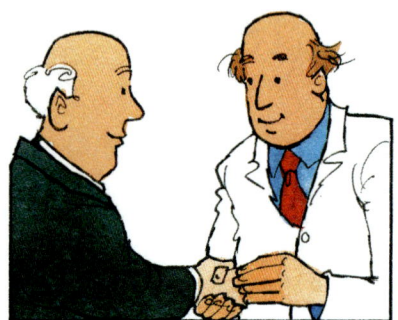

The Basics

1. What is meant by science and religion?
2. Which is more important, science or religion – and why? Use the reasoning you have just read in your answer.
3. 'Both science and religion are valuable in our world today.' What do you think? Give three arguments to agree and three in disagreement. Remember to explain each.

Religious, philosophical and ethical studies

The value of the world

You have already learned that most religious believers think God created the world. This part of the theme looks at key environmental issues, and how religious believers might think about these issues, or might try to be part of the solution to them.

Key concepts

All religious believers believe that life is sacred, or special. This must extend to all life and so the world becomes sacred as it is the home to all. It should be treated with respect.

The idea that God created the world means it has to be looked after. In fact, religious people believe they were given a responsibility or duty by God to look after the world (**stewardship**).

As the prime species, religious believers think that God gave them the right to decide what happens to the world and all the species in it. This is called **dominion**. Humans have power over nature by permission of God.

When people look at the beautiful things in nature, they can be struck by a sense of wonderment. They are amazed and 'wowed' by beautiful sunsets, landscapes, waterfalls and the power of nature. This is called awe. For religious people, that sense of awe makes them praise God even more because they believe God created the world. God is responsible for the things that make them feel this way. They want to worship God more as a result.

Is the world important?

Of course it is! We live on it. Our children will live on it after we have passed away. We need to look after it, if only because it is in our own personal interests.

For religious people, they also have the duty of stewardship, and the hope that they will be rewarded in heaven, or the next rebirth, for their positive work for the environment.

197

Abuse of the environment

Buddhism

Buddhist attitude to the environment

Buddhists believe that all life, in whatever form, should be respected. So, Buddhists should respect the natural world. Since everyone must live many, many lifetimes, it is important to protect the world for our own future, as well as our children's. Two key beliefs for Buddhists then would be respect and compassion.

The Dalai Lama has said:
- Destruction of nature and **natural resources** results from ignorance, greed and lack of respect for the Earth's living things … This lack of respect extends to future generations who will inherit a vastly degraded planet.
- The Earth is not only the common heritage of all humankind but also the ultimate source of life.
- **Conservation** is not merely a question of morality, but a question of our own survival.

Buddhism also teaches:
- Help not harm other sentient beings. (First Precept)
- Compassion for all life.
- There are karmic consequences to all of our actions.

Looking after the environment is about the people of the future, it is about the other forms of life now and in the future. Ignorance and greed are two of the Three Poisons which keep people from Enlightenment, and much environmental damage is because of people and business wanting more for themselves – money, space, anything.

You can find out more here: **www.earthsangha.org**

Pollution

Pollution basically means there is too much of something which is toxic and causes damage to the environment. It can affect air, water or land. We now even talk about light and noise pollution. Usually, it is a result of human actions.

Busy roads and factories cause air pollution. That affects our health and drives some wildlife away. It also produces acid rain, where chemicals dissolve in water droplets in the atmosphere so that when rain falls it poisons the land and water, and damages buildings and structures.

Factories can cause water pollution by emptying waste into rivers, poisoning them. Fertiliser running off farmers' fields can kill off all the fish, as it makes the algae grow too fast, taking the oxygen from the water. This is just one form of toxic chemical. Too much **pesticide** does more damage to the ecosystem than intended and can change its whole balance.

You have probably added to land pollution because of dropping litter. This does not just look bad, it also kills lots of wild animals who eat it or get trapped in it.

In towns and cities, you see fewer stars than when you are in the countryside. The lights at ground level block out the stars, causing light pollution.

People living near airports, for example, suffer from noise pollution because of the sound of planes taking off and landing. Even if it does not affect their hearing, it makes life unpleasant, and affects the value of their homes.

Pollution is a big part of the reason for **global warming** and climate change. Our waste produces greenhouse gases which heat the Earth.

The Basics

1. What is meant by pollution?
2. 'Pollution is a fact of life; it cannot be stopped.' Choose three reasons to agree with this statement and three to disagree, and explain each.

Religious, philosophical and ethical studies

Global warming and climate change

Climate change is the idea that the Earth's temperature is increasing and therefore causing more extreme weather, such as flooding and more storms. This is happening as temperatures everywhere are getting higher and this is what is meant by global warming. The questions are: why that is happening; what the consequences will be; and how we can try to stop it, because it is a problem.

Why is it happening?

The Earth's cycle is to get hotter and cooler over time. You have heard of the ice ages, when the Earth froze over; global warming is the opposite. So climate change and global warming are all part and parcel of the Earth's life. However, scientists know that the activities of humans over the last 250 years, and especially the last 100, have speeded up temperature change. They estimate that the surface temperature of the Earth will increase between 1.4 and 5.8°C before 2100. This is mainly because of greenhouse gases, particularly CO_2 released by burning **fossil fuels** for energy, transport and industry. Following the precautionary principle, scientists are telling us we need to act now.

What are the consequences?

Imagine British summers so hot you do not need to go to Greece for a sunshine holiday! It sounds good, so what is the problem?

Hotter usually means dryer and so plants and animals have to adapt or die. Hotter everywhere means some places become just too hot to exist in. The ice caps melt, so the seas rise and lands flood (and Britain is surrounded by the sea). If it gets too hot, the diseases found in hot countries come too, such as malaria, dengue fever, and so on. Everyone will need air-conditioning, which will cost money and resources. Hotter and drier also means a greater likelihood of wildfires, as we have begun to see in the UK in summer, but are seeing in greater numbers and size across the world in areas already used to them.

Climate change also means more extreme weather systems, bringing more damaging wind, flooding and storms. In the UK over the last few years, we have seen the evidence of this in terms of storms and floods.

> With a partner, work out what it would be like in school all year if climate change caused the place where you live to become too hot. What problems would there be? What solutions can you see?

Some effects of global warming: drought, melting ice caps and flooding

5 Theme B: Religion and life

Solutions?

Scientists say the key solution is to change our energy use. We need to find alternatives to fossil fuels (coal, gas and oil) so that the fuels we use do not add to the problem. This is called **sustainable energy** – in other words, we can keep using it without doing more harm. It is energy which meets the needs of the present without compromising the ability of future generations to meet their own needs.

> With a partner, list as many forms of renewable energy as you can. You have probably covered this in science – so use that knowledge here as well.

The Basics

1. What is meant by climate change and global warming?
2. Why do scientists think the Earth is getting hotter?
3. What is the main change we can make to try to slow this effect?
4. 'Religious believers should work harder to fight climate change.' Choose three reasons to disagree with this statement and explain each. Then choose three reasons to agree, and explain them.
5. 'Global warming is the biggest problem facing humans today.' Explain reasons to agree and disagree with this statement. Include religious arguments in your answer.

✝ Christianity

Christian attitude to the environment

Christians believe God created the world, and gave humankind stewardship – the responsibility to look after the world. Christians, in modern times especially, have seen the need to work to heal the world and look after the environment.

The Bible teaches:
- 'God made the world and gave the duty of stewardship to humans.' (Genesis 1:28)
- 'The Earth is the Lord's, and everything in it.' (Psalms 23:1)
- 'Respect for life extends to the rest of creation.' (Pope John Paul II)
- 'More than ever – individually and collectively – people are responsible for the future of the planet.' (Pope John Paul II)
- 'I want to awake in you a deep admiration for creation, until anywhere thinking of plants and flowers, you are overcome by thoughts of the Creator.' (St Basil)

Clearly, humans have a special role on Earth, which is to look after the Earth and animals. Since humans must face God on the Day of Judgement, all must carry out their given duties. If humans did not look after the world, or did nothing to stop its destruction, they should expect to be punished by God. Many Christians are motivated to do environmental work because of this belief.

You can find out more here:
www.greenchristian.org.uk

My house was flooded three times in two years. Torrential rain has made the river break its banks. I'm not the only one to suffer, but it has been devastating. We will have to move – but I have lived here all my life.

David

Destruction of natural habitats (deforestation)

You read about pollution on page 198. Pollution is one reason why natural habitats are being destroyed. For example, if a tanker spills oil into the sea it wipes out life in that area, and degrades the land for many years. Research the Torrey Canyon spill to get a better idea of this.

Another reason is deforestation, where huge areas of forest are cut down – for example, to create grazing land for cattle, or to create areas for building, mining and roads. The trees, of course, are the habitat for many species and so these species are affected; some are even dying out. Also, the trees take in carbon dioxide and release oxygen that we breathe, so they help the fight against global warming.

The rainforests also contain many plants which can be used as medicines, which are lost with deforestation. There are thought to be many species of animals and plants which we have not even recorded yet in the rainforests; they could become extinct before we have even studied them. Even without causing extinction, natural habitats are destroyed and species endangered.

> How could we make up for destroying these habitats?

Land is cleared in Borneo for palm oil plantations; orangutans lose their habitat, and are now an endangered species

ॐ Hinduism

Hindu attitude to the environment

Traditionally, Hindu life was very simple, and relied on nature. This was linked with beliefs about the **sanctity of life** and non-violence to form the religion, which is peaceful towards the environment. Brahman (the Ultimate Reality) is in all life.

Hinduism teaches:
- There should be respect for all life, including the created world.
- There should be ahimsa (non-violence).
- You should focus on environmental values. (the hymn, Artharva Veda)
- 'Trees have five sorts of kindness which are their daily sacrifice: to families they give fuel; to passers-by they give shade and a resting place; to birds they give shelter; with their leaves, roots and bark they give medicines.' (Varaha Purana)
- 'Everything rests on me as pearls are strung on a thread. I am the original fragrance of the Earth ... the taste in water ... the heat in fire and the sound in space ... the light of the sun and moon and the life of all that lives.' (Bhagavad Gita)

All life is seen as interdependent, and that includes animal and plant life. All life depends on the environment, so everyone has a vested interest in protecting and looking after it. Additionally, Hindus believe our souls will all be reborn into more lifetimes on Earth, so we have to look after it for our own future sakes. God is seen as part of nature, so protection and worship are important, as the Artharva Veda states.

You can find out more here: www.greenfaith.org

The Basics

1. What is meant by destruction of natural habitat? What does this lead to?
2. Give some reasons why this happens.
3. How could we avoid this destruction?
4. 'When God gave humans dominion over the world, it meant we could do what we like.' Explain reasons to agree and disagree with this statement.

5 Theme B: Religion and life

Use and abuse of natural resources

☪ Islam

Muslim attitude to the environment

Islam sees the creation in its entirety as the work of Allah. Humans are khalifah (stewards) of the world. Looking after the world shows respect to Allah.

Islam teaches:
- 'The world is green and beautiful, and Allah has appointed you His stewards over it.' (Qur'an)
- 'The whole Earth has been created as a place of worship.' (Qur'an)
- 'When Doomsday comes, if someone has a palm shoot in his hand, he should still plant it.' (Hadith)
- 'The Earth has been created for me as a mosque and a means of purification.' (Hadith)
- Prophet Muhammad gave the example of not wasting. He only ever washed in water from a container, not the river or other running water.

Humans are the trustees of Allah's creation. Trustees look after things, rather than destroy them.

The whole creation reflects Allah, and Allah knows everything that happens in it. He knows who damages and who looks after Allah's creation. So it is a good idea to look after the world, because those who do not follow their duty will be punished on Judgement Day by Allah.

The Muslim community is the ummah, a brotherhood, including those in the past and future. Everyone has a duty to their family and fellow humans to make sure they pass on to them a world fit to live in, not one damaged beyond repair because humans were so selfish as to think they could do what they wanted with it.

You can find out more here: www.muslimhands.org.uk

Natural resources include vegetation, minerals and fossil fuels. Humans are using these in greater quantities and at a faster rate now than at any other time in our history. This is because of how technologically advanced we are. We can take materials out of the ground faster and in greater quantities than ever before. Modern technology – for example, cars and all forms of transport, often needs more resources to run. More people use more technology more often.

Some of the fossil fuels (for example, coal) are already running out. These fuels are limited in quantity, and take millions of years to be formed. We have to find a different source of energy, which is renewable. If we do not stop using fossil fuels, they will run out, and we will have to find a new source anyway.

> Can you think of all the fuel sources we use? What new ones could we try? What will be the problems caused if, for example, oil runs out?

It is not just that these fuels are limited. They give off lots of greenhouse gases and pollution. The more we use, the more the problems stack up. So finding an alternative helps us with those problems too; it is not something we can hide from.

The Basics

1. What is meant by use and abuse of natural resources?
2. List the ways we use, overuse and abuse material resources.
3. Why do we need to find new ways to get energy?
4. What new energy forms could there be?
5. 'We must ban the use of fossil fuels now.' Explain reasons to agree and disagree with this statement.

Caring for the world

Sustainable development

This is the idea that new technological developments should all be infinite, or very long-lasting, as well as within the reach of all nations. Developments should support, not damage the environment. It would be no use swapping coal as a fuel for something else which will quickly run out. Similarly, it would be no good finding a new technology which was simply too expensive for anyone to use.

Conservation

Conservation means when we try to protect an area or species. Sometimes it involves repairing damage that has already been done – for example, to maintain the environment for an endangered species. It might include planting trees to protect an area from landslides. It might be declaring an area a nature reserve in order to protect wildlife and the environment there. This has happened in Borneo to protect orangutans.

It is becoming more common for people to take holidays which are based around conservation, either of animals, like working on a lion reserve for a few weeks in Kenya, or environmental, like rebuilding dry stone walls in Scotland to protect vegetation in fields beyond the pathways.

> Find out about a conservation project which is going on near to you.

Judaism

Jewish attitude to the environment

Jewish sacred writings begin with God's creation of the world, and go on to state that God gave humans the duty of stewardship. There are many mitzvot (rules) about looking after the environment.

Judaism teaches:

- The Genesis creation story. All is made by God and is good. Humans are given stewardship over the creation.
- The bal tashchit (do not waste) precept can be interpreted as an instruction to conserve resources. (Torah)
- 'The Earth and everything that is in it is the Lord's.' (Ketuvim)
- 'All that I created for you … do not corrupt or desolate my world … there will be no one to repair it after you.' (Midrash Ecclesiastes Rabbah 7:13)
- 'Love your neighbour as yourself.' (Leviticus)

So, clearly Jewish people have a duty to look after the world and should do this by treating it with respect. For example, land is to be left fallow on a regular cycle. Increasingly, Jewish people are becoming more active in environmental work and are linking existing Jewish values to the issue. For example, tikkun olam (healing the world) could be interpreted as tackling environmental problems; tzedek (justice) is being extended to mean justice for all of creation, including animals and the world itself. It is not possible to 'love your neighbour' if you are damaging the environment they live in.

You can find out more here: www.coejl.org

> *I was brought up to believe in tikkun olam, healing the world. I joined a local volunteer group, and have made lots of friends while helping with the cleaning of the local area. For example, we helped to get rubbish out of the local pond, and it is now attracting more birds. It feels good to be doing something good.*
>
> **Sol**

5 Theme B: Religion and life

What can individuals do?

Religious believers are like every other person on the planet and so can do what any other person can do. They can start from their own personal practice – for example, recycling, reusing, not wasting. They can join in local efforts, such as clean-ups, not buying certain goods, buying local produce. They can join in with campaigns, and donate to charities which try to resolve environmental problems. They might also work within their local religious community, encouraging others to also help or focusing worship on this issue.

The difference is their motivation, as you have already read. They have a religious motivation to look after the environment.

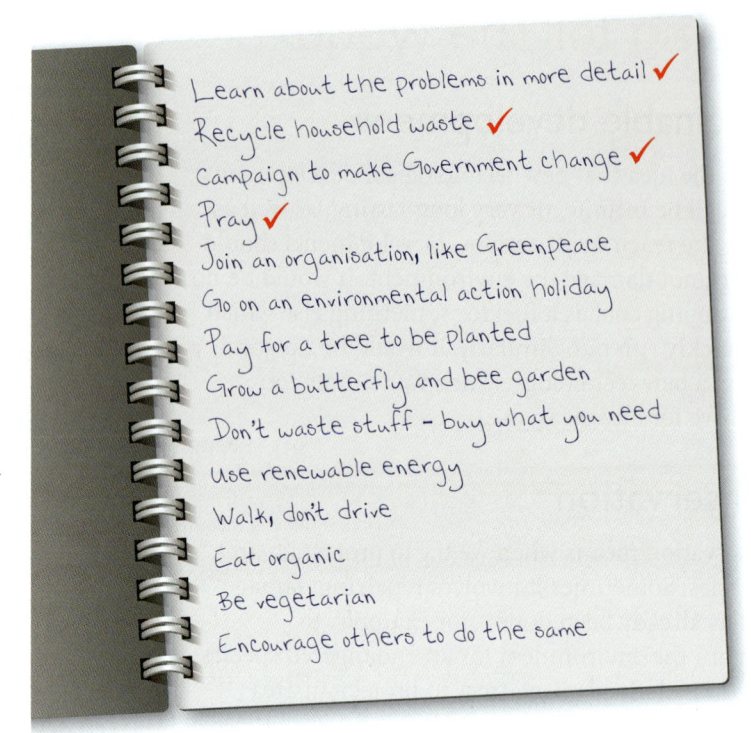

Learn about the problems in more detail ✓
Recycle household waste ✓
Campaign to make Government change ✓
Pray ✓
Join an organisation, like Greenpeace
Go on an environmental action holiday
Pay for a tree to be planted
Grow a butterfly and bee garden
Don't waste stuff – buy what you need
Use renewable energy
Walk, don't drive
Eat organic
Be vegetarian
Encourage others to do the same

The Basics

1. What is meant by sustainable development?
2. What is meant by conservation?
3. Explain why religious believers think they should look after the environment.
4. Explain how religious believers can help to solve environmental problems.
5. 'The environment should be everyone's first priority.' Do you agree? Explain your reasons, showing you have thought about more than one point of view.

I am part of the local ecology group. As I am the best with technology, I am the one who keeps the website up to date and running. I also keep environmental issues at the front of people's minds by putting up reports, displays and posters in church regularly. Everyone needs to help – it is their duty of stewardship.

Casey

I am a Sikh, and I have a job in scientific research. The projects I am working on are all about sustainable forms of energy. We need to stop using up the Earth's resources, and begin to show respect to our planet. God created this world, and it is sacred.

Japnoor

I know that when I go to be judged, I will be asked what I did for Allah's creation. I work in the local nature reserve one Sunday a month, helping to manage the plants and trees in there. Quite apart from being a good deed, it is really healthy, and I have learned loads.

Mo

Animals and animal rights

Religious people believe that animals are part of God's creation. All life, including that of animals, is sacred. Most religious believers think that they were given dominion over animals, so can make use of them for food, clothing and as working animals. However, animals should always be treated with respect, fairness and kindness.

> Think about all the ways humans use animals. Make a list of the ones which are fine – in your opinion – and those which are not. Now compare your list with a partner, and try to challenge the answers they give.

Many of the ways we use animals can be justified. The problem comes with how some people treat the animals, even in a use we find acceptable. So, for example, farming is fine, but battery farming may be thought of as cruel, given that the animals get very little space and a completely unnatural life. A religious person might choose never to buy produce which has come from a battery farm, choosing always free range.

There are specific issues which you have to know for the course. They are animal experimentation and the use of animals for food.

Sikhism

Sikh attitude to the environment

Sikhs believe the natural environment is a gift from God and that we have to take care of it. It only exists because God wants it to, so God could make it just stop existing.

Sikhism teaches:
- 'The universe comes into being by God's will.' (Guru Nanak)
- 'In nature we see God, and in nature, we hear God speak.' (Adi Granth)
- There should be respect for all life.
- 'God created everything.' (Guru Nanak)
- The Sikh ideal is a simple life free from conspicuous waste.

So, Sikhs should look after the environment out of respect for life, and as worship to God. Sikhs believe they must perform sewa (service) for others, and this can be understood to include the natural world. Of course, looking after the world means that it is safeguarded for future generations, so Sikhs are doing sewa for people in the future. They believe that it is not possible to care for the environment without thinking about society's needs too, because often environmental damage is a result of poverty.

The gurdwaras in India have signed up to a plan to replace fuel with solar power for their langars (communal meals) which feed hundreds of thousands every day.

Sikh gurus have said that God is within everything, so in some ways damaging the world is like damaging God.

You can find out more here: www.ecosikh.org

5 Theme B: Religion and life

Animal experimentation

When you mention animal experiments, many people instantly think they are very cruel. It is experiments on live animals which usually have this impact. The animals (mainly guinea pigs, mice, rats, rabbits, dogs and monkeys) are specially bred in farms.

However, animal experiments should be for the good of human beings, which is why many people, including religious believers, support them. Animal experiments further our medical knowledge so that surgical procedures are improved. They are used to test new drugs for effectiveness and so that they do not cause harm. They are also used to test new products – for example, cosmetics – for harmfulness (toxicity). Medical science has always used animals. Many surgical procedures, such as transplantation surgery, were perfected on animals. Some experiments just mean a change in diet; others cause injury or death. At the end of the experimentation any live animals left are humanely destroyed. Since 1986, in the UK, there have been specific laws to control animal experimentation.

Monkeys are bred and then used in live experiments

What are some of the issues?

1. It is cruel. Even scientists accept the animals suffer, though they believe it is for the greater good.
2. Modern science has now developed some other alternatives, like using human tissue cultures to test for toxicity.
3. Animal genetics and human genetics are different, and often reactions are not the same. So some animal experimentation is pointless as it tells us nothing helpful.

> ### The Basics
>
> 1. Explain why scientists do experiments on animals.
> 2. Explain why some religious believers disagree with animal experimentation.
> 3. 'Humans are misusing their power over animals.' Do you agree? Explain your reasons, showing you have thought about more than one point of view.

I work in a science research lab. We test new drugs on animals, before they go for human testing. These tests help us to develop drugs which can save lives. Although the animals must be tested on and must die at the end of the experiment, we have to use them. We couldn't just test on people without knowing anything about the effects of a drug.

Adil

As a Buddhist, I revere all life. However, I know that we need to protect life, and I think human life needs the greatest protection of all. I work in a research laboratory where we use human skin and tissue cultures to test products. This means that no animal is ever harmed, and that our products should be safer as all their testing has been done on human materials. Animals and humans don't always react the same way to the same things. It means I do not disrespect animal life in my work, rather I protect it.

Rita

While I know that all animals are part of the greatness of creation, I also know that humans are the highest form of it. God has given us the capacity to use animals for our own good. We can perfect surgical procedures on animals. Trainee doctors can learn how to be better surgeons – cutting, stitching, transplanting – all on animals, before they have to operate on people.

Daniel

Religious, philosophical and ethical studies

Use of animals for food

Why be vegetarian?

There are many reasons why people are vegetarian. They are usually to do with health, upbringing, religion and concerns about farming methods. Some people eat no meat or dairy products at all (vegans); some choose to eat no meat or meat products (vegetarian).

The Christian, Muslim and Jewish faiths all allow meat in their diets. Some Christians fast at certain times of year – for example, not eating certain foods during Lent. Many Christians do not eat red meat on Fridays out of respect for Jesus' sacrifice on Good Friday. Muslims and Jewish people may not eat certain meats, such as the meat of a pig, of shellfish, and of birds of prey. They may only eat ritually slaughtered meat (halal for Muslims, kosher for Jewish people). This reflects the idea that God/Allah gave humans dominion over animals, and so they could be used by humans, including as food. Hindus and Buddhists on the whole are vegetarian, reflecting two important beliefs: ahimsa (non-violence) and respect for all life. However, for Buddhists it very much depends on the culture in the country and on the available diet. For example, in Tibet a healthy diet is only possible if it includes meat. Many Sikhs are vegetarian to show respect for God's creation and the Sikh langar is always a vegetarian meal.

I don't like the taste.

I'm allergic to certain foods so I don't eat them.

I don't like the thought of how the animals are treated on the farms and at the abattoirs.

All living beings have a soul, even animals.

We should respect life, not eat some kinds of it.

I believe in non-violence, so eating meat is encouraging violence against animals.

The amount of food an animal eats would feed a lot more people than its meat would.

The Basics

1 Check pages 198–205 to find the religions you have studied. For each write any teachings which link with animals. Add any other ideas you have come across in your studies (for example, that God created all life).
2 Use what you have written to write a paragraph on the attitude of each of your two religions to animals.
3 Re-use those teachings to explain the attitude of each to eating meat.
4 Why do some people choose to be vegetarian?
5 'Eating meat is disrespectful to God's creation.' Do you agree? Give reasons and explain your answer, showing you have thought about more than one point of view.

Task

Find out about the dietary requirements of followers of the religion(s) you have studied.

5 Theme B: Religion and life

The value of human life

There is no doubt that religions say human life is the most important and special of all kinds of life. There are two key concepts: **quality of life** and sanctity of life.

Sanctity of life

This is the idea that all life is special. Many religions believe life is sacred because God created it (Christianity, Hinduism, Islam, Judaism and Sikhism). Some religions believe life is special because it is the way we can achieve Enlightenment (Buddhism and Hinduism). No one in the world believes that life is worth nothing. All the legal systems put murder as the worst crime you could commit, with the toughest punishments. All religions believe that life is special and deserves to be protected and cherished. Religions extend this belief to plant and animal life. Be sure to use this concept when talking about animals and the environment as well.

Quality of life

This is a description of how good someone's life is. It includes how comfortable they feel, how easy it is for them to live through each day, perhaps how much they have in terms of money and possessions. For this theme, it is about whether or not life is worth living because of the medical situation a person finds themselves in. Giving someone a good quality of life is part of the most basic teaching of all religions; we should treat others as we wish to be treated.

The status of human life

Religious believers think that humans are the highest form of creation, or that they are within the highest levels of spiritual development. For example, most religions believe that humans have a soul, whereas other forms of life do not (or have a lower form of one). This means that the value of human life is beyond measure, and as such it should be protected and cared for. Most religious believers are '**pro-life**' in many questions of life or death. For this part of the theme, you need to consider abortion and euthanasia. Abortion is the deliberate ending of a pregnancy so that no baby is born; euthanasia is the deliberate ending of a life for a compassionate reason based on the person having a terminal illness or a degenerative illness they can no longer cope with.

Task

Look at the scenarios listed below. In each case, decide if the key consideration is sanctity or quality of life, or both. Explain your decision each time.
- Sarah is pregnant, but has cancer and needs treatment. Treatment will lead to the termination of the foetus.
- John kills people who are dying of terminal illnesses.
- Gillian visits her mother regularly to make sure she has everything she needs and is comfortable.
- David does not agree with abortion because he says it is taking away a life God created.
- Kulpna is a doctor in the Intensive Care Unit. She makes decisions about life support.
- Jacob is very ill with cancer and is in a lot of pain. He is in a hospice.

The Basics

1. What is meant by sanctity of life?
2. What is meant by quality of life?
3. Explain why a religious believer might say that sanctity of life is more important than quality of life.
4. How might belief in sanctity of life affect the way religious believers behave?
5. 'Religious believers should always fight for life to be preserved.' Explain reasons to agree and disagree with this statement.

Religious, philosophical and ethical studies

Abortion

When does life begin?

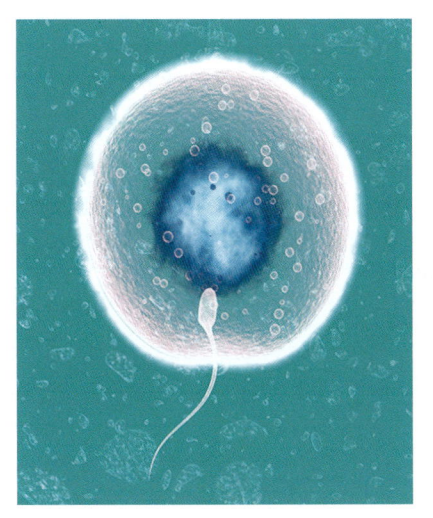

Is it at **conception**?

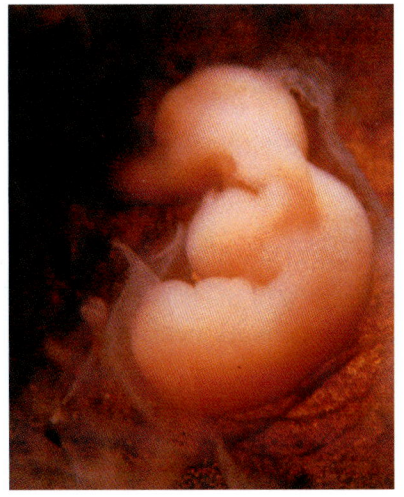

Is it when the foetus has a heart of its own, which beats?

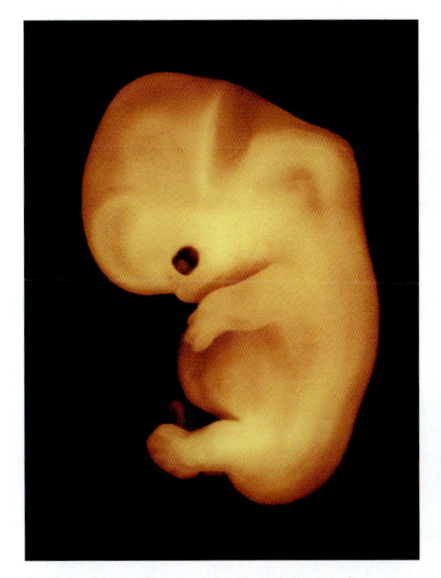

Is it when there is a backbone?

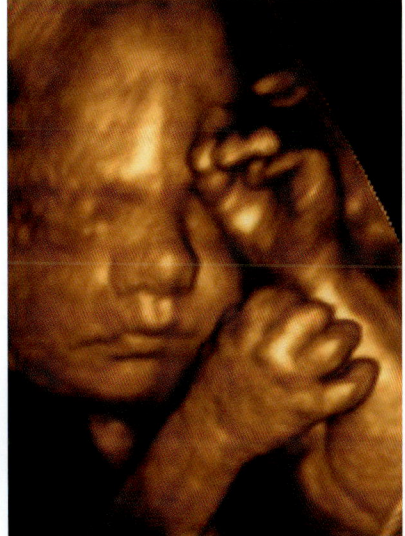

Is it when the foetus would likely survive if born prematurely (viability)?

Is it when it has been born?

The question of when life begins is key because many people see abortion as murder or killing, and there has to be a life before there can be a murder. It does affect whether or not we see an abortion as wrong.

By law, the life begins when the baby is born, but given that the Abortion Act (as amended in 1990) will not allow abortions beyond 24 weeks, is that when life begins? Many people think that when the foetus looks like a baby, it should be treated as such, whether it is fully formed or not.

What we *can* say is that at every stage the foetus is a potential life.

5   Theme B: Religion and life

The law on abortion in the UK

The law defines abortion as: 'The deliberate expulsion of a foetus from the womb, with the intention of destroying it.' It is different from a miscarriage, which has the same result (that the pregnancy ends without a baby living), because miscarriage is accidental, a turn of nature.

The law in the UK begins by stating that abortion is illegal. It then goes on to say that there are some exceptions.

Abortion can only be carried out if two registered doctors agree that at least one of the following is true:
- There is a danger to the woman's mental and/or physical health.
- The foetus will be born with physical and/or mental disabilities.
- The mental and/or physical health of existing children will be put at risk.

The abortion has to be carried out at a registered place, by a registered doctor, before the 24th week of pregnancy.

A registered doctor is a doctor who has passed medical exams and is recognised by the Medical Council. So a doctor who has been struck off the official list can neither give advice, nor carry out an abortion. A registered place is a hospital or clinic that has registration with the government, and can perform such medical procedures as abortion because of that registration. Any other place is not legal.

Breaking the law carries great penalties for all those involved.

The Basics

1. Explain what the UK law says about abortion.
2. Explain three situations in which a person might seek an abortion. For each, say whether a religious believer might agree with it.
3. Thinking about the belief in sanctity of life, how would you expect a religious believer to view abortion?

Some scenarios – what do you think?

> Before you look through these scenarios, there are some rules. You cannot just agree or disagree with any case, you have to explain why you agree or disagree. Also, you have to say what the consequences of each woman not having an abortion are because they are all asking for the abortion, even if they do not feel good about having to do that. Finally, you have to say whether you think they had another reasonable option and why.

I carry a genetic disease; doctors have tested my baby and it has the disease. If I allow it to be born, my baby will suffer greatly.

I am only 14 – too young to have this baby.

I was raped, which left me pregnant.

I am 46, and pregnant. My baby has Down's Syndrome.

I have cancer, and the doctors have advised me to have treatment (which will also end my pregnancy) for my best chance of recovery.

I am single and have no wish to have children – ever. I am pregnant because the contraception I used failed. I neither want nor planned this pregnancy.

Religious, philosophical and ethical studies

Reasons for and against abortion

Pro-life

Pro-life is the term we use for those arguments against abortion, usually in any circumstances. Pro-life pressure groups include PROLIFE and SPUC. Since they support the foetus' right to life, their arguments are all in favour of protecting the foetus to ensure it is born.

Read these comments and pick out the pro-life arguments in each one.

I believe that all life is sacred, and must be protected. So, abortion is completely wrong.

God has created life, and as stewards of this world, humans have to protect life.

Abortion is the murder of another human being. Murder is wrong.

The foetus cannot defend itself – so someone else has to.

When a foetus will be born with disabilities, we cannot say what the quality of its life would be, so should not decide to forbid it that life.

The foetus has a right to life and not to be discarded as if it is just waste.

Pro-choice

Pro-choice is usually associated with supporting the use of abortion, but it actually means the arguments which defend a woman's right to choose what happens to her body. Since they support the woman's right to choose, the arguments are about the woman, rather than the foetus. A pro-choice group is Vote for Choice (**vfc.org.uk**).

Read these comments and pick out the pro-choice arguments in each one.

A woman should have the right to decide what happens to her body.

Where a woman is pregnant as a result of rape or incest, it would be wrong to not allow her an abortion.

Some foetuses are so damaged that it would be cruel to allow them to be born.

If having a child is going to put a woman's life at risk, or is going to make her postpone medical treatment which she needs, then she should have the right to an abortion.

Up to a certain point, the foetus cannot survive outside the womb, so should not be thought of as a life in its own right.

If we banned abortions, women would still have them – but not in a safe way. We need to protect women.

Task

Find out about the work of a pro-life (against abortion) group and a pro-choice (for a woman's right to choose) group. In a presentation, explain what they do and how they campaign.

5 Theme B: Religion and life

Thinking about the lives involved

When we consider abortion, we are immediately thinking about the foetus involved. However, the law considers the woman first, not the foetus. Her life and well-being take precedence in law. So, how might her life become a greater consideration? Have a look at these examples:

> Jess has been told she has cancer of the womb. The only option is to remove her womb, which of course means removal of the foetus and the ending of the pregnancy. Without following this option, the cancer will be terminal.

> Saira has a heart defect, which means that any strain could be lethal. Obviously, pregnancy is difficult even for healthy women, especially in the last few months. The actual birth will also require a lot of work on her part. While she could have a caesarean section, the doctors are not sure her heart is strong enough to cope with that operation.

> Demi has a form of cancer which requires chemotherapy. The chemotherapy needed will affect the foetus, either by affecting its formation or causing miscarriage. If she does not have the treatment, the prognosis for her is very poor.

How would religions view the argument that a woman's life is at risk unless she has the abortion?

> *All religions believe in the sanctity of life and that life should be preserved/protected. Without the woman's life, the foetus has no chance of life.*

> *Buddhists believe the key intention must be compassion, so helping save a woman's life is compassionate.*

> *In Judaism and Islam, the life of the mother takes precedence – she is a fully developed human with responsibilities, whereas the foetus is not even born and will need everything doing for it.*

> *The Roman Catholic Church sees abortion as wrong, but where it is the 'side effect' of a procedure to save a woman's life, it can be accepted.*

> *The Church of England has said that abortion is a great moral evil, but that where the continuance of a pregnancy threatens a woman's life, then it is justifiable.*

> *In Judaism, before the birth, the foetus has no right to life over the mother.*

It seems clear, then, that religions believe the woman has the right to an abortion, albeit still considered a moral evil, if her life is at risk.

The Basics

1. Refer to page 210 to explain what the law in the UK says about the woman's right to an abortion. On what grounds does it support her rights?
2. Explain why religious believers believe a woman's life is more important than that of the foetus.
3. 'The only acceptable reason to have an abortion is when the woman's life is at risk.' Argue for and against this statement and use religious arguments in your answer.

Other questions about abortion

When students discuss this topic, they often get into debates in two areas not covered so far: whose right is it to decide that an abortion is the appropriate action, and what else could a woman choose to do to avoid abortion?

Looking at this, you can see there are a number of people who contribute to the decision. The woman is probably the first – after all it is her body. You would expect her to discuss it with the father. She might also discuss with her own parents or siblings – we often talk to them about issues. She will have to talk to a doctor – and under UK law, doctors are the ones who sanction and carry out abortions (without their say-so, she cannot have an abortion legally). The question is, who gets the biggest say and the final decision?

> What do you think? What rights do you think each person in the image has to agree or block abortion?

What other options are available?

If the woman has a medical condition, she may have no choice but to have the abortion or she forfeits her own life. That seems quite straightforward, but it is still difficult because it involves taking life.

A woman could decide against abortion, complete the pregnancy and have the baby fostered or adopted. At some point, by law, that child would be able to find out about their birth circumstances and might come back to the mother to ask questions.

Or, she could decide against abortion and continue the pregnancy. She would be choosing to work through, or in spite of, the problems which made her consider abortion. If there had been a risk to her mental or physical health, this is even more difficult.

> Can you think of the pros and cons of each of these alternatives to abortion?

Practising debate

Write arguments for and against each of these statements, giving at least three reasons for each side.

1. Only the pregnant woman should have any say in deciding to have an abortion.
2. Women in the UK should not be allowed to have abortions.
3. There is no need to have an abortion in the UK as there are better alternatives available.

5 Theme B: Religion and life

Euthanasia

Euthanasia is mercy killing. It is helping someone to die who is suffering from a terminal illness, or whose quality of life is less than they can bear, usually because of a degenerative disease. Euthanasia is done because of compassion or loving kindness.

The debates surrounding euthanasia have a long history. Hippocrates, a doctor from Ancient Greece, openly stated he would not prescribe drugs to help someone end their life. His stance has become the basis for the Hippocratic Oath, sworn by doctors in the UK, which says: 'I will give no deadly medicine to anyone if asked, nor suggest such counsel …' In 1516CE, Thomas More defended euthanasia as the last treatment option for doctors to give, if the patient wanted it.

In the twenty-first century, in most Western countries, groups exist to try to make euthanasia legal. In some countries – for example, the Netherlands and Belgium – it is legal.

Voluntary euthanasia is when the person who is suffering asks for euthanasia to end their suffering. This could be active euthanasia, for example being given lethal drugs to end their life so their illness does not kill them. However, it could also be a choice to stop taking medication, so that their illness kills them. This is passive euthanasia.

Non-voluntary euthanasia is when the patient is unable to say what they want to happen, and their family has to decide. It is usually that the person is on life support and will not recover. This is usually acceptable to most people, because actually the person is being allowed to die rather than being killed.

> I think active euthanasia is always wrong, but passive euthanasia is respecting natural law.

> I think euthanasia should be legal in the UK – only if a person wants it.

> It is unfair to not allow active euthanasia when a person's pain is so bad they couldn't opt for passive euthanasia.

Agree or disagree?

The law on euthanasia in the UK

Euthanasia is illegal in the UK. It can be seen as assisted suicide, so breaking the Suicide Act of 1961, which forbids anyone from helping someone else to die, and carries a 14-year jail sentence. It can also be viewed as manslaughter or, at worst, murder, which carries a life sentence.

Doctors do switch off life-support machines when patients have no sign of brain activity, and they do administer drugs to ease pain which also shorten life. Neither of these is seen as euthanasia in the UK.

The Basics

1. What is meant by euthanasia?
2. Using examples, explain the difference between active and passive euthanasia, and between voluntary and non-voluntary euthanasia.
3. What is the law in the UK regarding euthanasia?
4. 'Everyone should have the right to die if that is what they want.' Do you agree? Give reasons and explain your answer, showing you have thought about more than one point of view.

Tasks

Look at the scenarios below. Which ones are voluntary euthanasia and which ones non-voluntary?
- Ben's doctor agrees to inject him with a medicine to stop his heart and kill him.
- Carl's doctor turns off his life-support machine.
- Lisa stops taking medicine to fight a brain tumour, so that it will kill her sooner.
- Jean's husband suffocates her when she says she cannot cope with the pain anymore.

Religious, philosophical and ethical studies

The right to die

In society, arguments about euthanasia focus around the right of a person to choose their own death. On the whole, religious believers do not believe humans have the right to make this decision. You need to explore why people have these views. First, think of as many reasons as possible why people might agree with or disagree with euthanasia.

Arguing for the right to die

- It is my body, so should be my right to make decisions about it, after all I can elect for surgery, have tattoos, and make every other major decision.

- When you consider all human rights, the **right to die** naturally follows on from them.

- I am the only one who can really say when my life is no longer worth living.

- We see it as compassionate to put animals in pain to sleep, so should allow the same compassion to humans.

Arguing against the right to die

- To allow euthanasia would be to encourage it, so that people would force it on others for their own advantage – for example, making an elderly relative feel a burden.

- Life does not belong to us, it belongs to God – euthanasia is playing God.

- We should care for people in their last days, showing love, not kill them.

- Doctors and nurses take oaths to protect life, not to end it.

To find out about the more detailed reasons and explanations for and against euthanasia, look at some websites of organisations on the right to die, such as: **www.dignityindying.org.uk**; **www.carenotkilling.org.uk**.

Quality *versus* sanctity of life

Check out the definitions of these terms on page 225. Many people say that euthanasia is all about the quality of life and that for those who want euthanasia, they are suffering too much, they no longer have a good quality of life. Others say that, regardless of quality, life must be maintained because it is too special to end. *What do you think?*

> ### The Basics
> 1 Explain the reasons people give to support euthanasia.
> 2 Explain the reasons people give to disagree with euthanasia.
> 3 Explain why quality of life is an important issue in relation to euthanasia.
> 4 Explain why sanctity of life is an important issue in relation to euthanasia.
> 5 'The right to die should always take priority over the sanctity of life.' Explore this statement, giving reasons to agree with it and to disagree. Include religious arguments in your answer.

5 Theme B: Religion and life

Care for the dying – the hospice movement

Hospices are the preferred Christian response to the issue of euthanasia. A hospice is a home for those who are terminally ill (dying). They are for both children and adults of all ages – for example, those with cancer. People may go there until they die or to give their families respite from looking after them for a while. On average people stay there for two weeks.

Originally, hospices were places for travellers, the sick and the needy to stay. They were set up by Christians. Over time, some of them began to specialise in looking after those who were dying.

When someone is dying, they cannot be cured – only cared for. Hospices try to provide care for all aspects of a person's illness and suffering. Many religious people believe that if the care is good enough, then euthanasia would not even be considered.

The aims of hospices:

1. To relieve the physical symptoms of illness. In other words, to get rid of as much pain as is possible. This includes whatever it takes – for example, massage, meditation and relaxation. Often, medical treatment for the dying is very specialised. It is called palliative care.

2. To care for the emotional and spiritual well-being of the patient. Many dying people have unfinished business, which is a worry to them. The hospices help them to sort things out. Many patients are angry, asking questions such as 'why me?'; hospices help them to come to terms with dying. Many patients need to be listened to and often relatives cannot cope with this, but the hospices do.

3. To support the families of patients, who suffer too. Hospices provide many support networks and services for them, even after the death of the patient.

4. To educate others caring for the dying, and to work out new, better ways to care for the dying which will be invaluable in the future. The experience built up in hospices can be used in other places.

Religious groups see hospices as the way forward for terminally ill people. God wants us to care for these people, to look after them, to express God's love for them, not to kill them.

St Ann's Hospice (www.sah.org.uk)

This hospice was opened in 1971 and serves the Greater Manchester community. Its aim is to improve the quality of life of people with life-threatening illnesses. It aims to do this while supporting families and carers.

In a year, the hospice treats over 5,500 patients, of whom about 5,000 are outpatients. In 2018, it cost over £12 million to run St Ann's, meaning that the hospice has to raise £20,000 a day. The NHS provides only 37 per cent of funds, so most of the money comes from voluntary donations.

Ninety-five per cent of patients are suffering from a cancer-related illness. Each patient is given a personal care plan, which is tailored to meet their individual needs. This is what makes the support so unique and effective.

Task

Find out about a hospice local to your school. Learn something of the work it does, the numbers of people it helps each year, whether it specialises in certain illnesses or age groups. Produce a report on that hospice for others in your class.
www.hospiceuk.org.uk is the national charity for hospices. You can learn much about the hospice movement from that website.

Religious attitudes to life

☸ Buddhism

Buddhism tells us:
- Life is special and must be protected.
- The First Precept is to help not harm others.
- A primary guiding principle of Buddhism is to reduce suffering.
- The Dalai Lama has said: 'Where a person is definitely going to die, and keeping them alive leads to more suffering, then termination of life is permitted under Mahayana Buddhism.'
- Buddhists must show compassion (loving kindness) and practise ahimsa (non-violence).

The first and most important precept is not to take life; abortion and euthanasia both do this. So a first reaction might be that neither would be supported by Buddhism. However, the key element is the intention behind any action, and this may lead to the conclusion that either abortion or euthanasia is more of a right action than a wrong one. Every situation has to be judged separately.

Many Buddhists would point to the belief that suffering has come as a karmic consequence and so a person suffering may need to work through that so as not to face the same in a future life. It is important to make death as comfortable as possible, as our state of mind when we die is the key to shaping our next life. If we face death with anxiety, anger and upset, our next rebirth is negatively set. Facing death with acceptance is better. Hence, hospices which help people to face their death with calm are supported by Buddhism.

✝ Christianity

Christianity tells us:
- 'God created life in his own image.' (Genesis)
- 'Do not kill.' (Ten Commandments)
- 'I, your God, give life, and I take it away.' (Old Testament)
- The Catholic Church teaches that life must be respected from conception until natural death.
- Doctors do not have an overriding obligation to prolong life by all means possible. (Church of England)

It is clear that, on most occasions, Christians will not agree with either abortion or euthanasia. All life is believed to be sacred as it was created by, and belongs to, God. While death might mean going to heaven to be with God, it should not be hastened. Life should always be protected. For most Christians, abortion is always morally wrong. Some accept it rarely as a *necessary evil*.

In the case of abortion, where the mother's life is at risk, it is difficult because her life is also sacred. Most Christians would accept procedures which save her life, even if they lead to the ending of the pregnancy. Many would also point to the fact that in many cases there are options other than abortion – for example, adoption.

In the case of euthanasia, few support active euthanasia, regardless of what a person might themselves wish for. This is seen as killing, so wrong. However, in countries where euthanasia is legal, there are Christian groups who also agree with it. For example, the Dutch Protestant Church in the Netherlands, who see it as an act of love and compassion and a good use of the medical knowledge God has granted us.

Task

With a partner, come up with reasons for and against these statements:
- The mother's life is the most important in decisions about abortion.
- Abortion is always wrong.
- When it comes to euthanasia, quality of life is more important than sanctity of life.
- Euthanasia is just a form of murder.

5 Theme B: Religion and life

ॐ Hinduism

Hinduism tells us:
- 'Those who carry out abortions are amongst the worst of sinners.' (Arthava Veda)
- 'Compassion, ahimsa and respect for life are key.' (Hindu virtues)
- 'The result of a virtuous action is pure joy; actions done from emotion bring pain and suffering.' (Bhagavad Gita)
- 'The one who tries to escape from the trials of this life by taking their own life will suffer even more in the next life.' (Yajur Veda)

Life is very special and sacred, and must be protected. Hindu teachings are strongly against abortion. In each lifetime, a soul creates new karma for the next and 'pays off' the consequence of bad karma. By terminating a pregnancy, we deny the soul that chance to create/repay karmic consequences in a lifetime. So we block the soul's progress towards union with the Ultimate Reality. Some scriptures say that those who have abortions will themselves suffer that fate many times. Where a woman's life is at risk, abortion is acceptable as her life takes priority.

Many older Hindus see it as acceptable to refuse food and treatment so that they will die, rather than be a burden on their families. So, in this sense, passive euthanasia is acceptable. It is also expected that families will care for their elderly relatives as a mark of respect, which suggests euthanasia should not be necessary. However, active euthanasia is considered murder and wrong. Hindu principles support care for the dying, not the ending of their life.

☪ Islam

Islam tells us:
- 'Neither kill nor destroy yourself.' (Qur'an)
- 'No one can die except by Allah's leave, that is a decree with a fixed term.' (Qur'an)
- 'Each person is created individually by Allah from a single clot of blood.' (Qur'an)
- 'Do not take life – which Allah has made sacred – except for a just cause.' (Qur'an)
- 'Euthanasia is zulm – wrong doing against Allah.' (Shari'ah Law)

All life is specially created by Allah, and Allah has a plan for each life; both abortion and euthanasia go against these plans. Hence, for most Muslims, abortion is always wrong, as is any form of self-harm or self-killing.

There is a debate within Islam as to when ensoulment takes place (when the soul becomes part of the growing foetus). It is varyingly said to be at conception, at 40 days or at 120 days. Before that time, technically an abortion is acceptable because no life is being taken. Where a mother's life is at risk, most Muslims would defend the woman's right to life.

Prophet Muhammad told the story of a man who helped a friend die because he was in so much pain. The man and his friend were both denied paradise as a result. No one knows the plans of Allah, this is called al-Qadr or the predestination of Allah's will. In other words, Allah has planned for this experience, so it must have some value. Life will end when Allah wills it, so euthanasia is not acceptable. This does not mean that passive euthanasia is wrong; this would be accepted where there was no hope.

Task

With a partner, discuss whether the religion(s) you have studied would agree with abortion in these scenarios:
- a woman who is suffering from an ectopic pregnancy
- a woman whose pregnancy came about through rape
- a woman who feels unready to have a child.

Religious, philosophical and ethical studies

☪ Judaism

Judaism tells us:
- 'Do not kill.' (Ten Commandments)
- 'God gives life and God takes away life.' (Psalms)
- The foetus is 'mere water' until the 40th day of pregnancy.
- 'If there is anything which causes a hindrance to the departure of the soul then it is permissible to remove it.' (Rabbi Moses Isserles)
- The emphasis in Judaism is on life and new life, not the destruction of life.

In Judaism, life is sacred. Foetal life is not a life in its own right and does not have rights until it is born. Hence, there are many situations in which abortion would be allowed in Judaism – for example, if the woman's life is in danger, and for medical reasons (therapeutic abortion). Some rabbis have extended this idea of endangerment to include a woman's mental health being in danger – for example, after rape. Across the spectrum of Judaism, there are many different attitudes to what counts as therapeutic abortion.

Judaism believes death should be a calm experience, and attitudes to euthanasia vary greatly. The central question is whether euthanasia shortens life or shortens the act of dying. Shortening the act of dying, that is, not doing things which extend and prolong the pain, allows a person a 'good death', and so is acceptable. It is important to protect life and to care for the dying. Active euthanasia is considered to be wrong because it actually causes death. Euthanasia can be seen as throwing life away, which is absolutely and always wrong.

☬ Sikhism

Sikhism tells us:
- 'God sends us and we take birth, God calls us back and we die.' (Guru Granth Sahib)
- Life begins at conception.
- 'God fills us with light so we can be born.' (Guru Granth Sahib)
- 'All life is sacred and should be respected.' (Guru Granth Sahib)

According to Sikhism, all life is sacred and every soul is on a journey through many lifetimes to achieve liberation. That life begins at conception means abortion is generally considered to be morally wrong, as it is a form of murder. Abortion is also the destruction of God's creation and the opposite of Sikh ideals for life. This does not mean that a Sikh will never contemplate abortion – seeing it on some occasions as a necessary evil.

In Sikhism, there is no place for euthanasia. The Sikh gurus set up hospitals and many Sikhs work in the caring services because of the duty of sewa (service to others). This means looking after and healing, not harming or ending life. Active euthanasia is wrong, it is killing. Any suffering may be seen as working through the negative karma of previous lifetime(s), so must be lived through, not avoided. A Sikh's duty where someone is dying is to care for them until God decides they die, not to hasten their death.

Tasks

1. With a partner, discuss whether the religion(s) you have studied would agree with euthanasia in these situations:
   - a man on life support in a persistent vegetative state
   - a man suffering horrendous terminal cancer pain
   - a woman with end-stage motor neurone disease.
2. Read the information about the religion(s) you are studying. Explain what their attitude might be to: euthanasia, abortion and life support. Use religious teachings to support your explanation.

5 Theme B: Religion and life

Religious beliefs about death and an afterlife

Death is when our brain and body stop functioning permanently. No one recovers from death. Religious people believe that at death the soul/spirit/self leaves the physical body. Beliefs about what happens to it vary from one religion to another, but all believe there is a continuation and some other kind of life.

Buddhism

Buddhists believe in rebirth. There is no permanent soul, rather a mix of ever-changing skandhas: emotions, feelings, intelligence and so on. After the death of the body, this mix fuses with an egg and sperm at conception. The thoughts, actions and intentions of each life shape the quality of the next. The goal is to achieve Enlightenment and stop being reborn.

Hinduism

Hindus believe in reincarnation. Their atman (soul) lives through many lifetimes, each one shaped by the thoughts, words and actions of their past lifetime(s). Its goal is to achieve Enlightenment and become one with the Ultimate Reality, so stopping being reincarnated.

Judaism

Judaism focuses on this life, rather than the next. Some teachings mention a heavenly place. Jewish people talk of the 'world to come', which is when the Messiah will come to rule the Earth in peace. That is life after death because the dead will be woken to live through that time.

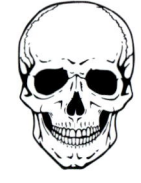

Christianity

Christians believe in the physical resurrection of the body. At death, the body waits until Judgement Day. Catholics call this purgatory. At judgement, each person faces God and Jesus to evaluate their deeds. If they were good in life, they go to heaven, which is paradise and wonderful forever. If they were bad, they go to hell for eternal punishment (see pages 12–15).

Islam

Muslims believe in resurrection. At death, the body waits in the grave (barzakh) and sees the events of its life. This can be quick or very slow and painful. On Judgement Day, people are sorted according to their beliefs and actions. The wicked are cast into hell; the truly good go straight to paradise. All others cross As-Sirat bridge, carrying the book of their deeds (sins make it heavier). The bridge is sharp and so they are purified from sin before going to paradise.

Sikhism

Sikhs believe in reincarnation. The soul is born into many lifetimes, whose quality is decided by the words, thoughts and deeds of the previous lifetime(s). The point of each life is to serve and worship God, so that eventually the soul can be reunited with God (waheguru) and stop being reincarnated.

> Think about this statement: If I believe any of these to be true, how might that belief affect my behaviour now in this life?

Contrasting beliefs

Abortion

✝ Roman Catholics

Roman Catholics believe that abortion is always wrong. They say **life is sacred** because it was created by God. They also believe that **life begins at conception**. This means life must be protected from conception, so any abortion is wrong. The Didache states 'Do not kill your children by abortion.' Vatican II says 'Life must be protected with the utmost care from the moment of conception.'

✝ Anglican

Many Anglicans accept abortion as a necessary evil. For example, the mother's life may be at risk (e.g. ectopic pregnancy) – her life is also sacred.

✡ Judaism

In Judaism, the life of the mother takes priority as hers is an actual life, while that of the foetus is only a potential life. Should there be any risk to her life, the principle of **Pikuach Nefesh** comes into play – an abortion should be carried out.

☪ Islam

In Islam, abortion is frowned upon. However, for many, **ensoulment** (when the foetus acquires a soul) only takes place at 120 days. Before this, it may be permissible to have an abortion.

Question

Explain two contrasting beliefs in contemporary British society about abortion.

In your answer you should refer to the main religious tradition of Great Britain and one or more other religious traditions. *(4 marks)*

Euthanasia

✝ Roman Catholic

Roman Catholics believe that euthanasia, especially active euthanasia (where action is taken to end life directly), is always wrong. They say **life is sacred** because it was created by God. The Old Testament says 'I, your God, give life, and I take it away', which shows that no one else has the right to end life – so euthanasia must be wrong. Also, the Ten Commandments clearly state 'Do not kill', and euthanasia would break this rule.

✝ Dutch Protestant Church

The Dutch Protestant Church believes that all life is sacred. However, for those with terminal illness their life can become very undignified. In these cases, they believe **God wants us to help the person** from their suffering.

✝ Christianity

Christians generally accept passive euthanasia (letting nature take its course) – for example, switching off life support. This fits with the Old Testament teaching 'There is a season for everything – a time to live and a time to die.'

Question

Explain two contrasting beliefs in contemporary British society about euthanasia.

In your answer you should refer to the main religious tradition of Great Britain and one or more other religious traditions. *(4 marks)*

✡ Judaism

For Judaism, euthanasia might be acceptable where it shortens the act of dying. So switching off life support would be acceptable. 'Anything that causes a hindrance to the departure of the soul is permissible to remove.' (Rabbi Moses Isserles)

Animal experimentation

✝ Christianity

Some Christians think experiments on animals are wrong because God gave us **stewardship** over animals – the duty to look after them. Experimenting on them and causing them to suffer is not stewardship. Pope John Paul II declared 'We must abandon laboratories and factories of death', showing that laboratories for experimentation are simply places of death. Many Christians believe that testing such as for **cosmetics is cruel and unnecessary**, bringing suffering to God's wonderful creation, and going against St Francis of Assisi's teaching that **as part of the creation, animals deserve respect and protection**.

✝ Roman Catholic

The Roman Catholic Church accepts experiments on animals 'within reasonable limits' and only if it is 'caring for or saving human lives' (Catechism of the Catholic Church).

✡ Judaism

Judaism recognises the duty to **improve the welfare and well-being of humanity**. This includes improving medical science. Where experiments are for this purpose, they would be acceptable, as **human life has more value**.

☬ Sikhism

Sikhism accepts experimentation which leads to improving human life. **Life is sacred**, and Sikhs have a **duty of service** (sewa) to others, so where **experiments advance medicine**, they are tolerated. Where experiments are repeating research already done, they are not acceptable.

Question

Explain two contrasting beliefs in contemporary British society about animal experimentation.

In your answer you should refer to the main religious tradition of Great Britain and one or more other religious traditions. *(4 marks)*

Getting prepared

Four-mark AO1 Influences questions

In your studies, it is not enough to only know and understand what religious people believe; you have to be able to write about how those religious beliefs and teachings affect the way believers act in our society today. The most obvious questions seeking this skill are 'influences' questions, and they are worth 4 marks each. You will have to answer one in each topic on the exam paper.

The crucial aspect of showing your understanding well is that you can explain beliefs and teachings in terms of the topic you are being asked about. So, for example, writing about abortion, you might use the teaching of 'Do not kill'. You could then go on to explain how that applies to the issue of abortion, and from there how that affects a person's decision about abortion. Where possible try to show how one teaching can be interpreted differently, depending on the circumstances; 'Do not kill' might seem to suggest abortion is always wrong, but what if the woman's life is at risk?

To answer these questions well you could use some key building blocks:

1. Know the key term and what it means.

2. Know the relevant beliefs and teachings which might be applied to this.

3. Know a general religious attitude to the term/issue.

Make sure you show how the beliefs and teachings actually influence the decisions made by the religious believer. That is the key element of the question. You could also combine the building blocks to show their influence.

The question might give you a belief/teaching to focus on in your answer. If it does this you must focus on that, or you will waste time. For example:

Explain two contrasting beliefs in contemporary British society about abortion. In your answer you should refer to the main religious tradition of Great Britain and one or more other religious traditions.

If all you do is list some teachings (like compassion, and Do not kill), you will limit your answer – so you have to make them relevant to abortion (showing how abortion could be seen as being compassionate).

You also have to present **contrasting beliefs**, that is, show that the attitudes of religions vary to any one ethical issue. The specification names three specific topics for each theme to be contrasted. Make sure you know contrasting views to each of those.

For each question complete the chart before writing a comprehensive answer.

5 Theme B: Religion and life

Definition of term	Potential beliefs and teachings relevant to this	General attitude
Abortion is …	In _____, it says …	This means that Christians agree/disagree with _____ because …

1 Explain **two** contrasting beliefs in contemporary British society about abortion. *In your answer you should refer to the main religious tradition of Great Britain and one or more other religious traditions.*

2 Explain **two** contrasting beliefs in contemporary British society about euthanasia. *In your answer you should refer to the main religious tradition of Great Britain and one or more other religious traditions.*

3 Explain **two** contrasting beliefs in contemporary British society about animal experimentation. *In your answer you should refer to the main religious tradition of Great Britain and one or more other religious traditions.*

For Theme C, the 'In your answer …' part changes. It says '*In your answer you should refer to the main religious tradition of Great Britain and non-religious beliefs.*' You are expected to show a secular attitude – what a humanist or atheist might say as your contrasting belief.

So what are the contrasting topics in each theme?

Theme A	Theme B	Theme C	Theme D	Theme E	Theme F
Contraception	Abortion	Visions	Violence	Corporal punishment	Women
Sex before marriage	Euthanasia	Miracles	Weapons of mass destruction (WMD)	Death penalty	Wealth
Homosexual relationships	Animal experimentation	Nature as general revelation	Pacifism	Forgiveness	Freedom of religious expression

As you study these topics, pay particular attention, and make sure that you learn contrasting views on each – that will mean you can cope well in the exam whatever topic is chosen.

Religion and life glossary

Abortion deliberate expulsion of foetus from womb with the intention to destroy it

Afterlife beliefs about what happens after we die to our self/soul

Animal rights the idea that animals should have rights because of respect for life

Awe an overwhelming feeling often of reverence with a link to God

Big Bang theory the scientific view of the beginning of the universe

Charles Darwin the man who put forward the theory of evolution in the nineteenth century

Conception when the sperm fertilises the female egg so allowing pregnancy

Conservation to repair and protect animals and areas of natural beauty

Creation the idea that God created the world/universe from nothing

Dominion the idea that humans have the right to control all of creation

Environment the world around us

Euthanasia mercy killing; ending life for someone who is terminally ill, or has degenerative disease; can be voluntary (a person deciding for themselves) or involuntary (being decided by others as the individual is incapable)

Evolution change in inherited traits in a species

Fossil fuels the Earth's natural resources – coal, oil and gas

Global warming a gradual increase in the overall temperature of the Earth's atmosphere, believed to be caused by the greenhouse effect

Hospice a place that cares for the dying, usually from an incurable disease

Hypothesis a proposed explanation of something

Natural resources the resources the Earth provides without the aid of mankind

Natural selection one of the basic mechanisms of evolution

Pesticide chemicals used to kill pests, especially on crops

Pro-choice pressure groups which campaign for the right of a woman to decide on abortion

Pro-life pressure groups which campaign against abortion/euthanasia

Quality of life how good/comfortable life is

Religious truth truth as understood by a religion, such as what God has said

Right to die the belief that a human being should be able to control their own death

Sanctity of life life is special; life is created by God

Science knowledge coming from observed regularity in nature and experimentation

Stewardship duty to look after the world, and life

Sustainable energy resources that are renewable, for example solar, wind and nuclear power

6 Theme C: The existence of God and revelation

Key elements of this theme

This theme is about God and experiencing God. It lets you consider some of the arguments for God's existence and whether they are effective arguments or not. It introduces you to how God is described (the nature of the divine), including some of the key terms used to describe aspects of God. It also takes a look at the concept of **revelation**, that is, how we might claim to see God directly and within the world, including whether what we think we have seen/experienced can be trusted. It is from this that we gain our ideas of the nature of God/the divine.

What is God like? What is your idea?

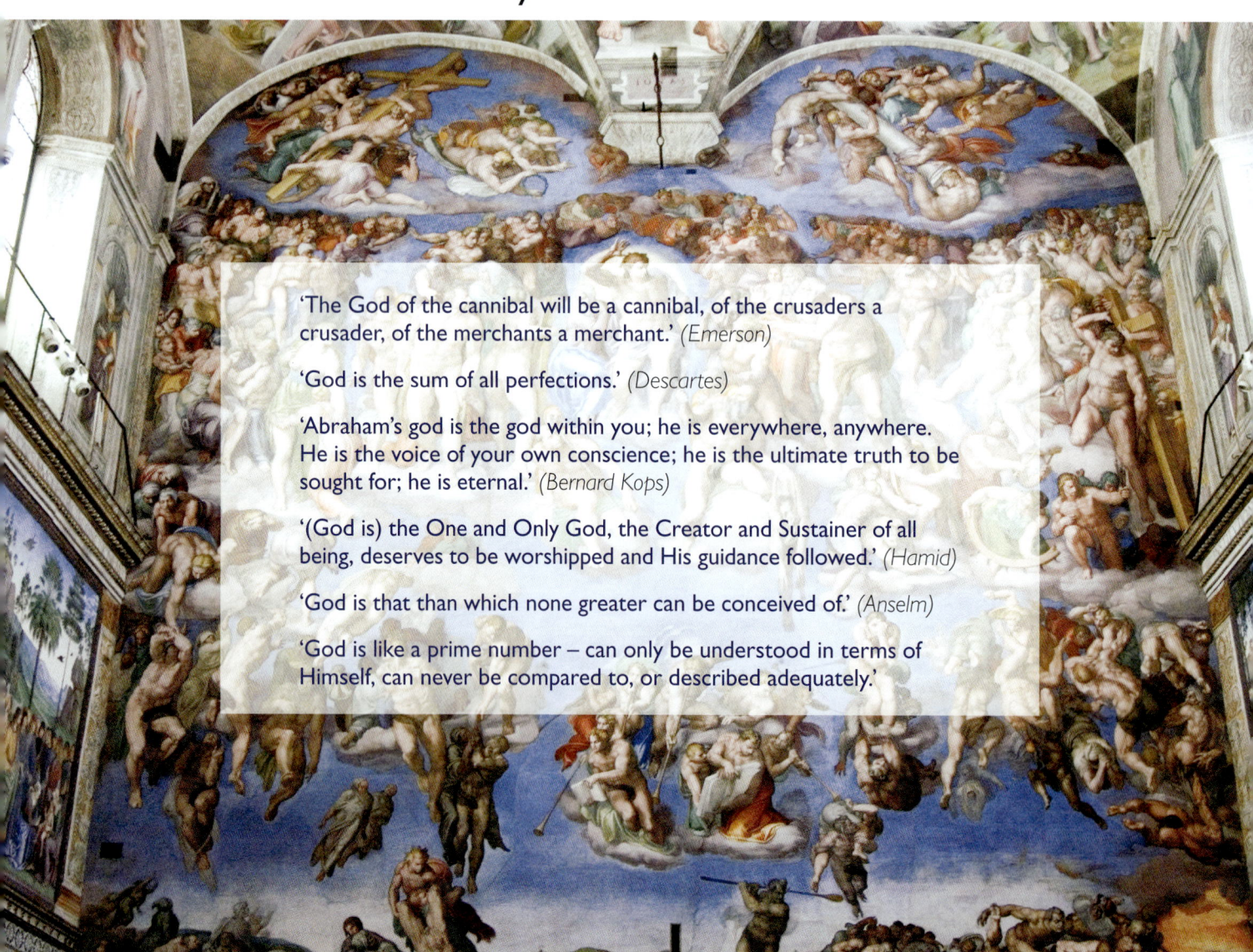

'The God of the cannibal will be a cannibal, of the crusaders a crusader, of the merchants a merchant.' *(Emerson)*

'God is the sum of all perfections.' *(Descartes)*

'Abraham's god is the god within you; he is everywhere, anywhere. He is the voice of your own conscience; he is the ultimate truth to be sought for; he is eternal.' *(Bernard Kops)*

'(God is) the One and Only God, the Creator and Sustainer of all being, deserves to be worshipped and His guidance followed.' *(Hamid)*

'God is that than which none greater can be conceived of.' *(Anselm)*

'God is like a prime number – can only be understood in terms of Himself, can never be compared to, or described adequately.'

Religious traditions of God

Religions have their own ideas about God and this is the key difference from which flow many other differences. On these pages we are looking at the idea of God as expressed differently in three religions.

✝ Christianity

What do Christians believe about God?

The main belief of Christianity is that God expresses himself in the form of the Trinity. This is one God, but three forms or persons. Forms or aspects are not individual gods. For Christians, God is One.

In the Apostles' Creed, we see an explanation of Christian belief. It includes descriptions of the three aspects of God: the Father, the Son and the Holy Spirit.

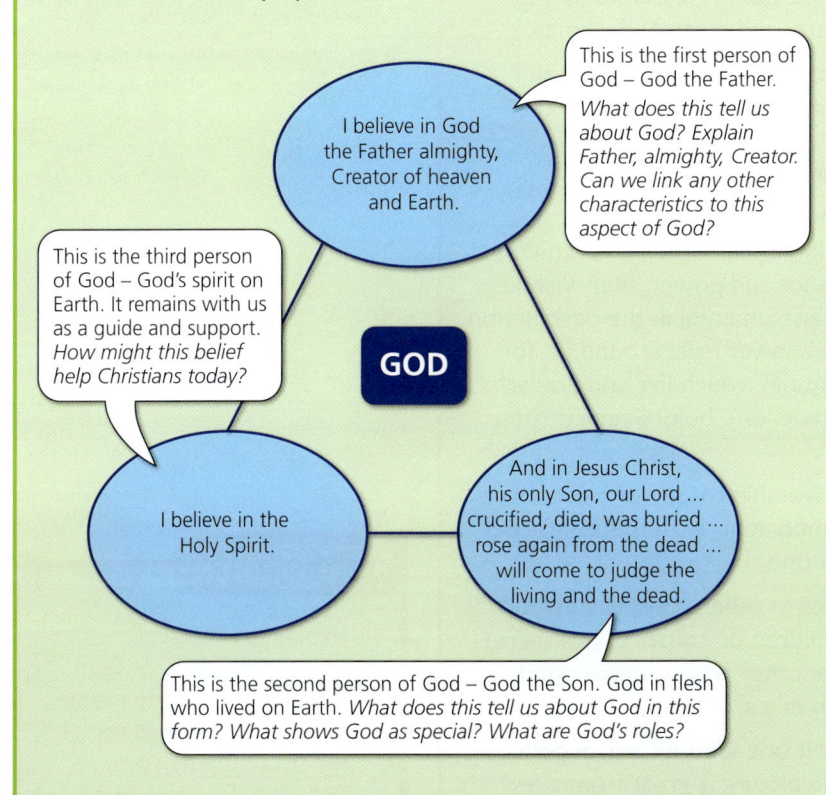

- I believe in God the Father almighty, Creator of heaven and Earth.
  - This is the first person of God – God the Father. *What does this tell us about God? Explain Father, almighty, Creator. Can we link any other characteristics to this aspect of God?*
- I believe in the Holy Spirit.
  - This is the third person of God – God's spirit on Earth. It remains with us as a guide and support. *How might this belief help Christians today?*
- And in Jesus Christ, his only Son, our Lord … crucified, died, was buried … rose again from the dead … will come to judge the living and the dead.
  - This is the second person of God – God the Son. God in flesh who lived on Earth. *What does this tell us about God in this form? What shows God as special? What are God's roles?*

GOD

God is all three of these; they are all aspects of God. They each have different roles, but are still the same God. Think about yourself for a moment. Are you exactly the same when in school as you are when at home? What about when with friends? What about at a club you belong to? We have different personas for the different situations we are in. We can use this analogy to help us to understand the aspects of God. God expresses himself in many ways but it is always the same God.

For more detail see pages 8–9 in Christianity section.

☪ Islam

What do Muslims believe about God?

> 'Say He is Allah the One. Allah is eternal and absolute. None is born of Him, nor is He born. And there is none like Him.'
> *(Surah 112, Qur'an)*

One of the basic beliefs of Islam is Tawhid, that is, the Oneness of God. Allah is the name of the Muslim God; it means one God. Allah cannot be split up in any way. Islam follows strict monotheism.

There are many names for Allah. The Qur'an lists 99 names, such as the merciful, the compassionate, the preserver. There is a story that there are 100 names, but only the camel knows the hundredth. It is just to show that we can never completely know Allah.

Allah is seen as the Creator of the universe, which means Allah is all-powerful and all-knowing. Allah is eternal, so was never born and will never die. Allah does not change, because Allah is perfect. Allah is our guide through the Qur'an and the prophets.

6 Theme C: The existence of God and revelation

ॐ Hinduism

What do Hindus believe about God?

Hindus believe in the **Ultimate Reality**, which they call Brahman. Brahman is eternal and unchanging. We cannot understand Brahman, we can only understand parts and ideas of Brahman.

Many Hindus believe that Brahman can be split into three major parts (the Trimurti). This lets us try to understand three of the major roles of God/Brahman. These are Brahma (Creator), Vishnu (Sustainer) and Shiva (Destroyer).

Hindus believe that the universe is in a continuous cycle of creation and destruction, then creation again. When it is time for the creation, Brahma has most influence and power, then Vishnu sustains the creation before Shiva is instrumental in the destruction. We can see this sharing of power on a lower level around us, for example seeds grow into plants (creating), which live and flower/fruit (sustaining), and finally die (destruction), before rebirth after winter or through their seeds.

Hindus usually devote most of their worship to one of these three. They see that element as the most important, with the other two as lesser expressions of their chosen one.

You may have seen statues or pictures of other gods. Ganesha, Lakshmi, Parvati and Durga are all children or consorts (partners) of the Trimurti. They are really just another way to understand Brahman, through the roles Brahman takes.

How can we understand this idea? Is it one God or lots of gods? Imagine sitting in front of the TV. The picture is great from a few metres away, you can see the whole scene; it makes sense and you can understand what you are seeing. Now try sitting ten centimetres away. All you see are lots of dots of colour, which do not make sense, except in their own right. This is rather like the Hindu idea of God. We as humans do not have the capacity to see God in God's entirety, so we can only make sense of bits of God. So Hindus create gods of the bits of God, but they still all point to the One Reality of Brahman.

With a partner, discuss these ideas:

God is way beyond our human brains to understand.

The idea of God contradicts what we know of the world we live in – God wouldn't let humans do this to His world.

Holy books give us everything we need to know about God.

The Basics

1. Explain contrasting (different) ideas of God.
2. Explain what it means to believe God has many forms, and why some believers find this helpful.
3. Explain why some religions say it is wrong to think of God in many forms.
4. 'Humans could never understand God.' Explain reasons to agree and disagree with this statement.

Religious, philosophical and ethical studies

One God – many gods – no God – aspects of God

If I believe in one God, I am a **theist**.

If I believe in many gods, I am a **polytheist**.

If I do not believe in God or gods, I am an **atheist**.

If I do not think it is possible to prove or disprove the existence of God, so am unsure, I am an **agnostic**.

Do not forget that some religions believe that one God can be split into different forms or aspects – for example, Hinduism and Christianity. Others, like Islam, believe there is only one God who cannot be broken into elements.

> Read the following statements. Which definition word from the left is an appropriate label for each?

I do not know whether there is a God or not. Sometimes I think there is, other times I am sure there is not.

God is all around us, in everything.

You cannot prove God, so as far as I'm concerned there is not one.

I believe there is a God for each one of us.

When someone proves God exists, then I will believe.

A god of the moon, a god of the sun, a god of the trees – all forms of God.

God is a crutch for the weak to lean on.

God is here now.

God is nowhere.

There are different gods for every element of life.

So, I am an atheist – what does that mean?

To start with it means 'I believe there is no God'. It is a more definite attitude than 'I do not believe in God', because we can say we do not believe in something yet it may exist. An atheist will base their attitudes and actions on things other than God and an afterlife in which we can be rewarded/punished.

But isn't that a humanist?

Well, humanists also do not believe in a God. The universe and all of nature are seen as totally without design or creator. Humanists trust **science** and can see how it is used to help our development. They believe in the fundamental value of each human and that we should make the most of the one life we have. We have the opportunity and responsibility to be decent human beings based on our ability to reason and empathise with others. Humans are the key, and what we can do to and for each other. There is no reliance on a divine being to get us out of trouble etc. So, you could say that being an atheist is actually a strand of being a humanist, but actually **humanism** is much more than just an idea about 'no God'.

> Religious people follow rules set by God, for reasons including what will happen when they die. What motivation might humanists have for behaving in a positive way?

> Is the motivation for humanists more effective than that for religious people in your opinion?
>
> What explanation might humanists give for the stories of people meeting God, or seeing God through nature and the work of other people?

> *Interesting point to bear in mind …*
>
> Humanist opinion is a useful way to look at statements which you are asked to evaluate and argue. Do not forget to try to bring in the 'non-religious, but morally good' thinking of humanists.

229

6 Theme C: The existence of God and revelation

Immanent or transcendent ... or both!

Immanent

When talking about God, this word means God is involved and active in the world (**immanent**). This is possible because of God's almighty power. It is a sign of God's love for us.

> Why is immanence a sign of God's love?

Jesus was an example of God's immanence. Jesus was God on Earth, trying to show people the way to live and so to attain heaven. Jesus' ability to perform **miracles** was due to his divine status. This was God active in the world.

> Find out about one of Jesus' miracles.

Many people believe that God makes things happen which are naturally impossible, for the purpose of good. For example, a person is diagnosed with a brain tumour, which should kill them, yet it suddenly begins to shrink. When questioned, doctors can only say what it is doing (disappearing), not why. The person involved sees this as God's intervention.

> Do you know of any stories of modern-day miracles?

Examples of people meeting God or having religious experiences are also examples of God's immanence. This is known as special revelation (see page 241). God has to be involved in the world to be able to let people have these experiences, because humans live in the world and that is where they must meet him.

Transcendent

When we talk about God as **transcendent**, we mean God is beyond this world and its limits. That does not mean God is far away, not in distance terms anyway. It means that God is distinct from the world. God is not controlled by time, so is. God was never born, and will never die – birth and death are not applicable to God. Nor is God limited by space, so God does not have the physical qualities humans have, such as a physical body which can be damaged and can deteriorate. God is utterly and completely unlike humans or any form of life on Earth.

> What does this mean for any efforts to prove God exists by scientific means?

God does not need the world or rely on it, though the world needs and relies on God. Many religions describe the world as only existing because God wills its existence; God thinks about the world, so it exists. This means that if God did not exist, then neither would we.

It also means that we cannot ever hope to understand God because God is beyond our limited intelligence, which is exactly what you would expect of the being that created the world. This is why some people claim that we should not try to understand why God allows evil and suffering – we simply cannot.

> Why do you think religious believers try to understand God, if God is beyond our understanding?

The Basics

1. What is meant by immanent?
2. What does it mean to say that God is transcendent?
3. Make a list of reasons why people might prefer God to be (a) immanent, and (b) transcendent. What problems might each cause for religious believers? (Think of how people might feel, to help you answer these.)
4. Can God be both immanent and transcendent? Explain your answer.
5. Can a human have a meaningful relationship with either an immanent God or a transcendent God? Explain your answer.
6. 'There is no point believing in a God who cannot be understood.' How far do you agree? Explain arguments showing different points of view.

Personal or impersonal

Personal

If you have a **personal** relationship with someone, what does that mean?

It is about being close, about knowing someone, being able to speak with them and to confide in them. It is about knowing they are concerned for you and will listen to you.

When we say God is personal, we mean all those things about God. We can have a one-to-one relationship with God, and can experience God in our lives. We can each relate to God as a friend. God can have such a relationship with everybody at the same time because God is **omnipotent**.

God wants to have such a relationship with everyone because God is omnibenevolent (all-loving).

> In practical terms, what would this mean in the life of the believer?

It also means we can describe God in human terms, even though God is clearly beyond human comprehension. This is how we can call God Father, or speak of God with human qualities (loving, forgiving and so on).

> Do you know of any other such expressions for God?

Impersonal

When we use this term to describe God, we are saying that we cannot relate personally to God, because God is God.

God is utterly and completely unlike humans, far beyond us in any sense we could think of (power, intelligence, creativity, any abilities). St Anselm described God as 'that than which none greater can be imagined', and Descartes described God as 'the sum of all perfections'.

> Try to make sense of the ideas of St Anselm and Descartes – can you understand God from their definitions?

We can worship God, though, as a sign of our acceptance of God's superiority. We cannot describe God because our terms are inadequate for the vastness that is God. God is beyond our understanding. Some religious believers believe they can come to understand God in time through study and devotion, even if that takes many lifetimes. In this sense, God is no longer impersonal. Others believe they can never understand God, only show devotion to God and believe God will reward them for that.

> Why might religious believers think this of God?

Impersonal also means that God is distant from us, because God is not like us in any way.

God's influence is on the world as a whole, not on our individual lives.

> Does this explain why evil and suffering exist?

Tasks

1. You must learn these four words: transcendent, immanent, personal, impersonal. Can you spot which statement relates to each?
   a. Mr Smith says God is beyond our understanding, because we are human.
   b. This book says God is pre-existent – never born, never to die.
   c. The vicar says God came to Earth as Jesus to die for us.
   d. She believes God is with her all the time, listening and concerned for her happiness.
2. Try to make up more sentences which demonstrate each of the four words.

The Basics

1. What is meant by personal and impersonal?
2. Make a list of reasons why people might prefer God to be (a) personal, and (b) impersonal. What problems might each cause for religious believers? (To help you answer these, think of how a person might feel.)
3. Can a human have a meaningful relationship with a God described as either personal or impersonal? Explain your answer, showing you have thought about more than one point of view.

Theme C: The existence of God and revelation

Why the different ideas about God?

How people learn about God

If you belong to one religion and your friend belongs to another, it is likely you will have different ideas of what God is like. Look back to the pages about ideas of God in three faiths (pages 227–228) to see. How do they differ?

What a person is taught in their places of worship, through holy books or teaching from religious leaders, will differ. For example, in the Qur'an, we see that Allah is totally beyond man's reach (transcendent). In the Christian faith, however, God is very much accessible (an immanent God).

You might also meet others who claim to have met God. They might show you a different idea of God to which you have no access through your own faith.

Probably your first impression of God comes from your parents. Upbringing is our number one influence.

How people experience God

People claim to have met God in various ways and at various times. This will affect their understanding of God.

If someone meets God when they are very unhappy (because of a tragic event, for example), they might feel that God is helping them through it. They might see God as a caring, loving figure, who is very much active in the world. That idea would help them through the difficult time, and encourage them to pray more often. On the other hand, if they have done something wrong, and they meet with difficulties in their life, they might see these as punishment from God. In this case, they might feel that God is like a judge, and to be feared, so they worship God more strictly.

> Can you think of any more examples?

Personal preferences

Maybe a person just prefers one idea about God to another.

They look around the world and see much suffering and evil. How do they reconcile this with the existence of the God they worship? They could say God is transcendent, because that helps with their dilemma. It makes the whole problem easier.

Alternatively, they might want to follow a God who is active in the world, so they do not feel alone. Even in the blackest hour, there is hope, because God is by their side.

> Can you think of any more examples?

Holy books inform believers about God

The Basics

1. In what ways do people find out about God? List them, and give examples to show your understanding.
2. Why might different people have different ideas of God?
3. 'It does not matter if people have different ideas about God.' What is your opinion on this statement? Explain some reasons to agree and disagree with it.

Religious, philosophical and ethical studies

Can we prove God exists?

When you have heard people say they 'believe in God', what do they mean? Is it that they believe God exists? Or that God will do something for them, or that God starts some religions, or is it something else? To 'believe in' God doing anything means you believe God exists in the first place, so what they are saying is they believe God exists. Not everyone believes God exists, so what is it that has proved God's existence to some people and not to everyone? Any ideas?

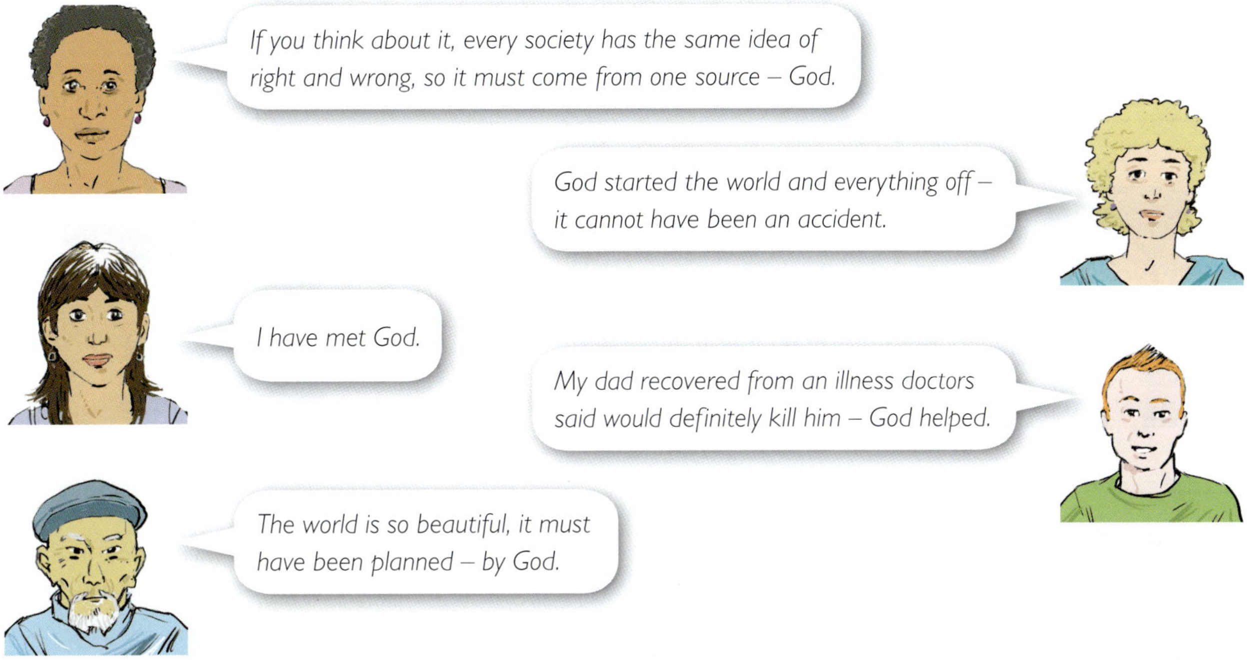

If you think about it, every society has the same idea of right and wrong, so it must come from one source – God.

God started the world and everything off – it cannot have been an accident.

I have met God.

My dad recovered from an illness doctors said would definitely kill him – God helped.

The world is so beautiful, it must have been planned – by God.

These five statements represent some reasons why people believe in God. Of course, people also believe because their parents, or some other significant person, told them God exists, or they believed what it said in a holy book. However, those reasons are not really useful to us as proofs. This course wants to know the 'proofs' of God's existence and whether they really are proofs or not.

The 'proofs' you are going to look at are summed up in the above statements. Can you can spot these arguments in the earlier statements?

- **First Cause** argument
- **Design argument** (**teleological argument**)
- argument from miracles

You are going to find out a bit more about each in this topic. You might be asked what the argument says, whose argument it is (because that helps you understand the way they thought), what is good about the argument (its strengths), and what is bad about it (its weaknesses).

Apart from saying what is wrong with the arguments, you also need to look at why people *do not* believe God exists. And lastly, the arguments you will meet are not the only arguments for God's existence, they are just the only ones covered by this course.

The Basics

1. Can you think of some reasons why people believe God exists?
2. Can you think of some reasons why people believe God does not exist?
3. What are the three types of arguments for God's existence covered by this GCSE course?
4. Write a simple explanation of each type. You could use the statements to help you.

6 Theme C: The existence of God and revelation

The Design argument (teleological argument)

1 This is **William Paley**. He said that the world itself was enough evidence of God's existence. It is too amazing to have just happened by chance.

Can you think of something amazing about the world? Why is that amazing?

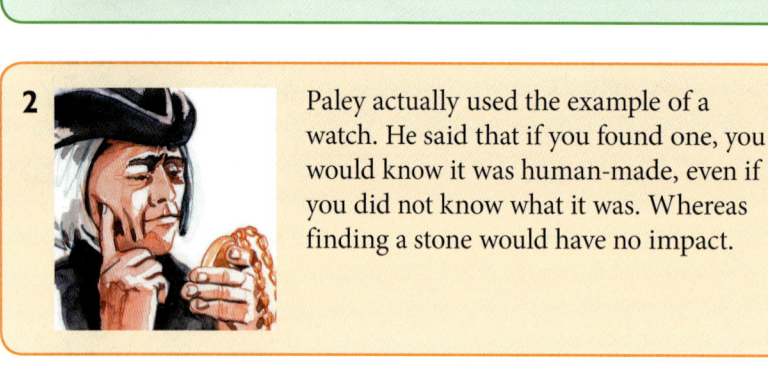

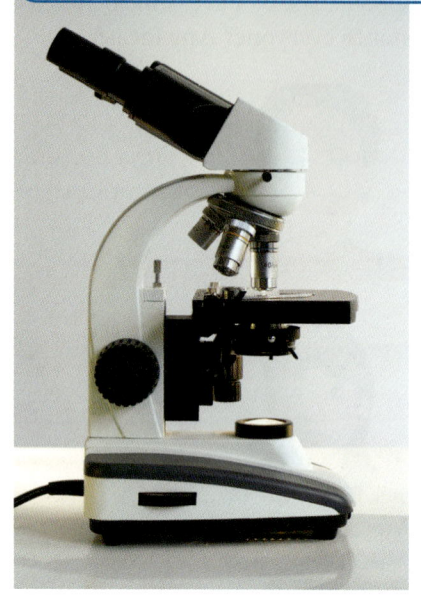

Look at this object. What is it? Has it got a purpose that you can recognise? Is it human-made or natural? How can you tell?

2 Paley actually used the example of a watch. He said that if you found one, you would know it was human-made, even if you did not know what it was. Whereas finding a stone would have no impact.

3 Paley said that the world is like that watch, or the object on the right. There is a difference though: he said the world is even more obviously designed.

You probably said that that object was not natural. Even if you do not know what it is, it is human-made. We can tell that things were deliberately made because they obviously have some sort of use and purpose.

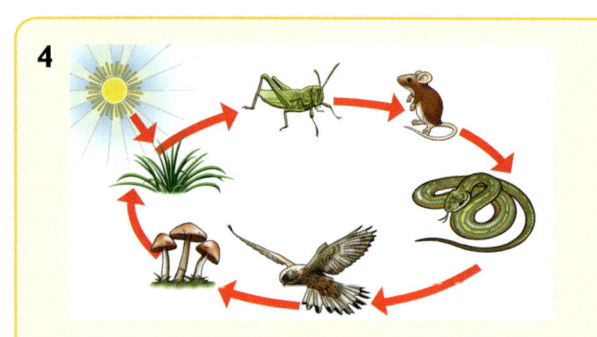

4 There are many patterns in nature, such as food chains and the seasons.

6 So many things seem perfectly suited to their environment, like polar bears, which have special fur and an extra layer of fat to keep them warm. Without this, they would not survive the extremely cold temperatures of the Arctic.

5 There are so many unique things – for example, each one of us, our iris pattern, our fingerprints, our DNA.

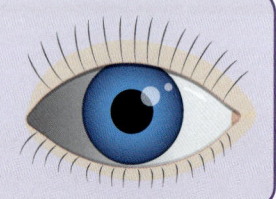

7 Paley said that the world is too amazing to have come about by chance. Something or someone must have thought about it all, and deliberately made it all. That someone must have been God.

Religious, philosophical and ethical studies

Doubts about the Design argument

> Answer these questions before you read on:
> 1 Outline Paley's Design argument for the existence of God.
> 2 Is that argument convincing to you? Explain your answer.

We could argue about whether the world does look designed. Here we are concerned with what is wrong with the argument itself. What do you think? Is this a strong argument? Does it convince you? Is it more convincing than other arguments such as First Cause when you read them?

You could get asked any of those questions, so you need to find out some of the flaws in Paley's argument to support your answer to them.

Think about what he is comparing at first: a stone and a watch. The stone is discarded because it has no design, but the watch has – it clearly has a purpose. Then at the end, he compares the watch to the world by saying the watch is designed, but the world is even more obviously designed. That's great, it makes sense, could it be a proof? Small question – is the stone (not designed) part of the world (very designed)? So, should it not also show design? It sounds like he changed the rules in the middle of his argument.

Something else – just because something looks designed, does that guarantee that it really was designed? Penicillin, which is brilliant as a medicine, was discovered by accident. You might have learned in science that it is a form of mould, created accidentally but becoming perhaps the most important medical breakthrough ever. The person who made Post-its® was trying to invent a glue which bonded two sides forever and never came unstuck! The person who invited nylon was trying to make a waterproof fabric. The list goes on … So, things that look designed might not have been.

Further consideration might lead to these ideas. Perhaps God just designed the world, but no longer exists. Also our world could just have been one of many different designs. Looking at the world, there are many reasons to suggest that God's design of this world wasn't as perfect as Paley claimed.

Person profile

The most famous person to use the Design argument to prove God's existence was William Paley. He was an eighteenth-century archdeacon in Carlisle. He wrote many books, including *Natural Theology*, which contains his 'proof'. His argument followed the process described on the previous page. It is basically saying the world looks designed, so it must have been, and God was the designer.

The Basics

1 Explain some of the problems with Paley's argument.
2 Do you think the problems make his argument weaker? Is it still as convincing as it was to you before you explored its problems? Explain your answer.
3 'Paley's Design argument proves God exists.' Do you agree? Explain arguments showing you have considered more than one point of view.

Extension tasks

1 Find out about other Design arguments. For example, Newton talked about the design of the thumb being proof enough for him.
2 Find out what 'teleological' means.
3 Which of the Design arguments do you find most compelling? Explain why.

6 Theme C: The existence of God and revelation

The First Cause argument

Person profile

St **Thomas Aquinas** was a Christian monk, who lived from 1225CE to 1274CE. He wrote several books, including *Summa Theologica*, which gave his proofs of God's existence. He spoke of five different proofs. The second is about God being the Uncaused Cause, the First Cause of everything else. So, according to Aquinas (using the steps of the argument on this page) God was the cause of the universe. However, Aquinas, being a monk, could be accused of bias; of course his solution to any question about the cause of the universe would be God, it is his job to say that.

Aquinas' argument

Step 1 – We can use the idea of the dominoes. Why do they fall? If nothing pushes them or acts on them to make them fall, will they ever fall? Now, think about the world around you and all the things in it. What causes each thing? Can you think of anything which is not caused by something else? Anything that is totally independent, not relying on something else for its existence?

Step 2 – Bet you could not think of anything. It seems that everything relies on something else so that it can exist, or be. For example, that row of dominoes does not just fall over, something has to make the first domino move, so that the whole chain of dominoes falls in a sequence. Usually someone pushes it.

Step 3 – So, we have to accept everything is caused by something else. But, how did the universe start? It had a beginning, it did not cause itself, so what caused it?

Step 4 – So if there was a beginning to the universe, we have to have something to start it all off. That something had to be Uncaused – had to just exist. At some point in the history of the universe there had to be something which is not caused by anything else – an Uncaused Cause, Aquinas called it. Can you guess what he said it was?

Step 5 – Some people say it was God. Thomas Aquinas said *everyone* did (but then he was a monk, so we should expect that).

Some might say: 'Of course, it is the Big Bang! The Big Bang is the First Cause.' But, then the question is 'what caused the Big Bang?' Do you think it might have been God?

The Basics

1. In your own words, explain the idea of God as First Cause. You could use the domino idea to help you explain.
2. Do you think Aquinas is right to say 'everyone believes the Uncaused Cause to be God'? Explain your answer.
3. Can you think of anything else that might be the First Cause other than God?
4. How convincing an argument for God's existence is this for you? Explain your answer.

Extension task

Research Aquinas, and try to find out the other 'ways' he used to prove God exists.

Religious, philosophical and ethical studies

The trouble with Thomas Aquinas

You need to consider some of the weaknesses in the arguments for the existence of God.

Can you see any flaws in it? Remember Thomas Aquinas was writing hundreds of years before the internet and modern science. Also remember he was a monk, so more inclined to believe in what the Bible said and see God as the explanation.

Use these clues to work out some of the bigger problems with his argument:

> **a** Who does he say believes the Uncaused Cause to be God? Is that realistic?

> **b** How does he know *everything* is caused by something else? What would be his evidence?

> **c** What is his God like? What does the God in this argument do and does that sound like the Christian God?

There are other problems, such as whether Thomas Aquinas was biased and so assumed certain things because of that.

Do you really think Aquinas could have asked everybody if they agreed with him? Hundreds of years ago there were no phones or internet. Even if he asked something totally obvious, like *do you think water is wet?*, he cannot really say everyone says yes, because he cannot ask everyone. He is making a claim, which he cannot prove.

There is a similar problem in clue b. Can anyone – in their entire life, doing nothing but study – be sure they have seen everything in existence? If he hasn't seen everything, how can he claim everything has been caused by something else? It is another claim he cannot prove.

What about clue c? His God causes the world – that is it. He could have just caused the universe and then ceased to exist. He might have caused an imperfect universe and not have been able to fix it. He could have deliberately caused evil. This God only has one role – to cause everything – which is a problem, because it leaves too many unanswered questions.

A word about *problems* in philosophy

You are going to see the word problem lots of times in this course. You just need to be sure you understand what it means in 'philosophy-speak'. It is not like a health problem, or a problem between people or a maths problem. It is one of those times where you say 'Yes, but …' and pose a difficult question for the person who is trying to explain something to you. You will have done it with your parents, or with your teachers. And when they cannot answer, we usually feel quite proud of ourselves! In this course, the problems are usually questions which challenge an argument or challenge belief. You will have to be able to talk about the problems (the flaws) in all the philosophy we cover, because that is part of the course.

> ### The Basics
> 1 What is meant by problems in philosophy?
> 2 What problems are there with Aquinas' First Cause argument?
> 3 Do you think the problems make his argument weaker? Is it still as convincing as it was to you? Explain your answer.

6 Theme C: The existence of God and revelation

Miracles

Many people believe that God reveals himself through miracles. They say God makes miracles happen, and the miracle is the proof God exists. The miracle is an example of God reaching into our world to help us. Religions are full of stories of miracles. Miracles can confirm what someone already believes, like a proof for their faith. They can also make someone believe in God; the trigger for belief. Without God there are no miracles.

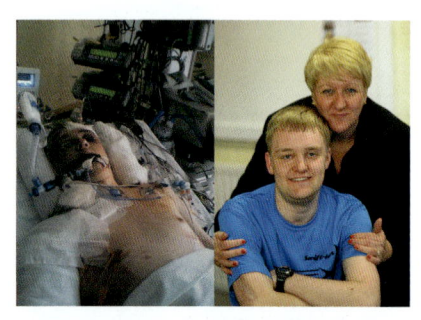

Brought back from death

The name of God in seeds inside an aubergine

Every single person survived

Statues of Ganesha drank pint after pint of milk

These events have all been called miracles. What is a miracle? From those images, how can you explain the idea of a miracle?

Chose the appropriate word from each pair below:

- expected/unexpected
- possible/impossible
- bad/good
- disaster/saving
- people/God

(You probably picked the second word of each pair; most people would. Can you explain why you picked each one?)

An 'act of God' means God did it. Many religious people believe God is immanent and that God interferes in our world through events like miracles. So, the family whose house is destroyed by a tornado while they sleep on is protected by an act of God.

When we say they go against what we understand of nature, we mean they seem impossible, like they should not have happened. If the doctors say someone is dying, with no cure, but they live, that is against nature.

Miracles are always good. God uses his power (omnipotence) to help because of God's love for us (benevolence). You would not call a plane crash in which everyone dies 'a miracle'. But you would if they survived, and you might even say God helped them.

Miracles are often very personal. The miracle proves God exists because the person thinks God intervened in their lives to help them. For example, if I believe I have been blessed with amazing luck, I might believe that luck came from God for me personally. This miracle has proved to me God exists and it does not matter what anyone else says, I believe in God.

The Basics

1. What is meant by miracle?
2. Give three different examples of a 'miracle'.
3. How does a miracle prove God exists?
4. If you recovered from a serious illness which should have killed you, would you think it was a miracle? Explain your answer.

Evil and suffering as an argument against God's existence

If we read the news, we might see a number of terrible events. Some are clearly caused by humans; others are definitely part of nature.

> Take a look at these headlines – which ones are the fault of humans, and which ones of nature?

ANOTHER COLLEGE SHOOTING LEAVES THIRTY-FOUR DEAD

Man jailed for torture and murder of his own baby

Religious extremists bomb tourist paradise

Hurricane Joe devastates Haiti – thousands missing

Tsunami death toll hits 9,000

Crop failure due to drought – a country starves

It is a fact of our lives that every day we are confronted with new stories of suffering where people have to endure mental, emotional or physical pain because of something that has happened. We also experience suffering personally. Suffering is a very real part of our world, which we cannot deny and which makes our lives more difficult on a number of levels.

Religious believers believe God has the following qualities:
- God is **omniscient** – God knows all there is to know, and all that can be known.
- God is all-loving – God loves each and every human as an individual and without reserve. Christians believe God even came to Earth as a human and died in order to make it possible for humans to enter heaven.
- God is omnipotent – God is all-powerful and can do anything. This is how it was possible for God to create the world and all in it.

Does the amount of evil and suffering prove there is no God? For many people it is obvious they know there is suffering as they see examples all the time. However, God is part of a **belief system**, and beliefs are not proven, so God may not be real. Many Christians struggle to explain why God seems to allow evil and suffering to exist, and this is a problem for their faith.

> *I see evil and suffering in the news all the time. Sorry to those that believe, but for me it proves there is no such thing as God. A loving, powerful God just wouldn't let so much of it happen.*

> *I lost all belief in God when my mum died. She had given her life to her religion, brought her kids up in it, done loads of charity work – a genuinely good person. She died horribly in extreme pain, ravaged by cancer. What kind of a God would allow that to happen?*

> *If God really loved us, God would make our world kinder and safer. After all, God must know about everything that is happening, and must know how to fix it. That God doesn't fix the mess, to me, proves God is either not loving or powerful, or simply doesn't exist.*

Task

Look back to pages 6–7 of Christianity where you can read how Christians try to resolve this problem.

The Basics

1. What is meant by evil and suffering? Give examples.
2. Explain why the existence of evil and suffering makes some people not believe in God.
3. 'God must not exist because of the suffering in the world.' Do you agree with this statement? Explain your ideas.

6 Theme C: The existence of God and revelation

Science as proof that God does not exist

Many people believe in science, and that science answers all the questions we have. Or that if it does not right now, it will at some point in the future. There is no need to believe in God.

> *Hundreds of years ago people didn't have the scientific knowledge we have now. I'm not surprised they believed in religion – it gave them answers to questions they puzzled over. But nowadays, we do not need to rely on a mystery being – we know how things work because science tells us.*

> *I know religious people believe God made the world, but to me I look at scientific answers. The Big Bang theory may only be a theory, but there is a lot of evidence. It makes more sense to me than some ultimate being. Science has evidence – I can relate to and rely on that; religion doesn't.*

> *Some people say God must exist because otherwise neither would we. They say the Big Bang was caused and controlled by God, that the conditions which made it happen, and the conditions caused by it (temperature of blast, distance from sun, and so on) are so precise, they had to be deliberately created. I just think we are here and asking questions because we are here – one big, lucky fluke, not God. So be a nice person and get on with it!*

> *When I prayed, nothing happened – I didn't get better. When I went to the doctor and got checked out, he gave me medicine – I got better. Science works, religion doesn't. Science is real, religion not.*

It is clear that for these people, science is more important and more realistic to them than religion.

Many religious people also believe very strongly in science; there are many religious scientists. For these people, science is how God works in the world, or is a description of God's natural law (which we are still learning about). To them, scientific advances just add to the glory of God.

The Basics

1. Explain why some people believe science disproves God's existence.
2. 'It is impossible to believe in both science and religion.' Refer to pages 190 and 196 in Theme B to help you argue for and against this statement. Explain your points.

General and special revelation

Many people say they will only believe in God when they meet God. Maybe you are one of them. Think about this though; if you met God, could you prove it?

Could you prove it to yourself or anyone else? Would you later dismiss it as an **illusion** or something other than God?

Revelation is when God reveals himself, so that humans can know something about God. There are two kinds:

Special revelation

Direct revelation, God communicating directly with you (as an individual or a group). For example, talking to you in a dream or hearing God's voice while you are praying.

General revelation

Indirect revelation, the revealing of God through other things – for example, nature, people, events. You interpret what you see as being linked with God, and this leads you to say you have experienced God. Your interpretation is based on a feeling.

Learn these terms. You may be asked to explain them.

Try to guess some of the questions we can ask about revelation. Then as we look at some examples of different types of revelation, we can keep those questions in mind. Philosophy is about those questions and our efforts to find solutions.

Sort these questions into the ones which apply to **special revelation**, and those which apply to **general revelation**. Some might apply to both.

- Where is the concrete proof that this really happened?
- Can you believe someone who already believes in God?
- Are our feelings and interpretations always right?
- Is there any other explanation?
- Does a particular place or context make us see things in a certain way?

Try to answer some of the questions.

6 Theme C: The existence of God and revelation

Special revelation

Special revelation is a direct revelation. God comes directly to the person involved and makes himself known. It is not that we guessed God did something, like cure someone because we prayed for it. It is that God spoke directly to a person. The event can have a massive impact on the life of that person. Unfortunately, there is no scientific evidence of this experience being true which we can show to someone else, or even for ourselves. We cannot prove it was real by using science or forensics. So why do we believe our experience was real? How can we show others that it was real?

If we cannot prove God by scientific means, we will not be able to prove that someone did meet God. All we can do is listen to their account of what happened and judge the impact it had on them. Then we have to decide if we believe that they met God or not, and from that if we now can say God exists.

Let's look at an example from Christianity:

1. Saul was Jewish and rounded up Christians to be executed as blasphemers against the Jewish faith.
2. On his way to Damascus, he was blinded by a light which only he could see, and from which came Jesus' voice: 'Saul, why do you persecute me?'
3. For three days he was blind; then a Christian came to cure him, saying 'God has sent me to give you back your sight'.
4. He immediately became a Christian, changing his name to Paul. He travelled around the Mediterranean spreading the message of Christianity: 'I speak to you of Jesus Christ, Son of God.' His teachings form the basis of much of the Christian faith.

We can say that Saul became enlightened through this experience; he learned religious truths through it, which then changed his life. He was also the beneficiary of a miracle: his blindness was cured. To be enlightened is to have a new understanding or insight. In religions, we are always talking about religious understanding. For some religions – for example, Buddhism, Hinduism and Sikhism – the aim of religious study is Enlightenment; to fully understand the true nature of things. Achieving Enlightenment in Hinduism and Sikhism means to be reunited with God; it brings revelation and knowledge.

You may need to be able to describe special revelations from each of two religious traditions. There is another example on the next page. When you read the examples, think about the impact they had on the person involved. What difference did special revelation make to their lives?

Religious, philosophical and ethical studies

More about special revelation

> The religion of Islam began from a revelation. Here is the story of an event celebrated by Muslims today as Lailat ul-Qadr (the Night of Power).

1. Muhammad was a business man. He would go to a cave in the hills to pray and to think about life.
2. On one of these visits, he was met by a huge man who ordered him to read.
3. Muhammad could not read, but the man grabbed him and squeezed him tightly, and again ordered him to read.
4. This happened three times. On the last time, Muhammad read – as if the words were burnt onto his heart and he knew them already.
5. The man was Angel Jibril, and he told Muhammad that Allah (God) had chosen him as a prophet (the final prophet) of Islam.

> If you had been either Paul or Muhammad, what would you have believed had happened? Explain why.

> Do you think that this type of direct experience is the best evidence for God's existence? Explain your view.

When someone has a direct special revelation, they feel they have met God in some direct, clear way. Maybe they have spoken to God, maybe they have heard God, or felt God's presence. Whatever happened, they are convinced this was God, and they know God through this meeting. For them, their personal experience was so strong that it is a proof of God – regardless of any argument or evidence to the contrary. Indeed, all they have is the memory, emotions and feelings of the experience.

What we can say is that these experiences are so profound they often lead a person to make massive changes in their lives. In the two cases you have just read, both men completely changed their lives, and put their own lives at risk many times because of their new beliefs.

Can we prove what happened though? To ourselves? To anyone else? That is a problem. But, why would anyone lie about these experiences? Would you tell anyone if you had such an experience? If not, why not? It is a big deal to describe these experiences to anyone because of how sceptical we all are.

But then again – TV space, 15 minutes of fame and money; all of these are enough to encourage some people to lie, or see things that happen to them in a certain way. So maybe some of these experiences are 'invented'. Can we trust people who believe in God already? Do they expect it to be God, so are biased and unconsciously invent these experiences? Plus, there is always the fact that our senses can be deceived by many things, such as drink and drugs, tiredness, illness.

Extension Tasks

1. Find out in more detail about either/each of the two examples of direct revelation, particularly how their life change was not an easy one to have made or to stick to.
2. Find out some other examples of people who have claimed to have met God.

The Basics

1. What is meant by revelation?
2. What is the difference between special revelation and general revelation?
3. Write accounts of two direct revelations of God and state which religious tradition each comes from.
4. What problems can you find with the idea of direct revelation?
5. 'We should always believe it when someone says God spoke to them.' Do you agree? Explain the reasons for your answer.

Enlightenment as a source of knowledge about the divine

Enlightenment means awakened. It is a term used to describe a person who has come to understand religious truths. The course wants you to know how Enlightenment helps believers know, and perhaps understand, the nature of God or the divine. It is a term used mainly in eastern religions, such as Buddhism and Hinduism, although the religious study by Orthodox Jews is also designed to gain a similar insight.

Buddhism began through the Enlightenment of the Buddha, so Enlightenment is crucial to the religion, and is an aim of all Buddhists. The Buddha's was a complete Enlightenment, so that he understood the true nature of everything. These are the key points of his Enlightenment:

1 The Buddha sat beneath a Bodhi tree and made a commitment to meditate until enlightened.
2 He was visited, tempted and threatened by the demon Mara along with Mara's daughters and armies, to stop him from meditating.
3 The Buddha called to the Earth as a witness that he was ready for Enlightenment and was able to see all his past lives (as human and animal) in evidence that he was fit for this step forward in his spiritual nature.
4 He finally understood the true nature of all things and of suffering, and how suffering could be ended. This meant he was fully enlightened.

Believers are realistic enough to realise that it takes much to achieve full Enlightenment (for the Buddha, thousands of lifetimes). They aim to achieve lesser levels of Enlightenment. Imagine standing behind a wall. A small hole gives a glimpse of what is behind – this is like a partial Enlightenment. Destroying the whole wall to get the full view and so properly understand would be like full Enlightenment.

Religious believers can study and learn about God, and the insight they gain from their study, meditation and worship may give them an insight (a partial Enlightenment, or an insight into a religious truth). From this they understand more about God and the nature of the divine. Some Hindus devote their whole lives to the study of the divine through their holy books – Enlightenment is seen as the main aim of their whole life. Hinduism splits life into four Ashramas (age-based life stages) – the first is that of student, where the beginning of studying sacred texts happens, while the last two are focused entirely on religious study and the pursuit of Enlightenment. In Hinduism, Enlightenment leads to moksha, which is a release from reincarnation completely and reunion with the divine.

The enlightenment of the Buddha

The Basics

1 What is meant by Enlightenment?
2 What do religious believers hope to gain from Enlightenment?
3 'Religious believers should make it a priority to gain Enlightenment.' Do you agree with this statement? Explain your arguments.

Religious, philosophical and ethical studies

General revelation – knowing God … through nature

Nature is beautiful.

Nature is complicated.

Nature is clever.

It seems that there is design and purpose in nature.

These ideas provoke a sense of awe and wonder in many people.

Make a list of examples of how nature is each of these things.

Many people would say that the sense of awe and wonder they feel when experiencing nature is a sense of the divine on Earth. It could be seen as evidence that God is immanent, because God is visible through God's creation, or in the workings of it. This idea can be difficult to understand. Let's explain it in a different way. If you like art or music or film or books, you may like a particular person's work. There is something about their style which draws you to them. Even when you have not heard or seen or read their latest work, you might buy it. You can also recognise their work, because of the style. When you get used to their style, you may feel it tells you something about them as a person; their thoughts or feelings. *Can you think of any examples of this?*

This is very much how some people see the world. It is God's creation, and so is full of hints about God. Generally speaking, the world and nature are good, so God is good. The elements of the world, although we try to use the ideas and imitate them, are vastly greater than those we could devise. We could, therefore, say that God is much wiser, cleverer, and more powerful than we are.

Can I prove that whatever I feel is the correct interpretation of what I see? Can I use it to prove God's existence to anyone else? In other words, is it real or illusion?

Religious believers often believe that the world is God's creation

The Basics

1 How can we know God through nature? Give examples to support the points you make.
2 How strong a proof is nature for God's existence? Explain your answer.
3 How strong a proof is this for God? Could we ever prove it was real (or illusion)?

6 Theme C: The existence of God and revelation

General revelation … through holy books, scripture and religious writings

The Basics

1. What are holy books and religious teachings? Give examples of each.
2. What can we learn of God from these? Give examples.
3. How useful is either in helping us to know about God? How well can we know God through these?

That holy books and sacred writings are a form of general revelation seems obvious – after all, holy books and religious writings are meant to be about God. The words in holy books are explained for us by religious leaders, such as the Pope and the Dalai Lama.

Holy books (scripture)

What do we learn about God from holy books?

The Qur'an gives 99 names for Allah. The Bible describes God in many ways.

The Torah gives the Ten Commandments, plus 613 mitzvot (laws). Qur'anic law forms the basis of Shari'ah (Muslim law).

The Old and New Testaments mention God in historical events.

The holy books are all about God, but these three elements stand out: what God is like, how God has acted in the history of the world to influence it, and how God wants us to live our lives.

We can look at holy books in many different ways. Indeed, their believers make different claims for them. The way we view a holy book will decide how closely we follow it, how we treat it, and how we understand what it tells us about God. If I take a book literally, for example, I believe every word to be accurate, so my God will be exactly as described.

Religious writings

How are these different from holy books?

They are the writings of religious people to explain what is written in the holy books, or their own experiences of God, or the teachings of their religious tradition.

Do we really need people to do this for us?

Perhaps the most famous religious leader in the world is the Pope. As head of the Catholic Church, every Pope has written papers about Church teaching. They are also said to be speaking the infallible word of God when speaking 'ex cathedra'. Roman Catholics look to the teachings of the Pope for guidance in their religious lives.

The Dalai Lama, leader of the Tibetan Buddhist faith, is respected worldwide. He has written and published many books which try to put ancient Buddhist teachings into modern language, to make them accessible and readable for the West. One of his books, *Ancient Wisdom, Modern World,* was top of the bestseller list for many weeks.

Religious, philosophical and ethical studies

The value of revelation

Special revelation, general revelation – what is the value of either?

> Read these statements and make a list of all the ideas they give you about why revelation is important and valuable.

Shaun: I had a religious experience – I saw God in a **vision**. I now have absolute proof that God exists and that I am right to live my life by following a religious code. It has given me the strength to keep living that way, even when I meet difficulties – as if that experience is my protection and security.

Narindar: I am aware of God often every day. God's presence is in everything all the time. I try to link everything to God – my thoughts are on God, and my actions devoted to God. Through this I feel comforted and protected.

Jacob: Through the scriptures, I learn about God. They give me insight into God's nature and what God wants from me. The rabbis of old explained the scriptures, and these religious writings, like the Talmud, help me to understand more clearly and deeply. By understanding these, I can live more closely following my faith – I get it right and that is important.

Helen: The beauty of nature reassures me that God is immanent, and that the world is a wonderful creation. This has encouraged me to be more aware and active in environmental work.

Djimi: Prophet Muhammad received the Qur'an through revelations. That has given us our religion. Without the revelations, we would not know about Allah or how we have to act in Allah's world – they were crucial to starting our religion, and are crucial in knowing how to secure a place in paradise in the afterlife.

Megan: I am studying for a PhD which focuses on some religious writers of the middle ages. These people claimed to have had revelations, and the truths they learned through those revelations are given in their work. The revelations are important because they educate other people through them.

There are many reasons why revelations are important. Perhaps the single most important is that most religions are based on one or more revelations; they are central to a religion. For an individual, perhaps the most important factor is that they confirm their faith and they provide personal proof of what they believe in, often against a context of many reasons not to believe.

The Basics

1 Explain why revelation is valuable.
2 Do you think special revelation is more important than general revelation? Explain your reasons.

247

6 Theme C: The existence of God and revelation

The problem of revelation

That is all great, but … is it all real? If we do not know God exists, how can we know this is all God's work? I know loads of people who do not believe there is a God – they'd all say this was someone putting a spin on things, and getting it wrong! These revelations tell us different things about God. Who or what should I believe?

That is a valid point. Is it all **real** or just an **illusion**?

The big question is whether people have really met God, or have just imagined it. **Reality** is what has really happened – you existing is a reality. Illusion is a false or misleading perception; you think you saw a leprechaun in your garden, for example.

Some people say religious experiences are real. Some people say religious experiences are illusions. Some say they can be either and it all depends on the person and the circumstances.

If someone does not believe in God, they will think all religious experiences are illusions. You cannot meet something that does not exist. These people say there is no proof of God. They also say there is no proof of the experience, it is just what someone says. That person could be mistaken or ill, or deliberately lying. They could make themselves believe something that was not real, because they are so desperate to see God. They might interpret something as God that was not, like if someone was very ill but got better. They would see that as God, but the atheist would not. There is no proof of either, in spite of how strongly convinced they each may be. That is the big problem with religious experiences – they cannot be proved, they can only be persuasive.

> Can you work out why each of the people on the page might be disbelieved if they said God revealed himself to them? While most people claiming to have met God are not like these people, the reasons you give for not believing the characters on this page are routinely used against perfectly ordinary people who make the same claims.

The Basics

'Religious revelations are all illusions.' Explore reasons to agree and disagree, before writing a justified conclusion.

What about general revelation? There is even less evidence of that; everything is an interpretation. I might be convinced that God exists because I read a holy book, but was I really reading God's words (so having a revelation)?

For the individual, a special revelation is strong evidence, and general revelation may be less so. However, many millions follow religions based on revelations, so maybe we can say this is strong enough evidence.

The person who has the experience might be convinced that it was God, even if they cannot prove it. We trust our own instincts and feelings. We cannot prove them to anyone else. We might be able to persuade someone else that we met God because of what we say. To the person meeting God, their experience is real, although others might see it as an illusion.

Religious, philosophical and ethical studies

Thinking about revelation

You have seen a range of examples of special and general revelation. These all tell us some things about God and that we can know God.

> Are we really seeing God or are we deluding ourselves? Can we explain religious experiences in any way other than God? If God is transcendent, can we expect to meet God? If we can meet God, does that mean God cannot be impersonal?

This page is designed to get you thinking about these questions. Look upon it as a sort of brain aerobics session!

I had been reading all about Saul, and later God came to me.

Choose the simplest answer and that's usually true.

I only trust my gut instincts.

I'd believe anything she told me.

There's got to be another answer.

Do you know anyone? Really know them? How can you justify that answer?

Do you think you could 'really know' God? Explain yourself.

How well can you know God? What makes it difficult?

Are revelations real or illusion? Which types of revelation are more likely to be real? Why?

If I cannot prove a revelation happened, did it happen at all?

If I am religious, can you trust what I claim to have seen?

Why do different people have different ideas about God?

Does accepting that revelations are real lead to any problems for believers?

Why do believers have different ideas about God?

When I meet God, I'll believe in God.

If God's not physical, can we prove God?

How well do you know yourself? Do you really know how you'd respond in every situation?

If a tree falls in a forest, and no one hears it fall, and no recording is made, does it still make a sound?

She's my best friend. We went to primary school together.

The Basics

1. What is meant by real and illusion?
2. What other explanations could someone give for a 'religious experience' other than God?
3. 'God is an illusion.' Do you agree? Explain reasons to agree and disagree with this statement.
4. 'As revelation is based on belief, it will always be subject to doubt.' Do you agree with that statement?

Contrasting beliefs

Visions

✝ Christianity

Visions are a **form of revelation** from God, allowing humans to **better understand God and have a relationship with God.** Many Christians have written about their revelation, and gave insight because of it – for example, St Teresa of Avila (sixteenth-century nun), Bernadette Soubirous (nineteenth century), and Fred Ferrari (twentieth century). Christians believe **God speaks to humans directly** through these revelations, telling them religious truths, and helping them understand God's wishes. The vision often has a **profound impact on their lives, causing great change**, so for example, Fred Ferrari became an evangelical Christian, having been a dangerous criminal.

Humanism

Humanism takes a non-theistic stance, and does not look for supernatural explanations for events. A vision may be caused by hallucination, illness, drugs, or many other reasons – but not a divine being.

☪ Islam

In Islam, **Allah does not reveal himself directly to humans**. It would be impossible for humans to be able to look upon Allah. Any message has been sent through the medium of an angel.

Atheism

Atheists might see these experiences as **hallucinatory**. They believe there is **no God, and so there can be no source for the revelation** other than our own brain.

Question

Explain two contrasting beliefs in contemporary British society about visions.

In your answer you should refer to the main religious tradition of Great Britain and non-religious beliefs. *(4 marks)*

Miracles

✝ Christianity

Christianity has recorded many miracles, **where God has intervened in the world to make something good happen, often healing** the incurable. Mother Teresa was a Christian nun who had devoted her life to helping the poor and needy in Calcutta. On the **first anniversary of Mother Teresa's death**, a non-Christian Indian woman was **cured of a huge abdominal tumour** – it simply disappeared overnight as she slept. Members of the Missionaries of Charity had **prayed to Mother Teresa** for this cure. The belief is that the prayers showed the necessary faith to allow Mother Teresa's soul to bring God's power to this problem. Doctors have been unable to find any other explanation.

Atheism

An atheist would **dispute that God performs miracles**, as (to them) **God does not exist**. They might see this event as **something which can occur naturally (spontaneous regression)** though is not yet understood by medical science.

Humanism

A humanist would look to a **non-supernatural answer** for this event. They can show that events previously classed as miracles are now **explainable through medical science**, and that those calling them miracles had already a **religious-bias** to affect them.

Buddhism

In Buddhism, the mantra is to resolve issues from one's own resources and strengths. The **Buddha told his followers not to look to some supernatural being for help or answers**. It is believed miracles are possible for **any person who has mastered higher forms of meditation**.

Question

Explain two contrasting beliefs in contemporary British society about miracles.

In your answer you should refer to the main religious tradition of Great Britain and non-religious beliefs. *(4 marks)*

Nature as general revelation

Christianity

Revelation is when God reveals himself. Nature is seen as a source of revelation by Christians because it is **God's creation**. Just as an artist leaves clues of themselves in their work, so God had left **clues in God's creation** – for example, in the beauty of nature, the fact that it seems to have been designed, the patterns found in nature (the seasons, life cycles, etc.). **William Paley** tried to prove God exists by using the world and nature as his evidence. Many Christians believe that **in a beautiful sunset, they see God at work, in new life they see God at work** – this is nature revealing God.

Humanism

A humanist would say that as there is **no such thing as God**, then a non-existent being cannot be revealed in any way – nature or otherwise – as there is **nothing to be revealed**. We should **just appreciate** the beauty and the patterns.

Humanism

Further, a humanist might say that seeing God in nature is **simply a person's interpretation of things, and not the reality**. There are many reasons why they might **interpret something as God**, but no proof it ever was. Hence their interpretation is wrong.

Atheism

An atheist would say that as much as nature might reveal to a believer that there is a God, **it reveals nothing to others, especially those who believe there is no God or divine being**.

Question

Explain two contrasting beliefs in contemporary British society about nature as general revelation.

In your answer you should refer to the main religious tradition of Great Britain and non-religious beliefs. *(4 marks)*

Getting prepared

Command words

These are the words which instruct you what to do in the exam. Understanding what they mean helps you to know what the question requires. They are not the key terms (like 'special revelation'), they instruct you (like 'Explain').

Explain – when you make a point, expand it

Give – same as 'write down' or 'list'

How – same as 'in what ways', like 'how do religious people work for animal rights' is asking 'in what ways' they help animals – practical answers are required

Name – is asking you for the actual technical word or actual name of something

Refer to ... – include in your answer. For example, you will often be asked to refer to religious beliefs and teachings or to examples, so you have to include some to meet the requirement of the question. Scripture and sacred writings just means the holy texts of a religion – for example, the Bible, or another text that a religion gives special respect to, such as the Talmud for Jewish people

What is meant by ... – say what something means – a definition usually

Why – give reasons for something – for example, why people choose to fight in a war

Contrasting beliefs – the two beliefs cannot be the same. You are being asked about attitudes to an ethical issue, and the diversity to how religious people approach it

Influences – this is how a belief, for example, affects the way a person behaves

Importance – significance; why something is important either in itself or to/for something else

In your answer you should refer to the main religious tradition of Great Britain and one or more other religious traditions – this is telling you to give an answer from Christianity, as that is the main religious tradition of Great Britain. You could choose another attitude from within Christianity, or from another religion to give the contrasting view (which the earlier part of the question has asked for).

Evaluate this statement – this is only found in the 12-mark questions. However, the bullet points which follow will help you develop the skills needed to tackle these questions:

- **give reasoned arguments to support this statement** – reminding you that you must give a number of reasons, and must explain them for one side of the argument; using the word 'reasoned' suggests you have to do more than a simple explanation, you really have to apply the points you make

- **give reasoned arguments to support a different point of view** – reminding you to give a second side, again with well-explained arguments for that view

- **should refer to religious arguments** – there has to be a lot of religion in your answer – try to get it on both sides of the arguments you pose. It will not be enough to give one simple religious point

- **may refer to non-religious arguments** – there are probably good arguments you can use from non-religious traditions, such as what atheists and humanists might say, or what any ordinary person on the street might say

- **to reach a justified conclusion** – this is the final bit asking you to draw a conclusion – which side is strongest from the arguments you have put forward, when considering the statement?

Make sure you learn these words and phrases so that you do what the question asks of you. That will guarantee your answer is stronger. It is no use knowing lots of information if you do not know what the question wants you to do with it!

The existence of God and revelation glossary

Agnostic a person who believes there is not enough evidence to say whether a God exists or not

Atheist a person who believes there is no God

Belief system those beliefs which a religion is based on

Design argument the idea that the world is designed so God exists as the designer, also known as the teleological argument

First Cause the idea that the world was the result of something causing it i.e. God

General revelation indirect revelation – for example, through seeing God through nature

Humanism a belief system which does not include God, but sees as central the morally good behaviour of humans

Illusion something that is not real, but a trick of the mind

Immanent that God is at work in the world – for example, performing miracles

Impersonal that God is beyond human capacity to understand; distant (in intellectual and emotional terms)

Miracles good events which are considered impossible, so should not have been able to happen, and are inexplicable by science

Omnipotent all-powerful

Omniscient all-knowing

Personal relatable; humans can meet and connect with God

Polytheist person who believes in more than one God

Reality what is real or actual

Revelation God revealing himself

Science the collection of knowledge from observation and testing

Special revelation direct revelation – for example, seeing God in a vision

Teleological argument an argument for the existence of God based on a perception that the world has been designed

Theist a person who believes in God

Thomas Aquinas an Italian philosopher and Catholic priest in the thirteenth century, who wrote five arguments for the existence of God, including the argument from Cause

Transcendent that God is beyond space and time, controlled by neither

Ultimate Reality the idea of one God which is absolute

Vision an image seen in the mind or a dream, especially as part of a religious or supernatural experience

William Paley an English clergyman who in the eighteenth century put forward the Design argument for the existence of God

7 Theme D: Religion, peace and conflict

Key elements of this theme

The first part of this theme considers the religious concepts relating to **violence**, **terrorism** and **war**. You need to know the key concepts of **peace**, **justice**, **forgiveness** and **reconciliation**, and the religious beliefs and teachings about these. You also have to explore religious beliefs and teachings about violence and terrorism, both of which some religious people are involved in. We need to look at beliefs and teachings about war itself and attitudes to fighting war, including when religious believers will go to war. We will also look at how religion causes **conflict**, and religious attitudes to **nuclear war**. We also need to understand religious attitudes to peace, including how individuals have fought for peace and how religions support victims of war.

Key concepts

Justice – this means fairness; making right and fair a situation which has been unjust. Religion is meant to bring justice to the world, and to fight injustice where it is seen. Many wars are about, or include, the abuse of justice, so many religious people feel duty-bound to fight against that. For example, Sikhs vow to fight injustice.

Peace – this has to be the aim and goal of all people, as it means to live in harmony and without fear. Many religions talk about a time to come where there is peace. It may be the Kingdom of Heaven, paradise, or Enlightenment, but it is a goal for all to reach and work towards. Having peace on Earth (no wars) is a step towards that.

Reconciliation – most religious people will be involved in reconciliation after war. The Quakers are pacifists who try to bring sides together and help them resolve issues so they can live peaceably. If we do not bring the opposing sides together and get their issues resolved, how can we expect any peace to last?

Forgiveness – this is the belief we should be able to move a relationship forward with someone who has done wrong to us, by accepting their apology and putting the wrong-doing behind us. It is a central teaching of Christianity and important in all religions.

Conflict – before the actual fighting starts, there is conflict. Conflict is disagreement; armed conflict is the actual fighting. Religious people might have been involved in trying to resolve the original disagreements, but might also then get involved in the armed conflicts as often as they feel they have no other option. For example, Dietrich Bonhoeffer, a German pastor, was involved in a plot to kill Hitler. Many religious people have died in battle.

> ### The Basics
> 1. Give a definition for each of the following words: justice, reconciliation, peace, conflict.
> 2. For each definition, give an example to demonstrate its meaning.
> 3. Do you think war is the biggest problem in the world today? Explain your reasons.
> 4. 'The most difficult thing to do is reconcile after conflict.' How far do you agree with this statement? Explore arguments for and against it, explaining the arguments you give.

> ### The Basics (for page 255)
> 1. Explain religious teachings about justice.
> 2. Explain how justice applies to war.
> 3. 'Justice is an impossible ideal when it comes to war.' How far do you agree? Explain arguments for and against.

Religious beliefs, teachings and attitudes about the meaning and significance of justice

In terms of justice there are two elements to justice:
- to put right injustice; making right a situation which has been unjust
- to carry out this fight in a just way.

Buddhism

Buddhists believe in preventing and diffusing conflict (a pacifist approach). However, out of compassion, Right Speech and Right Action, injustice must be challenged. It is important for justice to be found through negotiation. This is significant because war does not always bring peace and the threats of nuclear war/terrorism in the modern world environment are unacceptable for Buddhists. Justice is to understand the issues, respond with compassion and know that violence only breeds a cycle of **retaliation**. Buddhists will not fight through greed, hatred or ignorance; but for justice, Buddhists will act.

Christianity

Christians will fight for justice under the conditions of the **just war** theory, which is that war should be fought with justice too; the cause, weapons used and treatment of captured soldiers should all be just. While desiring peace, God also desires that humans should live in justice and freedom. However, some Christians believe that the conditions gained from war are never better than the injustice that started it. War goes against Jesus' teachings, but may be necessary for the greater good.

Hinduism

Holy books teach that it is necessary to be able to morally justify war in order to preserve the dharma. Arjuna, as a kshatriya, is reminded of his duty to uphold a righteous cause and that in fact there is nothing better than a righteous war. If the cause is just, Hindus will take up arms. Self-defence is justifiable; even nuclear weapons are acceptable because they are there as self-protection rather than as an aggressive act. Some Hindus have turned to terrorist activities to protect Hindu beliefs. The Arthashastra scriptures state that governments must act with a suitable moral approach, which implies a just one.

Justice

Islam

Muslims believe in Jihad, 'the striving for justice', which can mean armed conflict to protect the common good. Radical Jihad is not acceptable and neither is terrorism. Islam condemns violence and indiscriminate killing, so wars have to be carried out in the right way and there are set rules for warfare. People have the right to freedom and to defend that freedom in the right way.

Judaism

Justice is a key issue in Judaism, for example tzedekah is all about justice, even though people often think about it as charity. War in self-defence is justifiable where the Jewish nation is under attack, as this is about bringing justice. However, it must be carried out in a just way throughout. Even nuclear weapons are acceptable because they are there as self-protection rather than as an aggressive act.

Sikhism

Sikhs will fight for justice. Dharam yudh (a righteous war) is the idea that minimum force should be used; only enough to achieve an objective. Nuclear war and terrorism are never right as they indiscriminately take life, which is the highest expression of the Supreme Self, God. However, some Sikhs have used guerrilla tactics claiming the actions as 'rightful force' against oppression.

How do religious believers view justice in regard to war?

Religious beliefs, teachings and attitudes about the meaning and significance of forgiveness and reconciliation

Forgiveness and reconciliation are two of the most difficult challenges we have, both as individuals and nations, especially after a war or period of conflict. We hear much about the horrors of war, but what happens after it very rarely gets reported or seen. Nations very rarely apologise for their actions (as this would seem to say they were wrong to act in the first place) or forgive other nations, but reconciliation appears to just happen over time despite this.

However, on an individual basis there have been many stories of people coming to terms with war, their action and the actions of others by both seeking forgiveness and indeed giving it. This has then led to a kind of reconciliation. As a religious person of whatever faith, it is looked at as the right thing to do … to forgive.

Look at these two examples of people who have forgiven others for their actions in war.

Corrie Ten Boom was a Dutch girl who helped save Jewish lives in Holland in the Second World War. She was caught with her father and sister, both of whom were killed by the Nazis. She was for some reason released – an act of God, she claimed.

Later, when giving talks about the Holocaust, she met the SS man at a church in Munich who had guarded them in Ravensbrook concentration camp. As he held out his hand to shake hers, all her memories flooded back. She kept her hand by her side, even though she had preached many times that we should forgive those who hurt us. She recalled the treatment in the camps, her anger growing alongside a desire for revenge. Then she felt that her emotional state was a sin, and began to tell herself off because she believed Jesus had died for all, including this man. So she prayed for God to help her forgive him. She tried to smile and to raise her hand to shake his. However, she still could not engage with this man, so she prayed again for the help from Jesus. This time, she said, when their hands touched, it was as if a current was flowing from her to him and she felt love (agape) for this man who had formerly been her cruel guard. Corrie interpreted this to mean that the rifts in the world are healed by God's love. She believed that through Jesus' command to his followers to love their enemies, the ability to love enemies also comes from Jesus.

Eric Lomax was a British soldier who was tortured by the Japanese while a prisoner during the Second World War, but who was able to forgive one of his tormentors. He was one of thousands of British soldiers who surrendered to the Japanese in Singapore in 1942. Many were relocated to Thailand and forced to build the Burma Railway, also known as the Death Railway. After his captors found a radio receiver he had made he was repeatedly tortured; multiple bones were broken and water was poured into his nose and mouth. One of his constant torturers stood out: Nagase Takashi, an interpreter. 'At the end of the war, I would have been happy to murder him,' Eric told *The New York Times* in 1995. Eric had actually searched for the man, and his wife wrote a letter to arrange a meeting between the two in Thailand. He learned that after the war Nagase had become an interpreter for the Allies and helped locate thousands of graves and mass burial sites along the Burma Railway. 'When we met, Nagase greeted me with a formal bow,' Eric said on the website of the Forgiveness Project (a British group that seeks to bring together victims and perpetrators of crimes). 'I took his hand and said in Japanese, "Good morning, Mr. Nagase, how are you?" He was trembling and crying, and he said over and over again: "I am so sorry, so very sorry."'

Corrie Ten Boom spent many years after the war travelling in Germany and Europe, visiting schools and groups to talk about her experience. She did not hold a grudge against the German people for her suffering and loss, but found strength in her faith to be able to forgive. Her work was important in bringing other people to forgive each other, and reconcile.

Eric Lomax had gone to the meeting with his former guard with absolutely no sympathy for his former torturer, but was turned around by the complete humility Nagase showed. In the following days they spent a lot of time together, talking and laughing, and became good friends. That friendship remained until their deaths.

'I haven't forgiven Japan as a nation,' Eric told *The New York Times*, 'but I've forgiven one man, because he's experienced such great personal regret.'

When people forgive they start to heal and move on from their wartime suffering. All religions would commend these two individuals for what they were able to do. Whether it is religion inspired or simply human action, Corrie Ten Boom and Eric Lomax set an example for others. Neither found it easy, but both had the strength to do it.

> You can read Corrie Ten Boom's story in *The Hiding Place*, and Eric Lomax's in *The Railway Man*.

Religious ideas about forgiveness

Holding on to anger is like grasping a hot coal with the intent of throwing it at someone else – you are the one who gets burned. (Buddha)

To be a Christian means to forgive the inexcusable, because God has forgiven the inexcusable in you. (C.S. Lewis)

The weak can never forgive. Forgiveness is the attribute of the strong. (Gandhi)

Dispelled is anger as forgiveness is grasped. (Guru Amar Das)

We achieve inner health only through forgiveness – the forgiveness not only of others but also of ourselves. (Joshua Loth Liebman, American Rabbi)

Although the just penalty for an injustice is an equivalent retribution, those who pardon and maintain righteousness are rewarded by God. He does not love the unjust. (Qur'an 42:40)

The Basics

1. What is meant by forgiveness?
2. Explain two religious teachings about forgiveness.
3. How does the story of either Corrie Ten Boom or Eric Lomax show forgiveness?
4. 'Religious people should always forgive those who do wrong to them.' Explain arguments for and against this statement.

Religious beliefs, teachings and attitudes about violence, including violent protest

☸ Buddhism

Buddhism does not believe in any sort of violence and any **protest** should be non-violent. Protests have taken place and speaking out about injustice can be seen as Right Speech and Right Action. Trying to change injustice is a compassionate act. The Dalai Lama has said that peace can only happen with mutual respect. However, there have been occasions where Buddhists have used violence in protests – for example, against the Chinese occupation of Tibet and the very famous incident of Thich Quang Duc, who was a monk who set fire to himself to protest during the Vietnam War.

✝ Christianity

Christianity again teaches non-violence, as Jesus said 'Blessed are the peacemakers' and told his followers to turn the other cheek in the face of violence. Christians are told to love their enemies and love each other. However, God gave humans free will and choice, and sometimes non-violent protest is ignored, so violence might be used to force change for the common good.

ॐ Hinduism

Hinduism believes that non-violence is the only way to achieve anything long-term. The principle of ahimsa is key to Hindu life but even so, injustice should not be tolerated. Protest done for the right reasons can be seen as a religious act in itself and Gandhi himself protested about equal rights, apartheid in South Africa and against British rule.

☪ Islam

Islam means peace and Muslims should act in a peaceful manner, but violence may be used in self-defence. Muslims have a duty to protest about anything unfair and in the UK we have seen protests over wars and issues in the Middle East, what is perceived as Islamophobia, terrorism and racism issues. Some have become violent in nature. For example, in 2015 in Palestine, Muslims threw missiles at the Israeli police/army in protest over the shooting dead of a 13-year-old boy.

🕎 Judaism

Judaism does allow protest against injustice, as Jewish people believe that God made them stewards and having been the subject of persecution they want to help others in the same situation. The books of the Nevi'im have stories of the prophets protesting. Jewish people have protested about (perceived) anti-Semitism and issues in Israel. Quite often civil disobedience (active refusal to obey certain laws) is used, but violence is not. However, in spite of teachings, sometimes violence does erupt as emotions run high.

☬ Sikhism

Sikhism believes in not harming others but at the same time is a warrior religion. The Sikh Khanda symbol includes crossed swords. There is a willingness to violently fight for justice if necessary. We have seen this in India with Sikhs defending themselves against Hindu attacks. Sikhs believe in sewa (service) and as such they will defend the persecuted. The intention is always peaceful, but again, in practice, violence can happen.

The Basics

1. What is meant by violent protest?
2. Why might religious people feel the need to protest?
3. 'It is always wrong for religious believers to protest violently.' Do you agree with this statement? Explain reasons, giving examples to illustrate your arguments.

Religious teachings, beliefs and attitudes about terrorism

Terrorism is an act of violence which is intended to create fear. A terrorist is anyone who plans or carries out such an act. Terrorist acts are often directed at civilians and because of this many consider them to be unlawful acts of war and violence. The United Nations Security Council regards terrorist attacks as criminal:

> 'Acts intended to cause death or serious bodily harm to civilians or non-combatants with the purpose of intimidating a population or compelling a government or an international organization to do or abstain from doing any act.'

In the modern world there have been many recorded acts of terrorism. Al Qaeda's attacks on the World Trade Center Twin Towers (11 September 2001) and the Sri Lankan Easter church attacks (April 2019) are just two of the many recorded examples of suicide bombers around the world. White racists have been responsible for gun attacks – for example, in Norway (2011) and New Zealand (2019), murdering many. However, not all terrorist attacks are like this – often the terrorists attack and kill others, not giving their own lives, such as the murder of journalist Lyra McKee in Northern Ireland by the Real IRA in 2019. There have also been other kinds of attacks, such as on the internet and against governments and businesses (Charlie Hebdo in Paris in 2015), and attacks on historical sites (for example, Islamic State destroying the ancient site of Palmyra in 2015).

Why do terrorists carry out attacks? They claim that:
- they are fighting against social and political injustice, where a group of people are being denied their human rights
- they are fighting against poverty
- they are fighting to assert their religious beliefs, especially where they feel these are denied to them.

When people are fighting for a cause they believe in, some are prepared to go to any lengths to have their voice heard. It has been said that 'One man's terrorist is another man's freedom fighter.' There are many examples where a person was classed as a terrorist, but later seen as a legitimate leader – for example, Martin McGuinness in Northern Ireland and Nelson Mandela in South Africa.

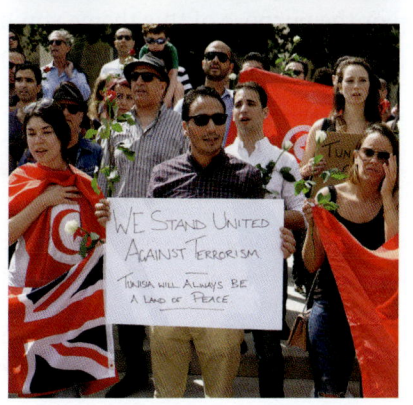

TERRORIST THREAT BRINGS FEAR TO OLYMPICS

White racist kills 51 worshipers in mosque shooting spree

Terrorists use hospital as base to launch bombs

Muslims in UK now fear being labelled a terrorist

Museums of ancient history destroyed by terrorists

The Basics

1. What is meant by terrorism?
2. Give two reasons why many religious people would consider terrorist acts wrong. Explain your reasons.
3. Use the images and headlines on this page to describe the effects of terrorism.
4. Why do some people feel they have to carry out terrorist acts?
5. 'Terrorism is never right.' What do you think? Explain reasons to agree and disagree with this statement.

7 Theme D: Religion, peace and conflict

Religious teachings, beliefs and attitudes about reasons for war

At any point in time there is always a war happening somewhere in the world. We have fought wars throughout history and there is little sign of them stopping. Wars between nations, **civil wars**, threats of futuristic wars, including nuclear and cyber wars, all threaten our existence on a daily basis. We have progressed in terms of weapons and types of war to a point where weapons exist that could destroy us all.

All religions promote peace and the majority of the world's people would claim to have a religious belief … so why do we continue to have conflicts?

We can examine history for the reasons.

> Name as many wars/conflicts as you can from the last 100 years.

Have you written a long list? It is probably true to say you know something about each of them, but do you know the reason why they started? Many reasons have been used to justify wars, but whether they are valid reasons is debatable. This could depend on the side you support, previous events in history, where it is happening and of course whether you find yourself in the middle of a war zone.

> There are many reasons why wars begin – can you think of any?

Your list might include: disputes over land, in self-defence, to get power, to re-establish human rights, for resources, or to keep an agreement (treaty) with other countries. There are many reasons. However, which reasons are valid, and which are just about greed? It all depends on your viewpoint.

For the purpose of this theme you need to focus on three reasons: greed, self-defence and retaliation.

Greed

This is war to gain, for example, more land, more power or more resources. Most religious teaching would not support this as a reason. Greed comes from selfishness, which are both characteristics not approved of by religions. Considering the numbers of soldiers and casualties in war, greed could never be seen as a justifiable reason for it.

Self-defence

Religious holy books and texts describe wars. The Old Testament, the Qur'an, the Bhagavad Gita and the Guru Granth Sahib all suggest that war may be necessary in self-defence. If a country or religion is under attack, then conflicts can happen. It would be seen as entirely right and proper to defend your own country against attack. The problem comes when the response is disproportionately large, and self-defence turns into aggression for its own gain.

Retaliation

At times, a country will be attacked in a way which provokes retaliation. For example, the First World War began as retaliation against a political assassination. The problem with retaliation is that it is often a spontaneous reaction which leads to the escalation of a situation, and hence war. Religions would all say that peaceful negotiation and discussions to resolve issues are better than simple retaliation because they diffuse rather than exacerbate issues.

The Basics

1. Give some reasons why wars begin. Which, if any, are appropriate reasons in your opinion?
2. Use religious teachings from pages 255, 258 and 262–264 to explain whether war can be justified.
3. Explain religious views about fighting in self-defence.
4. 'Greed is never a good reason for war for religious people.' What do you think?

Religion and belief as a cause of war and violence

When asked the question about causes of war, religion is always an answer. Is this true or not though?

Religion/religious teachings themselves do not cause violence or war. How they are put into practice or how they are interpreted is the problem. Religious teachings are all about peace and understanding, but sometimes teachings can be ambiguous or difficult to understand, which may cause problems. The Bible/Torah say 'Do not kill' but also 'an eye for an eye'; the Qur'an allows Muslims to fight for the name of Allah, yet 'the greatest sin is to take another man's life'. All of this means that for some people there is room for violence/war in the name of religion, and as long as people believe that, then innocent people will die in war and great mistrust will continue to grow between peoples of different cultures. Some may think they are fighting for their religion but for the people at the top organising the fight/war, perhaps their own power is the most important.

> **Task**
>
> Find out about the work of an organisation which tries to work for peace – for example, Médicins san Frontières, Pax Christi, Buddhist Peace Fellowship.

1. It is definitely true that religion is involved in war – for example, when two countries of different religions are fighting each other: Israel *vs.* Palestine (Jewish people *vs.* Muslims), the Syrian civil war (Sunni Muslims *vs.* Shi'a Muslims). However, both these conflicts are more about politics than about religion. The War on Terror has been seen as a conflict between Muslims and other religions in the West, yet the West would say that it is the politics not the religion that the war is against. So religion is not the actual cause.

2. Also, throughout history religious beliefs have divided people. Where splits have occurred violence has erupted. Actual examples show that, for example: when people broke from Hinduism to form Sikhism many died in the violence; after the death of Muhammad there was a terrible violent struggle for power resulting in the Sunni-Shi'a split; the Bosnian war in 1995 saw Christian ethnic cleansing of Muslims. Therefore, we can say religious beliefs sometimes do cause violence.

3. People are quick to discuss the differences, yet if we look more closely, the similarities between religions and what they want for the communities are far greater. This is what we need to hold onto to bring people together in faith and understanding. There are many people who are doing exactly that. For example, there are many who are working across religious divides to help others, save lives, solve conflicts and bring peace, and these people are in far greater numbers than those who are causing the conflicts. True religious beliefs do not cause war and these people are a testimony to that.

> Is it right to say that religion causes war? Explain your ideas.

Religious attitudes to war and peace

☸ Buddhism

Buddhism, war and peace

Buddhism is a religion of peace. Although Buddhist countries have armies, they usually exist for defence purposes and as a secondary police force.

Buddhism teaches:
- The First Precept – to refrain from harming others; this is ahimsa and is a core principle of Buddhism.
- The Noble Eightfold Path – for example, Right Action and Right Awareness.
- 'Hatred does not cease by hatred, hatred ceases by love.' (Dhammapada)
- 'He should not kill a living being, nor cause it to be killed, nor should he incite another to kill.' (Dhammapada)
- 'Peace can exist if everyone respects all others.' (Dalai Lama)

The message of Buddhism is one of peace, not war. Buddhists believe their actions have consequences for their future rebirths. It is wrong to harm others, yet soldiers must kill. Buddhists believe all peaceful means must be tried, because war can lead to greater problems than it solves. War is often the result of the Three Poisons (greed, hatred, ignorance), and war also encourages them, whereas Buddhism seeks to get rid of them. The Dalai Lama is the spiritual leader of the Tibetans; his country was invaded by and made part of China. He believes the only resolution can be a peaceful one. He won the Nobel Peace Prize in 1992.

✝ Christianity

Christianity, war and peace

The teachings of Christianity are peaceful. Jesus taught a message of love and Christianity has a strong pacifist tradition. However, many Christians accept that there are circumstances when it is necessary to use armed conflict and will fight in a just war. No Christian denomination would support the use of nuclear weapons.

Christianity teaches:
- 'Put away your sword. Those who live by the sword die by the sword.' (Jesus, Matthew 26:52)
- 'Blessed are the peacemakers.' (Jesus, Sermon on the Mount)
- 'Love your enemies, and pray for them.' (Jesus, Sermon on the Mount)
- 'Peace I leave with you, my peace I give to you.' (Jesus, John 14:27)
- 'Everyone must commit themselves to peace.' (Pope John Paul II)

Christianity is a peaceful religion if we look at the teachings of both Jesus and St Paul. The Kingdom of Heaven is a place of peace and love, not violence and fighting. The earliest Christians were pacifists and most Christians today are pacifists. The Quaker Movement is a good example of this attitude.

Many Christians only agree with war in certain circumstances – for example, to defend against an invading force. Many Christians disagreed with the war on Iraq (2003–2011) because they felt the reasons for it were wrong, and that it led to many innocent people being killed. Where Christians accept war, it has to be the last resort after all peaceful efforts have failed.

Task

Hold a class discussion about this statement:
'Peace is an impossible dream.'
Take a vote at the end of the debate.
Which side won? What arguments were the most persuasive?

ॐ Hinduism

Hinduism, war and peace

Historically Hindus were split by caste (social division). One of these was the kshatriya caste, which means 'to protect from harm'. They are a warrior caste. Even though Hindu society does not so rigidly follow the caste system today, it still has influence. Hindus believe in following dharma (duty), so for kshatriyas fighting is acceptable in just wars. However, Hinduism promotes ahimsa (non-violence) and tolerance as key virtues, which are against fighting.

Hinduism teaches:
- Kshatriyas (warrior caste) are expected to be the first to battle, and the bravest in battle; their main duty is to defend and protect others.
- 'Even an enemy must be offered appropriate hospitality if he comes to your home.' (Mahabharata)
- Key Hindu virtues include ahimsa (non-violence), tolerance, compassion, and respect, as well as protection of others.
- 'The pursuit of truth does not permit violence being inflicted on one's opponent.' (Gandhi)
- 'If you do not fight in this just war, you will neglect your duty, harm your reputation and commit the sin of omission.' (Bhagavad Gita)

So, where a war is seen as just – for example, in defence against an invading nation – kshatriyas must follow their duty and fight. Not doing so would gain bad karma, and negatively affects future rebirths. Where it is necessary to protect others, fighting may be the only way, and so is acceptable.

However, Mahatma Gandhi stressed that justice can be achieved through non-violence. Since all life is sacred because Brahman is within all (the atman) war destroys this ideal.

☾ Islam

Islam, war and peace

One meaning of the word Islam is peace. Allah has 99 names known to Muslims. One of them is As-salaam, which means 'the source of peace'. It is said that if all people followed the Muslim way of life, there should only be peace. Muslims should work to keep the peace; war should only occur when all peaceful means have been exhausted. Only then do Muslims have a duty to fight in the defence of Allah and the weak and oppressed.

Islam teaches:
- Greet others salaam alaikum, which means 'peace be upon you'.
- Greater jihad is every Muslim's personal struggle to follow Allah; the lesser jihad is **holy war** in defence of Islam.
- 'To those against whom war is made, permission is given to fight.' (Qur'an)
- 'Those who die in the name of Allah will be rewarded with paradise.' (Qur'an)
- 'Hate your enemy mildly; for he may become your friend one day.' (Hadith)

When Muhammad was alive, the Muslim community had to defend themselves by fighting. If they had not, they would all have been killed. Allah ordered Muslims to fight back when attacked, so holy war became a duty for Muslims. The Muslim religion realises that sometimes to defend people's rights or to change a terrible situation, we have to fight.

Task

Working with a partner, write a discussion between two believers, one who will fight in a war and one who says it is wrong to fight. Remember they could both be in the same or different religions.

7 Theme D: Religion, peace and conflict

Judaism

Judaism, war and peace

Judaism does not question the right to defend a just cause by war. The Talmud says that whoever sheds the blood of man, by man shall his blood be shed. However, in fact there are rules which exist for fighting war only as a last resort. It is forbidden to take delight in the war or its victory, and Jewish people believe that when the Messiah comes, all weapons will be destroyed and turned into peaceful tools. Peace remains the ideal.

Judaism teaches:
- The Jewish greeting is shalom – peace.
- 'Get ready for war. Call out your best warriors. Let your fighting men advance for the attack.' (Ketuvim)
- 'The sword comes to the world because of the delay of justice and through injustice.' (Talmud)
- 'It shall come to pass ... nation shall not lift up sword against nation, neither shall they learn war any more.' (Nevi'im) (about the future before God's kingdom is established)
- 'When siege is laid to a city, surround only three sides to give an opportunity for escape to those who would flee to save their lives.' (Maimonides Code)

In early Judaism, war was a religious duty. There are many descriptions of wars fought in the Bible, where God is on the side of the righteous Israelite army, and they win. The Ark of the Covenant was taken into battle with them as a talisman. Today, war is still acceptable, but as a last resort, and only for just reasons (for example, self-defence) or when the Jewish people or Israel are threatened.

There are rules about fighting the wars, including that chances for escape and surrender must be given, that there is no scorched earth policy, and that civilians and prisoners are treated with dignity.

The ideal is peace, and justice is vital for peace.

Task

Use the information provided to create a booklet that explains the religious teachings about war and peace for the religions that you are studying.

Sikhism

Sikhism, war and peace

Sikhs have duties to fight for justice and to protect minorities. War should be a last resort and should be fought in a just manner.

Sikhism teaches:
- The Sikh Khanda includes two swords, and Sikhs wear the kirpan showing a willingness to fight when necessary.
- 'When all other methods have failed it is permissible to draw the sword.' (Guru Gobind Singh)
- 'A true warrior is one who fights for the downtrodden, the weak, and the meek.' (Guru Granth Sahib)
- 'The Lord is the haven of peace.' (Guru Granth Sahib)
- Peace is believed to come from God.

While Sikhism aims for peace, it also allows fighting, particularly in self-defence and for justice. Early Sikhism saw many threats from other communities, including the rulers of the land in which they lived. Being able to fight was the only way Sikhism could have survived. Several of the Sikh Gurus instructed Sikhs to do physical and military training. Guru Ram Das swapped prayerbeads for two swords, showing a stance against oppression and injustice. Guru Tegh Bahadur led the Sikhs, Hindus and some Muslims in a national non-violent protest for the right to religious freedom. After this resulted in Guru Tegh Bahadur's execution in 1675, Guru Gobind Singh organised the Sikhs into an effective army after setting up the Khalsa, whose members were prepared to give up their lives for their religion. Even in the modern world, many Sikh men are soldiers and very highly regarded for their skill and effort, fighting for the country in which they live, so for example, there are Sikhs in the British Army.

This does not mean that Sikhism looks for wars to fight. Peace through justice is the ideal. However, there is an obligation to fight to get justice, where necessary.

Some Sikhs are pacifists out of respect for the sanctity of life and the belief that God created all life, so that it deserves both respect and protection.

Religions allowing war – holy war and just war

We have seen that all religious traditions believe in peace not war. However, most also accept that there are times when it is necessary to go to war to avoid a greater evil. Within religious teachings there are contrasting views on war and so religious believers must use their conscience in deciding if they believe a war is morally justified.

There are three possible stances a religious believer may take:

pacifist – believing all war and killing is wrong

holy war – believing it is right to fight a war in the name of God

just war – believing it is right to fight a war in the interests of justice and the greater good.

Within some religious traditions there is clear guidance on the rules and legitimacy of wars.

✝ Christianity

'Declare a Holy War, call the troops to arms.' (Old Testament)

Holy war

Within Christian history there was once a strong concept of holy war. In the Old Testament there are many examples of wars fought in the name of God. The soldiers believed God was on their side and indeed had influence over the outcomes of battles. For example, Joshua's army followed God's commands to blow trumpets and bring down the walls of Jericho. The Crusades (1095–1291) were fought to capture control of the Holy Land. The Christian soldiers believed they were fighting for a sacred and noble cause. They believed God was with them, and the Muslim Turks they were fighting against were the pagan enemies of God.

Just war

'It is impossible to conceive of a just war in a nuclear age.' (Pope John XXIII)

St Paul said Christians should obey their rulers, who had been given power by God. When those rulers demanded Christians be soldiers, a compromise had to be found. St Augustine was the first to try to write a set of rules regarding this, and eventually the just war rules were written in detail by St Thomas Aquinas. The message is clear: sometimes if you do not fight, you allow a greater evil to happen than a war would have caused, so you have to fight.

Christian just war rules

- War must be started and controlled by a proper authority such as a government.
- There must be a just cause for the war. It must not be aggression towards an enemy.
- The war must have a clear aim to promote good and overcome evil.
- War must be a last resort. Every effort must have been made to resolve conflict peacefully.
- There must be a reasonable chance of success. It would be wrong to risk lives with no chance of success.
- The war must be conducted fairly. Only reasonable force should be used and the risk to civilians minimised.
- There must be a good outcome and peace restored.

7 Theme D: Religion, peace and conflict

☪ Islam

> 'Fight in the cause of Allah those who fight you, but do not transgress limits ... if they cease let there be no hostility.'
> (Qur'an)

Lesser jihad also means holy war. Remember the Qur'an uses the word jihad to describe a personal struggle against committing sin. Holy war is a lesser meaning of the term. In a disagreement with another nation, if talking fails to sort the problem, then war becomes a religious duty for Muslims. (Look at page 263 for more detail on this.)

Holy war

For Muslims a holy war is a just war. There are rules for how Muslims should fight a war. These are in the Qur'an, and were written in more detail by one of the caliphs (rulers). A jihad may only be fought as a last resort and must never be against another Muslim nation.

1. Who fights?
   - Muslims have a duty to join the army and fight, if a just leader begins a war.
   - Not all Muslims have to fight. Muhammad said one man from each two should fight, so that there are still men to defend and look after the towns and villages.
   - Men (not boys) who are not insane, and whose families can cope without them, must fight.
   - Soldiers on the battlefield must fight; running away is wrong, because that makes it more difficult for other soldiers.
   - If a town is attacked, everyone (men, women and children) has to fight back.
2. How is the war fought?
   - It may only begin when the enemy attacks and it ends when the enemy shows they want peace.
   - Civilians must not be harmed, attacked or mistreated.
   - Crops should be left alone. Holy buildings especially should not be damaged.
   - Prisoners of war should be treated well. Money collected for zakat can be used to pay for food for them.
3. How does the war end?
   - When people regain their rights.
   - When the enemy calls for peace.

Sikhism

Just war

When Guru Gobind Singh formed the Khalsa it was his intention to create an army of warrior saints committed to the cause of justice. Accepting the need for Sikhs to be prepared to fight, he outlined the teachings of a just war. In Sikhism this is called dharam yudh, which means in defence of justice.

- WAR IS ALWAYS A LAST RESORT
- THE CAUSE MUST BE JUST. A SIKH DEFENDS HIMSELF, HIS NATION, AND THE WEAK
- WAR SHOULD BE FOUGHT WITHOUT HATRED OR A WISH FOR REVENGE
- TERRITORY MAY NOT BE TAKEN
- ALL SOLDIERS MUST BEHAVE JUSTLY CIVILIANS MUST NOT BE HARMED
- THE MINIMUM FORCE NECESSARY SHOULD BE USED
- ONCE THE AIMS OF THE WAR ARE MET, ALL ATTEMPTS TO ESTABLISH PEACE MUST BE MADE

Guru Hargobind set up an armed Sikh warrior order, called nihangs. Male and female Sikhs are part of this order which still exists today. They are devoted to God and train to a very high level in Sikh martial arts, ready to fight when called.

The soldiers were to be sant sipahi (saint soldiers). As well as their training, they had an obligation to do nam simran and meditate daily. In other words, they had to practise their religion devotedly, as well as do their military training and preparations. Guru Gobind Singh once said: 'Without power, righteousness does not flourish, without dharma everything is crushed and ruined.'

The Basics

1. What is meant by holy war?
2. Why do you think some religious believers would fight in a holy war?
3. Choose either Christianity, Islam or Sikhism. Write a detailed explanation of their teachings about a just/holy war.
4. 'There can be no such thing as a just war, because the innocent always suffer.' Do you agree? Give reasons to argue more than one point of view, including religious arguments in your answer.

7 Theme D: Religion, peace and conflict

Victims of war

War has obvious consequences – soldiers die, civilians die.

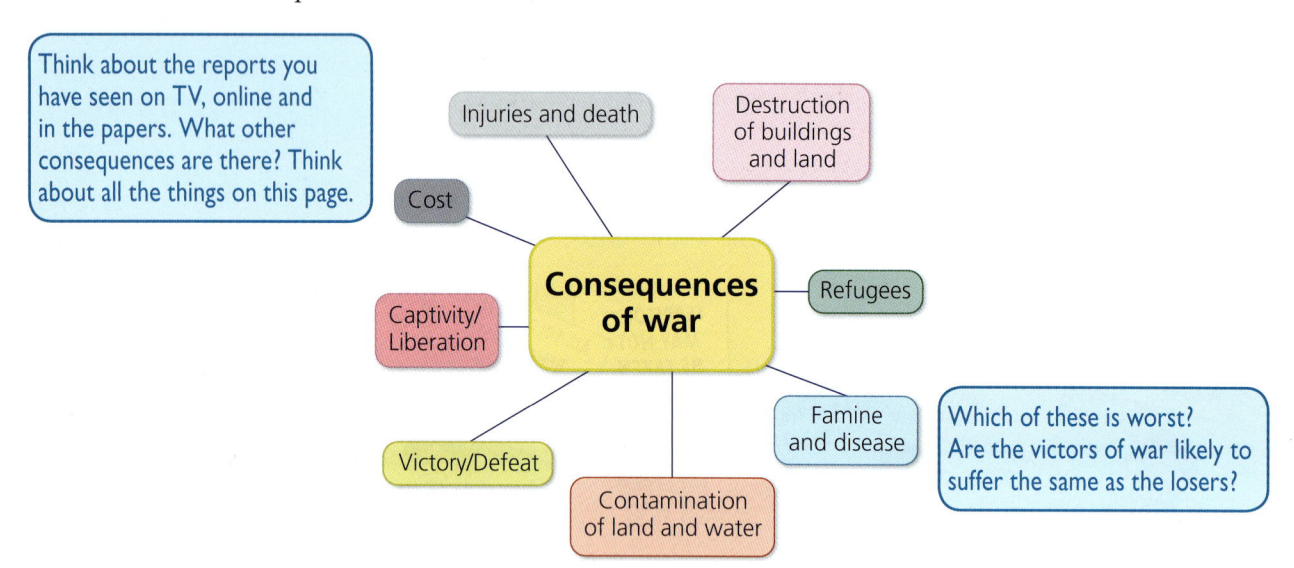

> Think about the reports you have seen on TV, online and in the papers. What other consequences are there? Think about all the things on this page.

Consequences of war:
- Injuries and death
- Destruction of buildings and land
- Cost
- Refugees
- Captivity/Liberation
- Famine and disease
- Victory/Defeat
- Contamination of land and water

> Which of these is worst? Are the victors of war likely to suffer the same as the losers?

Helping the victims of war

There are many organisations which try to help the victims of war, both when war is happening and after it. Part of that is to try to bring about peace. It is part of all religions to help those in trouble and defend those who cannot defend themselves, so it is natural that religions will try to help the victims of war. To do so fits with the basic teaching of the Golden Rule, 'Treat others as you would be done by', which every religion follows.

Christian Peacemaker Teams (www.cpt.org) was founded in 1984 by three historic pacifistic Churches – the Mennonite, Church of the Brethren and Quaker, though now has support and membership from a wider range of Christian denominations. They send small teams to work on peace-making in conflict zones (third-party non-violent intervention) trying to end conflict between sides by peaceful means, and bring aid and support to the victims of war.

The Buddhist Peace Fellowship (www.buddhistpeacefellowship.org) was founded in 1978, and works by applying Buddhist principles to issues in the world, and Buddhist teachings to resolve them. It speaks publicly to raise awareness of issues, tries to strengthen leadership in the areas where there are issues, and acts with other groups to make change happen. This supports victims of war, by helping bring peace back to an area. It also does relief work for victims of war.

Khalsa Aid (www.khalsaaid.org) was set up in 1999 as an international organisation. Its work is based on the Sikh principles of selfless service (sewa) and universal love. It has provided relief assistance to victims of war, funded through donations from Sikhs all over the world, as well as other disaster and relief work.

The Basics

1. What do we mean by 'victims of war'? Give examples.
2. Describe how different religious organisations try to help victims of war.
3. 'Not enough is done for victims of war.' Do you agree? Explain arguments to show different points of view.

Religious attitudes to weapons of mass destruction and nuclear weapons

Most religious people disagree with **weapons of mass destruction** (WMD), and many have joined protests against these. WMD are capable of killing and maiming large numbers of people. They can also cause massive levels of destruction to both the natural landscape and human-made structures. It is almost impossible to use such weapons solely to target military operations. They are controlled from far away, either in the form of missiles or as bombs dropped from planes. This means that whoever releases the weapon does not experience or see the weapon's effect directly. It is very different to soldiers on the battlefield. There are several types of these weapons:

1. Nuclear weapons – atomic bombs – cause immediate destruction of all life and structures within their range. The radioactive 'fallout' has long-term effects.
2. Biological warfare – also known as germ warfare, uses living disease-causing bacteria or viruses such as anthrax, to harm or kill people.
3. Chemical warfare – uses non-living toxins such as nerve agents and mustard gas, to cause death, incapacity or illness in people.
4. Radiological weapons – 'dirty bombs' – are weapons that use **conventional** explosives to create bombs that can disperse radioactive material. As well as killing people, they make the impact area useless because of contamination.

Religious attitudes

No religion agrees with the use of nuclear weapons and other weapons of mass destruction. They are seen as too extreme, and uncontrollable, and do not fit with any just or holy war theories, or with ideas of moral behaviour in war.

Religious people believe in the sanctity of life and so the effects of these weapons go completely against this belief. When the USA used a chemical called Agent Orange to defoliate trees in the Vietnam War, this powerful chemical destroyed people's crops, and got into the ecosystem and into people's bodies (including US soldiers') causing devastating and deadly health problems and birth defects. The chemical has also infected the landscape and more than 50 years on, people are still being affected with birth deformities, cancers, and so on.

Religious people also believe that wars should be fought to gain justice for the people. These weapons are considered unjust because they arbitrarily kill and maim civilians. During Saddam Hussain's reign in Iraq, his government ordered the use of nerve gas on the Kurds and the Shi'a Muslims at Karbala – a tool of oppression to bring terror upon the people who opposed his rule.

Nuclear deterrence

Some religious believers accept the existence of nuclear weapons to deter attacks by others, without any intention to use them. They help to keep the peace. Most religious believers, however, think nuclear weapons are completely unacceptable. They cost huge sums of money, which could be better spent. Also, if the technology gets into the wrong hands, there is no guarantee they will not be used. The fact that they exist means they could be used, which is immoral.

> ### Roman Catholic Church
> 'Though the monstrous power of modern weapons acts as a deterrent, it is feared that the mere continuance of nuclear tests, undertaken with war in mind, will have fatal consequences for life on Earth ... nuclear weapons should be banned.'
> *(Second Vatican Council)*

The Basics

1. What are weapons of mass destruction?
2. Explain religious attitudes to these weapons and their use.
3. 'WMDs should be banned.' Explain your opinion.

7 Theme D: Religion, peace and conflict

The role of religion and beliefs in war and peacekeeping in twenty-first-century conflicts

Religion causes all wars.

Do you agree with John? Does religion start wars? Is religion the defining factor of each side? Does religion play a part in ending war or keeping the peace? Let's consider evidence for each of those.

What involvement has religion had in twenty-first-century wars?

Does religion cause wars?

Yes …

… on occasions people have claimed that religion is the cause of a war by claiming that their religion is under attack. Many Muslims have claimed that the Gulf Wars and the troubles in Israel and Palestine are because the West were, or still are, making a direct attack on Islam. Some fundamentalist groups like the Islamic State believe an actual Islamic state needs to be created; however, many would say that what they have tried to create is not an Islamic state. Also troubles such as those in Israel cannot strictly be called a 'war', as they are not ongoing and engulfing everyone from both sides.

Ah but …

… if it was the religion under attack in these cases wouldn't someone just bomb their holy city, and hit the religion directly?

No …

… it is more true to say that religion rises to the surface in conflicts whereas power, land and self-defence are the real causes. War creates tensions and religious divisions surface. Also people claim religion as the cause to get support (money/people/weapons) from people of the same religion around the world.

Mmm however …

… perhaps it is religion, but countries do not want to admit it.

Is religion the defining factor between sides in a war?

Yes …

… religion may not be a cause directly, but often religion becomes a key issue as communities are divided. Israel and Palestine is an issue over land and living conditions yet it is defined as a Jewish *vs.* Muslim conflict. In parts of the Middle East conflicts in civil war have an element of Sunni *vs.* Shi'a to put groups on sides.

Ah well …

… it's just easier to see who is fighting who by separating on religious grounds, isn't it?

No …

… although many claim it is. Historical divisions often rise to the surface even between members of the same religion, but this is secondary to the root cause(s). Tensions bring out the worst in people and religion often gets caught in the middle. All religions speak of peace not war, especially with people or nations of the same religion.

Mmm true …

… but if it rises to the surface so easily does this not say it could be the root cause?

Religious, philosophical and ethical studies

Does religion play a part in ending war?

Some people would say yes …

… religious leaders often call for the end of conflict. For example, the Pope has called for the end of conflict in Syria and in Northern Africa where groups like Al-Shabab and Boko Haram wage war against Christians and indeed other Muslims. Also, he has called for peace in Russia and Ukraine. In 2013, the Archbishop of Canterbury appointed Canon David Porter as a Director of Reconciliation. His role is to make a powerful contribution to transforming violent situations around the world. Many religious leaders and groups are involved in bringing resolutions to war or speaking out against violent actions.

Mmm …

… but the Pope calling for the end of the war does not actually end it, does it?

Some people would say no …

… where religious extremism is concerned, groups often want to perpetuate war and they only want to see an end if everyone conforms to their demands. Even then they will find another excuse to continue their violence because of their need for power.

Ah …

… but extremists are only a small part of a religion … the majority in the religion do want to see the war end.

Does religion keep the peace?

Some people would say yes …

… Christianity teaches to 'Love your neighbour'; Islam means 'Peace'; Buddhism has the idea of non-harm in its precepts; Hinduism has the concept of 'ahimsa'; Judaism says 'Do not kill' in the Ten Commandments; Sikhism in the words of Guru Nanak says 'No one is my enemy'. If all these were adhered to, then there would be peace. Religious groups are regularly involved in peace-keeping in war torn areas and in negotiations to prevent wars happening.

Mmm …

… it may be true to say teachings want peace, but many believers ignore these teachings and start wars!

Some people would say no …

… sometimes even with all the best efforts, religion cannot keep the peace because there are greater overriding factors, such as the craving for power, the need to react to attack or to join allies to protect others.

True …

… but without the efforts of religions there would be more wars, so is it win some, lose some?

Tasks

Answer the following evaluation questions. Explain reasons to agree and disagree with each statement.
1 'Religion does not cause war.' What do you think?
2 'Religion does not keep the peace.' What do you think?
3 'Religion cannot end war.' What do you think?

Okay, maybe it isn't quite as simple as I thought it was. You have given me lots to think about. Maybe religion doesn't start all wars, and maybe it does help solve some of them, but then maybe I was right in the first place. I will have to think more about this.

7 Theme D: Religion, peace and conflict

Religious attitudes to peace and pacifism

Peace is not just the absence of war, but is a state of harmony, where justice exists for all and freedoms are respected. All religions teach the importance of peace on Earth and encourage their followers to live peacefully. Throughout history there have always been people prepared to refuse to use violence or fight in wars, even if it meant they faced imprisonment for their beliefs.

Pacifists believe that all violence is morally wrong. They will not participate in any war, regardless of the reasons for that war. **Conscientious objectors** are people who refuse to participate directly in fighting wars on the grounds of conscience. However, they will assist in non-military ways such as medics, relief work and mediators. Many believe they have a peace-making role.

Look back to pages 262–264 to reread the attitude of the religion(s) you have studied to peace.

Working for peace

The Quakers

This is a pacifist group within Christianity. As a Church they believe they are following the true teaching of Jesus by maintaining a completely pacifist stance. Their Peace Testimony makes clear that they will not use violence under any circumstances. It says that they denounce all violence, whatever its form. They totally oppose all outward wars and strife, and fighting with outward weapons, for any end, or for any reason. They believe that all relationships should be loving ones, including those between countries. During wars they will take on peace-making roles, such as mediating for peace between the warring nations. They also do non-combat work such as training to be, and acting as, medics for any side, and doing work with refugees and victims of war.

Gandhi

For over 30 years, the Hindu leader of India, Mahatma Gandhi, used a policy of non-violence and civil disobedience to oppose British rule in India. His belief in the Hindu concept of ahimsa (non-violence) underpinned his leadership of the Hindus. Through actions such as protests, marches, speeches, sit-ins and hunger strikes, he eventually led his country to independence. He demonstrated that **pacifism** does not mean you have to just put up with violence and intimidation; when used effectively it can be as powerful as any physical force.

Dietrich Bonhoeffer

Dietrich Bonhoeffer was a Christian living in Germany during the rise of the Nazi party. He believed in pacifism and helped found the Confessing Church, which spoke out against the human rights abuses of the ruling Nazis. As the war continued, he believed even more strongly that helping the oppressed was a test of faith. He defied Nazi rule by helping Jewish people escape the death camps and also worked to overthrow the Nazi party. Eventually, even though he opposed all killing, he felt that he had to be prepared to sacrifice his principles and even his life, and joined a group that planned to assassinate Hitler because he believed it was necessary for the greater good. He was eventually arrested and executed for treason by the Nazis.

Religious, philosophical and ethical studies

The Dalai Lama

The Dalai Lama is the spiritual leader of Tibetan Buddhists. He is recognised around the world as a symbol of peace. When the Chinese invaded his country, Tibet, he was forced into exile. However, despite this injustice he refuses to condone physical fighting against the Chinese. He says that hatred and violence will lead to more hatred and violence. He believes peace will only exist when everyone respects each other. He received the Nobel Peace Prize in 1992. Buddhist monks in Tibet have maintained peaceful protests against Chinese rule despite being subjected to threats and violence.

The Golden Rule

Buddhism
'I will act towards others exactly as I would act towards myself.' *(Udana-varqa)*

Christianity
'Treat others as you would like them to treat you.' *(Jesus)*

Hinduism
'This is the sum of duty: do nothing to others which if done to you could cause the pain.' *(Mahabharata)*

Islam
'None of you truly believe until he wishes for his brothers what he wishes for himself.' *(Prophet Muhammad)*

Judaism
'What is harmful to yourself do not do to your fellow man.' *(Rabbi Hillel)*

Sikhism
'As you value yourself, so value others – cause suffering to no one.' *(Guru Granth Sahib)*

Think about these statements. How do they fit with the idea of going to war? Or, being a pacifist?

The Basics

1. What does pacifism mean?
2. Explain religious teachings about peace and pacifism.
3. Describe different ways that religious believers have worked for peace.
4. 'The Golden Rule is not powerful enough to build a peaceful world.' How far do you agree? Explain arguments for and against before writing a justified conclusion.

Contrasting beliefs

Violence

✝ Christianity

While Christianity follows Jesus' teachings of peace, there are Christians who see war as **acceptable in given situations**. Catholic, Orthodox and Anglican denominations accept the just war theory, which provides **conditions within which war may be fought**. Certain groups believe it is acceptable to chastise children physically ('Whoever spares the rod hates their children, but the one who loves their children is careful to discipline them,' Proverbs 13:24). Most Christians would accept the **use of violence in self-defence**. Some agree with the **use of the death penalty** out of a sense of abhorrence for what that criminal had done.

✝ Roman Catholic

The Roman Catholic Church stance is that there is dignity to being human. Inflicting violence on them, or receiving it, is a denial of that dignity. Pope Francis has spoken out against the death penalty.

☸ Buddhism

The Buddha gave the Five Precepts, including to **not harm other sentient beings**. The skilful way to keep this is to help others – not to hurt them. **Violence breaks several of the Precepts** (sexual immorality, being untruthful and stealing being forms of violence), and is **against many of the Noble Eightfold Path** (e.g. Right Action).

✝ Quaker

The Quaker Society is **non-violent**. They **refuse to participate** even as soldiers in times of war. They will carry 'no outward weapon'. They claim the 'Spirit of Christ will never move us to fight.' There is **something of God in every person**, and appealing to that **resolves issues better than violence** can.

Question

Explain two contrasting beliefs in contemporary British society about violence.

In your answer you should refer to the main religious tradition of Great Britain and one or more other religious traditions. *(4 marks)*

Weapons of mass destruction (WMD)

✝ Roman Catholic

The Roman Catholic Church does not agree with the use of WMD but thinks they are acceptable as a deterrent.

✝ Quaker

The Quaker Society **utterly condemns WMD**. Quakers are pacifists, and no outward weapons are acceptable. WMD are **indiscriminate and beyond control**.

Religious, philosophical and ethical studies

Buddhism

The stance of Buddhism would be that **WMD bring death and suffering on a massive scale**, so their use **can never be justified** under the **Precept of not hurting other sentient beings**. Not only do these weapons impact now, they **would impact negatively on many generations in the future**.

Hinduism

Hinduism would argue that use of WMD goes against the teaching of **ahimsa**. It **is not possible to restrict the impact** of WMD, and they affect humans, animals and nature alike for very long periods of time. There is no justifiable reason for this destruction and the suffering caused.

Question

Explain two contrasting beliefs in contemporary British society about weapons of mass destruction.

In your answer you should refer to the main religious tradition of Great Britain and one or more other religious traditions. *(4 marks)*

Pacifism

Anglican

The Church of England is **not a consistently pacifist** church. Go into any cathedral and it is clear that **soldiers have been supported and are honoured**. The Church accepts the **just war theory**, and **sees war as necessary** in certain conditions, **especially in situations where war is waged to fight injustice**. It is seen that pacifism is the ideal to which we should strive, but given that others exploit and abuse, and **pacifist methods seem not to have made a difference, then war may be sanctioned**. For example, against Nazi Germany in the Second World War, **Anglican chaplains served in all the armed forces units**.

Quaker

The Quaker Society is pacifist. They **do not join armies, and refuse to participate in any violence**. They are **committed to peacemaking**. As Jesus said 'Blessed are the peacemakers, for they will be called the children of God.'

Hinduism

Although Hinduism has a warrior caste, for whom fighting is a duty, Hinduism is a peaceful religion. It is based on **ahimsa (non-violence)**. Key virtues include **tolerance, compassion, and respect for all life** – all qualities leading to pacifism.

Buddhism

Buddhism is a pacifistic religion. The **Five Precepts** demand a pacifistic approach to life. The **Noble Eightfold Path** seeks positive (hence peaceful) ways to live. The Dalai Lama said that 'Peace can exist if everyone respects all others.'

Question

Explain two contrasting beliefs in contemporary British society about pacifism.

In your answer you should refer to the main religious tradition of Great Britain and one or more other religious traditions. *(4 marks)*

Getting prepared

Attitudes

In the five-mark part of each question you will be asked to 'explain two beliefs/teachings about' one of the ethical issues discussed in the theme.

Here are some examples from each of the six themes:

Theme A: Explain **two** religious beliefs about the use of contraception. Refer to sacred writings or another source of religious belief and teaching in your answer.

Theme B: Explain **two** religious teachings about euthanasia. Refer to sacred writings or another source of religious belief and teaching in your answer.

Theme C: Explain **two** religious beliefs about revelation. Refer to sacred writings or another source of religious belief and teaching in your answer.

Theme D: Explain **two** religious teachings about holy war. Refer to sacred writings or another source of religious belief and teaching in your answer.

Theme E: Explain **two** religious beliefs about the aims of punishment. Refer to sacred writings or another source of religious belief and teaching in your answer.

Theme F: Explain **two** religious teachings about racial prejudice. Refer to sacred writings or another source of religious belief and teaching in your answer.

Scripture or sacred writings could include holy books like the Qur'an, Bible or Tenakh, or other respected religious texts, like Vatican II for Catholics. However, often holy books don't have specific teachings about these ethical issues, especially if they are issues arising from advances in medicine or science. This means that religious believers need to take the teachings of their holy books and other sources of authority and apply them to the issue. This is what shapes their attitudes.

What might be a good strategy for answering this type of question?

So, for example, let's take that question about the aims of punishment from above.

Holy books tend not to have direct teachings about the aims of punishment, rather they talk about whether and how we should punish, and the religion has a set of virtues its believers aspire to.

- You could start by giving a relevant teaching – 'Christians believe …'. We might use:

  > 'Christians believe there is something of God in everyone, because it says in the Bible that humans were made in the image of God.'

- Then you could show how that belief shapes attitudes to the topic, so for example, we have to apply that teaching. In this question then:

  > 'If this is the case, then punishment should aim to reform the person, as they are redeemable.'

- You could then develop your point further, for example:

  > 'This means that punishments which help the convicted person to improve their behaviour and become a good member of society are favoured by Christians.'

Here are some examples of questions for you to practise from this theme:

1. Explain **two** religious beliefs about helping victims of war. Refer to sacred writings or another source of religious belief and teaching in your answer.
2. Explain **two** religious teachings about war. Refer to sacred writings or another source of religious belief and teaching in your answer.
3. Explain **two** religious teachings about peace. Refer to sacred writings or another source of religious belief and teaching in your answer.

They can be marked against AQA's mark scheme, which can be found on the AQA website.

From the question wording and the mark scheme you can work out how to answer the question effectively. Each question is different, but in the case of the above questions you would:

- choose your two beliefs and then explain each one
- develop your explanations fully
- include a relevant teaching. 'Refer to sacred writings or another source of religious belief and teaching' means any book religious believers consider to be holy.

7 Theme D: Religion, peace and conflict

Religion, peace and conflict glossary

Civil war armed conflict between factions within the same country

Conflict disagreement which escalates

Conscientious objector a person who refuses to do something, here fight in war, because of their conscience

Conventional (warfare) war using conventional weapons – weapons acceptable under Geneva Conventions

Forgiveness willingness to not blame a person any more for the wrongs they have done

Holy war rules around fighting a war acceptable to Islam

Justice making things fair again

Just war rules around fighting a war acceptable to Christianity and Sikhism

Nuclear weapons/war a weapon/war of mass destruction

Pacifism belief that all violence is wrong

Peace the opposite of war; harmony

Protest voicing disagreement with something

Reconciliation making up between two groups after disagreement

Retaliation to pay back for harmful action

Terrorism use of violence and threats to intimidate, especially for political purposes to create a state of fear in a population

Violence causing harm to someone

War armed conflict between two or more sides

Weapons of mass destruction weapons which cause uncontrollable and untold damage – for example, nuclear weapons

8 Theme E: Religion, crime and punishment

Key elements of this theme

This theme is about **law** and **order**. It is about what we mean by **crime**, why people commit crimes, including the idea of **evil** people and actions, and the way society deals with offenders. It looks at the impact of crimes, the suffering they cause, and how we should help **victims** of crime. It is also about why we punish offenders and the debate about the death penalty. Key to the theme are religious teachings and beliefs about human nature, repentance and **forgiveness**. You must be able to show your understanding of religious attitudes to crime and punishment.

Key concepts

There are several concepts which underpin this topic and you need to learn them.

Law and order are about the rules of our society and how they are enforced. These rules exist to try to keep society a calm and safe place. They are based on ideas of right and wrong. Most of the rules are common sense really, and we usually agree with them most of the time.

Evil – an act which is very wicked or immoral. Many people associate these kind of acts with an evil being. They are not understandable to ordinary people, going beyond what most see as simply wrong or bad, and even sickening people.

Forgiveness – a process which a victim goes through, changing feelings of resentment, hate or vengefulness towards an offender in order to move on. It is a central attitude in all religions.

Justice – a belief in what is right and fair. It is also the main aim of any criminal system, that is to judge, punish the guilty and bring justice to the victims.

Suffering – a feeling of pain, harm, distress or hardship which is caused by the actions of others when they commit crime.

Morality – a person's or a religion's beliefs of what is right and wrong in terms of behaviour and actions. Most religious people have had their sense of morality shaped by their religion.

Conscience – the voice in our head that tells us right from wrong. It is also seen as the sense of feeling guilty when you have done something wrong. Many religious people believe it is God's guidance.

Sin – an act which goes against God's will; a religious offence. Many laws are there to enforce against sins – for example, taking life and stealing. For religious people, committing sin is a great wrong and can be punished by God in the afterlife.

The Basics

1. How might someone's conscience prevent them from committing a crime?
2. Why might it be difficult for someone to forgive a criminal?
3. How might criminal acts lead to suffering? Use examples in your answer.
4. Do you think that getting justice makes it easier to forgive someone? Explain your ideas.

8 Theme E: Religion, crime and punishment

Religion and rules

All religions have their own rules and laws that believers must follow. These rules give people a framework and guidance to help them live their lives correctly to achieve their spiritual aims. For example, the Ten Commandments apply to Jewish people and Christians, and Sikhs follow a code of conduct called the Rahit Maryada. When a believer does something that breaks one of their religious laws they commit a religious offence (sometimes called a sin). Just as in society when someone breaks a law they are punished, there is also the belief in religious traditions that believers who sin will be punished in some way. Ultimately their afterlife could be affected – for example, by going to hell or being reborn in a lower life form.

Deciding what is right and wrong can be a tricky business. Religious people have several sources of authority to guide them. However, they should always be guided by their conscience. This is sometimes described as the voice of God inside your head telling you what is right or wrong. Have you ever felt guilty, ashamed or disgusted with yourself because of a wrong action? Conscience is what causes these feelings.

Religious traditions accept that everyone makes mistakes, but they also teach the ideas of punishment for the wrong-doing, repentance by the individual and compassion from the victim which then allows them to forgive. To repent is to recognise that we have done something wrong and to be truly sorry. It involves learning from the mistake and doing our best not to repeat it. Forgiveness is accepting that a person is sorry for what they have done wrong and allowing them a second chance. Forgiveness can be given by a victim even if the criminal shows no remorse and therefore must continue with the punishment. Some people believe that forgiveness is the best way for both criminal and victim to rebuild their lives. Punishment, though, is a clear part of the process. Jesus discussed forgiveness on many occasions but that does not mean to the exclusion of punishment. When Jesus was on the cross his comments about the two criminals being crucified with him can be interpreted as forgiveness. However, there was no reference to their punishment being stopped or cancelled.

Most religions also instruct their followers to keep the laws of the country in which they live. They should only break a law in certain circumstances, such as to protect life, for example, or if they are being challenged to break a key principle of their own religion. Religions recognise that laws are for our own and society's good and safety and so must be right. Most laws are not unlike religious ones anyway. Some examples might be the ones in the blue box – *would you agree with them?*

> Do not hurt others.
> Do not steal from others.
> Do not damage other people's things.
> Do not tell lies about other people.

The Basics

1. What is meant by the terms: right and wrong, religious offence, sin, conscience, repentance, forgiveness?
2. Explain how the behaviour of religious people is guided by their faith.
3. 'Religious people should always forgive those who do wrong.' What do you think? Explain reasons to agree and disagree with this statement.

Different types of crimes

All societies have laws to protect individuals, protect property and make society a safe place for everyone. When someone breaks the law they commit a crime. In the UK, millions of crimes are committed each year. Many are not reported or followed up because they are considered trivial or the victim is too embarrassed or scared to say anything. Most crimes are committed by people under 25 years of age. Men are more likely to commit crimes than women. At some point in our lives most of us will experience the effects of crime.

There are two kinds of laws in the UK.

Bye-laws are made by elected councillors and apply to a local area. They cover things like parking restrictions, alcohol-free zones and environmental concerns such as litter and dog fouling. Breaking a bye-law can result in a fine, but you do not get a criminal record. Some laws are centuries old, and appear quite out-of-date, but as they have not been repealed, they are still laws.

Parliamentary laws are made by the government and apply to everyone in the country. These laws also put crimes into two categories. **Non-indictable offences** include minor crimes and driving offences. These are usually dealt with in a Magistrates' Court. **Indictable offences** are much more serious crimes. These are dealt with in Crown Courts with a judge and jury, and usually carry much harsher potential penalties.

> Why do you think there are local and national laws and not just one set for everywhere?

MAN DIES IN SUSPECTED HIT AND RUN

MUM KILLS AND BURIES HER OWN CHILD

THREE ARRESTED IN COUNTER TERRORISM STING

MAN JAILED AFTER SETTING UP CANNABIS FARM

BOY OF 16 PUNCHES MAN TO DEATH

CAR THIEVES TO DO COMMUNITY SERVICE

WOMAN CHARGED WITH FRAUD AFTER STEALING MONEY FROM HOSPITAL

There are three key types of crimes:
- **Crimes against the person** – offences causing direct harm to a person; for example, **murder**, rape, GBH and **hate crimes**.
- **Crimes against property** – offences that damage or deprive people of their property; for example, arson, burglary, trespassing.
- **Crimes against the state** – offences that potentially endanger everyone or affect the smooth running of society; for example, terrorism, selling state secrets, perjury.

It is very difficult to say which of these is the worst. The victim of an assault may say that crimes against the person are the worst as they have personal experience of them. Where a country is put at risk by someone's actions, millions can be affected, so maybe crimes against the state are the worst. Crimes against property, such as burglary, have very long-term negative impacts on the victims, and often these take longest to get over.

> With a partner, try to come up with reasons why each is the worst and also least bad. Thinking of examples often helps make those points.

The Basics

1. Write definitions for all of the bold key words/phrases on this page.
2. Using examples, explain the three types of crime.
3. Religion should dictate the law. What do you think? Explain your opinion.
4. 'Crimes against the state are the worst kind of crime.' Do you agree? Explain your reasons showing you have thought about more than one point of view.

Causes of crime

You have just looked at the types of crime that are prevalent in society today. More importantly, though, the question we should all be asking is why are they happening? If answers can be found, then society can try to prevent them in the first place.

Carry out the task in the box on the right.

Did you have any debates about where to place the crimes? You probably did, as there are not always separate reasons. For example, an addiction can be classed as a mental illness, or poverty might be about upbringing causing addiction. It is important to see these links.

> In pairs, make a list of the reasons people might have for committing crimes. Next, look at the diagram below. Can you place the reasons in your list under the correct headings?

Upbringing – This might include the environment a person is brought up in, the morals of the family/friends/neighbourhood, whether a person is surrounded by crimes or criminal activity and the social and financial status of the family.

Mental illness – The state of mind of a person may lead them into crime. They might have serious psychological issues with no understanding of right or wrong; might feel no guilt or compassion for others; might enjoy hurting others; might have educational learning issues and be easily led into crime; or are themselves victims of some event which has disturbed their minds – for example, depression or an abusive upbringing.

Opposition to existing laws – Some crimes are committed in protest about laws that exist that are considered either unfair or for the benefit of a select few in society. Sometimes laws have to be broken to get laws to be changed.

Reasons for crime

Poverty – A person might commit a crime because they see no other alternative way to survive. They may have no money, no job or cannot provide for themselves or their children.

Greed/hate – Emotions are often responsible for crime, our reaction to what goes on around us or what others have or do to us. We always want more so inherently we are greedy. People do bad things to us so hate leads us to take revenge and commit crimes.

Addiction – A person may have an addiction (for example, to alcohol, drugs, sex or money) which leads them into crime to feed their habit or their cravings. They may even be addicted to crime – for example, stealing.

What would religion say about this?

All religions would say that the law should be followed. St Paul tells Christians to 'obey the laws of the land'. In all religions, a law is a law and if you break that law, then punishment shall follow. However, although crime is never right, sometimes there are understandable reasons why it does happen. If all people lived by the principles of 'love your neighbour' or 'treat others as we wish to be treated' or the Buddhist Noble Eightfold Path or the Hindu idea of 'ahimsa', then many causes of crime might disappear. The phrase to 'hate the sin, not the sinner' can be used here. Criminals often need our help rather than our judgement. However, punishments have to be given or society would be chaotic but at the same time the causes of crime have to be removed.

The Basics

1. Explain briefly two of the causes of crime.
2. Explain religious attitudes to those who break the law.
3. What might a religious person mean by 'hate the sin, not the sinner'?

Good and evil

There are those who suggest that people who commit the worst crimes are evil. But what exactly is 'evil' and where does it come from? Similarly, what is meant by 'good' and where does that come from?

Definitions:
- Evil is something that is profoundly immoral and wicked and is usually seen as depraved and malicious.
- Good is defined as morally excellent, virtuous, righteous and pious.

Where does evil come from?

☸ Buddhism

Buddhism teaches that all unenlightened beings are capable of both good and evil acts. Evil acts are those strongly motivated by the Three Poisons – greed, hatred and delusion. Such acts cause suffering both to the person acting and probably to other people as well. We are each responsible for our actions and their consequences. How we manage our intentions, thoughts, words and deeds impacts other people for good or ill.

✝ Christianity

Evil is seen as the abuse of the free will God gave to humans which allowed them to choose right from wrong. In order to be able to see and appreciate good, then evil has to exist. Most Christians believe in a figure called the devil or Satan, who is an evil power, though ultimately less powerful than God. The devil continually tries to tempt people, encouraging them to behave badly. So, evil is a combination of internal and external factors.

ॐ Hinduism

According to Hinduism, there is a constant struggle in the universe, the world, and our individual selves between light and dark, good and evil. So good and evil are natural parts of the creation. Certainly, a human's free will allows them to do evil. Since people are ignorant of the reality of the world, their selfishness encourages them in the wrong direction as well.

☪ Islam

The Qur'an says that there is a devil who was an angel. Allah had ordered the angels to bow to Adam, but Iblis refused. Iblis was expelled from paradise, but was able to cause Adam and Eve's expulsion from Eden. Iblis continually tempts and pushes humans to be wicked. Humans fail to show self-discipline, and give in to Iblis' temptations. Evil is a mix of a powerful evil being and the weakness of humans.

✡ Judaism

In Genesis, we read the story of how Adam and Eve were tempted by the serpent to disobey God, resulting in the Fall (their expulsion from Eden). The serpent represents an evil malevolent force, which continues to subvert the behaviour of humans. However, we have free will, so there has to be evil – this allows us to exercise our free will for good or bad. By being obedient to the mitzvot (laws), a Jewish person avoids evil.

☬ Sikhism

Sikhism puts selfishness at the heart of evil. The concept of selfishness (haumai) is what prevents people from following their religion, and encourages them to break rules and hurt others. The more selfish a person is, the more evil they are capable of. So, for Sikhs, evil lies within the consciousness of any person, and the level of selfishness we have makes it more or less controlling of our actions.

8 Theme E: Religion, crime and punishment

What about other ideas?

If you do not believe in a devil or the Fall, or any other religious beliefs, you could still believe evil exists. Have a discussion with your partner. Can you think of any examples you would class as evil that you have heard of – what were they, and why do you label them as such?

Some people believe that all people have the capacity to do evil, that it is part of a human's make-up. We do not all show evil, and those who do, do it to different degrees. You might say that someone who murders their child is evil, but are they the same level of evil as someone who goes out hunting people only to torture and eventually murder them? Why isn't everyone evil? The argument goes that it depends on our upbringing, the influences in our lives (and when those influences occur), and experiences we have. Any of these can trigger or sow the seeds for evil to manifest in us, but evil is not a force within us, rather a psychological phenomenon. In all these, we are saying that it is the person themselves who is evil.

Evil person or evil action?

It is common to hear the phrase 'hate the sin, not the sinner'. This is making the point that it is actions which are wrong, not the person themselves. However, the fact remains that we cannot punish the action or sin, we have to punish a person *for* committing the sin or carrying out the wrong/evil deed. So, when we see something as evil, regardless of how we think that evil originated, we have to punish the perpetrator. Most religious people believe that people who do wrong are still redeemable, that they are not themselves evil, and can be brought back to good ways. Religions believe in evil actions rather than evil people.

How do we deal with evil?

Through a country's justice system, a person will be punished when found guilty of a crime. We will look at punishment later in the topic, but punishment in the UK takes a range of forms from **imprisonment** through to fines and exclusions. In other countries, punishment can be harsher, with **corporal** and **capital punishment**. However, crimes affect people beyond the actual event; they have an emotional impact, which can be very long-lasting. Evil events disturb people's sense of well-being and safety, so have even greater impact. The victims have to be helped, and everyone else reassured.

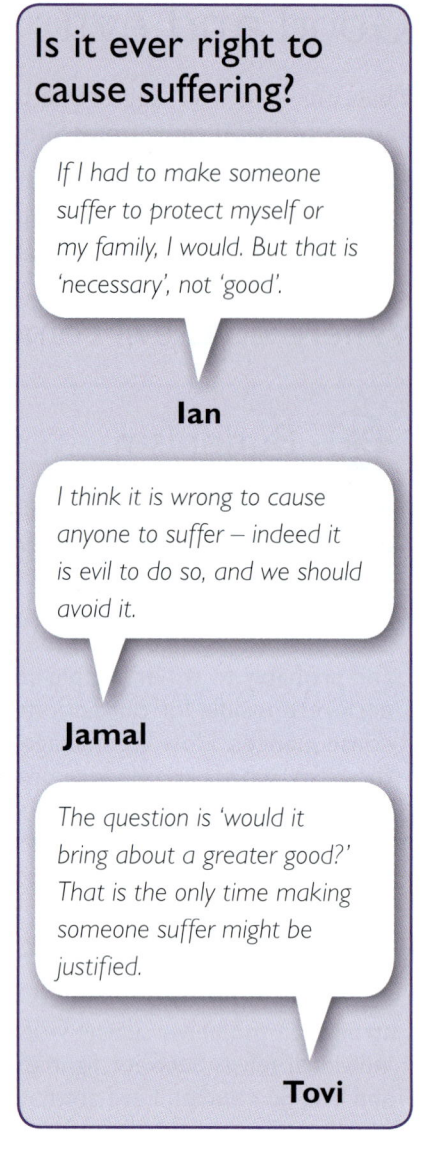

Is it ever right to cause suffering?

If I had to make someone suffer to protect myself or my family, I would. But that is 'necessary', not 'good'.
Ian

I think it is wrong to cause anyone to suffer – indeed it is evil to do so, and we should avoid it.
Jamal

The question is 'would it bring about a greater good?' That is the only time making someone suffer might be justified.
Tovi

The Basics

1. What is meant by good and evil?
2. For your chosen religion(s), explain how evil originates, and the relationship between good and evil.
3. Explain why some crimes are considered 'evil'. Use examples to help your explanation.
4. 'Following a religion prevents evil from happening.' Do you think this is true? Explain your answer, trying to show more than one point of view.
5. 'People are not evil, some just do evil things.' Do you think this is true? Explain your answer, trying to show more than one point of view.

What is the worst crime to commit?

For the course, you have to think about murder, **theft** and hate crimes. But, are you clear on what these are? Murder is the deliberate killing of someone; theft is to permanently deprive someone of something they own; hate crimes are any crimes motivated by prejudice in the negative sense. Religions are very clear about murder and theft, but hate crimes are not mentioned in any scriptures and are relatively new to the British legal system.

So which is worst?

Use these teachings plus information from page 283 and page 294 to work out what the religion(s) you have studied might say about each of the crimes.

All religions believe life is sacred, that it should be protected and cherished. So, any murder must be wrong by definition, as it is the opposite of that. They all include severe punishments for murder in their laws. There is no way to repair the damage; you cannot bring someone back to life, and their families suffer the loss for the rest of theirs. It is the biggest insult to God because it is deliberately destroying God's creation. Both Islam and Judaism describe the taking of a life as akin to the taking of the lives of everyone.

Theft is also against the laws of religions, but punishments are less harsh than for murder. Depending on what is taken, theft might have a bigger or lesser impact on someone's life. For example, to steal an old person's savings leaves them with only their pension to live on; whereas to steal a person's car might only be an inconvenience until their insurance replaces it. Theft shows disrespect to someone, and all religions preach equality and respect, therefore theft goes against fundamental ways of behaviour.

'Hate crime' really refers to the reason why the crime is committed, not the type of crime itself. You could say that because any type of crime could be a hate crime and be motivated by prejudice, then these are the worst type of crime. These examples are all considered hate crimes: the murder of Antony Walker in 2005, just because he was black; the theft of religious silver/gold from churches because of the belief the Church can afford it and there is no victim; the desecration of Jewish cemeteries because of anti-Semitism. It is also true that hate crimes go against fundamental religious teachings of equality and love, community and brotherhood.

Look at these examples. What is each an example of? Which do you see as worse, and why?

> David murdered John after he had an affair with David's wife.

> Siobhan stole £50,000 from her job in a hospital to pay for medical treatment for her sick son.

> Jayden poured petrol through a letterbox, and set fire to it. The family inside died. He did it because of the colour of their skin.

> Felix cheated an elderly couple out of their savings by telling them their money was going into Christian investments in developing countries.

The Basics

1. Define murder, theft and hate crime.
2. Explain why religious believers would disagree with each of murder, theft or hate crime.
3. 'Hate crimes are the worst type of crime.' Do you agree with this? Explain more than one point of view and include religious arguments in your answer.

8 Theme E: Religion, crime and punishment

Is crime linked to evil?

When you read stories in the newspaper or see some of the real-life programmes about what some people have done, you can be really shocked. Sometimes crimes are labelled as evil actions, their perpetrators as evil people. So, why do we use the word 'evil'? Usually it is because we are sickened by what we know has happened and we cannot imagine doing it so feel there must be something wrong with the perpetrator. Often their offences are against children or vulnerable people (or animals). Fred West, John Venables and Robert Thompson, Ian Brady and Myra Hindley are all people who committed crimes that might make us say they were evil.

So, why might some people be evil or behave in this way? Look back to the previous pages for the reasons behind crime. Many religious people also believe the devil is at work in the minds of these people, making them do terrible things and that this is where evil comes from.

> **Agree or Disagree?**
> 1 Only evil people do evil things.
> 2 There is no such thing as evil – just our interpretation of events.
> 3 Evil is just a label for the worst crimes.
> 4 People who commit evil acts should face the death penalty.

Crime and punishment exercise

Look at the list of crimes in the pink box. Identify the type of crime being committed in each case. Is it against a person, property or state?

Now look at the list of punishments available under the English law (the green box below). Which is the most suitable punishment in each case?

For each one, what do you think the punishment will achieve? Do you think any crime should have a different punishment? Explain why.

Would you class any crimes as 'evil'? Explain why.

> 1 A young woman who killed her husband after years of domestic abuse by him
> 2 A woman who beat her own child to death after a period of neglect and torture
> 3 A schoolgirl who stole items worth £85 from a department store
> 4 Four football fans who kicked a rival fan to death after a match
> 5 A schoolboy who covered a railway bridge with racist graffiti
> 6 A woman who defrauded £50,000 from a charity
> 7 A person who sold drugs in a school playground
> 8 A man who sexually abused a number of children
> 9 A gang of men who held up a train, stealing millions in bank notes being taken for destruction
> 10 A drunk driver who hit a pedestrian, leaving them disabled
> 11 A young man who raped a woman he had been dancing with all night at a club and had walked home
> 12 A couple who downloaded terrorist materials from the web

> Life imprisonment   Fixed term imprisonment
> Suspended prison sentence (only enforced if they reoffend)   **Community service order**
> Curfew order   Fine   Disqualification (e.g. from driving)   Electronic tagging
> **Probation order** (required to meet probation officer weekly)   Restraining order
> Exclusion order   Compensation order   Police caution

Religious, philosophical and ethical studies

The aims of punishment

On the previous page, it was important for you to justify the decisions you made regarding the choice of punishments. Society sets up rules and we have to obey them or face the consequences. However, what one person thinks is very wrong, another person might consider less so. That is why we have a judicial system that sets tariffs for punishments to guide judges in the sentences they hand down.

A judge will also know other information before they give a sentence. For example, whether the person has offended before, information from psychologists and perhaps about their home background.

There are six main aims of punishment and you probably came up with all of them in the punishment exercise. For the course, you need to know more about three.

> Think about your 'Crime and punishment' exercise from page 286. Would some of your decisions have been different if you knew more about the person? Did you think about the reasons why you were punishing someone? How might this have influenced the decisions you made?

Deterrence

A punishment is meant to be unpleasant and a **deterrence**, so that the offender is put off committing crimes in the future. A burglar who gets sent to prison for five years will hopefully not want to experience that again and will find some other legal means to obtain money and possessions. Also, we learn very quickly that when we do wrong we may be punished, so if they know what the punishment is going to be, many people would be put off committing the crime in the first place. For example, the penalty for drink driving in the UK is a minimum 12-month driving ban, a fine and potentially a prison sentence, which deters many people from drink driving.

Drink drivers lose more than just their licence

Task

Read these statements. How does each one demonstrate deterrence?
- Bilal – I lost my driving licence because of drink driving. No one got hurt, but I still got punished. That cost me my job as well, as I was a driver. I have really learned my lesson – so I won't drink and drive.
- Chris – I was sent to prison for 12 months. I never want to go back inside, so am working with my parole officer to make sure I don't.
- Jane – Even though I really needed cash, I didn't steal it when I had a chance, because of the consequences of getting caught.

Theme E: Religion, crime and punishment

BRING BACK HANGING FOR MURDERERS

Government to set up new prisons which aim to reform not just punish

Retribution

This is taking revenge on the offender; simply put it means 'getting your own back'. When people break the law someone somewhere is almost always hurt, even if it means they are just upset or angry. Most people follow the law so it is not fair that a few people want to just ignore the rules and do as they please. Society uses punishment to make the offender pay for what they have done and show support for the victim. They do this by demonstrating that the criminal has not got away with hurting them. In some cases **retribution** can be very severe. In the UK, criminals can receive lengthy prison sentences; other countries use capital or corporal punishment.

Reformation

Obviously society cannot simply lock up everyone who breaks the law and throw away the key. Many punishments are given to try to change the nature of the person who has offended. This is because most people who break the law are going to still continue to be part of society. It is important to try to make these people realise the effects their action had on others and then hopefully they will not do it again. A graffiti artist might be sentenced to work in the council parks and gardens department. In prisons there are usually education and work programmes to support offenders in their rehabilitation; this helps prepare them to rejoin society as a constructive member. Religious groups feel this is an important aim of punishment.

Task

Look at these punishments. Which ones suit each of the three aims of punishment? Explain why.
- Prison
- Large fine
- Corporal punishment
- Drink-drive rehabilitation course

Task

How might a punishment system based on each of:
- deterrence
- retribution
- reformation

influence criminals and society?

The Basics

1. Explain the meaning of deterrence, retribution and reformation as aims of punishment.
2. In what circumstances might each of the three aims be the best fit for the crime?
3. 'The only good aim of punishment is deterrence.' How far do you agree with that statement? Explore arguments for and against it, including religious arguments, before writing a justified conclusion.
4. 'Religious people should ensure all punishments reform criminals.' How far do you agree with that statement? Explore arguments for and against it, including religious arguments, before writing a justified conclusion.

The aims of punishment continued …

Although you will not need to know these in detail, there are three other key aims to be aware of. **Protection** – the whole point of having a legal system is to protect society. Some criminals are dangerous and society needs protection, and the criminal needs protection from society also. When a person shows no remorse for what they have done and continues to be a threat they have to be locked up. **Vindication** – the law has to impose proper punishments for crimes committed, so that the law is respected. If there are no penalties, then people will not keep to the law. Rules are rules and have to be justly applied to the crime done. **Reparation** – is a more modern aim designed at making up for what damage has been caused so the victim or society is compensated. Community service would be an example of this.

Religious attitudes to the aims

Deterrence

This is key for all religions, because if it works there is no need for any other aims as there would be no crime. Islamic law has tough consequences for the criminal in the hope that they will deter criminals. Christianity agrees with deterrence but not through such harsh punishment. For example, many Christians are against the death penalty. Judaism and Hinduism both have the death penalty as a deterrent. Breaking the law does not fit with Buddhist principles either, but Buddhism does not agree with harsh punishments that could harm the criminal. Positive punishments, such as community service or education programmes, would be used to deter future crimes.

Retribution

Religions have a similar view to this as they do to deterrence. The punishment should fit the crime which might make it seem barbaric at times (e.g. in the case of the death penalty). However, punishment should never be revenge, as revenge punishments are worse than the original crime. Islam, Judaism and Hinduism support a 'life for a life' for murderers where appropriate (though the Israeli Jewish state has carried out only one execution in its history). Many Christians believe that a criminal should serve their time, but that the death penalty makes the law as bad as the criminal which is not right or proper. Having said that, many Christians in the USA do support the death penalty, and it is used in half of the US states.

Reformation

All religions agree with this but in different ways. Under Shari'ah Law (in those countries practising it), harsh punishments like lashings and removal of limbs can reform the individual because the person sees the wrong they have done. Christians and Buddhists believe that many can be reformed through working with criminals, counselling, education programmes, and so on. Hinduism supports **reformation** to allow people to learn from their mistakes. Reformation as an aim has been central to all prison reform in Britain since the early nineteenth century. Quaker Christian Elizabeth Fry (1780–1845) was a major force in prison reform at the time.

> ### The Basics
>
> 1. Explain why some people commit crimes.
> 2. Using examples to illustrate your points, explain the different aims of punishment.
> 3. Look back at the punishment exercise on page 286. Which aim of punishment was most important in each case? Why?
> 4. 'Punishment should focus on protecting non-criminals.' Do you agree? Give reasons for your answer, showing that you have thought about more than one point of view and include religious arguments in your reasoning.

8 Theme E: Religion, crime and punishment

Suffering and religious attitudes to it

Suffering happens when people cause pain, hardship or distress to themselves or others. It can be physical or emotional. Crime may directly cause suffering because it is done to you directly (for example, you are assaulted) or indirectly (for example, your property or possessions are stolen or damaged). In some cases a country can suffer (the crime is against the state), or a whole religion. Rarely is it the case that only one person suffers because often their families and friends do too, as they see the effect of the crime on someone they love.

> *Who suffers?*
> 1 A bomb blast in a major city
> 2 An old person having their purse stolen
> 3 A young child being abducted
> 4 A house being broken into
> 5 A woman who is raped

> *Think about …*
> 1 Does the number of victims make the suffering worse?
> 2 Is physical suffering worse than mental suffering?
> 3 Should a criminal who makes many people suffer be dealt with more harshly than one whose crime involves only one person?

Religious teachings for you to think about …

Religions condemn suffering caused by human action towards others. Our wrong actions and decisions are unacceptable as they hurt other people. They are (often) a deliberate misuse of our free will, our ability to choose our actions. Religious teachings tell us it is wrong to cause suffering. There is also a responsibility to deal with people who cause this suffering. Buddhism stresses that suffering is everywhere and we all have to look within ourselves to stop this suffering, while other religions look to a God to help them overcome suffering or be forgiven for the suffering they have caused. Religious teachings give humans the path to righteous actions, but human nature (emotions, reactions and needs) makes it virtually impossible to choose the right actions all the time, so we cause suffering intentionally and accidentally, directly and indirectly to others in the world.

1 All religions have rules which are there to try to prevent suffering.
2 All religions have 'love your neighbour' or Golden Rule (see page 273) concepts to prevent suffering.
3 All religions stress how our emotions (for example, love, hate, greed and desires) easily lead to suffering and so they give us teachings to keep these in check.

Religions support the law to prevent suffering. However, they do believe that law-breakers should be punished fairly and with justice, and that victims must be helped. Religious people should care for all people, good and bad, even those who cause the greatest amount of suffering. The law must provide this help, while religions try to provide wrong-doers with the means to right their wrongs, be reformed, and heal suffering on both sides.

> **The Basics**
> 1 What is meant by suffering?
> 2 How can religion help prevent suffering?
> 3 Explain religions' attitudes to suffering.
> 4 'Those who cause suffering should not be helped.' What do you think?
> 5 'There will always be suffering caused by people.' Refer to religious ideas and different viewpoints in your answer.

Helping those who are suffering because of crime

Sometimes we get preoccupied with what should happen to the criminal and justice being done. However, there is the other side to crime … the victim of it. What happens to them? Is there support out there or are they just left to get on with it and move on?

If you are a victim of a reported crime, then the police will send you the contact details for 'Victim Support' (www.victimsupport.org.uk). Many victims of minor crime would not need this service but it is offered because we can never know how each individual may react to those crimes. You can use Victim Support for yourself to overcome the effects of the crime. Witnesses also get support, as the process of giving evidence can be quite traumatic, especially in the case of serious crime.

Victim Support

There are six key areas of support available:

- Emotional and practical support
- Practical tips to keep safe
- Specific support in certain areas – for example, abuse or rape
- The rights of a victim
- Help for young victims
- Help for foreign language speakers

> As a victim I didn't know where to turn … my house was broken into and I was a wreck, nervous and couldn't concentrate at all … Simply to talk to someone helped and getting advice about the criminal justice system gave me a way forward.

> As a victim of serious assault I could not come to terms with the crime. I didn't even know how to report the crime, how to write a personal statement to show how the crime had affected me, what would happen in court and what was meant by restorative justice. Victim Support helped me.

> The support I got was tailored to my needs … see I was abused as a child and only now can I talk about it. I needed someone specific to help me. Victim Support has given me that.

> As an adviser for Victim Support I am often contacted by victims who cannot speak English well enough to get the help they need. We can find interpreters in over 20 languages. They are victims just like anyone and I help them get the help they need.

> I suffered abuse on social media and no one understood how it made me feel … Victim Support did! Young people can react totally differently to an adult and so we need different support. The bullying made me feel helpless but now I get help.

> I didn't know I had rights! I do now though, thanks to Victim Support! There is a code for victims about how I should be helped and kept informed of my case which means I feel more secure and protected.

Task

Read the six cases above and use that information to explain why the work of Victim Support is important.

Forgiveness as an attitude to criminals

Forgiveness is a process that victims go through where they let go of the offence and the negative ideas of revenge, to move on and let the criminal move on too. It does not mean the victim condones, accepts, excuses or forgets the crime. Whereas society deals with criminals through punishment, victims can deal with it through forgiveness. To forgive is very hard to do and some never can, whereas others find it within themselves to do so. Some show forgiveness through words, others through actions.

Forgiveness is very important in Christianity, with Jesus saying we should forgive 'not seven times but seventy times seven' (Matthew 18:22). Islam states 'whosoever forgives and makes amends, his reward is upon Allah' (Surah 42:40). In Judaism, the Torah explicitly forbids Jewish people to take revenge or to bear grudges (Leviticus 19:18). In Buddhism, forgiving practises two essential virtues: compassion and understanding. Without it the world remains vengeful and troubled. Sikhism believes that 'forgiveness is as necessary to life as the food we eat and the air we breathe' (Guru Granth Sahib). In Hinduism, in the Rig Veda forgiveness is one of six cardinal virtues.

Although religions clearly teach forgiveness as a very important quality, they also teach justice when the law is broken. So for them, the law deals with the criminal as it has to. It can be described as a process: crimes committed → criminal caught and punished → time served → repentance shown (maybe) → new start. The crime is not forgotten, but the criminal has the opportunity to move on from that mistake. Some criminals, through their repentance, earn forgiveness as the victim can see that the criminal regrets what they have done and the forgiveness allows both parties to move on. However, forgiveness from the victim is not dependent upon the repentance of the criminal. A victim can forgive even though the criminal does not repent and this allows them, as the victim, to move on. Prayer is often used by Christians to help them forgive; they do so with the help of God. Most religions believe that forgiveness is a quality of God, to be copied by the believer. However, it is not an easy virtue to put into action as many people have suffered terrible crimes and will never be able to forgive, but at the same time the hatred can ruin their lives. Others have shown forgiveness and many positive things have come from it. Religion would always urge people to forgive, but never demand it as it is a personal decision. Those who are able to forgive need to be commended and those who cannot forgive need to be helped.

> 'Father forgive them' – Jesus calling to God of his executioners before his death.

> 'Allah is al-Afuw' – the forgiver.

> 'Forgiveness is one of the thirteen Attributes of God's Mercy' – Talmud.

The Basics

1. What is meant by forgiveness?
2. How does forgiveness allow victims to move on?
3. Explain religious attitudes to the forgiveness of criminals.
4. 'It is the religious duty of all victims to forgive.' Give arguments to support and arguments to disagree with this view. Explain your own views.

The treatment of criminals

Punishments in the UK

Custodial sentences	Locking the offender up
Prisons (adult)	The UK has different types of prisons. High security are category A and B and house the most dangerous offenders. Category C is for those serving shorter sentences and category D is open prisons for first-time offenders and those due to be released.
High security mental health institutions	House offenders with serious psychological disorders, who threaten the safety of others and themselves – for example, psychopaths, sociopaths, schizophrenics.
Young Offenders Institutions	House offenders classed as children (under 18 years of age). Routines are specifically targeted at children's needs.
Non-custodial sentences	Alternatives to prison
ASBO	An Anti Social Behaviour Order sets restrictions that the offender must stick to – for example, curfew, not go to certain places.
Community service/ payback	Unpaid work in the community, for up to 300 hours. They do not have a choice in what they do although their offence and experiences may influence magistrates.
Curfew	Must return home by a set hour, often used with tagging.
Electronic tagging	An electronic surveillance device attached to their leg.
Fines	A set amount of money must be paid for the offence.
Probation	Offenders must meet regularly with a probation officer who monitors behaviour.
Restorative justice	Young offenders attend sessions to look at their crime, why it was wrong and its effect on the victim; often including meeting and talking with their victims.

Look at pages 287–289 on the aims of punishments. What aims of punishment are met by each of the punishments described in the above table?

Attitudes of religions to offenders

For a religion to assess its attitude to offenders, various issues have to be looked at:

- the type of crime committed – lesser or serious
- the violence used and the suffering of the victim
- the reasons that caused the criminal to commit the crime
- who has committed the crime and their circumstances
- whether the criminal is old enough to be responsible for their actions
- the best punishment considered to serve the aims desired.

Each religion has general attitudes to punishments, but also has the belief that each case has to be assessed individually on its own merits. No crime is exactly the same as another and for that reason punishments can be different.

Task

Look at each of the issues above. Give reasons why you think each one could make a difference to the type of punishment that is given.

The Basics

1. Explain, using examples, the difference between custodial and non-custodial punishments.
2. What circumstances might be taken into account when deciding an appropriate punishment?
3. Using information from page 294 explain religious attitudes to punishing criminals.
4. 'Criminals must always get the punishment their crime deserves.' Do you agree? Explain reasons to agree and disagree.

Theme E: Religion, crime and punishment

☸ Buddhism

The law enforces rules and punishes when rules are broken. Punishment is a deterrent to put off criminals through a need for self-preservation; for example, not to murder because 'I' do not want life in prison. Buddhists believe that this is the wrong motive and rather that we should avoid criminality by thinking and acting in the right way (by thinking about the consequences of our actions). If this happened, punishment would not be necessary. Some Buddhist values are upheld by the law. For example, by prohibiting murder, the value of non-harm is maintained and by punishing thieves the value of 'not taking what is not freely given' is upheld. The types of punishments given do not always show compassion and understanding. Neither is the treatment of criminals carried out according to Buddhist teachings of compassion and the Noble Eightfold Path. It is not always easy to equate punishment with strict Buddhist principles.

✝ Christianity

Christians believe the law has a responsibility to punish and care for the criminal while trying to reform them. While prison removes freedoms, separates prisoners from families and removes their rights, it also has concern for their reform to be released back into society. Therefore, there can be conflict between severe punishments and the Christian belief in help, love and reform. Although some Christians want more of an emphasis on 'justice' based on the 'an eye for an eye' teaching from the Bible, most Christians do believe in people being treated humanely and fairly, giving them a chance to face up to their crime, serve a fair punishment and have a second chance to turn their lives around.

ॐ Hinduism

To punish is seen by smriti texts as a ruler's right and through fearing the threat of punishment all beings should follow their dharma. Punishment maintains social order. In the past, punishments allowed for compensation rather than for retribution. This allows for society and criminals to be reconciled and social justice to be restored. In modern UK law not only are punishments given by the state, but the victims need to be compensated too for loss or injury.

☪ Islam

The Qur'an emphasises the justice of Allah and the idea and accountability of one's actions. Also, it talks of mercy and forgiveness. The legal system prescribes punishments for crimes such as murder, rape and theft and punishments include capital punishment, imprisonment and lashings. Muslim scholars believe that extreme punishments are not used widely and that most Muslim countries have modern prisons and principles of fair treatment of criminals. Justice must be done though and the victims should be compensated equitably. Hence, victims can accept compensation from the criminal who then is given a lesser sentence, and Allah looks favourably on that.

✡ Judaism

Jewish people have to accept punishments dealt out for criminal acts. There is a strong belief in repentance and while a person can repent to God, this is pointless if they try to avoid the punishments from society. One of the seven laws of Noah states there is a need for a proper legal system to establish a moral society. With this in mind, treatment of offenders must be just and fair with a focus on reform. Revenge as in retribution, according to the Talmud, is not a Jewish principle.

☬ Sikhism

For Sikhs there are religious laws and criminal laws. For the former, community service in the gurdwara is used, with an emphasis on penance, humility and renewal of vows broken. Sikhs do not hold power in any state country and so do not determine punishments. Some agree with capital punishment to keep society safe, but many believe it is against the nature of God as God decides life and death. Punishments should be just and allowing for reform and forgiveness is consistent with trying to be like God.

Religious, philosophical and ethical studies

Focus on prisons

Prison is used as a punishment across the countries of the world as society needs to feel safe from dangerous people. There are many types of prison in the UK, from high-security to open prisons, and there are many crimes which result in people being given a prison sentence. There is great debate about the following:
- which criminals should be sent to prison
- the conditions that prisoners are kept in
- the work that is done with the prisoners to reform them
- whether prison actually achieves its aims, especially in the light of the high cost.

Christianity in Britain has played a big role in the prison debate. While Christians support their use, they are concerned about the way they are run and levels of reoffending. Many prisons contain troubled individuals who need social help, education, medical help, work and life skills and as Christians there is a **duty** of care and help which is based in religious teachings. Even criminals deserve fair and humane treatment and are more likely to respond positively to such. Other Christians have different views and believe that life in prison should be tough so it will act as a deterrent. If prison life was tough enough, then prisoners would not want to reoffend. The Islamic attitude agrees that a severe punishment can lead to reform better than reformative actions themselves. Within Judaism there is an organisation called Jewish Prisoner Services International (JPSI), which works to bring loving-kindness to prisoners; to treat anyone with mercy and humbleness is all part of being Jewish.

Organisation profile

The Prison Reform Trust was founded in 1981. It works to create a more humane and effective penal system. It provides advice, information, educational work, research and campaigning. Its work has been very effective in achieving change in prisons, as well as in the policies and practices of the penal system. Find out about this charity through its website. www.prisonreformtrust.org.uk

Fact! 54 per cent of prisoners have no qualifications

Fact! It costs £100,000 per year to keep someone in a Young Offender Institution

I work for the Prison Reform Trust and have direct experience of how damaging locking people up can be. It's easy to say that prison life is easy when you have never been inside one. The reality is very different. Conditions in some prisons are very poor – inmates can be locked in their cells for 23 hours a day. Problems such as over-crowding, lack of exercise, poor diet, boredom, violence and drug abuse are a daily experience. I think it is really important that prisoners have the opportunity to reform and the hope of reward for good behaviour.

I was imprisoned 20 years ago for armed robbery. It wasn't my first offence, I had done prison time before. I thought it was important to be hard and to stand up for myself. I got into a disagreement with a prison warden and ended up with another sentence for GBH. I should have been paroled by now, if it wasn't for that. Somehow it just doesn't seem important anymore. My wife divorced me by mail a few years back. Joey and Tina were just toddlers when I was sent down, I didn't see them grow up, I sometimes wonder what they are like now. Simple things like having a beer in the pub, driving a car, cuddling on the sofa are just distant memories. I'm used to life in prison, the routines, not having to make decisions and I've learned to just do as I'm told!

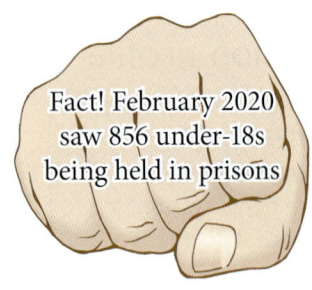

8 Theme E: Religion, crime and punishment

Fact! February 2020 saw 856 under-18s being held in prisons

I'm doing two months in prison because I allowed my teenage daughter to stay off school. I didn't think it would come to this. I was so frightened when they brought me here and embarrassed by the admittance procedures. I cried constantly for the first three days. It is hard to adjust to having your life run by someone else. I can't stop worrying about the kids. My mum isn't well so they have had to go into foster care. I know I'm going to lose my job too, because they don't know I'm in here, unless they have read the local papers. Going home will be really bad, everyone will know and they probably think I'm an awful mother.

Parole means that a person can be released early having served some of their sentence. When on parole they must live within the law and are supported by a parole officer, who will help them to reintegrate into society. The parole order may require them to have treatment – for example, for drug abuse. The aim is to help them avoid re-offending and become active and purposeful members of society.

Fact! Prisons spend on average just £2.02 on each inmate's food daily

Fact! 61 per cent of women prisoners have children under 16 at home

I'm in this Young Offender's Institute coz they want to change me, reform they call it. I have to go to sessions and talk about the stuff I've done and how it affects others. I've done loads of stuff. I've had warnings, three ASBOs, paid fines and done community service a couple of times too. I didn't do the last one though – it was boring. I'd have gone if it was working on cars or something like that. Me and the gang like twocking and hanging out in the street. I'm only in here after a copper saw me flashing a knife. I miss home and my mates and I'm well fed up with all the rules.

Fact! 63 per cent of young offenders were permanently excluded from school

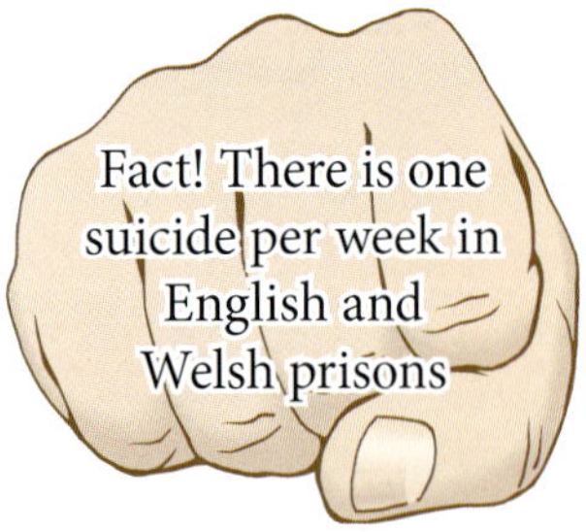

Fact! There is one suicide per week in English and Welsh prisons

The Basics

1. Describe the long-term and short-term effects of prison sentences on the offender.
2. Make a list of advantages and disadvantages of non-custodial sentences.
3. Explain three reasons why young offenders are dealt with differently to adults.
4. 'A life sentence should mean life in prison.' Do you agree? Give reasons for your answer, showing you have thought about more than one point of view.

Religious, philosophical and ethical studies

Community service as punishment

Payback is working in a local area and managed by a community payback supervisor. High-visibility yellow vests will be worn. Punishment time is between 40 and 300 hours dependent upon the crime and if the person is unemployed it might mean 3–4 days a week working.

Community service is also called 'community payback' when referring to it as a punishment. Community sentences can be given if the criminal is convicted of a crime but is not sent to prison. The punishments involve doing unpaid work in the local community, like cleaning up a park.

Aims – Community payback is intended to help with the problem that caused the crime and hopefully means that the crimes are not repeated. People could be helped with addictions, mental health, or simply learning new necessary skills. Payback programmes could include: counselling sessions, drug tests, anger management and mental health help, literacy skills and job applications. There is a positive nature to this type of punishment, as opposed to locking someone up in prison. Also anyone seen as dangerous to society would not be considered for such a programme. It is lesser punishment for lesser crimes.

Community sentences can be given for less serious crimes such as damaging property or drink driving. It is seen as more positive than prison and the judge might think that it could have a better effect than sending them to prison. Also, it allows people to carry on working and doing the payback in the evenings. This enables them to keep their job.

Religious attitudes to community service (payback)

If you look at the aims of payback, religions would support its use. Organised properly, it is suitable for the type of criminal it is designed to reform. Also, communities can benefit, with damage repaired or expertise shared. Prison can mean people mixing with individuals far worse than them and therefore it can have a negative influence. Also, separation from families and loss of jobs can lead to long-term problems, whereas community service does not have this impact. However, this punishment does not work for some people, and they get involved in further crime. Also, on some occasions the type of service or payback has not been suitable or indeed run very well. Some religions, like Islam, might believe it is too soft a punishment and does not bring the reform necessary or create the deterrent it needs to. If the punishment had been tougher, then perhaps further crime could have been prevented.

The Basics

1 Describe how community service works.
2 Why do religions support community service/payback?
3 Explain why some religious people believe community service might not be a suitable punishment.

Corporal punishment

What is corporal punishment?

Corporal punishment is to use physical pain as a punishment for a criminal act. It deliberately inflicts pain through whipping, branding or amputation (removal of a body part).

This type of punishment only remains in parts of Africa, the Middle East, Asia and South America.

Religious attitudes to corporal punishment

Most religious people today disagree with the use of corporal punishment, although many holy books allow it.

Buddhism

In Buddhism 'An action, even if it brings benefit to oneself, cannot be considered if it causes physical and mental pain to another being' (Buddha). Obviously, corporal punishment causes that pain, so should be considered to be against Buddhist principles. Buddhism believes that cruel treatment of an offender does not make right what they did, and does not improve them. The Dalai Lama said that hatred is not ended by hatred, rather by love – meaning that corporal punishment is wrong. It also harms the person giving the punishment as they are intentionally hurting another – so breaking a Moral Precept.

Christianity

Most Christians do not agree with it, believing it does not help reform criminals, as it is more about retribution and taking revenge. Jesus himself was flogged before he was hung on the cross. The quotations 'and a rod for a fool's back' (Proverbs 26:3) and Psalm 89, 'I will punish transgressions with the rod' allow some Christians to justify physical punishment of children as chastisement. No Christian country in the developed world uses corporal punishment in their justice system.

Hinduism

With Hinduism, corporal punishment has been used historically in cases where other forms of punishment have not worked. For example, where a sudra (lower caste) has injured a limb of a higher caste person, the punishment could be removal of the sudra's same limb; 'for someone who kicks out, shall his foot be cut off'. In ancient times, the Laws of Manu advised the removal of a thief's hand to prevent further crime. This was retribution and deterrent. In India today, the law does not support any physical punishment; it was outlawed as a state punishment under the Penal Code 1860 and the Juvenile Justice Act 2000. However, in some states it may be used under local justice systems.

It is not only the prisoners who grow coarse and hardened from corporal punishment, but those as well who perpetrate the act or are present to witness it. (Chekhov)

Islam

Islamic law allows corporal punishment: 'A thief male and female cut off the hand of both' (Qur'an 5:38), 'If a woman or man is guilty of adultery, flog each of them 100 stripes' (Qur'an 24:2). In many Muslim countries, the Law of Compensation can be used, which swaps corporal punishment for paying compensation. Some extreme Muslim groups do use these punishments quite freely, though.

Judaism

While used historically, Judaism is cautious about using physical punishments in the modern world. The punishment for breaking Torah Laws, and for showing contempt for rabbinical law, was to be whipped. The Old Testament does refer to floggings, but Judaism has moved on.

Sikhism

Sikhism does not agree with inflicting pain as a way of punishment. Within India, Sikhs follow Indian law. 'Show kindness and mercy to all life, and realise the Lord is pervading everywhere' (Guru Granth Sahib) – this suggests that corporal punishment would be wrong.

Reasons for its use
1 Some see it as a deterrent.
2 It can fulfil the aim of retribution and quick reformation.
3 Physical pain is a harsher punishment for more serious crime.
4 It would be more effective than prison as people fear pain.
5 Many parents believe they have the right to chastise their child using corporal punishment in order to teach them right from wrong.

Reasons for not using it
1 It is barbaric and inhumane.
2 Makes criminals more hardened and does not reform.
3 Revenge is wrong.
4 To purposely inflict pain is unacceptable.
5 The greater strength of an adult means that those who use corporal punishment on their child can easily inflict more pain and harm than they intend.

Sanctity of life in relation to corporal and capital punishment

Even the lives of criminals are sacred. Most religious believers agree there is an aspect of God to each individual. So corporal and capital punishment – as they damage/end life – are both incompatible with this idea. However, the offences committed have already disregarded 'sanctity of life', so do they deserve that consideration?

> Whoever spares the rod hates their children, but the one who loves their children is careful to discipline them.
> (Proverbs 13:24)

The Basics
1 What is meant by corporal punishment?
2 Explain why some religious believers agree with corporal punishment.
3 'Religious believers should never agree with corporal punishment.' Give reasons to agree and disagree with this statement, and explain them.

8 Theme E: Religion, crime and punishment

The death penalty – capital punishment

The death penalty is capital punishment. Where it is used, it is usually reserved for the most extreme offences, usually murder. Worldwide, other crimes such as blasphemy, adultery, drug offences, corruption, fraud, smuggling, treason, hijacking and war crimes are capital offences.

> Are any crimes so bad they merit the death penalty? What do you think?

Why use such an extreme punishment?

The crimes are seen as so bad that no other punishment would be suitable. People who commit such horrific acts must face the most severe punishment, so that justice is seen to be done and others are deterred from committing these crimes. It is the principle of 'an eye for an eye' and is seen as the law of equality of retribution in Islam. A murderer shows no respect for human life, so the state shows no respect for the murderer's life. Many holy books name certain offences as being punishable by death.

USA executions (1976–2018)

Lethal injections	1318
Electrocution	160
Lethal gas	11
Hanging	3
Firing squad	3

In 1977, the USA allowed individual states to choose whether they wished to use capital punishment. Currently, 29 states have re-adopted the death penalty. Texas is responsible for over one-third of all executions that take place. To date there have been over 1,512 executions in the USA since 1976. Right now there are over 2,650 people awaiting execution in America's death-row cells. Amnesty International has said that the USA is savage, barbaric, cruel, prejudiced and uncivilised. This is because the USA has executed: people who offended as a child; people who have mental illnesses; black people sentenced by all-white juries; and many other seemingly unfair cases. If this is what can be said about what is considered the most democratic country in the world, what might be the situation in other countries?

To find out more about the death penalty in the USA go to: www.amnestyusa.org

Facts and figures

- 144 countries have abolished the death penalty in law or practice.
- 58 countries retain and use the death penalty.
- This century, 88 per cent of all known executions have taken place in China, Iran, Iraq, Saudi Arabia and the USA.
- Between 1976 and 2003, the USA executed 22 people who were under the age of 18 at the time the crime was committed – more than half of those executed worldwide.
- In March 2005, the USA abolished child executions, affecting over 70 juvenile offenders on death row in 12 states.
- In the USA, since 1973, 156 prisoners on death row have been released after their convictions were overturned.
- Methods of execution worldwide include: firing squad, hanging, lethal injection, stoning, beheading, gas chamber, electric chair, crucifixion (Sudan).

> Discuss the information above. What issues does it raise about the death penalty?

Did you know? Over 1,300 people have been killed by lethal injection in the USA, some of them dying in excruciating pain. Victims have been seen gasping for air, convulsing, grimacing in agony and have received chemical burns 30 cm long. Some executions have lasted as long as an hour.

Did you know? In California in 2008, the legal system cost $137 million per year to run. Without the death penalty it would have cost just $11.5 million.

Did you know? Since 1973 there have been 166 death penalty exonerations in the USA – 29 of which were in Florida state.

Religious, philosophical and ethical studies

Find out more about the work of Sister Helen Prejean and the move to abolish capital punishment in the USA. Watch the film *Dead Man Walking*.

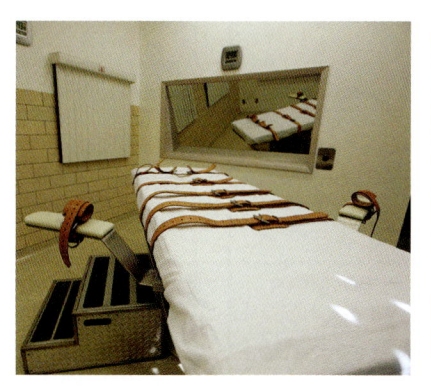

Should the UK reintroduce the death penalty? Discuss.

Some arguments for capital punishment

- An 'eye for an eye, life for a life' means that murderers should pay with their life.
- It is a deterrent, therefore it puts people off committing horrendous crimes.
- It brings justice for the victims and their families.
- Life sentences do not mean life; murderers walk free on average after 16 years.
- It is a waste of resources housing criminals for their entire life.
- This is the only way to totally protect society from the worst murderer who it is believed cannot be reformed.
- The Principle of Utility states that an action is right if it brings happiness to the greatest number of people. Capital punishment protects society at large and brings satisfaction to victims' families, so could be argued to be right under this principle.

Some arguments against capital punishment

- Retribution is uncivilised; two wrongs do not make a right. It is a contradiction to condemn murder and then execute (kill) a murderer.
- Most murders are done on the spur of the moment, so capital punishment would not deter these crimes.
- Victims' families still grieve; killing the murderer does not end the pain of loss.
- Legal systems can fail and innocent people can be executed.
- All life is sacred and murderers should be given the chance to reform.
- It is inhumane and degrading to put anyone through the mental torture of death row.

AMNESTY INTERNATIONAL

Amnesty International was founded in 1961 by Peter Benenson, a British lawyer. Today it is the world's biggest human rights organisation, informing the world about human rights abuses and campaigning for individuals and political change. Amnesty disagrees completely with execution, seeing it as cruel, inhumane and degrading. In its reports about the death penalty in the USA, it has highlighted the degrading nature of the system, giving examples of prisoners being taken from intensive care to be executed, wiring up prisoners who were still awaiting last-minute appeals, executing people who were clearly mentally ill, and a paraplegic being dragged to the electric chair. Campaigning against and monitoring the use of the death penalty worldwide is just one part of Amnesty's work. The organisation campaigns to end all human rights abuses and recognises the inherent value of all human life. Find out more about Amnesty International by visiting their website at www.amnesty.org.uk

The Basics

1. What is meant by capital punishment?
2. Explain three reasons why the death penalty is used.
3. Use the information from pages 302–304 to explain religious attitudes to the death penalty.
4. 'It is never right to execute a murderer.' Analyse and evaluate this statement. Explain reasons to agree and disagree, so that you show you have thought about more than one point of view. Include religious arguments in your answer.

☸ Buddhism

Buddhism teaches that people should follow the laws of the country in which they live. The Noble Eightfold Path relates to living life correctly. Each of the steps in the path starts with the word 'right' and they emphasise the importance of correct action. A life of crime would not be Right Livelihood and criminal activity would certainly be against the First Precept because it causes harm to other people. Furthermore, the motivation behind crime is often linked to selfish human traits and desires. Breaking the law would lead to bad kamma and this would affect future rebirths, preventing a person from achieving Enlightenment.

Buddhism teaches:
- Suffering is caused by attachment to the material world.
- The Three Poisons (greed, hatred, ignorance) are the cause of evil actions.
- The law of karma – the sum total of good and bad actions.
- Buddhists should practise metta (loving kindness) and karuna (compassion).
- The story of Milarepa illustrates that all people are capable of change.

Although Buddhists teach that all people can change and bad actions will have karmic consequences, they recognise the need to punish criminals. Buddhists would agree that the public needs to be protected from dangerous criminals. However, imprisonment should not prevent someone from changing and should provide opportunities for the offender to reform and be helped. It is true that many criminals re-offend after prison, showing they have neither changed for the better nor been reformed. The principles of non-harming, loving kindness and compassion mean Buddhists would not agree with punishments that were unduly severe or would cause direct harm to the offender. The Angulimala society provides support for prisoners.

Look up the stories of Angulimala and Geshe Ben. What do they teach about Buddhist attitudes to crime and punishment? https://angulimala.org.uk

✝ Christianity

Christianity teaches that the laws of a country should be followed unless they are unjust. The Ten Commandments concern both religious and moral practice. Many of them are reflected in the laws of the UK. St Paul taught that the state should be obeyed because it only has authority because God has given permission for it to exist. For Christians, law breaking would therefore mean they were committing sins as well as crimes. This could affect them in the afterlife because they believe they will be judged by God, who will decide if they are fit to enter heaven.

Christianity teaches:
- 'Love your neighbour' (Jesus – Mark 12:30–31) – Christian love (agape) should be shown to all people.
- 'Pray for those who persecute you.' (Jesus – Sermon on the Mount)
- The Ten Commandments – a law code that guides behaviour.
- 'Forgive your brother seventy times seven times' (Jesus – Matthew 18:22) – meaning that a Christian should always be prepared to forgive those who wrong them.
- The Lord's Prayer – recognises that everyone sins and needs forgiveness.

Christians accept that offenders must be punished to protect people from crime and deter people from offending. Punishments should be fair and just, offenders should be treated humanely. The Quaker Elizabeth Fry devoted her life to prison reform. Amnesty International, which was founded on Christian principles, works worldwide to campaign for the protection of prisoners' human rights. The story of Adam and Eve (the Fall) shows that human nature is such that everyone sins. Christians believe that people should have the opportunity to repent for their wrongdoing and make amends. They also emphasise that it is important to follow the example of Jesus and be prepared to forgive others. Hence most Christians do not agree with the death penalty. Some, however, follow the Old Testament teachings of *life for life* and *whoever sheds the blood of man, by man shall his blood be shed.*

Look up the Parable of the Lost Son (Luke 15:11–32) and the story of the woman caught in adultery (John 8:1–11). What do they teach Christians about repentance and forgiveness?

Religious, philosophical and ethical studies

ॐ Hinduism

Hindus believe all people should follow the law and rulers have a responsibility to ensure that justice is carried out and people are protected from offenders. In the Hindu scriptures dharma (duty), caste and the belief in karma are important influences on attitudes to crime and punishment. Every Hindu is born into a caste and has a duty to fulfil. Criminal activities bring bad karma and would cause a person to be reborn into a lesser life form. The principle of ahimsa (non-violence) would also be broken, since crime causes harm to others physically and/or emotionally.

Hindu teachings:
- Karma – all evil actions result in bad karma that influences rebirth.
- Reincarnation and moksha – the cycle of rebirth (samsara) depends on karma. Moksha can only be achieved through good actions.
- 'An eye for an eye and the whole world would be blind.' (Gandhi)
- 'When a person claims to be non-violent … he will put up with all the injury given to him by a wrongdoer.' (Gandhi)
- 'Murdering a Brahmin is the most serious of crimes.' (Laws of Manu)

Hindu teachings make clear that just punishments should appropriately provide retribution, deterrence and reformation. In the past the severity of punishment was greater the lower the caste of the offender. The scriptures state that a Brahmin could not be given a capital or corporal punishment. In modern times many Hindus follow the example of Gandhi and would expect offenders to be treated humanely and that punishment should make provision for the offender to learn from their mistake and reform. The Laws of Manu make clear that the death penalty is acceptable for crimes such as murder, theft and adultery, but in India today only murder and treason are capital offences.

Find out how Gandhi led a campaign of peaceful civil disobedience against British rule in India. Write a report on your findings.

☪ Islam

Muslim law, Shari'ah, is both secular and religious. It is based on the Qur'an, Hadith and Sunnah of the Prophet. An offender therefore breaks Allah's laws as well as man's law. To outsiders Islamic law can appear to be extreme. However, Islam is a complete way of life and all Muslims have a responsibility to each other and the community. For example, there is no reason to steal because zakat is provided for the poor. Criminal activity is an offence to Allah and will be punished on Earth and in the afterlife.

Islam teaches:
- 'A thief, whether man or woman, shall have their hand cut off as penalty.' (Qur'an)
- 'The woman and man guilty of adultery or fornication, flog each one of them.' (Qur'an)
- 'We ordained for them; life for life.' (Qur'an)
- Day of Judgement – Allah will decide who goes to paradise or hell.
- If a man is killed unjustly, his family will be entitled to satisfaction.

Crime in Islam can be divided into four groups. **Hadud** – the worst crimes; murder, blasphemy, theft, adultery, false accusation, treason, highway robbery and drinking alcohol. There are capital and corporal punishments for these offences. **Jinayat** – involve killing or wounding and the victims have the right to claim compensation. Offenders can pay **Diya** (blood money) as part reparation for their crime. **Ta'azir** – lesser crimes and punishments which are decided by a judge who will consider social pressures and change. **Mukhalafat** – covers laws related to the smooth running of the state, such as driving offences, and a judge decides the punishments. Punishments should ensure justice is served and Islam accepts there may be mitigating circumstances to be considered and allows for the forgiveness of offenders.

Find out more about the use of capital and corporal punishment in Islamic countries. Write a report on your findings.

303

8 Theme E: Religion, crime and punishment

Judaism

The Torah is the Jewish law book and includes 613 mitzvot (rules). These outline the conduct expected of all citizens. They include secular and religious guidance. All Jewish people are expected to follow the law and keep their religious duties and responsibilities. There is also guidance on repentance for wrongdoing. Jewish people believe that God will forgive and be merciful if a wrongdoer makes atonement – repents their sins and makes amends. They can do this through prayer, fasting and charitable giving. The Bet Din (Jewish court) makes decisions about religious matters.

Jewish teaching:
- The Ten Commandments.
- 'God created the world with justice and mercy so that it would last.' (Midrash)
- 'The Lord does not enjoy seeing sinners die, He would rather they stop sinning and live.' (Nevi'im)
- 'If anyone takes the life of a human being they must be put to death.' (Torah)
- Yom Kippur – the Day of Atonement when Jewish people make confession and atonement for sins.

Judaism teaches that society should be protected and that people should be deterred from committing crimes. Punishment should be just and rehabilitate the offender. The Torah does allow execution for some crimes and emphasises the need for corroborative evidence from two independent witnesses. The teaching of an *eye for an eye* is about making amends. The death penalty exists as a deterrent and it is rarely used. Judaism considers it important for offenders to have the opportunity to atone for their crimes.

Look up the Ten Commandments (Exodus 20:1–17). Explain how they guide religious and secular behaviour.

Task

For the religions you are studying; use the information you have learned in this topic to explain believers' attitudes to:
- the law
- punishment of offenders
- capital punishment.

Sikhism

Sikhs regard the law as important for ensuring justice and the protection of weaker members of society. All people need God's guidance to avoid the evils of anger, greed, lust, pride and attachment to worldly possessions. Human nature means that sometimes people fall into sin, but they should have the opportunity to repent and make up for their mistakes. Khalsa Sikhs follow a strict code of discipline (Rahit Maryada) when they commit to the community. If a Sikh were to break this code they would have to make reparation before the rest of the community. In society, Sikhism teaches its followers to be law-abiding, but to be prepared to fight against injustice and oppression.

Sikhism teaches:
- Law of karma – evil actions result in bad karma and lower rebirth.
- Kurahits – religious vows guiding personal conduct.
- Kirpan – a symbol of the fight for justice and truth.
- 'If someone hits you, do not hit him back, go home after kissing his feet.' (Guru Granth Sahib)
- 'He who associates with evildoers is destroyed.' (Guru Granth Sahib)

Sikhs believe in nirvair – trying to be without hatred. They accept that it is important to punish criminals in order to protect society and reform the offender. They do not accept physical or mental torture, as they respect the dignity of all human life and the essence of God within all. Many Sikhs support human rights organisations like Amnesty International and would offer support and counselling to convicts. Sikhs are told to follow their conscience and many would not support the death penalty because of the belief in the sanctity of life. However, some may regard it as a useful deterrent and just punishment for some crimes.

Look up the Sikh kurahits. Write a report on how they would influence a Sikh's life including the keeping of laws.

Contrasting beliefs

Corporal punishment

✝ Christianity

Christianity as a rule **does not support the use of corporal punishment**. Many point to the idea of **human dignity** and that this kind of punishment breaches that. As a form of violence it is seen as wrong by many as it is vengeful rather than merciful. The belief that **violence begets violence** means that criminals dealt with in this way will not be reformed. Christian groups such as the Quakers worked to reform this kind of punishment in UK law, so it is now illegal in the UK.

☪ Islam

In countries using Shariah, the Law includes the legitimate use of corporal punishment. The **Qur'an states that it must be proportionate, necessary and carried out publicly** (24:2). Methods sanctioned by the Qur'an include **beating/lashes, and amputation** (5:38). It is a punishment and deterrent.

ॐ Hinduism

Hinduism has **historically allowed corporal punishment. The Laws of Manu advise the removal of a thief's hand**, which prevents further crime, and deters others. It is not legal under Indian law today.

✝ Christianity

Some Christian groups allow parents to physically chastise their children for misbehaviour. This follows the teaching in Proverbs: 'Whoever spares the rod hates their children, but the one who loves their children is careful to discipline them' (13:24).

Question

Explain two contrasting beliefs in contemporary British society about corporal punishment.

In your answer you should refer to the main religious tradition of Great Britain and one or more other religious traditions. *(4 marks)*

Death penalty

✝ Christianity

Christianity generally does not support capital punishment. The Church of England was at the forefront of the move to end its use in the UK. It is seen as a breach of the commandment 'Do not kill', because a life is being deliberately ended. It also **denies the sanctity of life** as the life of the criminal can be taken, and is against their **human dignity**. There is no chance of reform of this person as death is too final.

☪ Islam

Islamic (Shariah) Law includes the use of capital punishment. The Qur'an states **crimes which are punishable by death** (5:32). The Qur'an insists 'Take not life except by way of justice and law', so the crime must be sufficient.

8 Theme E: Religion, crime and punishment

✝ Christianity

Some Christians believe it is right to use the death penalty for those criminals who have committed the **worst crimes**, such as murder. Since they have taken life, for example, they forfeit their own – 'An eye for an eye' (Exodus 21:24).

Question

Explain two contrasting beliefs in contemporary British society about the death penalty.

In your answer you should refer to the main religious tradition of Great Britain and one or more other religious traditions. *(4 marks)*

☰ Judaism

Judaism prescribes the **death penalty for murder**. This is seen as **justice** and essential to the **preservation of the community**. However, the state of Israel has only executed two criminals, one being the Nazi Eichmann, in its history, preferring to **commute death sentences**.

Forgiveness

✝ Christianity

Forgiveness is a central teaching of Jesus. When asked how often a person should forgive, in Matthew 18:22, he said 'seventy times seven' – in other words, innumerably. The Lord's Prayer includes the injunction to 'Forgive us our trespasses as we forgive those who trespass against us'. Jesus' **crucifixion was necessary so that humans could be forgiven their sins and so enter heaven for eternity with God**. Humans must try to follow Jesus' example, so should be forgiving.

☪ Islam

In Islam, while **forgiveness is a quality of Allah**, it is conditional. A human must be sorry, recognise the wrong, commit to not repeat it, and seek forgiveness. **Without these conditions, forgiveness cannot be given.**

✝ Christianity

Some Christians who have been victims of very serious crime – for example, having a family member murdered – **do not see a way to forgive**. They seek **justice rather than forgiveness** for these serious crimes.

☸ Buddhism

Buddhism recognises that while forgiveness is the ideal, it can be very difficult to grant. Where a person has suffered greatly, the negative emotions they hold because of that suffering can prevent them from forgiving.

Question

Explain two contrasting beliefs in contemporary British society about forgiveness.

In your answer you should refer to the main religious tradition of Great Britain and one or more other religious traditions. *(4 marks)*

Getting prepared

Using quotations for maximum effect

Every year, candidates do not make the best use of the quotes in their answers, leading to less effective responses. It is an important skill to learn and practise as it will improve your writing. Look at two examples, in each case the original answer is in black print, with improvements in purple.

Explain two religious beliefs about the treatment of offenders. Refer to sacred writings or another source of religious belief and teaching in your answer. (5 marks)

Christians say love your neighbour. They think everyone should be punished. So they think you have to punish them but fairly.

This candidate has mentioned one teaching and has indicated a value (fairness). Look at the next version. How do you think this compares?

Christians say love your neighbour, so while they think everyone should be punished, so they think you have to punish them fairly. They believe in justice which makes it important that treatment is fair and not cruel.

Explain two contrasting beliefs in contemporary British society about using the death penalty as a punishment. In your answer, you should refer to the main religious tradition of Great Britain and one or more other religious traditions. (4 marks)

In the Bible it says 'do not kill'. It also says that life is sacred. You should love your neighbour, not hurt them.

This gives us three valid ideas, but does not answer the question. Rather the reader has to work out the relevance of each point. Sometimes, it is not obvious enough. Make sure that you apply the quotes you use to the actual question. Compare that with this second version.

In the Bible it says 'do not kill'. Sometimes, a criminal has murdered someone, and they have broken this teaching so gone against a fundamental rule of Christianity. It also says that life is sacred. So we should always condemn and punish harshly when someone commits a crime against the person (which is always doing damage to someone). You should love your neighbour, not hurt them, so religious believers would say this kind of crime goes against this teaching by Jesus. All of these teachings show that when a person commits a very serious crime like murder, then the death penalty would be an appropriate punishment.

Do you think this second version is a better answer than the first one? If you do, what makes it better?

Religion, crime and punishment glossary

Capital punishment death penalty; state sanctioned punishment for what are considered the worst crimes; not part of UK law

Community service order punishment; criminal has to do a set number of hours of work in the community as their punishment

Conscience sense of right and wrong; usually the guilty voice in our head; some believe this to be the voice of God

Corporal punishment physically hurting the criminal as a punishment, e.g. by whipping them

Crime breaking the law; can be against a person (e.g. assault), against property (e.g. arson), or against the state (e.g. terrorism)

Deterrence aim of punishment; where the punishment puts someone off committing the crime

Duty something we are bound to do

Evil something (or someone) considered morally wrong; wicked; often linked to the idea of a malevolent force, for example the devil

Forgiveness letting go of anger towards someone for a wrong they have done us

Hate crime a crime committed because of prejudice, for example beating someone up because you think they are gay; in UK law, it can mean the doubling of a sentence if found guilty

Imprisonment locking someone up as a punishment

Justice making things fair again

Law the rules which govern a country to keep us safe

Murder the deliberate and unlawful killing of another person; carries the highest tariff of punishment in UK law

Order the enforcement of rules, for example by a police force

Parole release of a criminal from prison, but continuing to monitor their behaviour

Probation order punishment; monitoring of behaviour with the threat of greater punishment for offending again

Protection aim of punishment; to keep people safe

Reformation aim of punishment; helping the person to see how and why they should behave better

Reparation aim of punishment; making up for, compensating

Retribution aim of punishment; getting back at the person for what they have done

Theft taking something which does not belong to you with the intention to keep it/not to give it back

Victim the one against whom a crime is committed; someone who suffers as a result of a crime

Vindication aim of punishment; the punishment exists because the law does

Young offenders persons under 18 who commit crime

9 Theme F: Religion, human rights and social justice

Key elements of this theme

This theme is broken into three parts.

Firstly, **human rights** – what they are, why we should have them and how religious people may view them. From this comes the issue of **prejudice** – what it is and why it may happen; religious attitudes to prejudice and **discrimination**, both generally and in specific situations. Finally, **poverty** – both in the UK and across the world; why there is poverty; exploitation of the poor; religious attitudes to poverty and to helping those in poverty.

These themes can all be viewed through the idea of human rights and **social justice** – that society should be a fair place, and those who are victims must be helped and protected.

Key concepts

There are concepts which apply to all three aspects of this theme. Firstly comes the idea of **rights** and **responsibilities**. Many people argue they have a right to something, often without thinking of other people's rights. For you to have a right to something (for example, freedom of speech) you have to have the responsibility to speak appropriately, that is, not hurting others by telling lies about them. Where prejudice and poverty exist, it is often the case that someone somewhere is not meeting their responsibilities.

Given that people are individual and different, it is important to show **tolerance** to those others who are not the same as us. This means accepting their differences, and not making a big deal of it, especially not targeting them because of it. You can see that if we are tolerant, there is no place for prejudice. You can also see that where people are tolerant of each other, they can live in **harmony**.

All religious believers agree that life is special and sacred. Many believe we were all created equally by God. This means we have equal worth and value, and should enjoy equal rights (**equality**). Anything to deny these rights would be wrong.

Lots of people are disadvantaged in life for many reasons. Religious believers would see a need for systems to bring social justice to those people – they believe that things have to be made fair. They also call for all people to show **compassion** (loving kindness) to all others. This means giving help where it is needed, simply because it is needed.

Overall, religious people believe they have the duty of **stewardship** (a responsibility to look after the world and the people in it). If we are serious about this responsibility, we will try to defend the rights of all to live in harmony and in a just world.

> **The Basics**
>
> 1. Write definitions for the following words – tolerance; rights; responsibilities; justice; compassion; stewardship.
> 2. Explain how a religious believer who believes in tolerance, equality, justice, rights and responsibilities might view the following:
>   - prejudice
>   - poverty.
> 3. Explain how belief in compassion and stewardship might affect how a religious person lives their life in regard to others.
> 4. 'Rights are more important than responsibilities.' Do you agree? Explain your reasons, showing you have thought about more than one point of view.

9 Theme F: Religion, human rights and social justice

Social justice

This means **justice** in terms of **wealth** distribution, the law, equal rights and opportunities for all people. For social justice to exist, society must be fair to all regardless of race, age, **gender**, **sexuality** and disability. It also means that society has to be organised so that it is open to all in terms of education, health care, housing and social welfare. The United Nations' 2006 document *Social Justice in an Open World* states 'Social justice may be broadly understood as the fair and compassionate distribution of the fruits of economic growth'. Social justice is a reason why religions fight for human rights and against prejudice and exploitation of all people, including the poor and vulnerable.

Social justice in the modern world is difficult to achieve. Different political methods have been tried, but there are always those who feel things are not fair. Different political parties manage a country's economy in different ways, and promote social justice differently. It is probably true to say that there are people in society who can look after themselves despite political systems, but there are always those who cannot. Some will argue that the poor need preferential treatment and a society is judged on how it treats its most vulnerable. Others believe too much help can make people reliant on that help so they do little to help themselves.

All religions have teachings on social justice.

Buddhism
In Buddhism, along with the idea of selflessness, Buddhists believe that Right Action, Livelihood, Speech, Effort and Intention should, if carried out properly, lead to social justice.

Hinduism
In Hinduism within India, there is a conscious move away from the caste system, which separates people and has created a massive gulf between rich and poor.

Judaism
In *To Heal a Fractured World: The Ethics of Responsibility*, Rabbi Lord Jonathan Sacks states that social justice is central to Judaism. He explains that the concepts of simcha (gladness), tzedakah (the religious obligation to perform charity), chesed (deeds of kindness) and tikkun olam (healing the world) all allow for social justice.

Christianity
In the UK, Christians have fought for prison reform since the eighteenth century, organisations like Christian Aid work in inner cities, and the House of Lords includes clergy who discuss the law – all these are examples of involvement in social justice.

Islam
The Qur'an contains references to social justice. One of Islam's Five Pillars is zakat, or alms-giving. Charity and assistance to the poor (concepts central to social justice) have historically been important parts of the Islamic faith.

Sikhism
Sikh scriptures promote the message of equality of all beings and reveal that Sikh believers should deal with all humankind with the spirit of universal brotherhood and equality.

The Basics
1 What is meant by social justice?
2 Why is it correct to say that religions believe social justice to be important?

Religious, philosophical and ethical studies

What do we mean by human rights?

There are many descriptions and declarations of human rights. They are what humans should be able to expect as a minimum because they are human. They include basic rights and freedoms: right to life, to not be persecuted by others, to have a fair trial, to free speech, and also the right to have food, shelter, education, healthcare and work.

The UN Declaration of Human Rights starts with the most fundamental statement that:

> 'All humans are born free and equal in dignity and rights. They are endowed with reason and conscience and should act towards one another in a spirit of brotherhood.'

Everything else comes from that. Laws are built on it and our behaviour towards and with others should be governed by it.

Task

Imagine you and 99 others have been stranded on a bio-sphere which is on Mars. There is no hope for anyone else from Earth to get to you for many years. The bio-sphere allows for the production of food and recycling of all waste. It will sustain you all for as many years as you manage it properly (not over-using resources, and maintaining systems so that they do not break down). You all realise very early on that a set of rules needs to be drawn up which everyone will live within. You are a mix of cultures and nationalities, with different expertise and experience. Your rules will only work if they are designed to protect a set of human rights. Your task is to decide what the rights of humans on Mars should be.

Rights issues

Read these statements. In each case, do you think there is a human right being denied or broken? Which right(s)?

Luke was beaten up because he kept making extremely racist comments.

Chris was told by the council they could not house him after his parents had thrown him out aged 19.

Sash did not get into the school her parents chose because it was full – so they did not send her to another school.

Wayne was found guilty of murder and sentenced to death.

Rights ... and responsibilities

People have the right to voice their opinion. But that right brings a responsibility to also listen to the opinions of others, as they also have a right to their opinion. It also brings the responsibility of speaking in a responsible and respectful way, and of taking the consequences of exercising our right. It is the same for any human right. For example, if I have a right to education, then so do you; if I have a right to good healthcare, then so do you. We cannot say only we have rights, and we cannot say that we do not need to take responsibility for exercising those rights. Sometimes our rights affect others in a negative way, and we have to be mindful of that.

> *If I am to have my human rights, then I have to be prepared to respect and protect the human rights of others. If I am blessed with wealth, I should use my money responsibly – I have a right to my money as I earned it, but also a responsibility to help those in poverty. I have a right to live free from prejudice, but a responsibility to not behave in a prejudicial way as well as to actively try to fight prejudice and support victims.*

311

9 Theme F: Religion, human rights and social justice

The UN Declaration of Human Rights

Statements of rights have been written all through history. Britain's first was probably Magna Carta (1215CE), which stated the ruler's commitment to his people. Setting out a code of rights is perhaps the first step in building law and legal systems.

The United Nations Declaration of Human Rights was written and then adopted by many countries in 1948, coming about partly because of the atrocities which countries fighting the Second World War had carried out. Although countries adopt this Declaration, there is no binding requirement for them to keep it. These rights are in two distinct groups: civil and political rights, and economic, social and cultural rights. The UN claims that these are part of the way to build freedom, peace and justice in the world.

Here are some examples of human rights:

> Everyone:
> - is equal
> - is born free
> - should be treated in the same way
> - is innocent until proven guilty.
>
> Everyone should respect everyone else.
>
> Everyone has the right to:
> - legal protection
> - a public trial when accused of a crime
> - asylum
> - belong to a country
> - marry
> - own things and keep them
> - free speech
> - meet peacefully with others
> - vote
> - work
> - rest
> - an education
> - basic rights – water, food, shelter, healthcare
> - artistic freedom and to enjoy the arts.
>
> No one should be:
> - tortured
> - unfairly imprisoned.
>
> No one may destroy the rights of others.
>
> There must be laws to protect these rights.

> Do you think there are any rights missing? Or any that are wrong? Which do you think is the most important? Why? Do you think that everyone should always have rights? Is there ever a time when someone's rights should be reduced, or taken away?

> Look at the UN's website for more details of this topic – www.una.org.uk
>
> Look back to the four situations on the previous page. Use this list to work out if any of the UN's declared rights are being broken and who by. Look at the newspaper headlines below. Why is each one a human rights issue?

MAN CLAIMING ASYLUM TURNED AWAY AT AIRPORT

Tsunami victims denied help by their own government

More than one million children under 14 forced into prostitution each year

125 million children aged 5–14 work full-time to support their families

New laws rushed in to stop protestors

Racist fights for absolute freedom of speech for himself

The Basics

1. What is meant by human rights?
2. Explain how the United Nations Declaration of Human Rights came to be written.
3. List four human rights.
4. 'The most important human right is for everyone to be free.' Do you agree? Explain both sides of the argument.

Religious, philosophical and ethical studies

The Human Rights Act (1998)

The **Human Rights Act** (HRA) gave a legal standing in the UK to the fundamental rights and freedoms contained in the European Convention on Human Rights (ECHR). These are based on the UN Declaration. The HRA is supposed to ensure that people's human rights are protected and respected by public authorities. It makes it illegal for public authorities to act against a person's human rights. Everyone in the UK is protected by these rights.

However, the rights are not absolute. The government has the power to limit or control people's rights under certain conditions, such as in wartime. They also rely on people respecting each other, and not behaving in a way which would go against other people's rights. Respect is the key to everything, because respect for others leads to all those rights.

Respecting human rights as a religious citizen

A citizen is someone who is a member of a country or nation. You are probably a British citizen; you might have citizenship of another country, because some people have dual citizenship (usually because of having parents from different countries, or by living in another country for a number of years). Being a citizen brings rights within that country, but also responsibilities to respect and follow the rules of that country.

A religious citizen is simply someone who is a citizen, but has religious beliefs. Those beliefs should mean they respect the law of the country in which they live or have citizenship. Generally speaking, British law has as its basis the Ten Commandments. Both religious and secular laws are based on respect – that word keeps coming up, doesn't it? So religions would all agree with laws based around respect.

Sometimes the religious laws and secular laws do not match up. What happens then? Read these stories, and try to work out what the people did in the end. The answers are at the foot of the page for you to check.

David

My grandfather died suddenly. The doctors want to do a post-mortem. In my religion, we should not desecrate a body, and should bury it whole. The post-mortem goes against both of those beliefs. Should we agree to the post-mortem, or fight it?

Sarah

I belong to the Quaker faith. My grandfather was a Quaker, and when the Second World War started, he was called up to fight. Quakers are pacifists – they do not believe in violence. The draft papers said he had to join the army – in wartime, of course a soldier has to fight. What do you think he did?

Jane

I am a Christian. My teacher won't let me wear my silver ring which represents my vow to stay celibate until marriage – it breaks school uniform rules. I have not been to school while I'm banned from wearing it in school. I use the internet and books to help me study for my GCSEs. What should I do?

David's family did not give permission, but the law can take that right away. His grandfather's body was subject to post-mortem exam before being released to the family for burial.

Sarah's grandfather claimed his right to be a conscientious objector. He was given a job in the UK for the war effort, but was subject to much persecution and abuse, being called unpatriotic and a traitor.

Jane's case went to court, and the House of Lords. It was ruled that wearing a ring is not a religious duty for Christians, so the school need not respect that claimed religious right.

313

Freedom of religion and belief, including freedom of religious expression

In the UK today, the right to religious freedom is protected, and freedom from persecution because of religion is also possible, because of discrimination laws.

Freedom of religious expression – this is the right of any person to follow the religion of their choice and to be open about what they believe. In the UK, you cannot be told (legally) that you are not allowed to follow a particular religion, and none are banned. Nor can you be ordered by law to follow a particular group's interpretation of that religion, so you could not be told that the only legal denomination of Christianity is the Church of England. This was not always the case. For example, in the sixteenth century, first the Protestants under Queen Mary and then the Catholics under Queen Elizabeth I were executed for their beliefs.

Freedom from persecution because of religion – this is the right to be legally protected if someone targets you because of the religion you follow. They would have committed a hate crime, which is a criminal offence. So, for example, if a person attacked another person in the street, simply because they thought they were Muslim, then that would be a hate crime. That does not mean that a person who is refused the right to wear a religious symbol while at work is a victim of religious discrimination, unless the symbol is compulsory to their religion (like a Sikh's turban).

All religions will argue for their right to both of these freedoms. But do they also seek to protect the rights of others to their (different) religion?

Buddhism

Buddhism teaches that religion if properly understood is a way or means to realise the truth, and that there are many ways to the same religious truths. When asked for his religion, the Dalai Lama once said, 'The religion of kindness'. The Buddha himself, after Enlightenment, did not try to forcefully convert anyone; he explained and discussed what he had learned, allowing people to decide for themselves. Scriptures give many examples of where a non-Buddhist listened to the Buddha, and converted. Additionally, the Buddha did send followers out to spread his teachings. However, there have been occasions of Buddhist violence, in Sri Lanka, Myanmar (Burma) and Thailand, for example, against other religions.

Christianity

Many Christians believe that the only way to salvation (attain a place in heaven) is through belief in Jesus. This excludes all other religions, and is the main reason why Christianity has always been a missionary religion; trying to convert others. Some believe that as long as a person leads a morally good life, then they too can earn salvation, which opens the door to accept all other faiths, given their key principles fit with Christianity's. Whatever the belief about who can and cannot go to heaven, it is important to treat everyone equally and with kindness, so Christians should not be involved in any form of religious discrimination.

Religious, philosophical and ethical studies

Hinduism

Hinduism is a wide-ranging religion and is open to all other faiths. A famous Hindu, Saint Vivekananda, once likened religions to 'different paths to the top of the same mountain'. Hinduism does not agree with trying to convert others, and some Hindus have reacted negatively to perceptions of this being done by Christians and Muslims in India. It is also true that some practices of non-Hindus are seen as impure – for example, eating beef – which makes some from the Brahmin caste treat non-Hindus as inferiors. In India, Muslims have complained that the Hindu-based legal system discriminates against them, making them feel threatened.

Judaism

In Jewish thinking, other religions could be seen as either God-fearing or those who seek to deny or demote God. The latter will always be wrong. Jewish people are clear that Judaism is the best way to live, but they do not say others should not live how they choose to. To be Jewish is an accident of birth, not of design. Regarding non-Jewish people, the deciding factor is how they live their lives, not who they choose to worship, so there should be no intolerance or religious discrimination shown. It is true that the modern Palestinian–Israeli conflict has caused much trouble between what are Jewish and Muslim communities, and there is clear evidence that there is a religious basis to their disagreement. It has led to intolerance on both sides, and hence discrimination not just in Israel, but anywhere that Jewish people and Muslims live.

Islam

Islam sees Christian and Jewish people as 'People of the Book'. They have received revelations from Allah, although have allowed them to be corrupted. In essence, there is still a form of the right religion to their beliefs. Prophet Muhammad had to build relationships with people of each of these faiths, and a lot of his teachings show the principles of tolerance and peaceful coexistence, as well as inclusiveness and mutual acceptance. In particular, they were allowed to practise their own faiths in their own way. There is also a sense that those who are morally good will also be rewarded in the afterlife, so should be respected now. However, it is definitely the case that modern history, especially, has seen intolerance of other religions by certain Muslim groups, which has led to mass migrations and mass murder. While this is not supported by Islamic teachings or law, it is perpetrated by those calling themselves Muslims, and so makes non-Muslims feel this is a Muslim way. This has brought religious intolerance down onto Muslims as a result.

Sikhism

The Rahit Maryada states that 'Sikhs must in no way give offence to other faiths.' Guru Nanak said, 'There is no Hindu, no Muslim ... I shall follow God's path.' Guru Gobind Singh said that different clothes and cultures did not stop all being the same flesh and blood creations of God. There are many examples from the life of Guru Nanak where he shows there should be no boundaries and no discrimination because of religion – often rejecting the exclusiveness which others claimed for their own religion. But Sikh history does include examples of troubles with other religions; usually when ruled in an oppressive way by those of another religion. It is also true that specific Muslim practices, such as the eating of halal meat, are forbidden to Sikhs, and Sikhs may not marry non-Sikhs, which we could take to be a disapproval of one or more other religions.

Task

'All religions accept each other.'
Research your religion(s) of study to explore how true this statement is.

9 Theme F: Religion, human rights and social justice

Should religious people openly express their beliefs?

A public display of a person's beliefs can be as simple as how they live their life. You might not even notice they are religious, just that they are generally a good person (since all religions promote morally good behaviour). It might be something obvious – like wearing or having a particular symbol of the faith, perhaps a Jewish person wearing a kippah (skull cap), a turban by a Sikh or a Muslim carrying tasbi (prayer beads). It might be really overt – for example, someone talking to you about their religion and why you should convert.

Is there any problem with being open about what you believe in?

In the West, fewer people follow religions, and it seems acceptable to make fun of religious believers and their beliefs. Society is not guided by religion any more, so it has less authority.

> Read these real situations. What is your opinion on each? Do these show we live in a society tolerant of religion?

- An incident took place where a check-in desk worker at an airport was banned from wearing a cross and chain because it might offend passengers who were not Christian.
- A discussion took place as to whether shops should display Christmas cards in their windows because it might cause offence to non-Christians.
- A nurse was suspended because, as a Christian, she offered to pray for a patient who was in the hospital she worked at.
- A Muslim woman employed as a teacher was asked to remove her full face veil because it was deemed not appropriate when teaching young children.
- A secondary school has renamed Christmas holidays as 'Winter break' to avoid offending the Muslim students who attend. In contrast, the school has not reduced the length of the break so that it could make Eid a whole school holiday.
- A headteacher lost her job because she decided that all assemblies should be given to all students, and not split for particular religious or non-religious groups.

Is it easy to follow a religion in the modern world?

More and more countries are becoming more 'religion-rich', as immigration brings new faiths in, and new places of worship are built. The internet means anyone can access any religion, or group within it, for information or worship from their own home, without having to be part of a physical **community**. As a society, it could be said we know more about other faiths, so are more tolerant. Laws protect religious freedoms. All this makes it easier than ever to follow a religion.

The Basics

1. What is meant by religious freedom and freedom of religious expression?
2. Explain religious attitudes to other religions and people of other religions from the religion(s) you have studied.
3. What can make it difficult to openly express religion in our society? Use examples in your answer.
4. 'Freedom of religion and religious expression is not possible in the modern world.' Do you agree with this statement? Explain your arguments.

Religious, philosophical and ethical studies

Prejudice

The two key words for this part of the theme are prejudice and discrimination. If you can learn what they mean it will help with this whole theme. The two words are linked, but their meaning is slightly different.

Prejudice means to pre-judge something or someone usually without any real evidence to base that judgement on. In most cases it is negative. We use the word to describe a person's dislike of certain other people, when they have no good reason. We talk about prejudice against colour, religion, age (**ageism**), nationality, sexuality or appearance. Prejudice is about what we think – it is about the ideas in our head.

Discrimination is when we put these prejudiced ideas into action. We treat people differently or say things because they are not the same as us or what we know. We make known to them our dislike and therefore it can have a great effect on a person's life. In Britain it is against the law to discriminate against a person with certain protected characteristics in certain situations.

Prejudice and discrimination break people's human rights, because they stop them having the same chances as others and they lead to harm.

> What kinds of prejudice can you see illustrated here?

> What might be the attitude of religious believers to each of these, based on their beliefs in equality, justice and tolerance?

Positive discrimination

Discrimination can be positive as well as negative. Minority groups are often victims of prejudice and discrimination, and are under-represented in many aspects of our society. **Positive discrimination** is used to promote opportunities for minority groups in society, especially so that those groups are better represented in public services. For example, the police service may advertise specifically for black, Asian or gay officers – members of all these groups have an understanding of minority issues. The aim is to create a police force which better reflects and so can better serve our society, both locally and nationally. The Human Rights Act makes any kind of discrimination illegal, but it allows exemptions to be applied for in cases where positive discrimination will help.

> Can you see any examples of positive discrimination in the images on this page?
> Can you think of any examples of positive discrimination?

317

9 Theme F: Religion, human rights and social justice

What makes someone prejudiced and want to discriminate against others?

Everyone can show prejudice at times, even by accident, unintentionally and out of ignorance. Not everyone will discriminate against others though because of their prejudice. Which is the more serious – the thought or the action?

Prejudice can be a barrier which stops people living, working and learning together as a community. It is very unfair and it only takes someone to be 'different' to be singled out for discrimination. The victims are almost always in the minority and find it very hard to deal with or to fight against or get justice after.

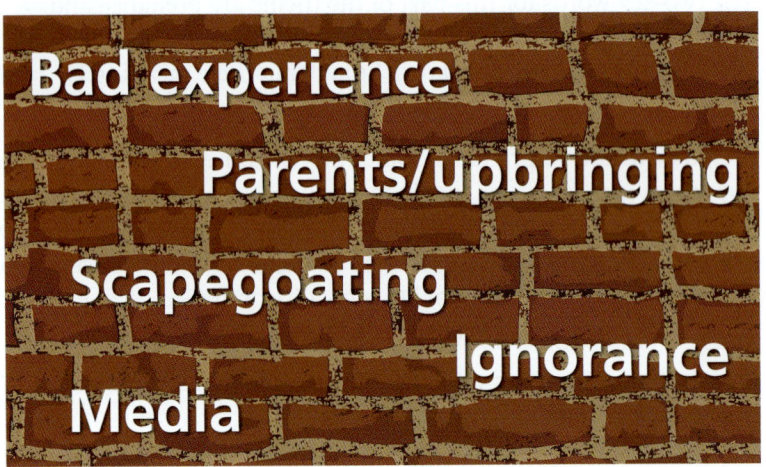

> Bad experience
> Parents/upbringing
> Scapegoating
> Ignorance
> Media

There are five main reasons for prejudice.

1. Having a **bad experience** with someone might make you think anybody else like them is like that. For example, maybe when you were young you were frightened by a grumpy old man and now you think all old men are grumpy.

2. Having been told bad things about a certain group of people by your **parents/carers**, you might be prejudiced without even getting a chance to know any differently. Their words and attitudes shape our own, so we copy and repeat them. Our upbringing has a big influence on us, and our parents' words have a huge effect.

3. Having seen something on television or read something in a newspaper (or other forms of **media**) that was very biased (it focused on only one fact or idea, taking it out of context), you might have believed it and so now are prejudiced.

4. When you do not have enough detail about something to base an opinion on, yet you think that you are able to judge someone, this is called **ignorance**. For example, having a negative opinion about a group of people who you have never met or actually learned anything about – you do not know them, but you insult them anyway.

5. **Scapegoating** is when you use others to blame or as an excuse for a problem. For example, Hitler blamed the Jewish people for the economic problems in Germany. He used the media and speeches to influence the German people so much that almost no one did anything to stop the Nazis rounding up Jewish people in Germany and taking them away to be killed. In actual fact, the German Jewish people had done nothing wrong.

The Basics

1. What is meant by prejudice and discrimination?
2. Explain how the pictures on page 317 are examples of discrimination.
3. Give some other examples of discrimination.
4. Why is tolerance important in helping prevent prejudice?
5. Explain some reasons why some people might be prejudiced.
6. Choose three of these reasons and give an example to demonstrate each one, which is different from the examples here.
7. 'You need to change the way people think to prevent discrimination.' What do you think? Explain reasons to agree and disagree with this statement.

Types of prejudice ... religious teachings

As a young person, you may have experience of prejudice/discrimination. What happened? How did it feel? Has it had a continuing impact on you?

Here you will see that each type of prejudice has been explained with some examples. The religious teachings given are general ones that can be applied to all forms of prejudice. *You only need to focus on the religion(s) that you are studying.* Think about how each teaching/religious idea can be applied to each of the forms of prejudice. Remember that tolerance, justice, community and harmony are key religious ideas too.

Sexuality

Some people are shown prejudice because of who they are attracted to. Traditionally, UK society expected men and women to be couples. Homosexuals often suffer **homophobia** because people do not agree with the relationships they have. It is often difficult to tell families (who may themselves be unsupportive, or even homophobic) and as a result there is little support available. For religious people who are gay, there are also fears of how their community might respond, and it may be the case that their religion forbids homosexuality. Also, many religions *do not agree* with these relationships, although they *do agree* that people *should not* be discriminated against. For religion, a key role of sex is to accept God's blessing of children – same-sex couples cannot do this naturally and in holy books there are teachings against homosexuality. In the UK, same-sex marriages are now allowed by law, and with the help of science, having children is also possible, so things are changing. Some religions do now accept that people are homosexual, but still disagree with them having sexual relationships.

Buddhism

Buddhism believes that as discrimination leads to suffering, it must be wrong and should be avoided.

- The belief not to harm others or use harmful language. (Precepts)
- Everyone should try to develop metta (loving kindness).
- Everyone is equal because everyone is welcome in the Sangha.
- Prejudice creates bad karma and has a negative effect on re-birth.
- The Dalai Lama stated that the best way to live life was to 'Always think compassion.'

Christianity

Christianity believes that all forms of discrimination are wrong.

- 'God created everyone equally.' (Old Testament)
- 'There is neither Jew nor Gentile, slave or free man, male or female. We are all equal in Christ.' (Galatians)
- 'So in everything, do unto others what you would have done to you.' (Matthew 7:12)
- Jesus told us to love our neighbour. (Sermon on the Mount)
- In the Good Samaritan story, the man is helped because of his need, not because of who he was or was not (in fact, the victim and helper were from enemy nations). (Luke 10:25–37)

9 Theme F: Religion, human rights and social justice

Disability

Sometimes people who have a disability are discriminated against. Remember, a disability encompasses a wide variety of conditions, categorised into two types: physical – for example, being blind, being in a wheelchair, or not having a limb; or mental – for example, having a learning problem or a mental illness. By law a disability is a long-term issue which has a significant impact on the day-to-day life of the person with the disability, so that they cannot do (some) things as normal.

People with a disability are often denied access to places. Could a person in a wheelchair access your school? Have you witnessed someone call another person names who is hearing or sight impaired? It is as if they are considered less of a person than someone fully able bodied in all aspects. Religion believes that all people are equal and God creates people in many different ways. We are all valued despite our differences. The picture at the top of the page is of Ellie Simmonds, multiple Paralympic champion, whose example shows that people can overcome difficulties and can reach the highest possible achievements despite their disability. In many cases this can be far beyond the levels an able bodied person could achieve. Such achievements should be an inspiration and make us realise we all have different talents to benefit society. Discrimination is totally wrong where disability is concerned.

Research the Disability Discrimination Act for more about this.

Hinduism

Hindu dharma is that Brahman is found in everything, so therefore any prejudicial thoughts or discriminative actions would be viewed as wrong.

- Hindus believe in non-violence (ahimsa), love and respect for all things.
- Compassion is a key belief with the desire to improve things for others, not persecute them.
- Hurting others can lead to bad karma, which affects future reincarnations.
- Hindus believe that the true self is the atman and as everyone has one this must mean everyone is equal.
- The Bhagavad Gita suggests that to reach liberation then you should work for the welfare of all fellow human beings.

Islam

Islam believes that Allah created everyone as equal but different. This was Allah's design, so discrimination is unjustified. (Qur'an)

- Allah loves the fair-minded.
- The Five Pillars (beliefs and actions) apply to all – equally.
- Muhammad allowed a black African man to do the call to prayer in Madinah and he welcomed anyone regardless of wealth, status or creed.
- The Muslim Declaration of Human Rights states that everyone is equal.
- On hajj (the biggest gathering of Muslims on Earth) everyone is equal in dress and action.

The Basics

1. How might people discriminate with regards to disability?
2. What is the religious attitude to any form of discrimination?
3. 'Discrimination is the worst thing a person can suffer.' What do you think of this statement? Explain your own opinion, then argue the opposite view.
4. 'Being discriminated against because of a disability is worse than sexism.' Explore reasons to agree and disagree with this statement, including religious arguments on both sides.

Religious, philosophical and ethical studies

Gender prejudice

People can often be discriminated against because of their gender. This is called sexism. Traditionally there are roles for men and roles for women in society and within religion. However, these have not been equal roles with equal opportunity. Religions would argue that the roles are equal but different. In society in the last 100 years the role of women has changed. There are far more women in top jobs, in male-dominated sports, in politics and in the armed forces. However, in terms of leadership roles in religion, most still are male-dominated.

Catholic Church reconfirms its position on the priesthood – no women allowed

First Anglican female Bishop appointed – 1960 years after Jesus died!

The Quaker faith welcomes anyone to speak in services – gender is not a barrier

March 2015 marked the start of the ministry of the first female Anglican Bishop. Libby Lane, who had been consecrated Bishop at York Cathedral in January 2015, began her work as Bishop of Stockport. This had been a long journey through a time of change for the Church of England. Before 1994, there had been no female vicars in the Church of England, and it took 20 years for one to become a Bishop. During that time, some Anglicans left the church in disagreement. Archbishop John Sentamu – at her consecration – said, 'In a few years' time, when more and more women will be Bishops, I predict we shall be wondering how we ever managed without them.' Libby Lane said, 'The Church has moved so quickly into a new normal where the appointment of women Bishops is as expected as the appointment of men.' Many Christians believe that women are suited to church leadership for the different skills they bring – such as empathy and personal skills which are valuable in a vicar's job. Other Christians believe a woman may not hold a leadership role in the church, as St Paul said women should obey men.

Refer to pages 182–184 for more detail on gender prejudice and gender in religion.

Judaism

Judaism teaches that prejudice and discrimination are incompatible with Jewish law. Over the years Judaism is the religion that has been the target of this to the extreme and therefore there are strong opinions on the issue.

- God created everyone equal. So prejudice is seen as an insult to God.
- The Torah tells Jewish people to welcome and not persecute strangers.
- The Nevi'im states God expects people to practise justice, love and kindness to all.
- 'Treat others as you wish to be treated.' (Old Testament)
- Jewish leaders stated that Jewish people should live in harmony with non-Jewish.

Sikhism

Sikhism believes in the principle of justice and to fight for justice where it does not exist. Equality and sewa (service to others) would clearly indicate that discrimination is wrong.

- 'Using the same mud, The Creator has created many shapes in many ways.' (Guru Gobind Singh)
- 'Those who love God love everyone.' (Guru Granth Sahib)
- 'God created everyone so all are equal so deserve the same treatment and respect.' (Guru Granth Sahib)
- The use of the langar suggests everyone is welcome – Sikh or not.
- 'God is without caste.' (Guru Gobind Singh)

9 Theme F: Religion, human rights and social justice

Racism

Racism is the belief that the colour of a person's skin, or their race, makes a person less valuable than others, so that they can be treated unfairly. We use the word 'racist' to describe someone who discriminates against people of other races in a negative way.

The slave trade in the seventeenth and eighteenth centuries was based on the belief that people of colour were somehow of less value than other people, and so could be bought and sold, and treated in any way, with no rights at all. It cost the lives of tens of thousands and destroyed many communities. This attitude of superiority still exists in the world today. The statistics in the UK show that if you are black, you are more likely to get excluded from school, to achieve less highly than others, to get stopped by the police more often, to get sent to prison, to be murdered – it goes on.

The police keep records of race-related crimes, which show that those of Asian heritage suffer most hate crimes, often because they are thought to be Muslim. This is in direct relation to society's perception of the nature of Muslims as portrayed by groups such as the Taliban, Al Qaeda and ISIL/ISIS.

> 'All human beings are born free and equal … should act in a spirit of brotherhood … everyone is entitled to all the rights and freedom.' (Universal Declaration of Human Rights)

Equality and justice

Religions believe in equality (that we all have the same intrinsic value, and are special beings) and in justice (that things must be made fair, and wrongs made right). So it seems impossible that religious believers could support prejudice of any kind. Prejudice clearly suggests a sense of superiority (not equality) and leads to injustice (not justice).

Positive discrimination though can help to bring about both as it tries to raise up the life and well-being, as well as the profile and status, of minority groups.

The Basics

1 List the types of prejudice covered by the course, and explain what each one is.
2 Use the teachings from pages 319–321 to explain what the attitude of the religion(s) you have studied might be to racism.
3 'Religious believers should fight racism more than other forms of prejudice.' What do you think? Explain your opinion.

Leaders from different faiths march together in protest in the UK

What does the law say in the UK?

There are laws in the UK to deal with discrimination. As prejudice is about the way people think, the law cannot do anything, but when that prejudice turns into discriminative actions then the law can act. However, discrimination is not always easy to prove.

The 1976 Race Relations Act (RRA) made it illegal to discriminate against anyone because of race, nationality, and ethnic or national background in four main areas: jobs, education, housing and the provision of services; or to use threatening or abusive language in regard to race. It also made it illegal to publish anything to stir up racial hatred.

The Commission for Racial Equality was set up to deal with cases of discrimination and to act as a watchdog against racism. In 2000, the RRA Amendment Act was introduced as a way of strengthening the 1976 Act. It stressed the need to promote harmony and tolerance among all people.

There have also been laws passed through the Equal Pay Act (1975), Sex Discrimination Act (1975), Disability Discrimination Act (1995) and the Sexual Orientation Regulation (2007). All these Acts have been superseded by the Equality Act (2010).

As well as the law there are organisations that support victims and try to improve awareness of the discrimination certain groups face, such as Stop Hate UK (www.stophateuk.org).

Religious groups take their responsibility to support victims and to work for a better world with more justice for all very seriously. This has led to them setting up many religious organisations which fight prejudice and which support victims. Here are two examples.

JCORE (www.jcore.org.uk) is the Jewish Council for Racial Equality. They believe that concern for social justice should be an important part of Jewish identity, and that Jewish people have a duty to work both with others and for others in the struggle against discrimination. They do a lot of work to educate Jewish children about this duty and to support asylum seekers in the UK.

FAIR (www.fairuk.org) is the Forum against Islamophobia and Racism. This organisation is all about making the UK less Islamophobic, less anti-Semitic and less racist. They see no place for attacks on Muslims and Jewish people in a civilised society, and reject the extreme actions of some Muslims as being against the religion. Part of their work is to encourage and facilitate discussion between Jewish people and Muslims, rather than fuelling hatred between the two or against them.

The Basics

1. Explain how discrimination affects its victims.
2. How does the law in the UK try to fight prejudice? Refer to the laws in your answer.
3. 'Not enough religious people stand up to fight prejudice.' Clearly explain arguments both for and against this statement, including religious arguments.

9 Theme F: Religion, human rights and social justice

Religious attitudes to wealth

What – to you – counts as being wealthy?

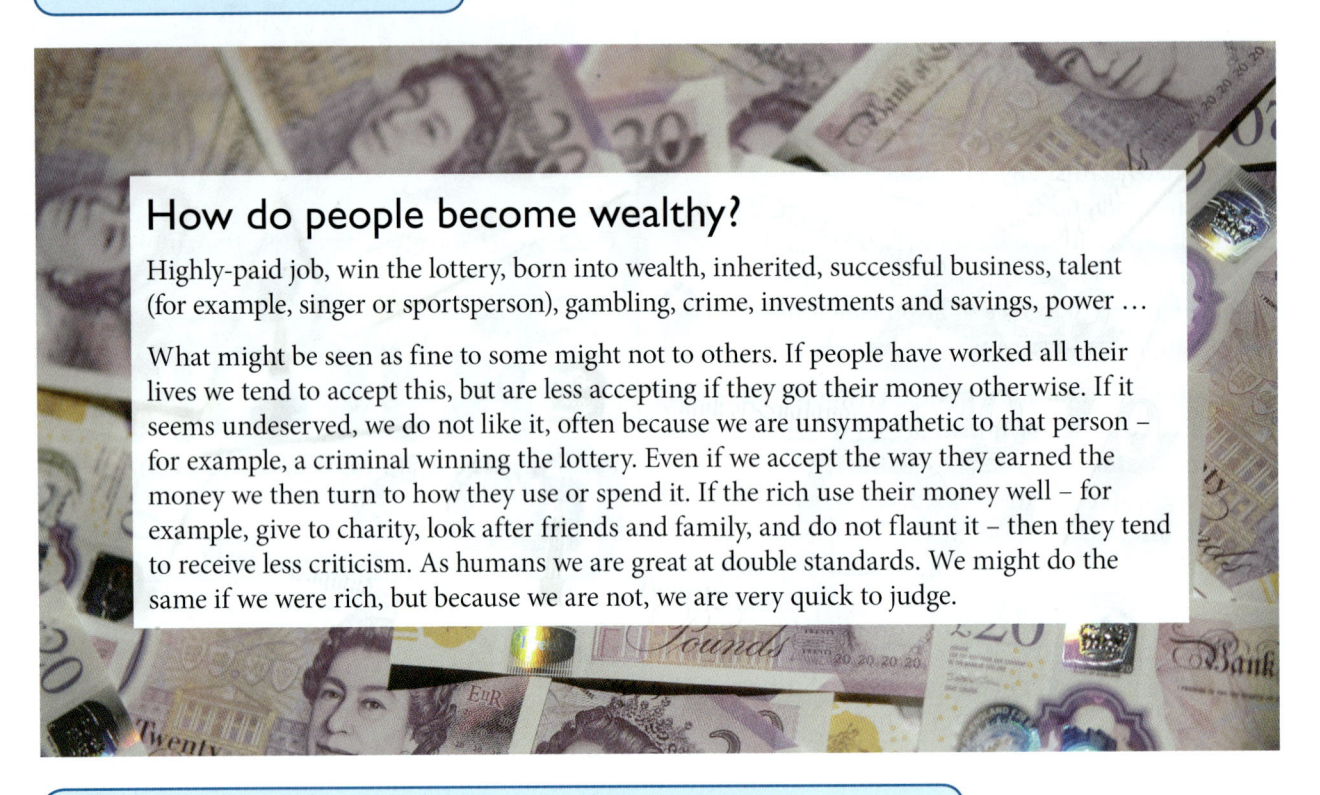

How do people become wealthy?

Highly-paid job, win the lottery, born into wealth, inherited, successful business, talent (for example, singer or sportsperson), gambling, crime, investments and savings, power …

What might be seen as fine to some might not to others. If people have worked all their lives we tend to accept this, but are less accepting if they got their money otherwise. If it seems undeserved, we do not like it, often because we are unsympathetic to that person – for example, a criminal winning the lottery. Even if we accept the way they earned the money we then turn to how they use or spend it. If the rich use their money well – for example, give to charity, look after friends and family, and do not flaunt it – then they tend to receive less criticism. As humans we are great at double standards. We might do the same if we were rich, but because we are not, we are very quick to judge.

Think about how people become wealthy. What would you see as the wrong ways and why?

Buddhism

Buddhism believes that there is essentially nothing wrong with having wealth; what is important is how it is used.

- 'Riches ruin the foolish … through craving for riches, the foolish one ruins himself.' (Dharmapada)
- 'Acquiring wealth is acceptable if, at the same time, it promotes the well-being of the community or society.' (Phra Rajavaramuni)
- 'Unskilful thoughts founded in greed are what keeps us circling in samsara, in an endless round of repetitive, habitual attachment.' (Kulananda, member of The Triratna Buddhist Order)

Buddhism encourages Right Action, Right Thought, Right Intention and Right Livelihood. For the wealthy to see poverty and ignore it would be wrong.

Christianity

Christians believe that there is nothing wrong with wealth in itself; it is how we use it that matters. We can use it for good and bad. Wealth is seen as a gift from God. Our money should come from lawful means. In the Bible there is the warning that the wrong attitude to money could lead people away from God.

- 'For the love of money is a root of all kinds of evil. Some people, eager for money, have wandered from the faith and pierced themselves with many griefs.' (1 Timothy 6:10)
- 'No one can serve two masters … You cannot serve both God and money.' (Matthew 6:24)
- 'Be on your guard against all kinds of greed: a man's life does not consist in the abundance of his possessions.' (Luke 12:15)

ॐ Hinduism

For Hindus, it is important to create wealth (artha) to provide for their family and maintain society. Rich devotees should not hoard wealth, but use it in a stewardship role. Excess wealth can bring problems as it can lead to over indulgence and materialistic rather than spiritual living.

- 'Money causes pain when earned, it causes pain to keep and it causes pain to lose as well as to spend.' (Panchatantra)
- 'Happiness arises from contentment, uncontrolled pursuit of wealth will result in unhappiness.' (Manu)
- 'Act in the world as a servant, look after everyone and act as if everything belongs to you, but know in your heart that nothing is yours – you are the guardian, the servant of God.' (Shri Ramakrishna)

Hindus believe that life is all about good deeds here and now. This not only helps the receiver but it helps the giver's own rebirth.

Islam

In Islam, all wealth is a gift from Allah; humans are caretakers of Allah's wealth, and will be judged by their use of it.

- 'Riches are sweet, a source of blessing to those who acquire them by the way – but those who seek it out of greed are like people who eat but are never full.' (Hadith)
- 'To try to earn a lawful livelihood is an obligation like all other obligations in Islam – no one has eaten better food than what he can earn by the work of his own hands.' (Hadith)
- 'It is not poverty which I fear for you, but that you might begin to desire the world as others before you desired it, and it might destroy you as it destroyed them.' (Hadith)

Islam teaches that wealth comes from Allah for us to use to benefit humanity.

Judaism

Judaism believes that wealth is a gift from God and can be used for the self and others. The Tenakh clearly states that money can only be earned in the correct way. Materialism can lead to people sinning – if your heart is filled with the desire for money then there is no room for God. The Talmud does see that a decent standard of living is needed for the well-being of the individual.

- 'Do not weary yourself trying to become rich.' (Proverbs)
- 'He who loves silver cannot be satisfied with silver.' (Ecclesiastes)
- 'He who has a hundred, craves for two hundred.' (The Midrash)

Money should not be desired but it is necessary.

Sikhism

Sikhs believe that anyone possessing riches has been blessed by God as they are able to help the poor. Livelihoods should be made by honest means. Anything that is earned dishonestly is seen as the 'blood of the poor'.

- 'One who lives by earning through hard work, then gives some of it away to charity, knows the way to God.' (Guru Granth Sahib)
- 'Be grateful to God for whose bounties you enjoy.' (Guru Nanak)
- 'Those who have money have the anxiety of greed.' (Guru Granth Sahib)

The Basics

1 Explain religous teachings about wealth – having it, and using it.
2 'The more important question is where a person gets their money from, rather than how they use it.' How far do you agree? Explain arguments, including religious ones, to show you have considered different points of view.

9 Theme F: Religion, human rights and social justice

Causes of poverty

Disease/disability Bad investments
Climate/natural disaster   Idleness/lack of effort   High-interest loan   People trafficking
War/corrupt governments   Addiction   Family and upbringing
Lack of education/employment   High taxes   Austerity measures   Debt
Immigration   Unfair trade/poor wages

> **Task**
>
> *Which causes apply more in the UK? Explain why for each of your choices.*
> We seem to believe the wealthy have a responsibility to help the poor. We are looking here at two areas: 'giving money' to help those in these situations, and preventing the underlying causes where we can. It is the creation of social justice we referred to earlier. Look at the list above – people are poor through one or more of these. Can you connect some of them? Solving one may not solve the poverty of an individual. Poverty is complex.

Religious teachings that tell us we have a duty to tackle poverty

☸ Buddhism
- Karuna (compassion) – wishing others freedom from suffering.
- 'Today everyone is looking for personal happiness. So, I always say, if you wish to be happy and aim for self-interest, then care for others. This brings lasting happiness.' (Dalai Lama)

✝ Christianity
- 'If anyone has material possessions and sees his brother in need how can the love of God be in him?' (1 John 3:17)
- 'If a brother has no clothes or food what good is it to wish him well without caring for his physical needs?' (James 2:15)

ॐ Hinduism
- Some believe by helping those in poverty, they can improve their own karma and rebirth.
- It is taught 'it is the same God shining out through so many different eyes. So helping others is no different than helping ourselves.'

☪ Islam
- 'He who eats and drinks whilst his brother goes hungry is not one of us.' (Hadith)
- 'For a debtor, give him time to pay – but if you let it go out of charity this is the best thing to do.' (Qur'an)

✡ Judaism
- 'You shall not burden your heart or shut your hand against your poor brother.' (Old Testament)
- The Torah forbids charging a fellow Jewish person **interest** on money.

☬ Sikhism
- 'A good person always seeks the welfare of others.' (Bhai Gurdas)
- 'A place in God's court can only be attained if we do service to others in the world.' (Guru Granth Sahib)

> **The Basics**
>
> 1 'If you have wealth you have a responsibility to tackle the causes of poverty.' Why might people agree and disagree with this?
> 2 Explain why religious people should be helping to tackle the causes of poverty.

How the poor are exploited

Fair pay

Fair pay means being paid at a rate that is appropriate for the work done, and that there is equal pay between men and women for the same job. It is a difficult issue because what is appropriate pay? Pay can be based on hours worked, qualifications needed, the necessity of the job and the type of job. A person might work a lot of hours but be low paid whereas another might work fewer hours at a highly qualified job and get paid more. There are some who are paid excessive wages, like the heads of big companies, whereas a nurse is paid much less. The **minimum wage** in the UK protects the very low paid. As of April 2019, the mandatory Living Wage was equalised with the minimum wage for those ages 25 and over. There are workers who are exploited in UK and there are those who do not deserve the wages and bonuses they get. Low-paid workers often do jobs of great necessity for our everyday living, so it is not as if the job is worthless, yet the wages they are paid by government or employers are unfair. Remember *fair* does not mean *equal* as this would be impossible to achieve.

In the UK religion has played a big part in campaigning for an increase in the minimum wage and working for the interests of the low-paid. Regular statements are made, particularly by Church bishops, to highlight this issue for the poor. There is a balance to be found as paying higher wages might mean fewer jobs, but even so there are too many people who are working really hard for long hours but little money.

> **UK minimum wage (April 2020)**
> 25 and over £8.72
> 21–24 £8.20
> 18–20 £6.45
> Under 18 £4.55
> Apprentice £4.15

> **UK National Living Wage (April 2020)**
> 25 and over £8.72

Excessive interest on loans

Those in poverty often take **loans** to pay for what they need. It might be to pay for Christmas as wages are not enough, or as a one-off item not budgeted for, such as a new fridge. Loan companies exploit this by offering same-day release of money, but the rate to pay it back can be huge – even thousands per cent interest. People paying weekly only at the minimum rate will see that what they owe actually increases rather than reduces. Each payment only pays off some of the interest on the loan, which gets bigger the longer it takes to pay the loan back. The poor often fall behind on payments and some take on additional loans to pay off the first loan. This is a vicious circle of increasing debt. The loan companies make a lot of money this way. In 2015, the UK government implemented restrictions on interest, but it was nowhere near enough and so poverty increased.

All religions disagree with these loans. In fact, Islam does not allow interest for fellow Muslims, nor does Judaism for fellow Jewish people. Religions accept that companies have to make profits, but disagree with the extent that loans can exploit people. They exploit their need, their inability to pay and their lack of understanding as to how the system works. The loans do not help; they make situations worse.

> *I needed cash quickly. The wages had gone and I had bills, so I took out a payday loan. I didn't read the small print carefully. I have already paid back ten times what I borrowed, and I still owe them money.*

9 Theme F: Religion, human rights and social justice

People trafficking

People trafficking is a modern-day slave trade. People are 'sold' for many purposes. Trafficking gangs take large amounts of money, but the people find themselves in awful situations that they cannot escape. Poor people in foreign countries are offered the 'chance of a better life' in another country. Their home might be war-torn or a place where there is little opportunity and a trafficker offers to take an individual to a wealthier country, if they can pay the price. This can be thousands of pounds and families will save up to give a person a better chance. Often these people find themselves in slavery and prostitution when they get to their 'better life' and are told they have to pay more, so are forced to work to obtain their freedom. Many live in fear as essentially they are illegal immigrants. They live in terrible conditions, often suffering violence and never achieving freedom from these gangs.

Some are trafficked to work, being 'bought' by rich families to work for very little. Again people pay, believing they will get a job and will be able to send money home to their families. It actually means they are being sold into slavery. They have no idea of what is actually going to happen and their families are given false promises. This sadly often involves children.

In recent years we have seen people trafficked across Europe. They are migrant workers who cannot get into the UK legally, so gangs offer to smuggle them in for a high price. Some pay it and get here, while some are caught and often deported back to their country of origin. Some are successfully smuggled only to find themselves at the mercy of the gangs who demand more money, which they have to work to get.

The year 2015 saw a new type of people trafficking, with many people trying to escape war-torn areas of the world like Afghanistan, Somalia and the Congo, Syria and Iraq. They paid for the right to a journey on a boat to get to Europe, from where they could try and make their way to a country which would accept them. The journey cost them vast sums of money and many of these people were not poor; they simply saw no other way to escape the horrors of their own countries, so paid what they were asked. Many of the boats were inadequate and they sank, killing men, women and children. Once in Europe, they had no right to claim status in any country – millions have been 'displaced'.

Religions see this activity not only as illegal, but as inhumane and totally unacceptable in a modern world. It goes against every kind of moral principle and religious teaching about our treatment of each other.

In 2019, global anti-trafficking campaign A21 hold their sixth annual walk for freedom calling for an end to modern day slavery

Another lorry load of illegal immigrants stopped in the UK

Death of a dream – smuggled people all die in the back of a refrigerated truck

The Basics

1. Why is fair pay an important practice?
2. Explain what 'excessive interest loans' are and why many religious people disagree with them.
3. Explain why religious people would believe people trafficking to be wrong.
4. 'The poor will always be victims.' Do you agree with this statement? Explain arguments on both sides, including religious arguments.

Think about the religious teachings you know already – which ones would tell us trafficking is wrong?

Religious, philosophical and ethical studies

Responsibility for those living in poverty

This section looks at who should help the poor.

The government
We elect a government to look after the best interests of society and this includes the poor. They provide for the needs of the country as a whole and for individuals.

They should help because they have the means to help: they collect the taxes to finance the running of public services. People will not vote them into power if they do not help.

They have the health services, educational services, welfare services, links to business and the means to bring all these together to help the poor. They have the money, expertise and the access to co-ordinate helping the poor. Also, their policy decisions on saving and spending directly affect the wealth of individuals – for example, cutting benefits or spending more on the homeless.

Charities
A charity by its very nature is set up to help someone or something. It collects money to help its cause and therefore has the means to help.

They should help because that is the reason they exist. They are set up on religious or humanitarian principles, that is, compassion and wanting to reduce suffering. People who belong to these charities perhaps just want to 'give something back' to society, to help those who have not had the same opportunities they had.

They fund-raise through organised events, national charity shops, donation collection and so on. They then decide through experience how what is raised is best spent.

Who should help the poor?
Why should they help?
How should they help?

Religions
Religions are about communities and helping each other. The worship of God has to be seen in action as well as in words.

They should help as the teachings of holy books tell them it is their duty. Famous leaders in history and today put the poor at the heart of their work. Also, helping the poor is seen as doing God's work, or showing loving kindness or bringing social justice to the world. God rewards such action.

Religions organise community events, donate to religious charities, work with the poor here and abroad, pray for them and are simply there for people in their times of need.

The poor
The poor need to want to help themselves or at least want help from others or the help is wasted.

The poor should not want to remain poor. They should want to improve their situation rather than staying reliant on society and charity. Often it is about believing that life can improve for them. Some people are poor due to their own action (for example, drugs), or inaction (for example, not gaining qualifications), so they do have a responsibility to themselves to change this.

They have to believe things can improve, take the help that is on offer and work hard to become independent again. Small steps can change things greatly. Many have made efforts to get out of poverty, but been knocked back (for example, job applications ignored many times) so it is up to society to make it possible for the poor to help themselves.

Task

In groups research one of these four areas. Make a case to present to the class that it is their responsibility to help the poor.

9 Theme F: Religion, human rights and social justice

Charity

☸ Buddhism

International Buddhist Relief Organisation

History – The aim is to give practical and direct help to all living beings anywhere in the world. It sees itself as having a duty, especially to the most vulnerable, particularly children to whom the future belongs. It sets up sponsorship for many children in many countries, trying to raise the standard of living and education for those children so that they have a better future.

Recent project – In Malawi, IBRO has financed the digging and building of wells so that the villages can get clean water. This has reduced water-born illnesses and their effects. Communities have been also able to redirect time previously spent fetching water into projects such as growing more food. They now have better diets and nutrition, so they are healthier. They can also sell some of this food. This is lifting them out of poverty.

www.ibro.org.uk

✝ Christianity

CAFOD

History – This was set up in 1962. Historically, Catholic churches generated charity funds on one specific day of each year. They themselves decided what to do with this money. CAFOD was the organisation set up to centralise this fund-raising, and be more effective and wide-ranging with it. Work which began as disaster relief and aid work now includes campaigning for a fairer world, and a vast array of educational work, including a school magazine, as well as church magazines.

Recent project – Nicaragua is the second-poorest country in the Americas. CAFOD is contributing to a range of revival and urban projects to transform people's lives – for example, projects to give emotional and educational support for women and girls so that they do not get forced into sexual exploitation.

www.cafod.org.uk

ॐ Hinduism

Sewa International

History – This is a UK charity, entirely run by dedicated volunteers from all sections of the community, working towards serving humanity. It funds long-term projects for economic development. It tries to combine modern and indigenous techniques to improve living conditions in affected disaster areas of India. It focuses on education, orphanages, village amenities and employment.

Recent project – The Women's Empowerment Project runs in Odisha, India. Its major focus is to form village women's committees. This tries to give women a greater say in the decisions made in their village. It also educates women, because it is proven that for every year of education a woman has, the better her children's lives will be and the better their life chances in the future. Her education encourages theirs and gives her more ideas for what they could do and more ambition for them.

www.sewauk.org

Tasks

1. Read about the six projects on this page and the next. In each case, how important do you think the work has been? Explain your ideas.
2. Do you think that any of them are more important than the others? Explain your ideas.
3. If these charities were all UK-based do you think they should focus on UK-based projects? Explain why.

Islam

Muslim Aid

History – Works in over 70 countries across Africa, Asia and Europe. It aims to help the poor overcome their suffering by reducing poverty. It responds to emergencies, where need is urgent and often life or death. However, at the same time it sets up strategic programmes to eliminate poverty, focusing on education and skills, provision of clean water, healthcare and ways to generate income. Also runs a qurbani programme whereby Muslims from all over the UK donate during Ramadan. This allows poor communities all over the Muslim world to receive food packages.

Recent projects – Beity Syrian Orphanage Appeal was set up in Turkey to take orphaned children from the Syrian crisis. Muslim Aid ensures there is an adequate supply of food and medicines at the orphanage, as well as the necessary furnishings and tools. It funds the employment of counsellors to work with the orphans who are often traumatised by their experiences. These children have a chance to rebuild their lives.

www.muslimaid.org

Judaism

World Jewish Relief

History – Was founded in 1933 to rescue Jewish people from the horrors taking place in Nazi Germany and brought 70,000 Jewish people to safety before the start of the Second World War. After the war, work began to respond to the needs of Jewish refugees and communities all over the world, with the aim of supporting Jewish people in distress. Its work involves empowering local communities by teaching them to be self-sufficient. Today, WJR stands as the leading UK international agency responding to the needs of Jewish communities at risk or in crisis, outside the UK and Israel. At times of major international disaster, it leads the UK Jewish community's response to others in need all over the world.

Recent project – WJR funds three centres which support over 100 former street children to give them a chance of escaping poverty. It provides food and shelter, and access to medical and social workers as well as trauma counsellors. It ensures they have an education and vocational training.

www.worldjewishrelief.org

Sikhism

Khalsa Aid

History – It is based in Slough, UK, as a humanitarian organisation run on Sikh principles, especially sewa (service to humanity). It runs entirely from donations and volunteers actually pay their own expenses. One of its aims is to strive to assist in any possible way to combat poverty wherever there is a need. Following the central Sikh belief in equality, Khalsa Aid will work with any group anywhere in the world, regardless of gender, age, religion or any other barrier. Khalsa Aid was one of the first agencies to help victims of the Grenfell Tower disaster.

Recent project – In the Punjab region there has been catastrophic flooding. Many villages have been destroyed and crops devastated. Khalsa Aid has responded by supplying food rations, blankets and clothes to affected people. It has also sent equipment to help ensure clean water is available. Khalsa Aid is working with the communities to help them rebuild, and to get them through to the time when their new crops can be harvested.

www.khalsaaid.org

The Basics

1. Give two reasons why the work of charities is important.
2. Why do religious people want to work for and give to charity?
3. 'The work of charities is the solution to poverty.' What is your opinion?
4. Research the work of a charity which helps internationally, and one which focuses its work in the UK.

9 Theme F: Religion, human rights and social justice

Poverty in the UK

There are some charities that focus on key areas of poverty in the UK. Sometimes when we see poverty in Africa, for example, we forget that actually there are plenty of poor people in the UK too.

Shelter

Shelter is the UK's leading housing and homelessness charity.

Shelter helps millions of people every year struggling with bad housing or homelessness with advice, support and legal services.

And they campaign so that, one day, no one will have to turn to them for help.

They are here so no one has to fight bad housing or homelessness on their own.

The charity was formed in 1966 by Bruce Kenrick (founder chairman) and Des Wilson (founder director), in response to the country's massive housing crisis. Their vision – along with co-founders Edwin Barker, David Reid, Rev. Eammon Casey and Lewis Waddilove – was to establish one organisation to speak for the millions of 'hidden homeless' living in overcrowded slums.

In 2019, a spokesperson from Shelter said that we are now again facing a national emergency that is the housing crisis, with 6 million households across England and Scotland denied the right to a safe home, or threatened with losing it.

The Salvation Army

You might have seen The Salvation Army at Christmas, in shopping centres playing music and with collecting tins. They actually work all year round:

- rebuilding lives – offering a hand-up to homeless people, a family tracing service, drug and alcohol rehabilitation, anti-human-trafficking services
- offering food parcels, holding lunch clubs for older people, supporting the emergency services during major fires and incidents, visiting prisoners
- giving people the chance to belong – youth clubs and music groups, for example.

As a Christian Church and registered charity, The Salvation Army also runs a Christmas Present Appeal each year for children, the homeless and older people who would have little or nothing at Christmas time. It runs homeless resettlement centres, care homes for older people, employment services for the long-term unemployed, support services to the armed forces and home-visiting services in local communities. All this is done by volunteers and ministers who believe in putting their Christian beliefs into action and to follow Jesus' example to help (not judge) anyone who is in need.

Issues with giving to charity – interesting dilemmas

Discuss the questions in pairs and share your answers as a class.

- Do we give to charity or directly to the individual?
- Do we give money to a beggar, for example, or buy them food?
- How do we know the money we give actually helps the people who need it?
- How much of each £1 we give to charity is actually spent on the poor?
- How much does it cost to fund the charity work?
- Which charities do we choose to give to when so many are so deserving?

The Basics

1. Explain the work of one charity that focuses on the poor in the UK.
2. 'The poor in the UK are just as deserving as the poor abroad.' How far do you agree or disagree?

Contrasting beliefs

Status of women in religion

✝ Christianity

Women have status in Christianity. Christians believe that **God made all people free and equal – in the image of God** (Genesis 1:27). St Paul said 'There is neither Jew nor Greek, male nor female, for you are all one in Christ Jesus' (Galatians 3:28) – demonstrating equality. The first people to see Jesus after his resurrection were female, and **early church leaders included women**.

✝ Roman Catholic

In the Roman Catholic Church, women **may not hold positions of authority**. While women could publicly pray and prophesy in church (1 Corinthians 11:1–16), they **could not teach or have authority over a man** (1 Timothy 2:11–14). These are **two essential functions** of the clergy, so women are **scripturally excluded** from these roles.

☪ Islam

A woman may study the Qur'an and Islamic law, but she **may not lead the mosque**, as prayers by men and boys would not be valid. The Qur'an states that women have rights, but **men have the final word and so greater status** (Qur'an 2:229).

✝ Christianity

In the Orthodox Church, women may not have leadership roles. Women have a **God-given role and task as a mother**; nothing is more important than this and nothing should detract from it.

Question

Explain two contrasting beliefs in contemporary British society about the status of women in religion.

In your answer you should refer to the main religious tradition of Great Britain and one or more other religious traditions. *(4 marks)*

Use of wealth

✝ Christianity

Many Christians believe in **tithing** – the giving to charity of up to a tenth of a person's income. Jesus taught the early community to give – 'Go sell everything you have and give it to the poor and you will have treasure in heaven' (Mark 10:21). In Luke 12:15, Jesus cautioned people **against greed, saying that life does not consist of having many possessions**. Wealth should be used to **benefit others, not just for selfish reasons**. There is **no fixed rate** of giving though.

☪ Islam

Shi'a Muslims give zakah (2.5 per cent) of their earnings each year, and also 20 per cent of their profit via khums. This is a very high level of **charitable taxation, which is compulsory** on them. They see it as a duty, not charity, and not giving will be problematic in the afterlife.

Sikhism

Sikhs should give 10 per cent of their wealth to charity (daswandh), with the expectation that they will give more where they can. It is more than a personal choice whether to give. 'One who lives by earning through hard work, then gives some of it away to charity, knows the way to God' (Guru Granth Sahib).

Question

Explain two contrasting beliefs in contemporary British society about the use of wealth.

In your answer you should refer to the main religious tradition of Great Britain and one or more other religious traditions. *(4 marks)*

Hinduism

In Hinduism, **wealth is seen as the consequence of previous rebirths**. Hence, a person's lack of it is also a consequence, and some might believe poor people **should not be helped, as they have bad karma to work through**. **Wealthy Hindus should act as custodians of wealth and feel responsible towards the needs of poor**. Being indifferent to the suffering of others is considered to be bad karma.

Freedom of religious expression

Christianity

Christians believe that **God made all people free and equal**. All were made in **the image of God** (Genesis 1:27). This entitles all to rights, including that of freedom of religious expression. **Dignitas Personae states that the 'human person has a right to religious freedom'**. They point to the fact that Jesus invited people to follow him, and did not force them – allowing them to choose their religious path.

Islam

In Islam, it is **acceptable to be a Christian or Jewish person – both are 'people of the book'**. However, converting to either religion from Islam is apostasy and carries the death penalty. The eastern religions are not accepted, and are seen as **blasphemy – for example, Hinduism as Islam argues that Hindus worship several gods**.

Hinduism

In India, there have been **examples of religious intolerance against Muslims and Christians**, which left people dead. 2015 proved a sad year in this respect. These are in direct contrast to what Hinduism teaches – **tolerance, respect**.

Most religious people would say that freedom of **religious expression is a vital element of society**. However, many would say that religious expression needs to be within reason – **not disrespecting or offending other religions, and not forcing one's own religious rules onto others**, for example.

Question

Explain two contrasting beliefs in contemporary British society about freedom of religious expression.

In your answer you should refer to the main religious tradition of Great Britain and one or more other religious traditions. *(4 marks)*

Getting prepared

Points of attack

Fifty per cent of your marks are for analysis and evaluation; that is, challenging or supporting statements. It is essential you have a good technique. For each topic, you have to answer a 12-mark evaluation question.

When faced with a statement, it is often the case that we can only think of one way to argue – either for or against – so our answer becomes either one-sided or very limited on a second side. There are ways to give yourself a better chance; let us consider some. The question might include one of these terms:

Best   Most   Everyone/All   Always   Must

Each of these words gives you an opening – a way to challenge the statement. If you always look for them, it also helps your brain to open up to more than one side of an argument. When we are faced with a statement that we feel very strongly about, our brains find it really difficult to think in a different way. By focusing on those words – if they are there – we open it up again. So, look at these examples:

'**All** religious believers should help the poor.' Should they really? **All** of them? What if the poor are poor because of activities like gambling (which is against most religions)? What if the religious believer is themselves poor (so they have nothing to give)?

'Religious people should **always** fight for human rights.' Should they really? Always? Are there any people who have forfeited some of their rights? For example, a murderer loses their right to freedom. What if those rights will lead to persecution or diminish their own rights – for example, allowing freedom of speech to the extent of religious hatred?

'Discrimination is the **worst** thing a person can suffer.' **Worst** ... really? What if the discrimination is very limited? Might there be other things more dreadful, like being wrongfully accused or convicted of a serious crime? Thinking about the potential repercussions gives you a huge scope for answers here.

Brainwork

Our brains are actually quite lazy, preferring not to have to think – which is actually quite hard. We know that our brains prefer to just go back to what they already know and have already experienced, rather than work things out anew. So a great phrase to help our brains open up to more options can come in the answer – '**it depends**'. Take a look at this:

'A special tax is the best way to solve poverty.' Well, it depends – if the tax is an affordable one, then yes. However, if the tax is a flat rate, so everyone pays the same – well that is not fair, and means even the poor have to pay (which is pointless!).

9 Theme F: Religion, human rights and social justice

Planning an attack on an evaluative question

When faced with an evaluative question:

- Make sure that you are writing about the statement and not just giving religious attitudes to the topic – there is no point writing what Christians and Muslims think about prejudice generally, if the statement says 'Prejudice is the biggest issue for the world today.'
- You have to give arguments to agree and disagree – giving a one-sided answer will limit your answer.
- You have to have a strong religious content – not just one religious argument or point.
- Use religious teachings to prove those religious arguments.
- You have to explain your arguments – just listing reasons to agree or disagree is not going to get you far enough. Each time you give a reason, explain it by extending the point – try to give examples to illustrate what you mean.
- Use examples to help support your reasons – they are very effective for showing the point clearly.

A useful checklist for checking your answers …

- Did you agree with the statement? What are your reasons?
- Did you explain all of those reasons?
- Did you include at least one religious argument which was explained in those reasons?
- Did you disagree with the statement? What are your reasons?
- Did you explain all of those reasons?
- Did you include at least one religious argument which was explained in those reasons?
- Is your opinion different? If so, add it.
- Did you write a short conclusion which focuses on saying which the strongest or most persuasive point of view is? This is really important because it concludes the whole answer and is often where the best evaluation takes place.

Let us practise …

Use the knowledge you have gained from this page and your notes to write detailed answers to the following statements:

'There is no point fighting for human rights.'

'Prejudice can never be ended.'

'Religious believers should make the ending of poverty their top priority.'

Don't forget to use the question checklist in writing your answer.

Religion, human rights and social justice glossary

Ageism discrimination on the grounds of a person's age

Community a group of people who belong together because of a shared characteristic

Compassion loving kindness; helping because help is needed

Discrimination actions based on prejudice, often negative

Equality the idea that everyone is equal, of equal value and worth

Fair pay payment which is appropriate for the work done

Gender the state of being male or female

Harmony living together without argument and conflict

Homophobia prejudice against someone on the grounds of their (perceived) sexuality

Human rights the rights a person is entitled to simply because they are human

Human Rights Act a law which protects the rights of all human beings and allows us to challenge when these are violated

Interest the money paid to a lender from a borrower on top of the initial sum borrowed

Justice making things fair again

Loan borrowed money which has to be paid back, usually with interest; excessive loans are where the rate of interest is very high

Minimum wage the legal minimum a person can be paid per hour in a job in the UK

People trafficking the illegal trade of humans for slavery; for example, in the sex trade or for work

Positive discrimination discriminating in favour of a person with a protected characteristic

Poverty having less than the basic needs of life, so that life is a struggle

Prejudice pre-judging someone based on a characteristic they have, for example their looks

Racism prejudice based on a person's racial/ethnic origins

Responsibility duty; for example, the responsibility to work to earn money

Rights entitlements; for example, the right to education

Sexuality a person's sexual orientation; for example, straight, gay or bi-sexual

Social justice justice in terms of wealth and opportunities in a society

Stewardship duty to look after, in this case, other people and those less fortunate

Tolerance acceptance of difference

UN Declaration of Human Rights a statement adopted by the United Nations organisation to protect all human beings

Wealth money and possessions a person has

Index

abortion 209–13, 217–19, 221
adultery 167, 169–71
afterlife 12–14, 220
age of consent 167
ahimsa 59, 74
Al Qaeda 259
Allah 227
allegory 11
Anglican Church 3, 28, 37
animal experimentation 206, 222
animal rights 205–7
Apostles' Creed 2–3, 16
Aquinas, Thomas 236–7
Archbishop of Canterbury 2
arranged marriage 172
ascension 16, 20
astanga yoga 96–7
atheism 229, 250–1
atonement 23
avatars 62–3
awe 193, 197
baptism 34–6
benevolence 4–5
bhakti yoga 96
Bible 2–3, 28
Big Bang theory 191
Bonhoeffer, Dietrich 272
Brahman 60–4, 67, 228
Buddhism
    abortion 217
    beliefs and teachings 164
    divorce 179
    enlightenment 244
    and environment 198
    euthanasia 217
    gender equality 183–4
    marriage 174
    miracles 251
    sex and sexuality 169, 185–6
    war and conflict 255, 258, 262, 274–5
Catholicism 2–3
    Mass 37
    pilgrimage 39
    see also Christianity; Roman Catholic Church
celibacy 167
charity 329–30
chastity 166, 169–70
Christianity
    abortion 217, 221
    afterlife 12–14
    animal experimentation 222
    atonement 23
    beliefs and teachings 2, 4, 164
    Bible 2–3, 28
    churches 2–3
    and community 45–6
    contraception 185
    creation story 10–11, 194
    creeds 2–3, 16
    divorce 179
    and environment 200
    euthanasia 217, 221–2
    events and festivals 3, 41–4
    evil and suffering 6–7
    gender equality 183–4
    Genesis 10–11, 194
    growth of 47–9

Holy Spirit 2, 9, 25
    marriage ceremonies 174
    miracles 250
    mission 47
    nature of God 2, 4–9, 227
    origins of 2
    practices 2, 28
    prayer 28–33
    sacraments 3, 34–8
    sex and sexuality 169, 185–6
    sin 21–2, 24
    Trinity 2, 8, 11
    visions 250
    war and conflict 255, 258, 262, 265, 274–5
    worship 28–31
    see also Jesus
Christmas 41–2
churches see worship
civil partnerships 177
climate change 198–200
cohabitation 177
commitment 166
community 45–6
community service 297
Confession 21
confirmation 34
conflict see war and conflict
conscience 279
conscientious objectors 272
consent, age of 167
conservation 203
contentment 119
contraception 168, 169–71, 185
contract 166
cosmology 68
courage 119
creation 10–11, 194
crime and punishment 279, 281–2, 284–306
crucifix 23
crucifixion 17–18, 23
Dalai Lama 246, 273
Darwin, Charles 192–3
death 12, 220
death penalty 300–4
    see also crime and punishment
deforestation 201
denominations 2
Design argument 234–5
deterrence 289
dharma 76, 78
disability 320
discrimination 182, 184, 317–23
divorce 166, 179–80
dominion 197
Easter 3, 43–4
empathy 75
enlightenment 244
environment 101, 198–205
equality 126–34, 182–4, 309–10, 319–22
    see also women's rights
Eucharist 17, 21, 34, 37–8
euthanasia 214–19, 221–2
Evangelical Christians 25
evangelism 47
events and festivals
    Christian 3, 41–4
    Hindu 59, 91

Sikh 145–50
evil 6–7, 22, 239, 279, 283, 286
evolution 192–3
families 173, 178
    see also marriage; parenting
family planning 168
First Cause argument 236–7
food banks 46
forgiveness 254, 256, 279, 292
freedom of expression 314–16, 334
Gandhi, Mahatma 100, 272
gender equality 182–4, 321, 333
global warming 198–200
God
    in Christianity 2, 4–9, 227
    elements of 229–31
    existence of 226, 229–51
    in Hinduism 58, 60–4, 228
    immanence 230
    in Islam 227
    in Sikhism 110, 112–17
    transcendence 230
Gospels 2–3
grace 24–5, 34
greed 260
Guru Granth Sahib 110, 115, 126, 131, 139–40, 143, 149
Guru Nanak 110, 114–15, 120, 127, 149–50
healing 34
heaven and hell 12, 14
heterosexuality 167
Hinduism
    abortion 218
    atman 70
    beliefs and teachings 58, 60–78, 164
    Brahman 60–4, 67, 228
    cosmology 68
    cow protection 102
    Cycle of Four Ages 68–9
    deities 62–3, 69, 85
    divorce 180
    enlightenment 244
    and environment 201
    environmental projects 101
    euthanasia 218
    events and festivals 59, 91
    four aims of life 76–8
    four paths 94–7
    gender equality 183–4
    karma 71–2
    marriage ceremonies 175
    nature of God 58, 60–4, 228
    origins of 58
    personal virtues 74
    pilgrimage 59, 98–100
    practices 59
    reincarnation (samsara) 71–3
    sex and sexuality 170
    stages of life 77–8
    temples 81–2
    Tri-guna 64–6
    Tri-murti 61–2, 65
    Ultimate Reality 62, 64
    Vedas 58, 67–8, 104
    war and conflict 255, 258, 263, 275
    women's rights 104
    worship 59, 81–90
holy books see sacred texts